International Development

Issues and Challenges

Third edition

Damien Kingsbury
John McKay
Janet Hunt
Mark McGillivray
Matthew Clarke

First edition 2008
Second edition 2012
Third edition 2016

Published by
PALGRAVE

Palgrave in the UK is an imprint of Macmillan Publishers Limited, registered in England, company number 785998, of 4 Crinan Street, London, N1 9XW.

Palgrave Macmillan in the US is a division of St Martin's Press LLC, 175 Fifth Avenue, New York, NY 10010.

Palgrave is a global imprint of the above companies and is represented throughout the world.

Palgrave® and Macmillan® are registered trademarks in the United States, the United Kingdom, Europe and other countries.

ISBN 978–1–137–42941–4 hardback

ISBN 978–1–137–42940–7 paperback

This book is printed on paper suitable for recycling and made from fully managed and sustained forest sources. Logging, pulping and manufacturing processes are expected to conform to the environmental regulations of the country of origin.

A catalogue record for this book is available from the British Library.

A catalog record for this book is available from the Library of Congress.

Printed in China

Contents

List of Figures and Tables

Figures

Tables

List of Abbreviations

BRICS	Brazil, Russia, India, China, South Africa
BSS	Basic Social Services
CEDAW	Convention on the Elimination of All Forms of Discrimination Against Women
CDF	Comprehensive Development Framework
CEIF	Clean Energy Investment Framework (World Bank)
CIS	Central and Eastern Europe and Commonwealth Independent States
DAWN	Development Alternatives for Women in a New Era
FAO	Food and Agriculture Organisation
FDI	Foreign Direct Investment
FTZ	Free Trade Zone
GDP	Gross Domestic Product
GEF	Global Environment Facility
GFC	Global Financial Crisis
GNP	Gross National Product
GNI	Gross National Income
GRB	Gender-Responsive Budgeting
GSP	Generalized System of Preferences
HDI	Human Development Index
HIES	Household Income and Expenditure Surveys
HPI	Human Poverty Index
ILO	International Labour Organization
IMF	International Monetary Fund
IPCC	Intergovernmental Panel on Climate Change
LD	Less Developed
LLD	Least Developed
MDG	Millennium Development Goal
MPI	Multi-dimensional Poverty Index (MPI)
MSG	Millennium Security Goal
NGO	Non-Government Organization
ODA	Official Development Assistance
OECD	Organisation for Economic Co-operation and Development
PPP	Purchasing Power Parity
PQLI	Physical Quality of Life Index

PRSP	Poverty Reduction Strategy Plan
SAP	Structural Adjustment Programme
SDG	Sustainable Development Goal
SWAP	Sector-Wide Approach
UNCTAD	United Nations Conference on Trade and Development
UNDP	United Nations Development Programme
UNHCR	United Nations High Commissioner for Refugees
UNICEF	United Nations Children's Fund
UNREDD	United Nations Collaborative Programme on Reducing Emissions from Deforestation and Forest Degradation in Developing Countries
WGI	Worldwide Governance Indicators (World Bank)
WID	Women in Development
WSF	World Social Forum
WTO	World Trade Organization

Introduction

Damien Kingsbury

The idea of 'development' of the world's poorer countries is contested in its meaning and, therefore, in approaches to it. This contestation has been reflected in varying approaches to the field over the period in which it has been studied, principally since the conclusion of the Second World War. Yet the idea of development is central to the processes by which countries, particularly poorer, developing and post-colonial countries, organize themselves. This book assesses the key issues that such countries are required to address as they try to work towards improving the living standards of their citizens, normatively to eliminate absolute poverty, as well as to construct a political and social environment in which such material benefit can take place.

If this book takes a particular approach to the subject, it is by trying to capture the key elements of the field in overview, identifying their main themes and some of the more normative approaches. It does not, however, try to suggest a singular approach to development, nor does it fall into the trap of the latest development 'fashion' being necessarily more valuable than those that have preceded it. Indeed, if there is one unifying theme, it is that the fundamental or underlying goals that have informed the development project – the qualitative improvement in the lives of the world's poor – have not essentially changed. How to go about achieving such improvement, however, has been proposed, questioned, challenged and re-invented. There are many answers, but no single or 'true' answer.

Origins of the 'development' paradigm

The post-Second World War period saw new states coming into being following the (often forced) withdrawal of European colonial powers from Africa, Asia and elsewhere. However, the aspirations that most former colonial states had for independence were often dashed upon the rocks of limited and, in many cases, reducing capacity. Existing

1

poverty was not always alleviated and in many cases was, along with corruption and inter-ethnic conflict, exacerbated (e.g. see Hirschmann 1987; Cornwell 1999; Englebert 2000; Luis 2000).

Combined with Cold War competition over the spread of competing ideological influences, the governments and often the peoples of most developed or industrialized countries acknowledged that they had and continue to have some responsibility to assist these poorer countries. The intentions were to support these countries' aspiration for economic development and to assist in establishing a stable and conducive material, social and political environment.

At one level, this was a simple matter of self-interest – if people in poorer countries have more income, they have more purchasing power and can generate more international trade and, hence, greater wealth all around, what has been referred to as 'enlightened self-interest' (Evans and Grant 1989: 12). At another level, a basic humanitarian sensibility leaves many people in wealthier countries feeling that to allow poorer people to continue to stay poor is simply unjust. Further, it has become increasingly clear, were there ever any doubt about it in the past, that poverty and underdevelopment have a direct correlation to a propensity for conflict, both within and between states. For much of the late twentieth century, development assistance was seen as a way to persuade poorer countries to come into one of the two major ideological camps that dominated the Cold War era – the West and the Communist bloc. The main powers of each bloc unashamedly used development assistance to maintain the support of poorer countries in order to keep them in their 'sphere of influence'.

By the early twenty-first century, this bipolar ideological orientation had evolved, with the Soviet Union no longer existing and China assuming a greater role as a development partner, if of a very particular and often overtly self-interested type. The fear that poverty could encourage conflict, perhaps on a global scale, was given a new lease of life by the preoccupation of the US, its allies and like-minded countries, following the events of 11 September 2001. This has led to a refocusing on at least some areas of development, intended to respond to a new perceived global 'enemy' – an anti-Western confederation operating under a banner of Islamist ideology, increasingly intended to establish an Islamic caliphate across claimed Islamic states.

Beyond this, even the brief era of a unipolar world, dominated by the US as the only remaining superpower in the period between the collapse of the Soviet Union and the early twenty-first century, has ended. The US has engaged in two disastrous wars, in Afghanistan and Iraq, and thus depleted its moral as well as its financial capital. The more limited re-engagement of the US, and its allies, in Iraq and Syria to combat the

self-styled 'Islamic State' can in large part be considered as a consequence of the errors made in its involvement in, and arguably its withdrawal too soon from, Iraq (Kilcullen 2015). This entanglement by the
US has been paralleled by the economic rise of China and its related
'soft power' diplomacy, and the reassertion of Russia as at least a powerful regional actor.

From the viewpoint of many of its adherents, a radicalized Islamist
ideology[1] has been seen as a foil to the perceived evils of global capitalism (or Westernism – defined as Christian, democratic or materialist,
or all three). And while some supporters of this form of Islam espouse
a purely religious (if arguably deviant) understanding of the conflict,
many are also driven by desperation, poverty, inequity and dispossession. This adds up to a deep – and in many cases well-grounded –
sense of injustice, raising the question of whether enhanced development leading to greater global equity might dampen the zeal of at
least the foot soldiers of the movement. The aforementioned 'enlightened self-interest', which was the principal ideological motivation of
Western donors fearful of the spread of Communism in the 1950s and
1960s, might provide a similar impetus for a renewal of development
assistance today, so that increased 'development' might be seen as one
thread in the 'war on terror' and beyond.

The economic and strategic rise of China, closely followed by India,
has more specifically shifted the world balance in trade and development. Developed countries, notably the US, are increasingly on the back
foot over the rise of these two powers, having shifted its global strategic
focus back towards the Pacific. The global financial crisis that began in
2008 and continues to reverberate through parts of the global economy
illustrated just how fragile the global economy can be. Development
suddenly seemed no longer a given, even for developed countries, while
developing states were in many cases buffered by these larger forces
over which they had little or no control. Many Organisation for Economic Co-operation and Development (OECD) states continued to
grapple with the effects of post-industrial decline well after the global
financial crisis was thought to have formally passed, with one major
area of impact being, in some cases, their relatively reduced level of
financial support for international aid and multilateral institutions.

The preoccupation with new competing forces and limitations upon
the extent to which external actors can effect positive change has
focused attention away from discussions about the meaning of 'development'. In the early post-war period, development was primarily, and
often exclusively, identified with economic growth, usually measured in
terms of the average income per head of population (per capita gross
domestic product (GDP)). However, as discussed further throughout

this volume, development has a range of meanings which, while in most cases are complementary or at least overlapping, may be quite distinct in the priority they give, for example, to economic equity, to political development and democratization, to gender, or to environmental issues. This then affects their implications for action.

Even the terminology of development has changed and is continuing to change. For example, the term 'third world', used in the early Cold War period to describe less developed countries, was coined to contrast them to the 'first world' of the West (largely corresponding to the OECD countries) and the 'second world' of the socialist bloc states (see Sauvy 1952). Although still, if more rarely, used, the term 'third world' has been effectively undermined by recognition of a 'fourth' world (indigenous peoples), the political collapse of the 'second world' and, more importantly, by its overly generic and hence indistinct meaning across a wide range of quite varied economic and political circumstances.

The whole approach to development, assumed for years to occur through a process of industrialization, which has occurred in some instances and not in others, has also been questioned. There is now a more nuanced approach to improving livelihoods, especially in societies whose capacity for industrialization is limited or, in effect, non-existent. The OECD countries, meanwhile, which 'industrialized' or 'modernized' in the nineteenth or the first half of the twentieth century, are now increasingly reliant upon service industries and higher technology rather than the heavy industrialized industries of that principally manufacturing-driven era. Some analysts suggest that the idea of 'modernism', which they see as corresponding to heavy industrialization, production lines and bureaucratic organization, has, for many countries, more or less passed with the advent of the increasingly diversified, globalized, high-technology types of work that now characterize the leading edge of developed economies. While some countries have successfully adopted industrialization, this wider change to economic organization suggests that the path to development may differ for countries now endeavouring to lift themselves out of poverty. Some may be able to 'skip' directly to a service industry, high technology approach.

Such considerations are, of course, a very long way from the commodity-producing and subsistence economies of most of the world's developing, less developed or least developed states, in which wages are low, employment conditions usually poor and unregulated, and in which many facets of modern (or postmodern) life taken for granted in OECD countries exist only as a dream. Such countries also often lack technical and organizational capacity, and have limited access to resources. There has been a trickle down of technology to developing countries, but for many people – around one in ten – clean running water is still not available, while health conditions remain poor, medical support is limited or unaffordable, literacy remains at marginal levels and opportunities for personal growth are virtually non-existent.

Varied development experiences

The notion of 'third worldism' as a formula to express the common interests and joint organization of developing countries has also been challenged and largely undermined by the increasing variety of development experiences between and within these countries themselves. Can there be said to be a common feature of countries as diverse as East Timor, Ethiopia, El Salvador and Bangladesh? Such countries are usually classified as less developed (LD) or least developed (LLD), with the latter status being used by the United Nations as a benchmark for entitlement to preferential assistance. The LLD countries, the poorest in the world, are those whose poverty is most profound, for whom special help is supposed to be available. Per capita GDP in such countries is generally less than US$2 a day and in some cases US$1 a day. What is more, for many of their inhabitants even these amounts would be regarded as a mark of wealth, as median incomes are invariably less than this. Examples of LLD countries include Laos, Cambodia, East Timor, Burma and many of the states of sub-Saharan Africa. LD countries include South Africa, Egypt, the Central American states and the Philippines.

Some countries previously regarded as 'third world' and generally classified as 'developing' have managed to rise above such levels, on account of beneficial location, natural resources (especially oil), colonial (or post-colonial) heritage and good governance, or, in more exceptional circumstances, the right mix of policies combined with a competent and honest government. The average income of their populations is considerably more than in the bottom two categories, yet they are still some way from the income levels of the OECD countries. Industrialization may be taking place, but it is not consistent, and their economies tend to continue to be dominated either by commodity exports or light or simple manufacturing, often combined with a high level of foreign investment and ownership. Thailand, Malaysia, Chile and Argentina all fall into such a category of 'developing' countries, as do China, Brazil and India, with each now rapidly industrializing and also moving into areas of higher technology.

Such a focus, however, privileges the economic above other aspects of life. The argument that it is difficult to consider other facets of life when one is hungry is persuasive, yet people in LD and LLD countries may still enjoy rich cultures and social structures, and deep religious beliefs, as well as strong and complex social and kinship ties. And, at least as importantly, their hopes and aspirations are equal to, and often greater than, those of more economically privileged people. For example, a person consciously deprived of freedom of political choice is likely to appreciate its political advantages more than a person who can take it for granted. So too with human rights and their suppression, including those most basic desires of ordinary people everywhere, to speak freely and to be heard, to assemble and to organize around issues that affect them, and to be free of punishment, including torture, arbitrary arrest and detention, inhumane and inappropriate prison sentences and death. Following this logic, rather than just looking to economic indicators as a measure of development, one might also consider the nature of the state: whether its agencies function adequately, whether they are corrupt or untainted, the extent to which the government is autonomous of vested interests, and whether the rule of law applies consistently and equally, and across the whole of the territory claimed by the state.

There is an assumption in such a discussion that, all other things being equal, such conditions – or opportunities to create such conditions – do or should apply to all people more or less equally. Yet fully half of the world's population suffers various forms of discrimination, ranging from the 'glass ceiling' experienced by women and minorities in developed countries, to forced abstinence from education or work in others, and the otherwise culturally imposed roles that women are often forced to undertake, their lack of rights to redress and their inferior status in almost all aspects of social, political and economic life. The role of women, their position in many societies and the tension over the evolution of such positions has been one of the most troubled aspects of the development debate, and while there has been encouraging movement in some areas there has been disturbingly little in others.

The issue of development, and especially material development, also implies the greater use of natural resources, often in ways that wilfully ignore the side effects, such as water pollution from industrial sources, but also in ways in which people are genuinely unaware of the consequences, such as deforestation. One might ask, leaving aside for the moment the question of resource distribution, if parents in a heavily overpopulated country where large families are favoured would understand that continuing with such a tradition, especially in an era of broadly increasing life expectancy, could directly contribute to the potential ecological collapse of their own local environment? Or, indeed, one might also ask whether a local logger engaged in deforestation is thinking about the longer term when immediate survival continues to press. And then there are those whose faith in technology and the potential 'fixes' that it might provide offers an easy rationale for not altering their otherwise ecologically unsustainable behaviour. The world is our home, yet many of the world's population seems to insist on crowding and despoiling it, with little thought for how, and if, we can continue to live in our current manner, much less what sort of 'home' we are leaving to our children, our grandchildren and subsequent generations.

Measuring development?

Within discussion about development, the idea of per capita GDP as the primary measure of development, as noted above, began to give way, in the 1970s, to a more widely inclusive Physical Quality of Life Index (PQLI). The PQLI emphasized development results rather than capacity for consumption, measuring infant mortality, life expectancy and adult literacy. This was, in turn, supplanted in 1990 by the Human Development Index (HDI) as a way of measuring development, which combined life expectancy (as a proxy measure for good health), per capita income and a mix of educational measures in an effort to measure capacity to make life choices. These measurements, in turn, are now being challenged by the additional development criteria of human dignity, religious freedom, cultural maintenance, political expression, participation and empowerment, which give meaning to the often abused term 'democratization', and other so-called civil and political 'rights'. In this broad field, issues of 'governance' have become paramount.

In this respect, notions of 'development' continue to evolve in ways that increasingly address the range of concerns that are expressed by people in their daily lives, most notably in those countries or regions where such daily lives are often a struggle for existence, or at least an adequate existence. In particular, the expression of concerns and values that contribute to an expanding idea of 'development' is the product of an increased level of community participation in the development process. The emphasis on development has increasingly moved away from what the 'experts' say 'development' is to what people seeking 'development' want it to be. In saying this, however, it should be understood that this process of change is only partial and not especially quick, in particular among the larger multilateral agencies like the World Bank or Asian Development Bank, and more traditional development planners.

The shift in the categorization of what constitutes development began not only to diversify 'ownership' of the meaning of development, but also to reflect the diversity of responses to the development process. Some more successful developing states, for instance, have moved up the HDI scale while others, for various reasons, have tended to languish or indeed slide further down the scale, and yet others have had responses that have been inconsistent, in turn reflecting a different mix of policy prescriptions and circumstances. However, it has become increasingly clear that while, for the purposes of broad study, there is some advantage to such general categorizations, as a methodological tool such a scale is only partially helpful. All countries respond to and are influenced by a range of criteria that include history, material resources, economic infrastructure, trading links, political systems, conflict and the environment. Against this, while there are similarities between some countries, no two places are exactly the same. Hence, the study of development as it applies to people in real circumstances must, if it is to be meaningful, grapple with the specific outcomes in particular contexts, and not just broad theories.

Development is, perhaps, the world's most critical problem, incorporating most and perhaps all of the world's pressing issues. At the same time, the subject of development has retreated to increasingly simple formulae in the minds of many of the people and governments able to address it meaningfully. Much has been achieved in the development field in improving the lives of many of the world's people, but for many others little has advanced. Based on the overall fall in official development assistance (ODA) from developed countries as a proportion of their GDP, it is clear that donor 'fatigue' has set in, and the global contest driving much work has ended. While many developing countries have shown real signs of improvement, the gap between still-growing developed countries and many developing countries continues to widen, meaning that the world is, for many, a less equal, rather than a more equal, place.

In part, the problems of developing countries in 'catching up' with the developed world, or, in some cases, even maintaining their existing position, are self-inflicted. Poor and often corrupt leadership with authoritarian or totalitarian tendencies has all too often been experienced by developing countries over the past half century. And a refusal informally to accept as equal citizens members of non-governing ethnic groups has riven many multi-ethnic developing societies, undoing the civic basis for state development. However, in many cases, the problems faced by many developing countries are also a legacy of colonialism, in which disparate ethnic groups – proto-nations – were lumped together by colonial powers based on geopolitical and military reach and with little or no regard for social cohesion, existing patterns of social organization or the need for social and capital infrastructure. Similarly, the style and method of colonial rule very often imparted to aspiring independence movements engendered little respect for, or understanding of, economic equity, legal principle or political participation. Further, the often brutal methods of maintaining political control by many colonial powers and their often violent intransigence towards decolonization also informed and deeply influenced many post-colonial states.

Yet, it would be a mistake to see developing countries simply as a product of these historical circumstances alone. Post-(or neo-)colonial economic relationships have dominated most developing countries since, constructing them as suppliers of primary commodities to an often oversupplied world market that, as a consequence, has driven down prices and hence income available to such countries. Foreign political intervention has also been used to maintain in power governments that served elite interests, rather than the mass of the people. This process was especially notable during the period of ideological contest between the West and the Soviet bloc. Very often regimes were installed or supported not because they addressed development issues but simply because they were regarded as loyal 'clients' of one side or the other. The economic and political fallout from this policy continues to reverberate to this day.

Most notably, for over half a century, developing countries have been encouraged to follow the industrializing lead of developed countries, borrowing heavily for (often questionable) major infrastructure projects and attempting to track along the path to economic 'take-off' expected by early development theorists. Indeed, this fixation with an often externally imposed model of economic development has often not suited the conditions of developing countries and has exacerbated existing political and economic problems, or created new ones, such as deepening levels of indebtedness. There have been some notable development successes, particularly in East Asia. But a closer reading of these successes reveals a complex set of conditions that make them the exception rather than the rule. Until recently, only one broad model of development – the so-called 'Washington Consensus', based on neo-liberalism, was promoted globally. But, and especially with the rise of China as a new economic power, the question remains whether or not there are potentially several development models rather than that which had been dominant. Does the experience of China offer an alternative model to the neo-liberalism of much of the West?

The 'aid', too, that has been offered to developing countries to help alleviate their problems can often be seen as a means of buying off the sense of guilt of those in developed countries whose conscience is not shackled by parochial identity. Aid policies frequently target spending of aid money in the donor country on goods or services that usually have a short lifespan in the developing country and are unable to be sustained once the donor has left. In only a few cases are skills and knowledge successfully imparted to local partners in aid projects, creating a legacy of unfulfilled hopes, failed expectations and political frustration. The best, though rarest, aid projects are those that impart knowledge and skills and leave in place technology that is sustainable in local conditions. This represents the slow and incomplete transition from patronage to participation.

If most of the post-colonial era has been marked by wide-ranging policy failure on the part of many developing countries, then the developed countries also continue to bear responsibility. The policies of infrastructure development and industrialization encouraged by developed countries that required massive overseas borrowings by developing countries left a vast number of countries with crippling and often unsustainable debts. The answer to this has been further, renegotiated debt, mortgaging not just the present but the long-term future of many developing countries. And the policies that have been imposed by Western governments as a condition of debt 'relief' have, in most cases, been onerous and narrowly defined, leading to cuts in basic social services such as education and health care.

The tighter economic embrace of global capital, particularly since the end of the Cold War, has left most developing countries with few, if any, options about the course that is supposed to lead to development. The largely 'off the shelf' economic model been handed down by organizations such as the International Monetary Fund and the World Bank was, in reality, simply not negotiable. Yet it has been precisely this patronizing and unilateral view of the options for development that have themselves failed in the past. The 'experts' continue to believe their own theories and, too often, to ignore the mounting evidence. The one or two that announce that the emperor (or the empire) has no clothes are invariably cast out (see Stiglitz 2002).

The failure of development

Yet what has been learned about development over the past half century or so is that much of the process to date has, based on a wider set of criteria, not worked especially well. Ideas in development have changed while the lives of many poor people remain much the same. It is now clear that investment in new industries to modernize the economy in the

1950s was inappropriate or inadequate; that investment in education alone (1960s) has in most cases not been sustained to reveal the benefits it could have delivered; that investment in basic needs (health, agriculture, etc.) in the 1970s has not been enough or sufficiently applied; that investment in 'getting policies right' to facilitate technology transfer (1980s) has been misguided, mishandled or was simply unsustainable; and that investment in alliances that were intended to achieve sectoral reforms, especially in finance and export-led development (1990s), has not achieved the sort of gains in development that have led to a sustainable reduction in poverty on a global scale.

Remarkably, and perhaps dangerously, little attention has been paid to the physical impact that various attempts at development have had on the planet on which we all live. According to the UN Department of Economic and Social Affairs, by 2050 the population of the world's 48 least developed countries will double and the global population is expected to be 9.6 billion people. In terms of economic distribution, around half of the world's population currently lives on less than US$2 a day, which as noted above is understood by some planners to constitute absolute poverty, while more than 150 million children remain undernourished and wider malnutrition affects more than a quarter of the world's population. According to various studies, around 80 per cent of the world's wealth is held by 15 per cent of its people, who also use a disproportionate share of world resources, while the world's wealthiest 1 per cent control as much money as the world's poorest three billion (see e.g. Thompson 2014). Natural resources, including arable land, forests and sea life, are diminishing at an unsustainable rate, while more than 11,000 species risk extinction, including a quarter of all mammal species and 30 per cent of fish species (WWF 2014). Remaining forests, which produce oxygen and absorb carbon dioxide, are estimated to reduce by almost half over the next 20 years. Global warming from the production of greenhouse gases continues and constitutes perhaps the single biggest threat to the survival of the planet. Scarcity of clean water affects more than a billion people, and water loss is becoming a major problem in Africa and Asia.

Facing a less forgiving international economic and ideological order, with little scope for error, traditional 'modernist' development is being challenged by models that are more reflective, more critical and more participatory. This development challenge is reflected in efforts by some practitioners to utilize more participatory approaches to development planning, and to challenge orthodox approaches to development project design, implementation and monitoring. Greater focus on the accountability of decision makers in developing countries also reflects these more recent trends. As a result, much of the focus has shifted to giving attention to governance issues which, it has been repeatedly shown, when ignored can be manipulated by sectional interests for narrowly defined personal gain.

Accountability, transparency and mandate are key themes in this more recent approach to development, with advocates for pro-poor policies, fairer international economic relations and sustainable poverty reduction challenging globalization and free-market capitalism for a greater sharing of the development agenda. This shift in focus and emphasis poses fundamental challenges to earlier conventional approaches to development, and redefines the roles that key stakeholders play in priority setting. Moral hazard and poor governance are two of the issues that are now attracting greater attention. Equally important are shifts in process that challenge development professionals to genuinely 'democratize' the development process and set out key performance indicators that do more than give lip service to the interests of the people it is intended to serve.

It is important to note that these trends were unlikely to have come forward while the Cold War continued. While developing countries remained pawns in a larger game, it was commonly regarded as too costly to the big powers to allow issues of governance, fairness or justice to play a real role in determining stakeholder influence. While there remain significant vested constraints, with the passing of the Cold War the pressures are different. Disenfranchised stakeholders are asserting their voices and poverty reduction can (and no doubt should) be a real goal of the global system.

About this book

This book is the third edition of the 2008 book *International Development: Issues and Challenges* which in turn replaced the 2004 text *Key Issues in Development*. In common with *Key Issues in Development*, it acknowledges that development is a contested and, in some senses, unstable idea, having progressed from the early post-war years when it meant little more than increasing average income, to, seven decades later, including a range of conditions and circumstances that impact on life in countries that continue to variously define themselves in the modern, or postmodern, world. A common understanding of a postmodern world that has evolved since the end of the Cold War is that which has transcended industrialization and largely relies on information flows and processes as the basis for its economy. Critics have argued, however, that postmodernism is in fact a variety of modernism which continues to rely on (sometimes offshore) manufacturing substrata and maintained access to primary commodities, while also using the higher level of information technology now available. That is to say, the world is increasingly locating economic sectors along state lines with different states playing different roles, i.e. high-technology information providers, industrial manufacturers and basic commodity providers. The primary categories continue to exist, if in an increasingly global, rather than local, economy.

Assuming, then, that the major global economic changes involve a reorganization of states as primarily differentiated contributors to commodity, manufacturing and information components of the global economy, the questions that arise revolve around the relative weightings of these sectors and the political judgements that consent to such a reorganization. In this there is a very real tension between the structural exigencies of the 'neo-liberal' (free market-led) global economic agenda, state-led developmentalism and the potential agency of politics in which allocation of resources reflects interest-based, rather than mechanistic, economic considerations. There is a suggestion in this that, following the economics-first approach, development is increasingly market- rather than state-led. However, this assumes that what markets achieve is development, broadly defined. The neo-liberal philosophy, itself under challenge by the statist approaches of China and to some extent India, which structurally links free markets (which are almost never actually free) and democracy (generically regarded as political development) fundamentally fails to note a long history of state intervention in markets within democratic contexts. It is also based on the assumption that markets, unrestrained, will deliver broadly distributed wealth, which is at best a moot point, and that competing neo-liberal economic practice is politically value-neutral which, demonstrably, it is not.

From this tension arises the question, yet again, what is the purpose of development? As discussed in this book, development continues to mean the material advancement of people, especially the world's poor. But material advancement, especially if understood as simple economic growth, is not enough by itself, and, indeed, may not even be realized without other component aspects of development which include the capacity to ensure adequate distribution of the benefits of such growth, ecological sustainability in the way the growth is achieved and the governance to ensure that the processes to achieve such growth are agreed in a politically inclusive manner and operate under the rule of law.

Development here is, therefore, understood as a process not just of growth or, at its most benign, poverty alleviation, but also of empowerment. The universalist claim to rights, for example, as a part of an overarching (although inconsistent) globalization of standards, also includes accountability and transparency. On the other hand, the growing tendency towards localism is increasing the pressure to put decision-making into the hands of the people. In this, it has been argued by some development commentators that there is a further tension between universal prescriptions and local conditions. As discussed in the chapter on community development (Chapter 8), the application of development practice must be attuned to local conditions. Yet there are also certain normative development outcomes, including the full and disinterested application of law, and active political participation and representation of people whatever their race, sex, creed or social status. These mutually reliant outcomes, which might be termed 'inclusive governance', both implicitly and sometimes explicitly underpin the contributions to this book. It is this underpinning, or philosophical orientation, that makes this book a somewhat more original contribution to the development debate than many others which have been far more equivocal about or disinterested in such matters.

For the purpose of the book, development means the process by which the people and states outside the industrialized world attempt to improve their conditions of life, through material and social means. Here, development implies change, affecting most, if not all, areas of life. The idea of development is a multidimensional and, by definition, interdisciplinary field in which economic, political, technological, social and cultural factors interact. In this respect, this book considers a wide range of what its authors believe to be the key issues in the development debate. These include definitions of levels of development, global influences on development, measurements of development, economic issues, the contribution of international aid, political and civil development, the issue of gender, the idea of development as 'modernization', theories of underdevelopment, regional variation, the environment and community development. The focus of the book is widely international and employs a geographically broad range of examples, other than where it addresses geographically specific issues (that themselves have wider implications for the field of study, such as the global financial crisis, sub-Saharan Africa's development challenges or United Nations-led state-building).

Mark McGillivray's opening chapter asks the question 'What is Development?' At one level this is a basic question, but, as intimated above, it can quickly descend into a complex and contested range of responses. This chapter is a mild revision of the previous iteration, given that what constitutes 'development', and, more importantly, the 'good', has not meaningfully changed. McGillivray's detailed discussion of what constitutes development locates at development's core the idea of poverty alleviation, and tracing its origins from the beginning of the post-Second World War era, some of the variations that have shaped the process over the intervening period. The focus on poverty alleviation as the core of what constitutes development addresses perhaps the most basic issue in the development debate: that if people remain hungry or without adequate shelter, education or other basic services, then all else becomes redundant. This establishes the basic premise for the rest of the book.

Any study of development must trace the key debates on its political economy since the beginning of the post-war era. John McKay updates and outlines these major trends and conditions within the global system, and the dominant ideas on the nature and genesis of development. At one level, the second half of the twentieth century was an era of unparalleled growth and prosperity, if with some economic stumbles in the twenty-first century. But this has only occurred within certain countries or regions. A key question then, which McKay seeks to answer in his revised Chapter 2, is why some countries have been able to prosper while others have stagnated or gone backwards.

McKay also addresses the continuing fallout from the global financial crisis, which has forced a rethinking of some assumptions about how development works, including 'trickle down' theory, although he notes it as coming under challenge as a result of the 'Beijing Model' of development and the global financial crisis. The survival of the neoliberal paradigm after it was widely discredited in the global financial crisis and as a result of an increasing gap in wealth distribution is also analysed and put into broader context. McKay also addresses the move towards greater solidarity among many lower income countries, as well as examining the increasing role of groups like the BRIC (Brazil, Russia, India, China).

The chapter explores the history of ideas about development, asking what has been learned from the last 60 or so years, in particular more recently, in terms of theory and the design of more appropriate policies. It looks at the motives for co-operation and assesses the current state and role of development co-operation in light of globalization and significant progress in reducing poverty in developing countries. It also considers the role that development co-operation has played towards the Millennium Development Goals (MDGs), which were replaced in 2015 by the Sustainable Development Goals, and what future role aid could play in a very changed development environment relative to other sources of finance.

Most notably, as McKay observes in Chapter 4, rapid economic growth, collapse and a resumption of high levels of growth in Asia, most notably China, have posed questions for both dependency theorists and the proponents of free-market policies, while the continued crisis in Africa continues as an indictment of the entire development 'profession'. This chapter examines these two very different crises, and considers in particular the nature of the crises in the two regions, and the various explanations that have been put forward to account for these serious events. Working with long-term data, McKay considers whether the crises in Africa and Asia were separate, unrelated events, or two symptoms of some basic problems in the global system which have reappeared in the global financial crisis.

Within this, McKay notes the variations between countries in terms of the severity and causes of the crisis, the policies that had been adopted, or had failed to be adopted, in the period leading up to the respective crises, and the relationship between them with the onset of crisis conditions. This then leads to consideration of the impact of trade, investment and other liberalization policies, the relationship between the crises and the nature of the global systems of trade, investment and finance, and the impact of the global financial crisis upon all of that.

Given expressions of broadly anti-Western sentiment in a number of developing countries, McKay then looks at the level and nature of resentment in Asia and Africa against the West, and its economic, political and strategic implications. And continuing with a theme developed in earlier chapters, McKay also considers the relationships in various countries and regions between democracy, transparency, good governance, economic development and the crisis. He explores the extent and nature of recovery from the crisis in various countries, especially in Asia, and the policies for restructuring and reform, including the role of international and regional agencies in facilitating recovery, the extent to which these actions were effective, and what has occurred since.

In discussion of the success or otherwise of the application of economic models, issues of governance and, hence, accountability have become critical. Kingsbury notes in the chapter that follows, on political development, some of the characteristics that have become identified with developing countries and why many of them are locked into a cycle of repression, reform and then a return to closure. As noted by Kingsbury, multi-ethnic states with low levels of institutional capacity and relative economic scarcity tend to default to patron–client relations and repression of objectors. Within that, as they try to transition out of such situations, there are a range of factors which can militate against the success of such transitions. Within this, there are debates about universal versus local values, the form and structure of the state, the principal model of political organization, about who should be included and who not and how and why, about the legitimacy of the state and the relationship between the government and the state. Case studies in this chapter include the mixed outcomes of the 'Arab Spring', reforms in Myanmar and political changes elsewhere. Political reform, as Kingsbury notes and addresses, is neither a given nor irreversible.

Within development, a major consistent focus has been on development assistance, usually referred to as aid. In Chapter 6, Janet Hunt critically reviews multilateral and bilateral aid, and the distinctions between official development assistance (ODA) and private aid programmes. This revised chapter assesses the contributions, styles and shifting orientations of the major multilateral aid organizations and aid donor countries, the international commitment to aid, how aid is employed in bilateral relations and the role of non-government organizations in the aid agenda/s and as contributors to the effective application of aid. This updated chapter assesses the impact of economic crisis in Europe and the US on promised official flows and on private flows, the changing landscape of poverty with the majority of the world's poor in middle-income countries, and hence raises some questions about the role of aid in regard to these people and, related to this, concerns about inequality in development.

There have been critical questions raised about the emphasis on aid effectiveness and results-based approaches, particularly in relation to the MDGs at the conclusion of their period of application, which Hunt also considers before moving to the debates going on about the post-2015 agenda for development and the role of aid within that. The question of aid and power relations raises the further question of who primarily benefits from aid, noting that aid is often far less benign than it initially appears.

Following from this increasing tendency towards globalization, in Chapter 7 Matthew Clarke examines the concepts, measures, trends and responses that have in large part come to define, if not the global standards, then at least the major development paradigms. As Clarke argues, at its base development seeks to improve the lives of the poor. Determining whether development has been successful in reducing poverty, however, requires an understanding of the meaning of poverty and, once it is understood, responses to how it can be measured. Clarke's chapter therefore begins with a review of how poverty is defined, and describes the movement from the long-held approach of it being solely a function of income to its more recent multidimensional understanding best encapsulated by the MDGs. Clarke then offers an assessment of the experience of poverty over recent decades, utilizing a large number of poverty measures and other data. He then analyses change in poverty measurements and outcomes, concluding with thoughts on how poverty might be further reduced through both local or community and national and international interventions.

Chapter 8 picks up on themes of the focus, purpose and methods of development raised by politics in developing countries to consider ideas of community development. Community development is intended to enhance the social and local decision-making process – the 'empowerment' – of people who are the target of development projects and to give them more practical political power over the goals and outcomes of the development process. Kingsbury posits that the movement towards community development reflects a fundamental reorientation of development towards a grass-roots or local-level process of democratization. Such an approach has been shown, in a number of cases, to produce real, tangible and appropriate benefits to people at the local level, as well as providing a greater sense of self-worth and the capacity to make many of their own decisions. It also has the benefit of working within and preserving aspects of local culture that give meaning to community life and which assist in maintaining and enhancing the social cohesion that is necessary when successfully engaging in a process of change.

This chapter is updated with examples of community development from recent studies in Timor-Leste, where the Community Development Program has largely failed to meet objectives or expectations, and from Aceh in Indonesia, where it has fared better. It will also consider the impact of community development programmes in conflict-affected states such as Iraq, Afghanistan and Syria. This chapter considers reasons for the success or failure of different community development projects, and looks at differing approaches to community development models, including participant-response analysis, grass-roots and pro-poor orientations, and so on. Related to community development or local empowerment is the development or empowerment of women within the development context. In Chapter 9, Janet Hunt focuses on the gender aspects of development, in particular how women have largely been 'made invisible' and left out of the development process. While policies have more recently sought to include women in development, the results have been mixed, progressing in some areas but going backwards or simply staying stagnant in others. Women have always carried the largest share of the domestic material burden in societies in developing countries, beyond child-rearing and home maintenance, including domestic husbandry and agriculture, and, more recently, in paid employment. Hunt also notes that men have been more readily accommodated into the cash economy, although the benefits of their access to cash have not always contributed to the welfare of family members.

As Hunt explains, gender is understood as the socially ascribed roles of men and women in any society based on their sex. Hunt examines how gender-defined roles have been differentiated traditionally and how the development process has influenced or changed this, and how this influence or change has impacted on gender relations and the distribution of the benefits of development, often to the detriment of women. Understanding the gender impacts of proposed development is a key issue.

Hunt's chapter links many of the issues raised in earlier chapters and views them through a gender lens. If development is to reduce poverty, then it must transform women's lives, since women are disproportionately represented among the world's poor.

While all of the preceding issues are critical to an understanding of development, it is the degradation of the earth's capacity to sustain life that presents short-term problems and critical long-term threats. That is to say, no development can take place outside the context of the physical environment, yet, until relatively recently, this has been the most neglected area in development debate. In Chapter 10, Kingsbury therefore considers aspects of the environment that increasingly demand to be thought of as fundamental parts of the development agenda. This demand has been partly as a consequence of the rise in the profile of environmental issues in developed countries and, hence, among many bilateral and multilateral aid agencies and aid organizations. It has also, in part, been in response to environmental issues that have arisen in developing countries due to increases in population and particularly as a direct result of a range of development processes. However, as Kingsbury notes, environmental issues such as global warming are not exclusive to particular countries but are now understood as constituting a threat to all. Kingsbury recognizes that the environmental record in development has, to date, been poor, and environmental degradation has continued at a pace that is unsustainable in absolute terms.

Given the world's focus on terrorism, the issues of underdevelopment that have been argued to give it fuel, and the various development (not to mention military) resources that have been allocated to combating it, the final chapter of this book, by McKay, reviews recent thinking about the causes of terrorism and violence, and the impact that the anti-terrorism effort is having on development. Although there had been little action up until this was being written, there had been considerable rhetoric about the link between poverty and terrorism, and the need therefore to tackle poverty.

This chapter is substantially revised and rewritten in the light of recent experiences and new theoretical advances. The impact of the wars in Afghanistan, Iraq, Syria – and the subsequent rise of Islamic State – the spillover of the Afghanistan war into Pakistan, and the expansion of anti-state militarism into other parts of the Middle East such as Yemen are considered. This then begs the question regarding the meaning of the word 'terrorism' and its capacity to impact upon development in ways not previously considered. McKay reflects on the new work on the concept of the failed (or failing) states, employing the Democratic Republic of the Congo as a relevant case study. The limits to effectiveness of international intervention in these matters have also become much clearer, and the implication of this is also evaluated.

As noted at the outset, much of the world continues to focus on issues of development and, when attention is properly turned, it is widely recognized that the problems of development are global in both their reach and their potential impact. Yet at the same time the urgency felt by some about such global development issues is far from shared by all, and has resulted in this retreat from tackling the complex issues. The reduction to increasingly simplistic formulae for addressing the continuing problems of development reflects the 'fatigue' that has, in various forms, beset many wealthier countries in relation to poorer countries. Much of this, in turn, can be attributed to the lack of ideological imperative that characterized the period from around 1950 to 1990. A new ideological imperative – that of neo-liberalism – has prevailed but it has been less generous, less sympathetic (and much less empathetic) and fairly inflexible in the choices that it has offered. It is also itself now under increasing challenge, as countries and the citizens within them reject imposed austerity which has been argued – and in some cases shown – to actually make their problems worse rather than better.

This book, then, attempts to discuss these key issues and explore some of the ways forward for development in this evolving period of global reorganization. If it provides questioning material to work with and to consider critically, it will have gone a long way towards achieving its primary goal.

Note

1. The common basis for this ideology is the fundamentalist Salafi interpretation of Sunni Islam, based on the first three generations after the Prophet Mohamad. A violent interpretation of Salafism is that which informs most so-called 'jihadi' organizations.

Chapter 1

What is Development?

Mark McGillivray

The term 'development' is one that has many different meanings. While many overlap, some inherently contradict each other. To many people development is either a process or outcome that is often bad in terms of its impact on people and the societies in which they live. Some others see development as both a process and an outcome, and as necessarily good. These people see development as something that should be actively sought after. And to complicate matters further, there are many others who define development in many different ways. This chapter broadly attempts to identify, explain and resolve those issues by introducing and outlining various conceptualizations of development. Such an exercise is an important one: if we are to study something, it is essential to first understand what we are studying. It is especially important in a study of development, for without a definition of this term we cannot determine whether a country is achieving higher levels of development, or whether it should be considered developed, developing or underdeveloped. It is also important for development practice. Development practitioners, irrespective of whether they are involved in policy, planning or in implementing development projects, need a working definition of what it is they are seeking to achieve.

This chapter looks at various definitions of development. Such an exercise necessarily requires an examination of theoretical material about what development is or ought to be. The chapter adopts a largely chronological examination, given that many new definitions are actually responses to earlier ones. To understand the latter, one first needs to understand the former. The chapter commences by introducing and critiquing various traditional or early meanings or conceptualizations of development. This is a deliberately brief discussion. More detailed treatments can be found in Leftwich (2000), Hunt (1989) and, in particular, Cowen and Shenton (1996). The chapter then examines more contemporary meanings of development, those which emerged from the late 1960s to the present. These meanings either treat development as the domination and exploitation of one group by another or as what might very loosely be described as 'good change'. The chapter favours the use of the second meaning, largely because it forces us to reflect on what sort of change or outcomes we want to see in all countries, rich and poor, providing a framework to compare actual changes against those we would like to observe. It also allows us to consider which countries, and, within countries, which people, should be prioritized in efforts to improve the human condition.

The chapter focuses predominantly on various conceptualizations that are consistent with the 'good change' approach, many that are provided by the literature on human well-being. This is followed by an empirical examination of the development record in a manner consistent with some of these conceptualizations. This involves looking at country achievements, or in some cases lack thereof, in health, education, income and related indicators. Finally, a balance sheet is provided that looks at what might be perceived as 'goods' and 'bads' and which asks us to judge whether 'development' has actually occurred. It is argued that this is essentially a subjective exercise, and a complicated one at that, which requires one to reflect on one's own personal values to judge what is important and what is not.

Traditional meanings of development

Historical progress and modernization

To many people, development means the use of natural resources to supply infrastructure, build roads and dams and provide electricity and other forms of energy, to productively utilize or exploit previously unused areas of land or to devise new forms of technology for productive use. For others, it can simply be an ordered or linked set of events or changes. It is not uncommon for someone to refer to the 'next development' in something, be it an individual's life story, a novel, a movie or a sports event or, more to the current point, a town or city, region or nation. These meanings correspond, arguably, with what most laypeople would mean by 'development'.

These layperson's definitions of development are broadly consistent, to varying degrees, with more formal definitions that were dominant in the academic and policy literatures and embraced by most development practitioners during the 1950s to late 1960s. They still appear in some literatures and are embraced by some practitioners even today, but are far less dominant. Some have their origins in literature dating back many centuries. Most, if not all, overlap to varying degrees and some are differentiated only by subtle variations. For our current purposes, it is sufficient to outline two that are arguably the most dominant. The definitions treat development as either historical progress or modernization. Let us briefly discuss each in turn.

Development as *historical progress* refers to the unfolding of human history, over a long period of time, in a manner that is thought to be progressive. The evolution of capitalism is often put forward as an example of historical progress. Key to this definition is what is understood as progress, and deciding whether certain historical changes are progressive is not a straightforward task. It is made all the less straightforward by many different conceptualizations of progress. The modern view of progress is based on a philosophical notion that is equated with a steady onward process, brought about by human agency, that results in a systematic transformation of the world. Human agency is in turn seen as the application of human abilities, such as intelligence and initiative.

Development, defined as historical progress, is very much linked to the Western European experience from the late eighteenth century onward. This experience saw the emergence of more materially affluent societies, the application of improved technologies that resulted among other things in better communication and transportation, greater human freedom and, in time, improvements in health and education levels.

Development as *modernization* has been described in many different ways. This very influential conceptualization of development is discussed in detail in Chapter 2 of this book, so here we provide broad details only. Modernization is a process whereby societies move through a fundamental, complete structural transition from one condition to another, from a starting point to an end point. The starting point is viewed as a traditional society which develops into an advanced, modern society. This is associated with a shift in the structure of an economy, away from a reliance on the agricultural sector. This shift sees a greater reliance over time on the industrial sector, with an increasingly large proportion of an economy's output coming from manufacturing activities. Eventually it also sees the rise of a services sector which includes the providers of health and educational services, finance, transportation and professional advice.

It should be emphasized that in its proper context modernization not only involves an economic transformation but profound social, cultural, ideological, institutional and political changes as well. In an influential paper, Huntington (1971) describes modernization as a process in which societies have more control over their natural and social environment due to the use of superior scientific and technical knowledge. Moreover, according to Huntington, the economic, social and political structures and processes actually converge over time.

Development defined as modernization or historical progress is evident in the works of two well-known writers, Walt Rostow and Karl Marx. Examining these works allows us to better understand these definitions. Rostow proposed what is known as the 'stages theory' of economic growth in his famous book published in 1960 (Rostow 1960). The growth to which Rostow refers is in the economy or economic growth, measured by year-on-year changes in the overall level of production. Rostow's theory is also discussed in the next chapter which mainly focuses on the context in which this theory was proposed. Here our focus is on the meaning of development implicit to the Rostow theory.

Rostow's stages of economic growth

Rostow's theory is that societies pass through five stages. A society or country can be considered to be *developing* as it passes through these stages and as *developed* as it reaches the final stages. And, as we shall shortly note, development is very much defined in terms of material advancement. Often this type of development is called *economic development*. The first is a *traditional society* stage. This stage is characterized by low levels of productivity and technology. The economy is dominated by the agricultural sector, with most people living and working on the land. The social structure of agricultural life is very hierarchical and there is little upward mobility: people who are born poor remain poor, and successive generations are often no better off than each other. Economic growth is very low or non-existent.

The second stage is when societies commence a process of transition. This is when the preconditions for what is termed 'take-off' into rapid and sustained growth are put in place. Accordingly, this is the *preconditions for take-off* stage. Entrepreneurial activity emerges, with a class of people willing and able to save from their incomes, thereby creating a pool of funds that can be invested. Banks and other institutions that facilitate these activities emerge, with an increase in investment in transport and communications. Modern technologies are also utilized.

The third stage is *take-off*. During this stage there are further technical advances in both industry and agriculture, the entrepreneurial class expands, new and profitable industries emerge and quickly expand and previously unexploited natural resources are increasingly used in production. This stage is characterized by two key factors which differentiate it from the previous stage. The first is that institutional resistances to steady economic growth are largely removed. These resistances might be, for example, a class of people whose interests are to retard general economic advancement, such as a landed or elite class that wants a pool of cheap labour. The second is that there are large increases in the incomes of those who not only save increasingly larger shares of this income but make these savings available to those wanting to invest in modern sectors of the economy. Savings increase by up to approximately 10 per cent of national income in the take-off stage.

Take-off is followed a long interval of sustained, although fluctuating, progress as the now regularly growing economy drives to apply modern technology throughout its entire economy. This is the fourth stage, known as the *drive to maturity*. Savings and investment is in the vicinity of 10 to 20 per cent of national income and the growth of national output and income regularly exceeds that of the population. The economy is now involved extensively in international trade. Commodities that were once produced at home are imported and purchased using funds obtained from exporting other commodities abroad. New industries emerge and older ones either disappear or taper off. The society adjusts its values and institutions in ways that support the growth process. Maturity is reached 40 or so years after the end of the take-off stage.

The final stage in the Rostow theory is the *age of high mass-consumption* in which the country or society is truly developed. Upon reaching this stage, societies no longer accept the ongoing application of modern technology as the fundamental objective. The consumer is king, with the economy being primarily geared towards the production of consumer durables and services on a mass basis. The leading sectors of the economy are those that supply these goods and services. Cars, television sets, washing machines, cooking equipment and leisure are the focus of productive efforts. Material prosperity is higher than ever and this modern society can unambiguously be considered as developed. Importantly, while this prosperity might not be very evenly distributed in this modern society, it would be enjoyed by all sections within it. Those who were once poor would no longer be so because economic expansion would ensure high levels of employment and a high demand for employees would ensure higher wages. This spreading of the benefits of growth to the poor is referred to as 'trickle-down', a crucial characteristic of theories such as Rostow's.

Marx's stages of historical development

Marx, in his writings first published in the second half of the nineteenth century, envisaged four stages of historical development (Marx 1970a,

1970b, 1970c, 1972). As with Rostow's stages, the implicit message from Marx's treatment of history is that a society is *developing* as it passes through each stage and achieves a higher level of *development* along the way. The level of freedom enjoyed by individuals and the ownership of private property differentiates stages. The first of Marx's stages is the *primal stage.* Individuals are overwhelmingly concerned with satisfying the most basic of human needs such as food, clothing and shelter. Higher notions such as self-expression and individual freedoms are not entertained until basic survival is ensured. All societies are thought to emerge from this primal stage.

The second stage of historical development is the *feudal stage,* in which private property exists but is held by the aristocracy. The aristocracy oppresses and alienates but at the same time is dependent upon the masses which are the subordinate serf class. This stage provides no freedom or opportunity for self-fulfilment, and increased production is achieved through the direct exploitation of the majority.

Feudalism is followed by the *capitalist stage.* The capitalist society provides private property and productivity capacity grows rapidly. An entrepreneurial, capitalist class emerges that seeks out commercial opportunity. A more modern and technically advanced economy consequently emerges that relies less on agriculture and more on industry. Marx was of the view that capitalism was best suited to achieve increases in the productive capacity of the economy. Individual freedom is, however, withheld from the proletariat working class. This class is both exploited and impoverished, and remains alienated through its submission to wage labour. The capitalist class is enriched by the expansion of the productive capacity of the economy.

Marx's historical stages of development culminate in the fourth stage, *communism.* The enrichment of the capitalist class and the impoverishment of the proletariat in the capitalist stage would ultimately lead to the latter overthrowing the former. The proletariat would, in particular, seize the means of production, transferring it to public or collective ownership, and encourage social relations that would benefit everyone equally. True freedom for the proletariat would then be achieved. This society would reject all previous values, realizing that class is an artificial creation and perpetuated by rulers interested only in ensuring their own self-interests and survival. That the productive capacity of the economy has been built up under the capitalist stage and the sharing of the benefits of this capacity are equal means that everyone's living standards in this society are relatively high.

A critique

Traditional meanings of development, implicit or otherwise, came under great scrutiny from the late 1960s onward. Understanding this scrutiny requires us to outline the main measures of development that corresponded to these meanings. Consistent with the traditional conceptualizations of development, in particular that which equated development with modernization, was the use of the rate of growth of per capita national income, be it measured in terms of per capita Gross Domestic Product (GDP), Gross National Product (GNP) or Gross National Income (GNI), as the main indicator of whether a country was developing. Some people went so far as to even equate per capita economic growth with development, defining the latter in terms of the former.

Also consistent with the early conceptualizations was the use of the *level* of per capita national income as the main indicator of the *level* of development that a country had achieved. The World Bank, for instance, classified countries on the basis of their GNPs per capita as either low, middle or high income. Countries belonging to the high-income group were widely considered as developed, while those in the low- and middle-income groups were often considered as less developed or developing countries. This does not mean that developed countries cannot also be developing, by achieving higher levels of development, just that the label 'developing' was assigned to the low- and middle-income groups. This practice continues today, but with the use of GNIs per capita for the year 2013. Low-income countries are defined as those with a GNI per capita of US$1,045 or less in 2013, middle-income countries are those with a GNI per capita of more than US$1,045 but less than US$12,746 and high-income countries are those with a GNI per capita of US$12,746 or more (World Bank 2014d).

It was observed in the late 1960s and early 1970s that many economies that had followed a broadly Rostow-type modernization-led growth (or growth via modernization) strategy had achieved high rates of economic growth, with some achieving rather high incomes per capita. But this growth was not uniform, both among and within countries. Among countries, it was observed that rates of per capita economic growth in high-income countries far exceeded those of their low- and middle-income counterparts. For instance, between 1961 and 1970 the per capita national incomes in the high-income countries grew at an annual average rate of more than 4 per cent while over the same period the middle- and low-income countries grew at annual average rates of just over 3 and just under 1 per cent, respectively.

These differential growth rates, combined with the fact that initial incomes in the high-income countries are by definition higher than those of the low- and middle-income countries, meant that international inequalities in per capita incomes grew over time. The rich countries were getting richer and the poor countries, while also getting richer on average, were falling further and further behind. Put differently, the poor countries were becoming relatively poorer over time. High-income country income per capita was 45 times that of the low-income countries in 1960, a ratio that many observers thought was obscenely high. By 1970, however, the former were 56 times richer in terms of per capita income than the latter and 70 times richer by 1980 (World Bank 2007).

Arguably more disconcerting were inequalities within countries. Despite the positive and often high rates of growth that were experienced by the vast majority of developing countries, there remained large sections of the populations of these countries that were largely untouched by this growth. The lives of these people were still characterized by crushing, abject poverty while tiny minorities benefited enormously. The widespread perception among observers was, therefore, that the poor benefited little, if at all, from the growth via modernization strategies that had been pursued in the 1960s and earlier decades. Indeed, there were many that believed that some groups within developing societies were actually worse off as a result of these strategies, if not in terms of the incomes they earned but in terms of social upheaval and displacement, a loss of identity and cultural dislocation.

Statistics, while never adequately capturing the plight of the poor, do back up the views of the late 1960s' and early 1970s' critics of growth via modernization strategies. The experience within Latin American countries is often cited, Brazil in particular. Like many other countries in its region Brazil experienced very high rates of per capita income growth – between 6 and 11 per cent per year during the late 1960s and early 1970s. Yet large sections of the Brazilian population remained impoverished, as implied by income distribution statistics. Throughout the mid-1960s to mid-1970s, it is estimated that the poorest 10 per cent of the Brazilian population received less than 2 per cent of their nation's income. The richest 10 per cent of Brazil's population during this period is estimated to have received a little more than 40 per cent. By the early 1980s, the corresponding numbers were 1 and 45 per cent, respectively. Income poverty data are hard to obtain for the 1970s but by 1981, after further high if not volatile annual per capita national income growth outcomes, 31 per cent of the Brazilian population, some 39 million people, lived in poverty (World Bank 2007). Brazil might well be considered an extreme example but it is broadly indicative of trends in the developing world as a whole. For instance, in 1981, after years of per capita income growth in the vast majority of countries, 67 per cent of the combined population of low- and middle-income countries lived in income poverty, some 2.5 billion people (World Bank 2007). Thus it appeared that while the developing world might have grown, the fruits of this growth were not widespread. In short, if there was any trickle-down it was clearly insufficient in its extent.

Such comments apply to those countries which followed what might broadly be considered a Rostow-type growth strategy. But broadly similar comments can be made about those countries that chose Marxism during the post-Second World War and subsequently Cold War era, the many countries that were part of the Eastern bloc of countries, including the Soviet Union. Most if not all of these countries had achieved industrialization and had overthrown their capitalist classes. But the freedoms expected for the masses, especially civil freedoms, were not enjoyed. Nor, in many cases, were the expected gains in material living standards.

Contemporary meanings of development

A number of alternative meanings of development emerged from the criticisms of the modernization strategies. Some of these meanings were implicit to alternative theories of development. By this it is meant that alternative explanations of the development experiences of countries were offered, and from these theories it is possible to infer a particular definition of development. In other cases, the meanings are the result of an explicit attempt to provide an alternative definition of development. Two broad types or classes of definitions emerged: those which defined development in a rather negative manner and those which defined it in a way that is necessarily good. Let us examine each in turn.

Development as domination and exploitation

That the gap in living standards between developed and developing countries had very substantially widened throughout the 1960s and 1970s and that many hundreds of millions of people still lived in poverty in the developing world led many commentators from the late 1960s to question some of the fundamental assumptions on which modernization theories and strategies were based. These commentators tended not to question the goals of modernization but the assumption that all countries could follow a largely homogeneous development path, and that in particular what happened in the industrialized Western world could be largely replicated in poorer developing countries. What these commentators instead saw were large volumes of foreign trade between developed and developing countries and large increases in developed country foreign development aid and investment to developing countries in the apparent absence of the gains that these flows were supposed to generate. They saw countries that were marginalized and locked into a situation of underdevelopment, in which they were peripheral and subservient to and dependent on a global economy dominated by developed and multinational countries.

A leading proponent of this view was Andre Gunder Frank. Frank, like many others holding the same view, drew on the experiences of the Latin American countries. As Leftwich (2000) points out, these countries had a long and intimate engagement through investment and trade with the developed world, but the processes and features of development were thought by Frank and others to be retarded and deformed, constituting what came to be known as *underdevelopment*. Frank argued that 'development and underdevelopment are the opposite sides of the same coin' (Frank 1967: 33). The school of thought to which Frank and many others belonged believed development was not about, in effect, rapid growth that led to the sorts of societies envisaged by Rostow and other proponents of modernization-led economic growth but, rather, about the domination and exploitation by the rich developed countries of their poor underdeveloped (as distinct from developing) counterparts. It was not something for poorer countries to strive for but something that should be avoided at all costs. Further details of this school of thought are provided in the next chapter.

Development as good change

In an extremely influential work published initially in late 1969, Dudley Seers rejected the view that development was an objective or positive concept that, for example, described what was necessary for a country to achieve higher living standards for its citizens. Instead, he thought that development should be seen as a concept that requires us to identify the normative conditions for a universally acceptable aim, which for Seers was the *'realization of the potential of human personality'* (Seers 1972: 6, emphasis added). This conceptualization was a direct challenge to strategies that relied heavily on economic growth or that implicitly equated growth with development. He actually thought that economic growth did not only solve certain social and political difficulties but could actually contribute to them.

Having defined development in terms of the realization of human potential, Seers' next task was to consider what was absolutely necessary for such realization. This led him to three related questions:

• What has been happening to income poverty?
• What has been happening to unemployment?
• What has been happening to income inequality?

Seers asserted that if all three of these phenomena had over time declined from high levels, then 'beyond doubt this has been a period of development for the country concerned' (Seers 1972: 7). He further asserted that 'if one or two of these central problems have been growing worse, especially if all three have, it would be strange to call the result "development" even if per capita income doubled' (Seers 1972: 7).

A reasonably clear case was provided for the singling out of these questions. Seers thought that human potential could not be realized without sufficient food, and that the ability to buy food is determined by income. Those living below an income poverty line cannot buy enough food to realize their human potential. Having a job – whether in paid employment, being a student, working on a family farm or keeping a house – was considered to be essential for the enhancement of one's personality and for self-respect. Inequality was linked to poverty. Seers argued that poverty could be reduced much more quickly if economic growth was accompanied by reduced inequality. He also saw equity as an objective in its own right, arguing that inequity was objectionable on ethical standards.

A point often overlooked in Seers' writings is that he thought that many other factors, in addition to the reduction of poverty, unemployment and inequality, were also important for the fulfilment of human potential. He thought that this fulfilment also required adequate education levels, freedom of speech and national political and economic sovereignty (Seers 1972).

The fundamental contribution of Seers was that development should be defined as a subjective or normative concept. Development is not about what actually has or will happen – as in the writings of Rostow and Marx who saw development as historical change, or those who defined development as exploitation and domination – but what ought to happen. In short, this is about differentiating between changes per se and that which we would like to see, that change which might simply be described as 'good'. This laid the groundwork for many new development conceptualizations proposed from the early 1970s through to the present. Let us now highlight some of the better known of these conceptualizations.

In the early 1970s, the International Labour Organization (ILO) focused attention on the importance of employment in developing countries for providing for basic needs (ILO 1976). The efforts of the ILO and others led to the emergence of a new meaning, which treated development as the fulfilment or satisfaction of *basic human needs*. The corresponding measure of development became the extent to which these needs were met. Basic needs are often thought to be confined to food, shelter and clothing. The ILO identified five categories of basic human needs which go well beyond these. They are:

- basic goods, including food, shelter and clothing;
- basic services, including education, health, access to water and transport;
- participation in decision making;
- the fulfilment of basic human rights, and;
- productive employment, that which generates enough income to satisfy consumption needs.

It should come as no surprise that the ILO's flagging of a list of needs was followed by much discussion about how they can best be fulfilled. There were those who believed that basic human needs could only be fulfilled through redistributive policies that result in a more equitable distribution of income, assets and power (Green 1978). Implicit to this view was that growth-oriented strategies could not satisfy basic human needs; strategies aimed at fulfilling the latter were actually a rejection of the former. The ILO, while not rejecting redistribution policies, was of the view that high rates of economic growth were essential for a successful basic human needs development strategy.

Many more elaborate needs were subsequently articulated in the years after the ILO came up with the basic human needs approach. They included those from Streeten (1979), Streeten et al. (1981), Stewart (1985) and, some years later, Doyal and Gough (1991). These articulations tended to focus more than the ILO on needs beyond the provision of basic goods and services, such as a sense of purpose in life and work, self-determination, political freedom and security and national and cultural identity. The issue of the universality of needs, across cultures and over time, was also examined. Doyal and Gough defined universal needs as preconditions for social participation that apply to everyone in the same way. They concluded that two universal basic needs do exist – physical health and autonomy. Autonomy was viewed as the capacity to initiate an action that requires, among other things, the opportunity to engage in social action.

Discussions on development strategies and corresponding meanings of development were rich and engaging in the 1970s and early 1980s. The same cannot be said of the remainder of the 1980s. The early 1980s was a period of great economic turmoil in the developing world, largely owing to steep declines in oil prices. Many developing countries experienced serious balance of payments problems, growing public and private debt, declines in investment and high inflation. All of these problems culminated in lower economic growth rates than would have otherwise been the case. The dominant view at the time is that the best way to deal with these problems was with what might loosely be described as neoliberal economic policies, often aimed at less government economic intervention and, above all, a primary focus on sustained economic growth. The World Bank was an active and influential proponent of similar views. Such an environment was not conducive to a more interventionist development strategy, including one aimed at satisfying basic human needs. Strategies aiming to put basic human needs satisfaction first, that were consistent with a notion of development as something other than or in addition to economic growth, were not high on the agenda of national governments and international development organizations. The 1980s can, in this sense, be seen as a lost decade in terms of the advancement of development conceptualizations.

This state of affairs changed in 1990, with the release of the UNDP *Human Development Report 1990*. In an attempt to shift development thinking and strategies away from what was thought of as an excessive preoccupation with economic growth as a goal for development policies, and back to what it saw as core values, the UNDP advanced its concept of *human development*. The UNDP defined human development as follows:

> Human development is a process of enlarging people's choices. The most critical ones are to lead a long and healthy life, to be educated and to enjoy a decent standard of living. If these essential choices are not available, many other opportunities remain inaccessible. But human development does not end there.   (UNDP 1990: 10)

The UNDP was at pains to emphasize that its concept of development was broader and more vital than mere economic growth that achieved higher average incomes. It made the powerful point that income is not an end in its own right but a means to an end. What matters, according to the UNDP, is not so much the level of income but the uses to which it is put. The UNDP invoked a powerful ally in advancing its position: the ancient Greek philosopher Aristotle. He had warned against judging societies by variables such as income and wealth that are sought not for themselves but desired as means to other objectives. Succinctly, Aristotle's view was that: 'Wealth is evidently not the good we are seeking, for it is merely useful for the sake of something else' (UNDP 1990: 9).

The UNDP not only proposed its own definition of human development but also a measure designed to show which countries had achieved the highest levels of this development and which had achieved the lowest. More generally, the measure provided a league table, a ranking, of countries in terms of the levels of human development they had each achieved. That measure is the now famous Human Development Index (HDI). A detailed technical description of the HDI is not necessary for our current purposes but it combined measures of longevity, knowledge and the material standard of living into a single index. The HDI has changed since its inception in 1990 but in the original version these measures were life expectancy (the number of years a newborn child would be expected to live in a country given prevailing patterns of mortality), adult literacy (the percentage of persons aged 15 and over who can understand, read and write a short statement on everyday life) and a measure of GDP per capita adjusted for differences in the cost of living between countries (UNDP 1990). The HDI is now arguably the most widely used and reported measure of the level of development among countries. HDI scores have been published annually and are now available for more than 170 countries. The higher the score, the higher is the level of development that a country is considered to have achieved. We return to HDI scores later in this chapter.

The UNDP relied heavily on the work of Amartya Sen in articulating and designing the HDI. Sen was winner of the 1998 Nobel Prize in Economics for his contributions to the field of welfare economics. In the late 1970s, Sen began proposing what became known as the 'capability approach'. This was in the context of how inequality should be judged, with Sen arguing the case for looking at inequalities, not in variables such as income but in what he referred to as basic capabilities (Sen 1980). Indeed, Sen had long been critical of the use of income as a measure of development; the level of income or its growth was not as important as what it was used to purchase (Sen 1985a). To this extent he was in agreement with Aristotle. Accordingly, as Alkire (2002) points out, development in Sen's capability approach is not defined as an increase in income growth, or for that matter in terms of enhanced education or health alone, but as an *expansion of capability*. Capability is treated as the *freedom* to promote or achieve combinations of valuable functionings (Sen 1990). Functionings, in turn, are the 'parts of the state of person – in particular the things that he or she manages to do or be in leading a life' (Sen 1993: 31). The link between freedom and development was a theme Sen articulated further in subsequent writings. In his well-known work, *Development as Freedom* (Sen 1999a), he argued that the expansion of freedom is both a primary end and a principal means of development. More precisely, he argued that development involved the removal of the 'unfreedoms that leave people with little choice and little opportunity of exercising their reasoned agency' (Sen 1999a: xii).

So, what are these capabilities that allow one to function? Sen resists identifying a set of capabilities on the grounds that it is a value judgement that needs to be made explicitly, in many cases through a process of public debate (Sen 1999a). We need to keep this point in mind later in this chapter. Yet many others have identified various lists of capabilities, or what might be interpreted as such. The UNDP has done so, in its definition of human development and choice of components of, or dimensions of development empirically captured by, the HDI. This was made clear in the *Human Development Report 1995*:

> The basis for selection of critical dimensions, and the indicators that make up the human development index, is identifying basic capabilities that people must have to participate in and contribute to society. These include the ability to lead a long and healthy life, the ability to be knowledgeable and the ability to have access to the resources needed for a decent standard of living. (UNDP 1995: 18)

A comprehensive list of often complex capabilities is provided by Martha Nussbaum, among others. Many of these are most applicable or easy to understand at the level of an individual but can also be applied in varying degrees to countries, based on the life situations of their citizens. Nussbaum's list has been revised many times but in 2000 consisted of the following: life, bodily health, bodily integrity, senses, imagination, thought, emotions, practical reason, affiliation, other species, play and control over one's environment (Nussbaum 2000). Nussbaum describes these as 'central human functional capabilities'. Many of the capabilities identified by Nussbaum are by no means simple in a number of respects, for example in assessing whether they have been achieved or designing policies aimed at achieving them. Clearly, the underlying or corresponding definition of development is far more complex than those outlined above. This is also evident from an examination of the equivalent lists provided by other writers, often described as dimensions of development, and numerous extensions of Sen's capability approach. Alkire (2002) provides an excellent and comprehensive survey of human development dimensions and of the research that has identified them. Oosterlaken and van den Hoven (2012), Scheffran and Remling (2013), Trani et al. (2011) and Elson et al. (2011) extend the capability approach to technology and design, human security, disability and human rights, respectively.

The work of Alkire (2002) and others, including Sen's contributions, belongs to the literature on what is now widely called *human well-being*. The capabilities that are identified in it are often called well-being dimensions, and this term will be used in the remainder of this chapter. Broadly analogous terms include the quality of life, the standard of living and, as the UNDP prefers, human development. It is now very common to equate development with these terms. Using the first, development is therefore seen as enhancing or increasing the level of achieved human well-being. This can be at the level of nations, in which it is the overall level of well-being of its citizens, or at the level of individuals.

A key characteristic of the Sen capability approach and its extension by Nussbaum, and indeed the basic human needs approach and the writings of Seers, is that development is seen to be *multidimensional*. It is just not about improvements according to a single criterion, but multiple criteria. The extent to which this had become appreciated in the early 1990s and onwards is evident in statements emanating from the World Bank. The World Bank had long (and sometimes unfairly) been seen as a vanguard of a market-friendly, economic growth-first approach to development strategy. It differentiated between what is referred to as 'economic development' and 'development in a broader sense' in its *World Development Report 1991* (World Bank 1991a). Economic development was seen as a 'sustainable increase in living standards that encompasses material consumption, education, health and environmental protection' (World Bank 1991a: 31). Development in the broader sense was articulated by the World Bank as follows:

> Development in a broader sense is understood to include other important and related attributes as well, notably more equality of opportunity, and political and civil liberties. The overall goal of development is therefore to increase the economic, political, and civil rights of all people across gender, ethnic groups, religions, races, regions and countries.   (World Bank 1991a: 31)

The pendulum had firmly swung, it seems.

The World Bank, in these quotes, refers to the various population sub-groups (delineated by gender, ethnicity and so on), sustainability and the environment. These issues have for a number of years been highly relevant to development theory and the definition of development. Let's deal with each in turn.

Inequality of incomes among people within countries was discussed above. This type of inequality is often referred to as 'vertical inequality' in that it refers to differences in incomes between individuals. *Horizontal inequality* refers to the existence of inequalities between groups of individuals, typically within countries. It is based on the twin recognitions that an intrinsic part of human life is group membership and that there is a universal human need to belong, to identify with a particular group or groups (Gellner 1964; Stewart 2001). Early usage of the term looked at inequality between culturally defined groups (Stewart 2001), but the same general notion can be applied to gender. Inequities between the sexes, members of different castes and between tribal, racial, religious or ethnic groups are considered to be different types of horizontal inequalities. As Stewart (2001) emphasizes, horizontal inequality is also multidimensional, not only relating to differences in economic outcomes (such as incomes) but to social and political outcomes as well.

Concerns for horizontal inequality were heightened in the 1990s for two main reasons. The first was the increasingly apparent inequities between population sub-groups. It is not uncommon for a man to be twice as likely as a woman to be literate in developing countries (UNDP 2006). One of the best-known cases of inequities among racial groups within countries is South Africa in the apartheid era, which ended in 1993. Some simple statistics bear this out. The average monthly salary of black workers was less than one-third of that of white workers in 1990. In 1980 the incidence of infant mortality (the number of infants dying before their first birthday) in the black community was six times that in the white community. There are of course many other examples from developing countries. These include differences between the living standards of or the rights enjoyed by the various Hindu castes in India, between Tamils and Sinhalese in Sri Lanka, between indigenous and Indian-origin citizens in Fiji, between citizens of Albanian and non-Albanian origin in the Kosovo territory of the former Yugoslavia and between Tutsis and Hutus in Rwanda. But horizontal inequities, like vertical ones, are clearly not the exclusive domain of developing countries. They can be observed in the developed group as well. Differences in the lives experienced by blacks and whites in the United States, Catholics and Protestants in Northern Ireland and between indigenous and non-indigenous groups in Australia are examples. Indeed, the

Australian example is among the more extreme in developed countries. Based on mortality rates at the time, in 2000 an indigenous Australian male could be expected to live 54 years, 24 years less than a non-indigenous Australia male. The second factor leading to a heightening of concerns for horizontal inequality related to its perceived consequences, particularly violent conflict. Such inequalities were thought to drive to varying degrees the conflicts in Northern Ireland, Sri Lanka and the former Yugoslavia, a series of coups in Fiji and the Rwandan genocide that resulted in an estimated 800,000 deaths.

Concerns over environmental degradation, the use of non-renewable resources and the like are well documented and there is little need to elaborate on them for our current purposes. They are accepted and known and are widely regarded as core issues of our time, affecting all citizens, albeit to varying degrees, worldwide. The more pertinent line of enquiry is to establish how these concerns relate to how development might be defined. At a simple level one might argue that they lead us to question whether it is possible to *sustain* development levels into the future. But this is an explanation of future development levels which treats sustainability as a determinant of them. It does not embed or incorporate sustainability into a definition of development. Put differently, it does not treat sustainability as being constituent of development itself. Anand and Sen (2000) provide the grounds with which one can incorporate sustainability into a definition of development. Earlier in this chapter, a view was put that change cannot be considered as development unless it is equitable. Anand and Sen argue that sustainability should be seen as a concern of inter-generational equity, or as they put it, 'a particular reflection of universality of claims – applied to the future generations vis-à-vis us' (Anand and Sen 2000: 2030). Anand and Sen further note that:

> We cannot abuse and plunder our common stock of natural assets and resources leaving the future generations unable to enjoy the opportunities we take for granted today. We cannot use up, or contaminate, our environment as we wish, violating the rights of and the interests of the future generations.   (Anand and Sen 2000: 2030)

Sustainability can reasonably easily be seen as development, in this context.

Sustainability has been at the forefront of development policy challenges for years, and now arguably the biggest issues in development. The Sustainable Development Goals (SDGs) were adopted by the international community at the United Nations Sustainable Development

Summit in September 2015. They reiterate and extend the Millennium Development Goals (MDGs), which were adopted by the international community at the United Nations Millennium Summit in 2000. There were eight MDGs, with most to be achieved by 2015. The principal goal was MDG1, which was to halve the proportion of people living in extreme income poverty from 1990 to 2015. There was one overtly environmental goal, MDG7, which was to ensure environmental sustainability through inter alia providing sustainable access to safe drinking water and basic sanitation facilities (United Nations 2015a). There are 17 SDGs, of which at least 13 focus either solely or in part on sustainability issues. They are to be achieved by 2030. SDG15, for example, aims to protect, restore and promote sustainable use of terrestrial ecosystems, sustainably manage forests, combat desertification, halt and reverse land degradation and halt biodiversity loss (United Nations 2015b).

Some comments on development as good-change definitions are warranted at this stage. It is abundantly clear that these definitions, and the interpretations or judgements that emerge from them, are far more complex than corresponding definitions implicit in modernization theories. A country according to this definition could be said to be developing if it was achieving economic or income growth per head of population. The larger or faster this growth, the more it could be said to be developing. Moreover, a country with a higher level of income per head of population than another was said to be more developed. And, as we have seen, certain levels or thresholds of income per capita have been used to distinguish developed from developing countries.

For a number of reasons, such judgements cannot be as easily made if the good-change definitions are used. Let us highlight two. The first is that many of the dimensions that have been identified do not lead to precise judgements regarding changes over time, or across people or countries. Put differently, it is far from self-evident that progress in them might have been achieved or what the levels of fulfilment or achievement might be. The second, and arguably more fundamental, reason relates to the multidimensionality of these definitions or the conceptualizations on which they are based. Seers pointed to this issue when posing the three questions outlined above. To illustrate, consider a situation in which a country is showing improvements in three of five key well-being dimensions, but is showing the reverse in the remaining two by the same magnitude. Is that country developing? Similarly, consider a situation in which we are asked to assess which of two countries has the highest level of development based on these five well-being dimensions. These two countries have identical achievements in the first three dimensions. But the first country has higher achievement in the fourth dimension and lower achievement, by the same magnitude, than the second country in the fifth dimension. Which country has the highest level of development? The answer to both these questions depends on the relative importance one attaches to the five dimensions. Returning to the first question, if we thought the remaining two dimensions were collectively more important than the first three, we would conclude that the country is not developing. Alternatively, if we thought that the first three dimensions were more important than the last two, we would conclude it was developing. For the second question, we would conclude that the second country was more developed than the first if we thought the fourth dimension was more important than the fifth and vice versa.

The issue of how to weight or assign relative degrees of importance to well-being or quality of life outcomes is a huge issue in the assessment of development levels and trends. In an ideal world, we would have the scientific information to be able to weight these outcomes. But we do not. We do not, for example, have the results of a worldwide survey in which people were asked to rank what outcomes are most important to them. Nor is there consensus on what determines well-being outcomes. This was an issue that the UNDP grappled with in the construction of the HDI. It is widely accepted that the weights attached to the component variables of the HDI should vary. Yet in the absence of information on how to assign values to these weights, the UNDP opted for the simplest alternative which was to give each an equal weighting. This means, for instance, that an improvement in health is just as important as an improvement in education or income of the same magnitude in assessing development changes based on the HDI. At this point it is instructive to recall Sen's view on identifying a set of capabilities, which was that this rests on a value judgement that needs to be explicitly made. The same point can be made about valuing development outcomes. In the absence of the required scientific information, one must ultimately make an explicit value judgement in assigning different values or weights to given outcomes on the basis of personal preferences, subjective or otherwise.

Applying development definitions

It is now appropriate to apply some of the development conceptualizations outlined in this chapter by looking at country classifications and development achievements. Specifically, we look at development achievements in terms of the modernization-led growth and good-change definitions. The former definition leads us to focus on income levels (as they reflect historical growth rates) and the latter leads us to look at achievements in such areas as health and education. This in many respects is an unavoidably empirical exercise. As such it is necessary to again invoke the caveat stated above, that statistics, while useful, do not adequately capture the plight of the poor. This does not mean that we ignore statistics, just that we recognize their limitations. We start by looking at how countries are classified.

Country classifications

For much of the second half of the twentieth century countries were classified as either First World, Second World or Third World. The First World countries were those that had industrialized and achieved high per capita incomes and belonged to the Organisation for Economic Co-operation and Development (OECD). The Second World countries were those that were part of the Soviet bloc and the Third World were in essence, all other countries. The First World countries were considered developed, so too typically were the Second World countries. The Third World countries were considered developing or less developed. While these classifications were influenced by political criteria, it was for much of the second half of the twentieth century that the First World countries were richer in terms of per capita income than those of the Second World, and the Third World countries were poorer still. So, to this extent, the division between developed and developing countries was consistent with the growth via modernization definition of development.

The usage of the terms First World, Second World and Third World came under increasing question in the late 1980s and 1990s. This was for two main reasons. The first is that many of the Third World countries were as rich as those in the First World group and richer than all in the Second World group. Indeed, there was so much diversity in the Third World group that people began to question the usefulness and usage of the term. The second reason was the collapse of the Soviet Union. Many of the countries that emerged from the Soviet Union as independent states were extremely poor and by income standards alone could clearly be labelled as developing. These classifications are still largely used today in official circles despite these changes. While the First World, Second World and Third World terms are not used, those that would have been labelled Third World are officially classified by the United Nations and other official international organizations as 'developing countries': 150 countries or territories were classified as developing in 2010. Most of the former Soviet bloc countries in this year were classified as Central and Eastern Europe and Commonwealth Independent States (CIS) countries (UNDP 2010a). Full lists of the countries belonging to these and all classifications mentioned in the remainder of this chapter can be found in the *Human Development Report 2010* (UNDP 2010a) and on the World Bank website: www. worldbank.org.

A number of changes in country classifications have occurred over time. The Czech Republic, Hungary, Poland and Slovakia are all former Soviet bloc countries that are now part of the OECD and as such are generally considered as developed countries. The Republic of Korea (South Korea, as it is more widely known), Mexico and Turkey have in the last decade moved from the developing to the OECD group. Many anomalies remain, however, and for this reason the developing countries group remains highly diverse. Many countries in the developing group should clearly be treated as developed. Singapore and Hong Kong have very high well-being or living-standards levels by international standards (Hong Kong has been in the top 20 countries in the world in terms of income per capita) and yet are still in the developing countries group in 2014. The reasons for this are largely political, as certain benefits in terms of access to concessional international finance and trade opportunities, for instance, accrue to countries in the developing group. In partial recognition of the diversity of the developing country group, the United Nations has for many years assembled a 'least developed country' group, based purely on developmental criteria, including income per capita. Countries in this group are those considered by the UN to have the lowest levels of development, as its name implies.

Two additional methods of classifying countries and the corresponding country groups are widely used. The first is to classify countries according to per capita income levels. This is how the World Bank arrives at its income group classifications. As mentioned, it has been common to treat low- and middle-income countries as developing or less developed and high-income as developed countries. The income thresholds used change over time, getting larger each year. In 2014, 75 countries were classified as high income, 105 as middle income and 34 as low income (World Bank 2014d). Singapore and Hong Kong are in the high-income group and yet as mentioned are still included in the UN developing countries group. The number of countries in the low-income group has declined over time owing to per capita economic growth and the resultant graduation of countries into a higher income group. In

2007, for example, 59 countries were classified as low income (World Bank 2007). The second method of classification is based on the HDI, with countries being divided into low, medium and high and very high human development categories. As such, these groupings are consistent with a multidimensional development conceptualization that is broadly consistent with the Sen capability approach, albeit taking into account a rather narrow selection of capabilities. In 2014, 49 countries are classified as very high, 53 as high, 42 as medium and 43 as low human development. Sub-Saharan African countries dominate the low human development group: of the 43 countries in this group, 35 are from this part of the world (UNDP 2014).

Development profiles

Let us now take a closer look at development levels by looking at the development profiles of individual countries and not just the group to which they belong. Which countries have the highest levels of development and which have the lowest? It would be particularly insightful to base this exercise on a comprehensive range of well-being dimensions (or capabilities) but the availability of information required to do this limits us to only relatively basic dimensions. Table 1.1 helps in this regard. It identifies the 20 most developed and 20 least developed countries based on both the HDI and income per capita. Income per capita is measured using Purchasing Power Parity (PPP) GNI per capita. Such a measure is adjusted to take into account differences in price levels between countries, and as such gives a better idea of the purchasing power of incomes across countries and hence in material living standards. For instance, if one country had a PPP GNI per capita that is twice that of another, a person earning that income in the first country can buy approximately twice the number of equivalent goods and services of someone earning half that income in the second country.

All of those in the top 20 HDI group are classified as high-income countries. The vast majority of countries in the top 20 HDI group are European. The top 20 income per capita countries is much more diverse geographically, but has high representation from countries that rely heavily on oil for their national prosperity. These countries are the Middle Eastern countries of Qatar, Kuwait, United Arab Emirates and Saudi Arabia, together with Brunei Darussalam and Norway. Both bottom 20 groups are dominated by sub-Saharan African countries. All 20 bottom HDI countries with the exception of Haiti and Afghanistan are from that region. The only bottom 20 income per capita country not

Table 1.1   *Top and bottom 20 countries, 2014*

Human Development Index (HDI)			*Income per capita*		
Rank	*Country*	*HDI*	*Rank*	*Country*	*GNI per capita ($PPP)*
1	Norway	0.944	1	Qatar	133,713
2	Australia	0.933	2	Luxemburg	86,587
3	Switzerland	0.917	3	Kuwait	84,188
4	Netherlands	0.915	4	Singapore	71,475
5	United States	0.914	5	Brunei Darussalam	71,080
6	Germany	0.911	6	Norway	62,858
7	New Zealand	0.910	7	United Arab Emirates	57,045
8	Canada	0.902	8	Switzerland	51,293
9	Singapore	0.901	9	United States	50,859
10	Denmark	0.900	10	Saudi Arabia	50,791
11	Ireland	0.899	11	Hong Kong, China (SAR)	50,291
12	Sweden	0.898	12	Austria	43,139
13	Iceland	0.895	13	Ireland	42,919
14	United Kingdom	0.892	14	Netherlands	42,453
15	Hong Kong, China (SAR)	0.891	15	Australia	42,278
15	Korea (Republic of)	0.891	16	Germany	41,966
17	Japan	0.890	17	Sweden	41,840
18	Liechtenstein	0.889	18	Denmark	41,524
19	Israel	0.888	19	Bahrain	40,658
20	France	0.884	20	Canada	40,588

→

from sub-Saharan Africa is Haiti. Note also that there is a lot of overlap between the groups: most in the top 20 HDI group are in the top 20 income per capita group and the same applies to the bottom 20 groups. Recalling that the HDI includes measures of health and education, this reflects the statistical reality that, in general, countries with higher levels of these variables also have higher incomes.

The development record

Let us conclude our empirical exercise by looking at the development record over recent decades. Has the level of development, worldwide, increased, decreased or remained the same? We again base this exercise on rather basic well-being dimensions, relating to health, education, income and sustainability. The answer to the preceding question is

Table 1.1 *(continued)*

Human Development Index (HDI)			*Income per capita*		
Bottom 20					
Rank	*Country*	*HDI*	*Rank*	*Country*	*GNI per capita ($PPP)*
168	Haiti	0.471	168	Mali	1,607
169	Afghanistan	0.468	169	Sierra Leone	1,586
170	Djibouti	0.467	170	Haiti	1,575
171	Cote d'Ivoire	0.452	171	Gambia	1,565
172	Gambia	0.441	172	Burkina Faso	1,528
173	Ethiopia	0.435	173	Comoros	1,493
174	Malawi	0.414	174	Rwanda	1,379
175	Liberia	0.412	175	Madagascar	1,378
176	Mali	0.397	176	Zimbabwe	1,337
177	Guinea-Bissau	0.396	177	Uganda	1,334
178	Mozambique	0.393	178	Togo	1,286
179	Guinea	0.392	179	Eritrea	1,180
180	Burundi	0.389	180	Guinea-Bissau	1,164
181	Burkina Faso	0.388	181	Mozambique	971
182	Eritrea	0.381	182	Central African Rep.	964
183	Sierra Leone	0.374	183	Niger	884
184	Chad	0.372	184	Liberia	782
185	Central African Rep.	0.341	185	Malawi	739
186	Congo, Dem Rep	0.338	186	Burundi	737
187	Niger	0.337	187	Congo, Dem. Rep.	451

Source: Data from UNDP (2014).

not at all straightforward. 'It depends' is probably the way to respond. The development balance sheet, shown in Table 1.2, helps illustrate this point. It distinguishes between what might be called good change, progress or development from less pleasing changes. The former are labelled alternatively as deprivation, disparity or, consistent with the development as domination and exploitation paradigm, underdevelopment. If we look at the development record over the last 45 to 50 years, we cannot help but be impressed by the substantial progress that has been made in many areas. The left-hand side of the balance sheet in Table 1.2 makes this abundantly clear. People are now living much longer, many less children are dying before reaching their fifth birthday, far more people are literate, incomes have increased tremendously and consciousness of environmental and sustainability issues has increased substantially in recent years. To these extents, the development record

Table 1.2   *A development balance sheet*

Progress, good change, development	*Deprivation, disparity, underdevelopment*
Health	
• The life expectancy of a person born in a developing country in 1961 was 47 years. By 2012 this number had risen to 69 years. Worldwide, average life expectancy increased from 52 to 71 years over the same period.	• A person born in a high-income OECD country in 2012 is expected to live 26, 21 or 13 years longer than one born in the same year in sub-Saharan Africa, a least developed or a developing country, respectively. • In many OECD countries life expectancy had exceeded 80 years of age in 2012. Life expectancy in 2012 was 46 years in Sierra Leone and 49 years in Lesotho.
• The number of children in the world dying before their fifth birthday fell by 134 deaths per 1000 children between 1961 and 2013. In developing countries it fell from 218 to 50 deaths per 1000 children over the same period.	• In 2013 6.3 million children still died before their fifth birthday. Roughly half these deaths occurred in sub-Saharan Africa. • A child born in a least developed country in 2013 is 19 times more likely to die before reaching its fifth birthday than one born in the same year a high-income OECD country. A child born in sub-Saharan Africa in 2013 is 20 times more likely to die before its fifth birthday than one born in the same year in the European Union.
Education	
• The percentage of developing country adults who were literate rose from 64 in 1970 to 80 in 2010. In the least developed countries it more than doubled between 1970 and 2010, from 26 to 59 per cent.	• One billion adults were illiterate in the world in 2013. • In many developing countries more than half of all adult females and in 10 sub-Saharan African countries more than seven out of every 10 females were illiterate in 2013. • It is not uncommon in developing countries for a male to be almost twice as likely as a female to receive a secondary school education.

→

Table 1.2 *(continued)*

Progress, good change, development	*Deprivation, disparity, underdevelopment*
Income and wealth	
• Developing country per capita income (measured using GDP per capita in 2005 prices) increased more than fourfold between 1961 and 2013, from US$575 to US$2,479. World per capita income increased over the same period from US$3,134 to US$7,850.	• More than one billion people – one-fifth of the world's population – live in conditions of extreme income poverty, surviving on less than $1.25 per day. In at least 12 developing countries more than half the population lives in extreme income poverty. • Income per capita (measured using GNI per capita adjusted for purchasing power) among OECD high-income countries in 2013 was 5, 13 and 21 times that in developing, sub-Saharan African and least developed countries, respectively. These gaps have increased over time. Qatar's purchasing power parity GNI per capita in 2013 was an incredible 296 times that of the Democratic Republic of Congo. • In 2013 the richest 10 per cent of the world's population held 86 per cent of world income, while the poorest 50 per cent held 1 per cent. • In 2013 1 per cent of the world's adult population held more than 46 per cent of the world's personal assets.
Environment and sustainability	
• Environmental consciousness has increased worldwide in recent decades and most countries have ratified the major international environmental treaties, including the Kyoto Protocol. Official national targets to limit greenhouse gas emissions are not commonplace and the concept of 'green growth' is widely accepted.	• World carbon dioxide emissions rose from 3.1 metric tons per person in 1961 to 4.9 metric tons per person in 2012. In OECD high-income countries they rose from 7.9 to 11.3 metric tons per person over the same period. • The world's largest carbon dioxide emitting country over the decade from 1998 – which contributed more than one fifth of total world carbon dioxide emissions during these years – still refuses to ratify the Kyoto Protocol.

Source: Data from various issues of the UNDP *Human Development Report* (New York: UNDP) and the World Bank *World Development Indicators* (Washington DC: World Bank), the UNICEF *Levels and Trends in Child Mortality 2014 Report* (New York: Unicef) and from the Credit Suisse *Global Wealth Report 2013* (Zurich: Credit Suisse).

is impressive, levels of development are higher than ever before (at least in recorded history) and the world is a better place as a consequence.

But it must be emphasized that this picture is an average or aggregate one. It does not necessarily apply to all people in all countries of the world and ignores a number of disparities. It is, in short, a partial story as the right-hand side of the balance sheet reveals. Despite improvements in child mortality and literacy, 6.3 million children died in 2013 before reaching their fifth birthday, one billion adults are illiterate and one billion people live in extreme income poverty, on less than $PPP.125 per day. Disparities have also grown, quite substantially in some cases. Finally, the increase in environmental awareness notwithstanding, carbon dioxide emissions are still on the rise worldwide and some countries have not ratified key international environmental agreements.

The main conclusion emerging from Table 1.2 is that despite the progress that has been made, the world remains a place of widespread deprivation. Much more still needs to be done, and the world could be a much better place.

So, let us ask our question again. Has the level of development, worldwide, increased, decreased or remained the same over recent decades? If one looks at the general picture and ignores disparities, then on balance the answer to this question based on the evidence just presented is probably 'yes'. It might differ, of course, if one looked at information based on a large range of well-being or related dimensions. But if our conceptualization of development includes a concern for equity, the answer is not so clear. Recall what Seers wrote about development: that if unemployment, poverty or inequality has grown worse, it would be strange to call the result development. Inequality seems to have grown worse. Has there then been development? To emphasize a point made above, the answer will depend on how highly we value equality. If it has an especially high value, then we might conclude that the level of development in the world has declined, and not risen as many would assert.

Conclusion

This chapter outlined various meanings or conceptualizations of development. It commenced by looking at traditional conceptualizations. This included the definition implicit in the modernization approach to development, which saw development largely as economic growth. The chapter then examined more contemporary meanings of development, those which emerged from the late 1960s to the present. These meanings are those which either relate to the domination and exploitation of one group by another or to what might very loosely be described as 'good change'. Most attention was devoted to the latter; this was on the grounds that these definitions are particularly useful because they force us to focus on and consider what sort of change or outcomes we want to see in all countries, rich and poor, providing a framework to compare actual changes against those we would like to observe. The fundamental premise of the chapter is that defining development, and deciding what is development and what is not, or whether development has actually occurred, is a necessarily subjective exercise. It is also a rather complicated exercise, requiring one to reflect on one's own personal values to judge what is most important and what is not as important.

Given this, let us conclude with some more questions, in addition to those asked in the previous section of this chapter. What is your definition of development? Is it based on multiple dimensions or on a single dimension? Put differently, what criteria does a country need to satisfy to be considered to have achieved higher levels of development? It might be useful to write down your own definition (ideally limiting it to a sentence) and revisit it from time to time as you work your way through this book, and especially when you have completed reading it.

Chapter 2

Reassessing Development Theory

John McKay

In this chapter we explore the key ideas put forward, especially in the last half-century or so, on development and underdevelopment, and place these concepts in the context of the major trends, conditions and prevailing ideologies within the emerging global system. The dominant ideas on the nature and genesis of the very process of development have themselves gone through a series of transformations during this period, but strong counterarguments have also emerged constantly. Thus the history of ideas on development can be characterized as a series of revolutions and counter-revolutions, and in many cases the key ideas from a particular period have re-emerged in a new guise at a later date. While successful development concerns much more than just economic processes or outcomes, economic issues have dominated much of the literature as well as the policy debate, and these key questions relating to economic development are explored in detail in Chapter 3. We also argue that most fundamental changes take place in response to crises of various kinds that challenge accepted paradigms, and the Global Financial Crisis (GFC) – discussed in detail in Chapter 4 – has since 2007 shaken the foundations of the global economy and has had a major impact on our thinking about competing theories of development. The GFC was the result of some fundamental changes taking place in the global political economy, and in turn the crisis itself caused some further transformations to the structure and operation of the overall system, and these changes, their causes and their impacts will be explored at various points in Chapters 3 and 4 and in this chapter.

One question that these global changes have forced us to consider is whether the traditional distinctions between 'developed' and 'underdeveloped' regions, between 'North' and 'South', and between 'rich' and 'poor' nations are still valid. It could be argued that one result of new patterns of production that have emerged under complex processes of globalization is that discrepancies in wealth within both 'developed' and 'developing' countries are much greater than in the past. Thus John Saul (2004), for example, has suggested that old binaries based on geography should certainly now be questioned. Rather, while much poverty can still be explained with reference to a spatially defined global hierarchy, significant segments of societies in all parts of the world are equally at the mercy of exploitative forces now operating at a global scale. Thus conventional geographical divides need to be considered alongside other social, political and economic binaries. This is another key issue to be dealt with in the next three chapters.

Notwithstanding periodic episodes of crisis, the last 50 years have been characterized by unprecedented growth and prosperity, but only within certain countries, regions and social groups. A basic question, then, must be why some countries, groups and individuals have been able to achieve spectacular progress while others have stagnated or even gone backwards. Within mainstream economic thought there has been a strong assumption throughout this period that growth in successful regions will eventually 'trickle down' to the more peripheral areas, given appropriate policies. Thus, poor countries can catch up and benefit from the earlier growth experiences of others, and pass through a similar process of development, albeit at a later date. This is the essence of the theories of modernization that were popular in the 1950s and 1960s, and which, in a modified form, made a return to the mainstream of policy-making in the 1980s. However, these prescriptions have come under sustained attack ever since the 1960s from a number of different directions. The first criticisms came from what became known as the 'dependency school', originating especially in Latin America: the underdeveloped world could not develop in this 'trickle-down' manner, because the very processes of global change that gave rise to prosperity in the North resulted in the simultaneous impoverishment of the countries of the South.

These ideas were in turn criticized, partly because of their overreliance on global rather than national factors, but more particularly for their alleged inability to account for the very rapid growth that was going on in parts of East Asia at the time. If growth at an unprecedented rate was possible in South Korea, Taiwan and the other 'Tiger' economies, there could be nothing wrong with the global system as such, it was argued: the problem must rest with the internal policies of the poor countries. The onset of the Asian financial crisis in 1997 gave support to this view, however the onset of the GFC a decade later has once again challenged this dominant view: the ability of the Asian nations to rebuild their economies so quickly after their own crisis, and now their emergence relatively unscathed from the GFC, have again forced us to think anew about the Asian development model and the rapidly growing global influence of a number of Asian countries.

Mainstream ideas of modernization have also been criticized from quite different directions. Several authors have questioned the often unspoken assumption that the aim of development is to deliver to every global citizen a lifestyle similar to that now prevailing in the rich countries. They have dismissed the idea that development must always be the same as 'modernization', which is in fact nothing less than 'Westernization'. This perspective has also been taken up by the growing environmental movement which has argued that it would be physically impossible for everyone in the countries now poor to live the sort of lifestyle now prevailing in North America or Western Europe. The costs in terms of resource depletion, pollution and general environmental degradation would simply be too great.

Still other commentators have suggested that in the development debate there has been far too much reliance on economic factors alone, and that in fact processes of political and social change are equally relevant. Indeed, many would argue that for effective development to take place it is usually essential to consider a range of social and political factors.

This chapter will explore these major currents of thought and will evaluate some of the major theories that have been advanced. However, the main focus will be on what we have learned from the last 60 years of development theory and how this might be reflected in the design of more effective policy approaches.

The global context for development ideas and policies

Ideas in development theory and practice cannot be divorced from the broader assumptions, aspirations and beliefs of any age. These more general modes of thought set the scene for more specific discussions of what development is, or should be, and the most appropriate policies and methods that can be harnessed in the search for this elusive promised land of happiness and prosperity. It could be argued that debate about development, its nature and how to achieve it, is *the* central issue in the whole of Western social science. The early towering figures in the field, writers such as John Stuart Mill and Karl Marx, were essentially theorizing about development. The Enlightenment was fundamentally concerned with progress towards an ideal society, and how the harnessing of rational thoughts, policies and actions might allow the realization of this goal. But similar ideas of progress can be found in other non-Western modes of thought. In Japan, for example, a distinctive approach to the philosophy of economics was developed with a focus on 'administering the nation and relieving the suffering of the people' (Morris-Suzuki 1989), a notion close to the concerns of development. In traditional China, Confucius (who died around 479 BC) was convinced that he lived in an age of acute crisis and his entire project was concerned with the ways in which a better society might be built and governed (Leys 1997). Interestingly, the Chinese government is now reviving Confucian ideas as a way of stabilizing a society undergoing rapid change (Bell 2008).

The genesis of modern development thought in the West is usually dated to the end of the Second World War: the European colonial empires had expressed some concern earlier for the improvement of their subject peoples, but it was really only after 1945 that development was recognized as a worldwide priority. The initiation of the Marshall Plan for the reconstruction of Europe, a similar plan for Japan, and the establishment of the major Bretton Woods institutions, notably the World Bank and the International Monetary Fund (IMF), signalled a new determination to avoid the economic and social problems of the 1930s that heralded a global conflict. However, there have been numerous changes of fashion in development thought since 1945, reflecting the ebb and flow of a series of wider debates.

The first of these concerns the position and role of the nation-state as the fundamental unit of analysis and policy-making. The system of international relations that emerged in the post-war world centred on the United Nations, and related institutions enshrined the special position of the sovereign state as the recognized authority over the space defined by its national boundaries, as the legal body able to pass laws and initiate policy, and as the only legitimate user of armed force to ensure its stability and will. Thus the field of development studies generally uses the nation as its primary unit of analysis, and most statistics are collected on this basis. However, the growth of broader economic and political units such as the European Union as well as the ratification of significant international treaties has challenged some of the traditional powers of the state. At the same time a large number of regions within individual countries have been campaigning for, and in some case achieving, much greater autonomy. Thus the powers of national governments are being whittled away from above and below, a process which some have called the 'hollowing out of the state'. However, in the aftermath of the GFC some commentators are questioning whether such processes will continue. Responses to the crisis have dominantly involved actions by national governments to shield their economies, shore up key corporations such as banks and stimulate employment. A related question concerns the extent to which the government of a nation can act as the most important catalyst for change and the key controller and co-ordinator of all kinds of development programmes. In the 1950s and 1960s, there was a general assumption that governments must play these key roles and be the organizers of a wide range of services; however after the 1970s there was a long period in which the private sector was seen as much more important. The conviction that markets can deliver the benefits of development more effectively than governments is a central tenet in the neoliberal paradigm that has held sway for so long, and which has resulted in what Toye (1987) has called the 'counterrevolution' in development thought. There were always important differences between opinions in various countries here. Support for the minimalist state came most enthusiastically from the United States, the United Kingdom and Australia, while much of Western Europe retained its traditional range of government responsibilities. The transformation of Asia into an economically powerful region also suggested new creative possibilities for government activities, with governments central to progress in Korea, Taiwan and Singapore, and more recently in China. Some writers have even suggested that the Asian model of development brought together the most useful aspects of the capitalist and socialist systems into a new 'third way' that was the most efficient method yet devised of generating growth (Johnson 1987; Wade 1990). For some time after the Asian financial crisis of 1997 many commentators dismissed the continued value of this Asian development model, but the continued growth of Asia, the realization that many aspects of this model have still survived, including in China, plus the impact of the GFC have now reopened discussion of this whole area.

Notions of power are central to development thought – some would even argue that power is the pivotal concept in the whole corpus. During the Cold War, both the United States and the Soviet Union saw aid and development programmes as a major weapon in the battle to gain support for their ideologies and systems. Genuine independence of policy was not favoured by either side, hence the rise of the non-aligned movement. However, some leaders were able to play off one side against the other, gaining benefits from both. The end of the Cold War saw the demise of both these constraints and opportunities. Whole regions of the globe, especially in Africa, suddenly became peripheral to the global system and were simply ignored by Western politicians, businessmen and investors. This situation has changed again after the terrorist attacks on the US on 11 September 2001. In the 'war on terror' we have returned to the Cold War slogan that 'either you are with us or against us'.

In the period since the end of the Cold War it has become common to regard liberal democracy as the only viable economic and political system in the modern world. Francis Fukuyama (1992) called this the 'end of history', in the sense that the long period of conflict between rival ideological systems was over, raising again the question of whether there is only one way of achieving development and creating a modern nation. However, this assumption has come under sustained attack. The whole debate about 'Asian values' at a time when growth rates in that region were clearly superior to those prevailing in the West was one form of questioning. The environmentalists' view that not all nations can possibly have the lifestyle dominant in the West has already been mentioned, but other authors are now raising some rather different but just as difficult questions. Hernando de Soto (2000) has asked why capitalism has triumphed in the West but has been so spectacularly unsuccessful in a number of other regions. Oswaldo de Rivero (2001) has raised the prospect that not all economies can ever aspire to sustained growth and development: many are simply non-viable. Thus the old assumption that development can be achieved by all if the 'correct' policies are implemented is being increasingly questioned.

These debates raise further questions about democracy, freedom and the involvement of local communities in the process of development. Nobel Prize winner Amartya Sen (1999a) has proposed that we should regard development as freedom from tyranny, poor economic prospects, social deprivation, inefficient public facilities and so on. Freedom and democracy are of course noble aims, but open to a wide range of alternative interpretations. Not surprisingly, a number of Asian commentators, confident in the economic success of their region, have proposed that Asia can develop its own form of democracy and its own definition of human rights. These concepts would not be the same as the Western ideals but would be just as valid (de Bary 1998; Mahbubani 1998; Bauer and Bell 1999; Bell 2000). Finally, the question of democracy and freedom raises the question of how far we see development as being a process initiated and implemented by outside forces and actors, or as an essentially an internal transformation fuelled by local initiative and self-help. The emphasis in the field on the role of outside 'experts', the inculcation of new and foreign values and methods, and the central role of aid all have conspired to downgrade the role of local mobilization. This is especially true in an era of globalization, when many commentators predict that cultural and economic convergence on some kind of international best practice is bound to take place. In the present era, the whole question of the relationships between globalization and development theory is opening up as a new battleground in the conflict of ideas and ideologies (see, for example, Jomo and Nagaraj 2001; Petras and Veltmeyer 2001; Schuurman 2001; McKay 2014).

Theories of modernization

None of the complexities, counterarguments or self-doubts introduced in the previous section was allowed to cloud the simple but powerful message espoused by the proponents of modernization theory. During the 1960s and part of the 1970s, within all of the social sciences there appeared studies in aspects of modernization, each couched in the distinctive language and concepts of the particular discipline but all carrying the same beguiling promise: all nations, however poor, were able, with the implementation of 'correct' policies, to achieve a modern standard of living by following exactly the same growth path as that pioneered by the Western nations.

Examples of such studies can be found in sociology, geography and political science; however, it was in economics that the seminal work was published, with the appearance of Rostow's *The Stages of Economic Growth* (1960). But this is more than just a study in economics, which is part of the reason for its influence over the years. Rostow, as he has made clear in some of his later reminiscences (Rostow 1984), has always had a strong interest in economic history and he has also written in detail on the importance of politics in the development process (Rostow 1971). Yet, somewhat paradoxically, his many critics have derided his attempts to produce a universal theory of development, one largely divorced from the historical and institutional realities of particular societies, and have been particularly scathing about his political positions.

Rostow proposed that the path to development and modernity involved the movement by any nation through a series of stages:

- the traditional society
- the pre-take-off society
- take-off
- the road to maturity
- the mass consumption society.

The framework is full of hope – every nation has the capacity to pass through these stages and achieve mass consumption. The image of take-off is particularly evocative, as the nation is able to launch itself into a bright new future. The book was also written as a deliberate counter to the numerous Marxist theories that were appearing at this time. The subtitle of the book – 'a non-communist manifesto' – written at a time when Communist expansion was feared in all parts of the underdeveloped world, emphasized that successful development could be achieved without revolution. The most important mechanism in the whole process, the fuel needed to achieve take-off, was investment derived principally from domestic savings. If the savings rate could be moved from the normal 5 per cent of GDP to 10 per cent or more for a sustained period, then take-off could proceed. Rostow was at pains to point out that there was nothing automatic or inevitable about these processes: unless economic policies and political systems were managed effectively, then a nation's move from one stage to another could stall.

Rostow (1990) has claimed that history has entirely vindicated his theory: the fall of the Soviet Union has demonstrated the unviability of the Communist alternative, while the success of East Asia has underlined the importance of high rates of savings and investment. Certainly these theories matched the mood of their time. There was much discussion in policy circles of the need to escape the 'vicious cycle of poverty'. Low rates of growth meant that savings and investment rates were low, ensuring that low levels of growth persisted. Funds were not available for better schools, universities or hospitals, ensuring that the nation could not find a way out of its poverty through investment in its human resources. Lack of investment in roads, ports and other infrastructure kept the economy working at low levels of efficiency. A way out of this persistent cycle of poverty was needed, and the modernization theorists provided a hope that this might be possible.

The Harrod–Domar growth model, which also became popular at this time, provided some economic sophistication to the emerging propositions (Hettne 1995). Growth could be self-sustaining, leading to a 'virtuous cycle of growth'. Increases in output and income would be accompanied by a higher marginal propensity to save, leading to more investment and a new round of expansion and income growth. This model, based on Keynesian theory, also proposed that initial impetus for growth could come from foreign aid, providing the first round of investment in the absence of domestic savings.

The emphasis on modernization within economics was mirrored by a range of other (and some would say complementary) studies in other social sciences. In politics, for example, there was much research on political modernization and the generation of more effective political institutions, inevitably made in the image of the West. In geography, a number of studies concentrated on 'spatial modernization', involving the spread of infrastructure and other symbols of modern life, and the gradual expansion of the *core* into the more backward *periphery*. In psychology, too, there was an attempt to explore the ways in which more 'modern' personality traits could be engendered and fostered. Perhaps most influential was the work going on at this time in sociology, and most important here was the work of Talcott Parsons (1937, 1951). He attempted to develop a grand theory of 'social action', seeing human activity as voluntary and intentional but set within a symbolic realm and a natural environment. He identified four major functional subsystems – the economy, the polity, the social community and the fiduciary system – and argued that as societies modernize these systems become more elaborate and the roles of individuals are increasingly differentiated. It is not surprising, then, that Parsons has been called 'the theorist of modernity' (Robertson and Turner 1991).

There were, however, some genuine attempts to make modernization theory more sophisticated through what has become known as *dialectical modernization theory* (Martinussen 1997). This attempted to unravel the complex relationships between the 'traditional' and 'modern' sectors. Gusfield (1976), for example, argued that traditional institutions could be revitalized through contact with modernizing influences in other parts of society. This represented a significant advance over the numerous studies of the 'dual economy' that saw a much clearer distinction between the modern and more traditional parts of the society.

Some assumptions in the rather optimistic modernization framework were questioned by Gunnar Myrdal (1957) and Albert Hirschman (1958), both of whom demonstrated that both 'virtuous' and 'vicious' cycles could operate simultaneously to produce growth in some areas and stagnation in others. Earlier economic theory suggested that inequalities would not persist because labour would migrate from low-wage areas to regions where rewards were higher. Similarly, capital would move to regions where the returns were higher, usually in areas which were currently backward but had high investment potential. Thus, growth would take place in the more backward areas, removing the initial inequalities. Both Myrdal and Hirschman attacked this kind of equilibrium analysis. Myrdal suggested that two kinds of forces would be at work. *Spread* effects would serve to distribute growth from richer to poorer regions or countries, while *backwash* effects tended to intensify existing inequalities. The relative strength of these two forces would depend on a range of circumstances and policy frameworks: thus processes of *circular and cumulative causation* could often lead to ever-deepening levels of inequality.

Many of Hirschman's idea were quite similar, but he developed a particular analysis of the role of government in the management of these processes. He argued that development is by necessity an unbalanced process, and it would also be unrealistic to expect government planners to invest in various sectors of the economy in a finely balanced way. In particular, he considered the balance between investment in *directly productive activities,* such as factories or plantations, and the infrastructure needed to support these facilities, which he termed *social overhead capital.* Growth may occur by concentrating on the development of infrastructure, thereby reducing production costs and encouraging further investment in production, or the reverse may be preferred. If production is privileged, inefficiencies in infrastructure will appear, forcing catch-up investment. Either strategy might work, and the choice of the more appropriate would depend on local circumstances. The work of Hirschman and Myrdal grew out of the tradition of modernization studies, and used some of the same theoretical assumptions, but their attention to the persistence of inequalities provides a direct link to some of the more radical critiques that began to appear in the 1960s.

The challenge of dependency theory

During the 1960s it became clear that inequalities were not being narrowed as conventional economic theory had predicted: rather, the world was becoming increasingly divided between the powerful *core* regions and the impoverished *periphery.* In Myrdal's terms, the *spread* effects were being overwhelmed by the much more powerful forces of *backwash.* One of the regions where this reality was most pronounced was in Latin America, and it was from here that an influential set of new theories began to emerge – what became known as the *dependencia* or dependency school.

Much of the initial impetus for this mode of thought came from the work of the United Nations Economic Commission for Latin America, and in particular from the work of Raul Prebisch. The central argument – now known as the 'Prebisch thesis'– was that the basic assumptions of neoclassical economics did not exist in the real world: the economic landscape did not primarily consist of small producers and buyers, each operating in a perfect marketplace with none able to exert power over these market processes. Rather, global commerce took place between the rich and powerful developed economies and the weaker peripheral countries. Not surprisingly, the rules of the trading system were systematically manipulated in favour of the powerful Western-based corporations (DiMarco 1972). In particular, Prebisch rejected the orthodox Ricardian arguments in favour of each nation specializing in the output of goods for which it had a particular comparative advantage and trading these goods through the international system. He argued that none of the 'late industrializers', such as the US, Germany and Japan, had been able to use such a strategy for their development. Rather, they had gone through the early stages of industrialization behind protective tariff walls until they felt competitive enough to confront the global market on equal terms. Specialization would not encourage industrial development of the kind needed in Latin America; instead the region would be condemned to a peripheral position as a supplier of primary products.

These arguments were taken a stage further, and given much greater exposure in the English-speaking world, by Andre Gunder Frank, who in 1967 produced his classic *Capitalism and Underdevelopment in Latin America*. According to Frank, development and underdevelopment are simply two sides of the same coin: the rich countries achieved growth by systematically exploiting their colonies and the rest of the underdeveloped world and this process had been going on for several centuries, at least since the Spanish penetration of the New World. By the twentieth century, no part of the globe was too remote to remain untouched by the impacts of the international economic system of imperialism and domination. Thus it was nonsense to regard, as Rostow had done, the underdeveloped world as in some kind of pristine initial state. The poor countries had in fact been *underdeveloped* in the process of incorporation into the global system, and the structural changes that had been imposed upon them made future development of a real and autonomous kind much less likely. Once the goods in which they specialized were no longer needed by the world market, or if a cheaper source was found, they would simply be discarded without the possibility of returning to their old internally oriented system of production. The poorest regions of Latin America were not those that had been ignored by the world market: rather they were those that had in the past had a very close relationship but had outlived their usefulness. Latin America as a whole, he suggested, had progressed most during the two world wars when the countries at the core of international capitalism had been otherwise engaged and the periphery was left to develop in its own way.

Many similar ideas were developed at roughly the same time by Celso Furtado (1964), who argued that capitalism had expanded throughout the globe, particularly after the industrial revolution in Europe: no region was left untouched, and in all cases new hybrid structures were left behind, with profound implications for future development prospects. The penetrated economies were generally characterized by the existence and interaction of three distinct sectors:

- a 'remnant' economy consisting mainly of subsistence farmers, but with a small amount of cash crop production;
- a domestic sector producing goods and services for local consumption;
- the internationally oriented sector producing goods for the world market.

This classification was used as the basis for a later analysis of the Brazilian situation (Furtado 1965), written at the time of political and economic crisis. Here he dealt with the class implications of the structures of underdevelopment. Many earlier theorists had dismissed the role of the elites in Latin America as simple collaborators with international capitalism in the exploitation of their lands, but here Furtado presents a much more nuanced analysis, pointing out that there is a real diversity of class interests in Brazil. Particularly lacking was an elite committed to the generation of autonomous industrialization, and institutional arrangements would need to be flexible enough to allow such a group to assume power – a crucial advance in development thought that we will take up again with reference to the successful industrialization of East Asia. Furtado himself then returned to a general analysis of Latin America (Furtado 1969), which represents one of the fullest statements of the dependency thesis. The export of primary products, he urges, cannot advance development at all, but more importantly the structures of the economy and the society strongly inhibit any movement towards a more productive and sustainable future. He called for a complete reform of institutional arrangements, of political power and of relationships with the outside world. New technologies must be developed and harnessed internally, and in the early stages at least the state sector needed to play a leading role as a catalyst for development. The countries of Latin America could achieve many of these difficult tasks more easily by developing productive arrangements for regional co-operation. While these basic assumptions and propositions were generally accepted by many later theorists, a number of writers developed particular components of the analysis in more detail. Three of them, all of whom have particular relevance for current debates, are considered briefly here: Arghiri Emmanuel, Samir Amin and Immanuel Wallerstein.

Emmanuel (1972) produced what at the time was a very influential analysis of the ways in which international trade reinforces income inequalities at a global level. Goods exported from high-wage countries have a consistently higher price on the world market compared with exports from underdeveloped countries that have much lower wages, not because these first-world exports are inherently more valuable but because rich countries have the political power to manipulate the markets and set prices favourable to their own products. This argument, although widely criticized in several quarters, is still repeated by some authors in the current debate about globalization and the supposed benefits of large-scale expansion of world trade.

Amin's particular contribution, on the other hand, was to elaborate Furtado's analysis of the internal structures of underdeveloped countries (see, for example, Amin 1976, 1977). He looked at the development of both the export-oriented and domestic sectors, and at the linkage (or lack of it) between the two. Areas involved in export activities, usually of primary products, would have higher wages than found in the rest of the economy, but the multiplier effects of these investments would be far less than in developed economies. Most of the supplies of specialized machinery would come from core countries, as would even some of the food and more luxury items consumed by the labour force. This lack of productive linkage meant that the two parts of the economy were quite isolated from each other. The export sector would in fact have its closest relationships with the areas to which its output was exported, again in the core countries, a characteristic which he termed *disarticulation*. The obvious gaps between rich and poor would inevitably cause deep resentments that could lead to political instability and, to ensure the maintenance of order, large sums would have to be spent on the import of military hardware and on rewards to local elites and the military forces to ensure their loyalty. This would exacerbate a balance of payment situation already made dire by the progressive decline in the relative value of the primary products being exported. The shortfall in hard currency could only be met by opening up yet further mines, plantations or other export activities, but this would lead to yet another spiral of deepening disarticulation and internal inequality.

Wallerstein's contribution has been voluminous and has partly involved some very detailed historical analysis of the development of the global economy, founding a whole school of analysis that has become known as *world systems theory* (see, for example, Wallerstein 1974, 1979, 1984, 2011; Hopkins and Wallerstein 1982). But he is also important for his introduction of an entirely new category into the debate about the structure of the core and the periphery. He pointed to the need for a category of countries that acted as go-betweens or mediators between the rich and the poor nations, and could help to diffuse any tensions that might arise from global inequalities by providing examples of what could be achieved within the system. This group, which included countries like Australia, Canada, Spain and South Korea, he termed the *semi-periphery,* and their role was to demonstrate that revolution or even drastic reform was not at all necessary.

As we have seen, in much of dependency theory there was the assumption that external forces were all-powerful and simply swept away any lingering remnants of the old structures. As a number of critics pointed out, this is clearly too extreme, and even in the newer versions of modernization theory important interactions between the modern and traditional sectors were postulated. A number of the later dependency writers attempted to remedy this shortcoming, notably Fernando Cardoso (Cardoso and Faletto 1979; Cardoso 1982). In these writings, they point to the complex configuration in various Latin American countries of competing or co-operating groups and classes, each influenced by external forces and each attempting to use these external elements to their own advantage, although no class or group is strong enough to control this environment.

A number of Marxist scholars have taken issue with the methods and assumptions used, suggesting that they are a misrepresentation of the true Marxist position. Bill Warren (1980) has argued that while it may have a number of abhorrent features, capitalism is necessary to strip away the original feudal situation found in most underdeveloped regions, and this can only be accomplished by outside imperialist forces that are essential for its establishment, which is in turn a prerequisite for the transition to socialism. From the other side of the ideological spectrum, several critics have pointed to gains that have been made in the development of a number of countries, especially in Asia. These have been contrasted with the performance of those countries that have attempted a more self-reliant approach, and it is to this 'miracle' of growth in Asia that we now turn.

The Asian miracle: challenges for modernization and dependency approaches

It has been claimed, with justification, that the spectacular growth that has taken place in East Asia since the 1960s represents the most profound and rapid economic, social and political transformation that has ever taken place. Former US Treasury Secretary Larry Summers has calculated that during the Industrial Revolution in Britain, within an average human life span, standards of living rose by perhaps 50 per cent, a noticeable improvement. But in contemporary Asia a person may well have experienced an increase of living standards of some 100 fold, or 10,000 per cent (Mahbubani 2008). It is little surprise, then, that the Asian experience should have attracted so much attention and presented such a challenge to all existing theories of development (see, for example, Berger and Borer 1997; Rowen 1998; Leipziger 2000). The recent history of the region has generated an enormous literature and spawned a number of comparative studies seeking to explain why Asia has been so much more successful than either Latin America or Africa (Gereffi and Wyman 1990). However, there is still no agreement about the Asian experience and what its implications are: each side in the debate has attempted to enlist the Asian success story to support its own entrenched position.

The modern-day descendants of the modernization theorists have stressed the importance of adherence to neoclassical postulates in countries such as South Korea, Taiwan and China. Protectionist tendencies were avoided, with the entire emphasis being on exports as the engine of growth. International competitiveness in export required close attention to labour and other production costs, the careful management of macroeconomic policy and exchange rate settings and ongoing programmes of reform, resulting in progressive privatization of government enterprises, trade liberalization, structural adjustment, reforms in corporate governance and the fundamental democratization of the political system.

The responses of the adherents of dependency theory have also been predictable. In the early stages of the developments in South Korea, for example, a number of critics questioned how 'real' this development was, arguing that this was a classic example of dependent development, relying on politically motivated support from the US and essentially exploiting low-cost labour resources. Unflattering comparisons were made with North Korea's emphasis on self-reliance. Yet as the evidence of continued progress mounted, and as the North Korean competition faltered, the emphasis switched to the lauding of the South Korean model of autonomous development. It was emphasized that the early stages of industrialization took place behind high tariff walls, and the government played a very important role as initiator and co-ordinator of new initiatives (Amsden 1989; Wade 1990). Peter Evans (1995) has argued that East Asia has been far more successful than Latin America because the state was both *autonomous* and *embedded*. Unlike its counterparts in Latin America, the state in Asia has not been hostage to particular vested, class interests, but has been autonomous and able to act independently in the interests of the whole nation. Yet the state has been closely integrated into society, positioned to receive messages from all parts of the community and able to interact on all of these levels, and, in particular with the business community, to ensure that plans and targets were effectively met.

Yet, the Asian experience has also presented some different challenges to development theory by highlighting some factors that are outside all of the major existing theories. One set of writers has highlighted the role of culture in development, and pointed to the wide variety of experiences in different parts of the world, thus questioning the generality of any development theories. Much has been made of the common Confucian heritage in Korea, Taiwan and China. This philosophy emphasizes the ethical responsibilities of both rulers and the ruled and was useful in instilling a high level of work ethic and response to authority in these countries. Confucianism also places great reliance on education and self-cultivation in the development of society, and as a result the level of investment in education has been extremely high.

Some commentators have also pointed out that both Korea and Taiwan had a special strategic position during the Cold War, being American allies on the frontline against Communism. This allowed them to gain special advantages from the US, including access to military and development aid, and preferential access to American markets for their products, especially in the early stages of growth. The Western world generally turned a blind eye to the blatant copying of products and technology, something that would not be tolerated today.

Rather than supporting one of the existing models of development, a number of researchers have suggested that the Asian model of growth is in fact a case unto itself. Asian companies have been energetic and entrepreneurial, have concentrated on improving their productivity levels and have been able to develop new product lines and penetrate new markets as older lines become less profitable. At the same time, some of the strengths of more centrally planned economies were utilized, especially in the early stages of development. The state was both active and efficient, avoiding the lethargy and waste that characterized the Soviet system. Importantly, the population felt that it was involved in a great and vital national enterprise, and was willing to work enormously hard and make sacrifices in the interest of future generations.

But this successful experience and the later onset of the Asian crisis leads us to two further questions, both of which are concerned with the question of the applicability of this model to other parts of the underdeveloped world. First, several commentators, as well as policy-makers from around the world, have urged various governments to adopt the Korean or Taiwanese models of development but it is far from clear whether such a transfer can work. Cultural values in regions such as Africa are very different from those in Korea, and countries could not now expect to derive the economic advantages that Korea and Taiwan were able to derive during the Cold War. A second and related question is: even if it were possible to transfer development models in this way, do nations that adopt such a high-growth path to development risk the sort of damaging crisis that befell Asia in 1997? Is it possible to adopt these methods in the early stages of growth and then undertake a careful and appropriately sequenced series of reforms that can avoid later instability? This latter question is of great relevance to China at the moment. Many features of the Korean model, including the creation of some large conglomerates based on the example of the Korean *chaebol*, have been adopted but there are fears about how the economy will be adapted and reformed in the longer term.

The rise of neoliberalism: globalization and development theory

Since the 1980s, development thought and policy has been dominated by what has become known as neoliberal thought, or what Toye (1991) has called the New Political Economy, a movement that gained much momentum from the fall of the Soviet Union and the consequent discrediting of socialist alternatives to capitalism. A more self-confident West became willing to reassert many of the elements of the old modernization model (Colclough and Manor 1991). In the core countries of the developed world the rise of neoliberalism followed the election of Ronald Reagan in the US and Margaret Thatcher in Britain (Peck 2010), but these ideological currents also flowed into the developing world (McKay 2013).

Certainly, there are many elements that demonstrate a simple return to modernization, notably the often unstated belief that there is one path to development which all nations can follow in a series of stages. The goals of development are also portrayed as unproblematic, involving a simple movement toward the modernity that is portrayed as so successful in the West. It could even be argued that development economics as a distinct discipline has been declared redundant by those arguing instead for some universal recipes for successful growth and change. All good comes from external sources, with outside norms and methods being essential to the breaking down of traditional barriers to growth. Many of the core mechanisms for growth are also similar to those cited in the earlier period. Savings rates are still a central element, supported by foreign investment. But the role of government is simply dismissed. Elites and politicians in particular are uniformly portrayed as rent-seeking villains, willing only to look after their own narrow interests rather than the good of the entire society (Toye 1991). Thus, while markets may not be perfect, they are portrayed as infinitely preferable to governments controlled by a 'kleptocracy'. Market failures are seen as resulting from an excess of government interference in the economy rather than from a dearth of regulation. Government services, even including health and education, must be pared back in the interests of balancing the budget and creating an environment conducive to foreign investment, and where possible government-owned services and assets should be privatized in the interests of efficiency. Similarly, foreign exchange rates must be managed (i.e., devalued) to encourage export competitiveness.

Many of these policy measures have been promulgated by international institutions, notably the IMF, to deal with the periodic crises that have plagued much of the underdeveloped world. But it is also true that much of the neoliberal doctrine is embedded in the large body of literature supporting the move towards globalization, and it is this set of beliefs that was so fundamentally challenged by the onset of the GFC.

In the early years of the new millennium, the central talking point, both among policy-makers and the general public, was globalization. There even seemed to be a general agreement that this new wave of change was inevitable and that all nations must either seek ways of accommodating the new reality or risk irrelevance as the rest of the world marches into this glittering future. Yet there was surprisingly little consensus on exactly what the term meant. At one level, it can simply involve the expansion of economic activities such as trade and investment across national boundaries. But it is frequently used to highlight closer economic integration, greater policy reform and openness and greater interdependence between countries. More controversially, the term has sometimes been used to describe (or predict) tendencies of convergence by all countries towards similar political systems, lifestyles and even tastes in entertainment or fast foods. There were certainly dissenting voices even at the height of enthusiasm for this new order, but the onset of the GFC in 2007 added a whole new dimension to the debate – underlining old warnings and raising completely new ones. A significant impact of this crisis has been to hasten the shift that was already taking place from the old centres of economic and political power in Europe and North America to the 'developing economies', and particularly those in Asia, nations with rather different priorities and strategies. In the process the whole notion of development is being redefined as well the theoretical and policy frameworks utilized in achieving progress.

Given the looseness of the concept of globalization, it is not surprising that a number of voices have long been raised to criticize several of the claims that have been made in its name. John Gray (1998) has challenged one of these basic tenets, that this is a new era involving a profound set of changes to many aspects of global economy and society. Rather, Gray suggests, there have been several similar periods before in world history – in the mid-nineteenth century and again in the years leading up to the First World War in particular – when there were high levels of international trade and investment. In these earlier cases, the experiment with laissez-faire economics proved to be short-lived, principally because of the extreme levels of income inequality that were generated in the process. This polarization led to political instability that quickly forced new systems to be adopted. Thus, Gray argued, globalization is merely the return to a failed experiment, and this current incarnation is bound to disappear in the same way, and for basically the same reasons.

Not surprisingly, the remnants of the old dependency school have also criticized globalization as yet another manifestation of the Western desire to dominate and exploit underdeveloped countries. The existing world order is being remade to serve the greed and class interests of a small elite, and the capitalist state is being restructured to serve this new kind of imperialism (Petras and Veltmeyer 2001). Many groups have felt marginalized and even exploited by this powerful set of global forces, and we have witnessed a number of mass demonstrations against globalization and what are regarded as some of its key institutions, the World Trade Organization, the IMF and the World Economic Forum, for example.

Moving beyond these arguments, a number of elements of a new agenda for development have been proposed by some writers; importantly the whole modernization approach has been seriously questioned by those seeking to go beyond what they regard as an outmoded modernist paradigm. Any attempt to impose a unidirectional or single path to development has received harsh criticism from those researchers using a postmodern approach that stresses a whole new agenda concerned with knowledge, identity, meaning and the like (Schuurman 2001; Parfitt 2002). Some have gone so far as to suggest that the whole development project is now moribund or at has at least reached a serious impasse, and we have entered an era of 'post-development' (Sachs 1992; Rahnema and Bawtree 1997).

In part, this introduces a whole new set of concerns into the debate but in the process many of the older issues are also rejected or turned on their head. The assumption that the underdeveloped world can be treated as a homogeneous and undifferentiated whole is completely dismissed. The development path of a society, and indeed its choices about the goals of development itself, are historically conditioned and are heavily influenced by the pattern of institutions that has emerged over the years. We should not regard any set of institutions, not even the market, as indispensable or the best choice – everything depends upon the context and the historical legacy. Similarly, the overarching belief in progress that characterized the modernist approach has been replaced for some by a greater sense of pessimism or a desire to avoid the most dangerous risks. The state, regarded for so long by many as the guardian or even the catalyst of development, is now seen by this group as part of the problem. Rather, they argue, our real hope is with civil society and its struggle for emancipation. This of course raises some serious issues about the old methods of development assistance and the role of aid and the 'expert'. The process of development is here conceived as a form of discourse, one shaped by disparities of power. Escobar (1995) has argued that development is not a set of aims or knowledge that is gradually uncovered and acted upon, but an imposed set of constructs and values. The Western concern has been to win markets, gain access to raw materials and avoid being swamped by massive increases in the populations of impoverished countries. The West, with its blind faith in technology and the effectiveness of planning, has treated the Third World as a child in great need of guidance. Accordingly, this school argues that all earlier categories of development thinking have fallen into the trap of paternalism, or what is often now called 'trusteeship' (Cowen and Shenton 1996; Parfitt 2002). The aim of development must be to escape from this 'impasse' and reflect the real needs and goals of the people involved, although it is far from clear how this is to be achieved (Sharp and Briggs 2006; Simon 2006; Sylvester 2006).

Another important element in the current debate concerns the role of different kinds of political and economic regimes in encouraging or inhibiting growth. The neoliberal mainstream argues that Western-style democracy is essential to progress, although some interesting counter-arguments are now appearing (see, for example, Clague 1997; Rodrik 2011). Not surprisingly, some new ideas are coming from Asian countries, which see themselves as being successful but not necessarily following conventional or Western models. In an interesting study, Sylvia Chan (2002) argues that the common label of 'liberal democracy' contains two different elements that may in fact be contradictory – many of the strongest supporters of economic liberalization are opposed to many democratic ideals. Similarly, we need to recognize three key elements of 'liberty' – *economic, civil* and *political* liberty – and three key conditions that need to be achieved to promote growth – *security, stability,* and *openness and information.* After surveying the Asian growth experience, she concludes that such liberties and outcomes have in fact been achieved under national systems that are not democratic in the Western sense but are more congruent with local histories and institutions.

The global financial crisis and emerging challenges to neoliberalism

While these arguments were still raging, the global economy entered a new and extremely unstable phase culminating in the GFC and its numerous aftershocks that are continuing right down to the time of writing. For some, as will be explored in Chapter 4, the entire edifice of neoliberal thought has been shown to be worthless or even reckless and dangerous, and has brought the entire global financial and economic system to the brink of disaster (McKay 2013). However, there have been concerted attempts by many with a strong vested interest in retaining the pre-GFC system – with the finance houses of Wall Street and the city of London very much to the fore – to drag public opinion and policy-makers back to 'business as usual'. The economics profession in particular has shown itself to be generally unwilling to rethink any aspects of neoclassical orthodoxy and has carried on as if nothing had happened in the real world: as Mirowski (2013) has put it, economics makes no pretence to describe the world as it is but rather the world as some important vested interests would prefer it to be. Yet in spite of these efforts it does seem that the old modes of neoliberalism have been seriously wounded. At the very least, as Robert Wade (2009) has put it, even if there are strong pressures from powerful elites to return us to the familiar ways of thought and action, it is now more possible to consider some alternative paradigms and policy agendas. For some, the basic problem is that although neoliberal approaches have been roundly attacked, no well-articulated alternatives have so far emerged (Rodrik 2006), however as Streek (2014a) has argued it is possible that the current system may collapse under the weight of its own contradictions even in the absence of any clear new direction. What we are certainly now seeing is a healthy reappraisal of the entire architecture of development theory, with some key elements of the old received wisdom now being re-thought. This process is far from complete, but a new approach may well emerge built around the following central questions that are briefly introduced here and will be discussed in more detail in the chapters on the economics of development and on the impact of the global financial crisis and of economic instability more generally.

Perhaps most basically, the inherent superiority of market mechanisms for the allocation of resources and the design of a whole range of policy instruments in all areas of development – something that as we have seen has been an article of faith for some time – is now under serious question. It is not just that markets were patently incapable of dealing with the crisis of 2007 – and for many critics they were seen as being central to the problem – but some key theoretical constructs backing up long-held assumptions about the role and efficiency of markets have been shown to be shaky to say the least.

Related to this point, the neoliberal slogan that governments were part of the problem rather than the solution has also been challenged. With the widespread and catastrophic failure of markets, governments were the only line of defence against complete system failure, and were forced to pump billions of dollars into their economies. This has generated widespread taxpayer anger, and there have been many calls for much stronger regulation regimes. Just how far this political process goes depends upon how much longer the crisis continues – at the time of writing continued fears about Europe suggest that the instability still has a long way to go, with unpredictable consequences – but it is clear that debate about the appropriate role of the state in the whole process of development has returned to centre stage (Tanzi 2011). The intense examination of neoliberalism that has taken place in the aftermath of the GFC has shown that in fact the whole edifice of neoliberal thought and action depends on the existence of a powerful and active state, but one that is diametrically opposed to the aims and methods of the developmental state that has been so vital to the emergence of the Asian powerhouses (Peck 2010; Mirowski 2013). Thus the debate is now not just about whether state action is vital, but also what kind of state serving whose interests and pursuing precisely what kinds of aims. The UNDP (2013) has made its position on this issue quite clear, arguing that progress in developing nations is ultimately dependent on the presence of a proactive and responsible developmental state with a long-term vision and the ability to design shared norms, values, rules and institutions.

One clear dimension of the developments leading directly to the global crisis was the 'unhitching' of the financial sector from the 'real' economy. Both Satyajit Das (2011) and Costas Lapavitsas (2013) have noted that once upon a time economies were about making useful things, but now we construct complex and artificial financial structures that give immense riches to a few but put at the risk the vast majority of the population. Virtually all aspects of the economy – and indeed society more generally – have been 'financialized' and brought within the realm of the market. Goods and services that were once thought of as unambiguous public goods – for example water supplies – have been privatized in many countries. Similarly, many food staples now traded on world markets have attracted the interest of speculators, and speculation on wheat, rice and other basic items has been seen by many as being a major contributor to the rapid increases in food prices in the last few years.

A number of authors have raised the wider question of the impact of the dominance of neoliberalism on the psychological health of individuals and on the texture of entire societies. Michael Sandel (2012) has suggested that societies are significantly weakened in a moral and psychological sense because non-market norms have been crowded out by market values in almost every aspect of life. Even more provocatively, Paul Verhaeghe (2014) has argued that the market-driven world is bringing out the worst in all of us. We were promised that the market would emancipate us and herald an age of autonomy and freedom, but instead we live in a world of atomization, loneliness and unbounded selfishness.

Overall, it could be argued, the world is now much more unstable than it has been for some time, and this is creating a lack of security across many dimensions for many millions of people, but especially the most vulnerable. As part of the debate about the causes and consequences of the GFC it has been argued that the processes of financial sector growth and the increasing reach of the market have exacerbated degrees of inequality at all levels, and this inequality has been a major contributor to the rise of instability and the generation of crisis (Vandemoortele 2009). The creation of a small number of very rich individuals and a mass of poor people has reduced aggregate levels of demand and simultaneously created dangerous levels of social and political instability. The recent publication of a detailed study by the French economist Thomas Piketty (2014) has stirred enormous interest. He argues that current levels of inequality have not been seen since the latter part of the nineteenth century, the era of the unbridled 'robber barons' in the US and some parts of Europe. Wealth, he stresses, is not determined by income alone but more importantly by possession of a wide range of assets, including housing and land, many of them inherited. As Christine Lagarde, the head of the IMF, is fond of pointing out, the 85 richest people in the world now control as much wealth as the poorest half of the global population – that is 3.5 billion people!

This incredible level of polarization in the global economy has been made worse by the inability of most countries to create nearly enough well-paid jobs, so that the World Bank (2012) is arguing that jobs, and in particular jobs for vast numbers of unemployed young people, are now a key global priority. As the Bank stresses, jobs not only provide income but also largely define who people are, and contribute enormously to the maintenance of social and political stability. Similarly, the use of austerity measures to balance the budgets of many nations that had spent vast sums to ameliorate the impacts of the GFC by bailing out their banking systems has had a serious effect on the poorer segments of society while not achieving any of the benefits predicted by supporters of neoliberal policies (Blyth 2013).

One important component in the growing scepticism about the neoliberal position especially as it relates to developing countries is the shift in the position of some key international institutions, notably the World Bank and the IMF. The support of these bodies has always been crucial, since the advice they give to governments – and often the conditions that they impose in return for financial assistance – set the parameters for policy and in the process entrench particular ideological positions (McKay 2014). Shifts in the position of the World Bank have been particularly interesting to observe. As the GFC engulfed the global economy sharp differences emerged between the World Bank and the IMF as to the most appropriate policy responses, with the IMF adopting a much more conventional approach. Recent appointments to senior positions, and in particular those of the president and the chief economist, seem to be at the centre of this change in policy. The change of president to Robert Zoellik in 2007 was significant, as was the accession of the current president Jim Yong Kim in 2012. Kim is a physician and anthropologist with a long history of work on HIV/AIDS within the World Health Organization and thus brings to bear a much broader perspective on development priorities. He has been particularly outspoken on the problems created by the intensification of inequalities at all levels and the need for a development paradigm that has at its core a strong sense of ethics and basic human rights. Under his leadership the Bank has adopted the goals of ending extreme poverty by 2030 and boosting shared prosperity among the poorest 40 per cent of the citizens of developing countries. The chief economist position at the Bank has also been important in setting both the tone and the detail of the international development agenda. Joseph Stiglitz, who occupied the position from 1997 to 2000, was fired for expressing dissent from Bank policies, but since then he has published a number of influential books on the problems of globalization, the causes and consequences of periodic economic crises and the costs of inequality (for example, Stiglitz 2002, 2010, 2013) and in 2001 he was awarded the Nobel Prize for Economics. Clearly, his lasting influence at the Bank should not be underestimated. Also significant was the appointment of Justin Lifu Yin to the position of Chief Economist from 2008 to 2012, a crucial period in the Bank's response to the GFC. With a doctorate in economics from the University of Chicago, one of the key intellectual centres of the entire neoliberal movement, his credentials as a supporter of conventional economic theory and policies were not questioned – and indeed he steadfastly supported the role of market mechanisms in the efficient allocation of resources – but he also introduced some interesting new elements into the thinking of the institution. Undoubtedly, as he has stressed in much of his writing, his position owes much to his experiences as a child in Taiwan, and more recently in China, resulting in an interesting hybrid of conservative and progressive thought (Lin 2012a). His championing of what he calls a new 'structural economics' will be discussed in the next chapter. Lin's successor, the Indian-born Kaushik Basu, is still regarded as a relative newcomer to the Bank, but he has expressed strong support for the emphasis on shared prosperity rather than simple economic growth.

At a more general level, the GFC has forced everyone to think about the politics involved in financial and economic policy issues; the need to take what some regard as the old-fashioned field of political economy seriously may be one of the most important consequences of the crisis in terms of development theory and policy. In considering the new global political economy one key impact of these recent events has been the hastening of the transfer of global power from the West, and in particular the US, to the rising powers of Asia, and notably China. This will have all kinds of implications, many of them quite profound. It has always been clear that dominant theoretical and policy paradigms can only be established and maintained with strong pressure from a major global power. The US exerted the power necessary to establish and defend the neoliberal orthodoxy, but with the decline of Washington and the rise of Beijing things may be very different. China is of course actively promoting its interests and the strengths of its development model with a deliberate campaign to enhance its 'soft power' through a well-financed 'charm offensive' (Kurlantzick 2007).

A key consequence of this renewed attraction of Asian approaches to development policy and planning is that the role of the state – and indeed the very nature of the state – has returned as a central issue of our age. The fact that China's economy is still under very direct control of the state, that a significant proportion of its economy is still state-owned, that the nature of China's links with the global economy are tightly constrained and that the country was able to weather the GFC so well, has not gone unnoticed in the rest of the developing world (Subrahmanian 2011). The need to strengthen state capacity and regulatory reach has emerged as one of the key lessons of the GFC: the state should now not be seen as a key problem but as an indispensable part of any viable solution. Markets unaided cannot be relied on to deliver the benefits of development since market failures are endemic, even in developed countries. This lesson is certainly being heeded in a wide range of countries where various kinds of 'state capitalism' have been established. Aware of the economic power of capitalist systems but unwilling to trust the operations of uncontrolled markets, several countries are using carefully regulated markets to create wealth but are ensuring that the funds are used as the government sees most appropriate (Bremmer 2010).

This re-evaluation of the role of the state also raises questions about the future of democracy. If the dominant model of capitalism is concerned more about profits than the creation of jobs, and as we have seen is now producing incredible levels of inequality at all levels of the economy, it may be that capitalism and democracy are not really compatible. As Wolfgang Streeck (2014a, 2014b) has argued, we may be witnessing a conflict between capitalism and democracy, and if, as he predicts, capitalism will be the victor in this battle then the future may be extremely unstable. Halper (2010) fears that with the rise of China authoritarian forms of government will again become more attractive, but Dani Rodrik (2011) presents a rather different kind of argument about the future of democracy. He suggests that after the GFC we now realize that the simultaneous pursuit of democracy, self-determination and economic globalization is not feasible. If nations need the ability to defend their own economies and citizens at times of financial crisis, and if the frequency and impacts of such crises are to be lessened, then it is the nature of globalization that must be redefined: we must return to the idea that international economic rules need to be subservient to domestic policy, not the other way round. A less ambitious globalization would be better for the vast majority.

At a rather different scale of analysis, the fundamental shifts in global power that are in process have given rise to a series of important studies on why, some two centuries or so ago, the West rose to a position of unchallenged world dominance, what factors were crucial, and how this leadership position of the North Atlantic powers is being challenged by developing Asia. Kenneth Pomeranz (2000) has shown that at the time of Britain's industrial revolution some areas of China were equally well positioned to take off but were left behind by a rapidly expanding Europe. The explanation for this 'great divergence', he argues, was that parts of Britain had easy access to high quality coal deposits essential for early industrialization, but even more important were the major advantages, including raw materials of various kinds, provided by the acquisition of extensive new colonies. Taking a much longer historical perspective, Ian Morris (2010) similarly concludes that the biggest advantage that the West had was one of geography, and in particular easier access to the vast resources of the New World. Geography will continue to be an unequal force in the future, but he speculates that the uneven consequences of climatic change will be a major factor in future development, and Asia's proximity to an arc of instability stretching through much of Africa through the Middle East and India and into South East Asia will cause many problems. Niall Ferguson (2011) has also weighed into this debate arguing that there were six major factors that allowed the West to gain global dominance – intense competition within Europe itself; the scientific revolution in the seventeenth century; the rule of law and representative government; the development of modern medicine; the emergence of the consumer society; and the work ethic. All of this allowed sustained capital accumulation, but by now the East has absorbed all of this technology and its associated lessons, while the West has sunk into a massive crisis of debt that could destroy the whole edifice quite quickly, a process highlighted and intensified by the GFC. At the same time there have been suggestions that Africa may also be embarking on a period of rapid development, driven by demands, particularly from Asia, for its vast reserves of mineral and energy resources, although the recent history of Africa clearly demonstrates that much of this potential wealth could be squandered (McKay 2012). Thus, development theory now has to grapple again with these large-scale and long-term issues, questions that were familiar in the writings of the Marxist historians, but which for some time were submerged by the more immediate analyses of the neoliberals.

For the first time for several centuries developing Asia is replacing the North Atlantic region as the main driving force of the global economy, and the G8 and the other cosy clubs of the rich nations are challenged by newer groupings such as the BRICS (Brazil, Russia, India, China, South Africa). Will the old imperial relationship between the rich and powerful be re-established, albeit in a revised form, or are, for example, China's relationships with Africa and Latin America very different from British or French colonialism, and will China emerge as the champion of the developing world rather than just the latest superpower? Many African leaders believe that China is not just interested in economic exploitation – offering generous assistance with infrastructural, health and educational development – and see China as offering a way out of the restrictive lending practices of the older international institutions such as the IMF (Ampiah and Naidu 2008; Michel and Beuret 2009). However, there is some evidence of popular resentment against Chinese practices in Africa, resulting in anti-Chinese riots in Madagascar and Zambia (Lee 2014).

Perhaps the most fundamental question of all for development theory relates to the whole nature of the debate – if indeed the developing economies are now poised to become the main driving force of global growth while the West is entering a prolonged period of austerity and low growth. Nancy Birdsall (2011) has even asked whether the GFC might mark the end of 'development' as an idea to be replaced by a more global agenda for co-operation. Certainly, if the developing world is to escape from what it sees as the tyranny of the neoliberal world order, and the dominance of the large multinational corporations and the escalations in inequality that go along with it, the revival of what for long was known as 'Third World Solidarity' will be essential. Unless developing countries form a united front then each of them can be used in turn by international corporations to provide cheap labour and resources, in a cut-throat competition that in the long run will harm all of them. Vijay Prashad (2012) has presented a detailed history of co-operation between developing nations, and argues that it is both essential and possible for some of the old momentum to be recaptured. Clearly, he suggests, neoliberalism has failed the developing world but under the leadership of China, India and other members of the BRICS a completely new narrative for the Global South is possible. It is far from clear whether this is simply wishful thinking, but there is no doubt that we live in extremely interesting times for our discipline, as the tsunami that was the GFC necessitates a fundamental reassessment of development's theoretical underpinnings.

Chapter 3

The Economics of Development

John McKay

While most of us accept that development is about much more than economics and growth, there is no doubt that academic and policy debates have been dominated by economic considerations. Work in this area has a long and conspicuous pedigree and has attracted some of the best minds in the history of analytical thought, and not only in the Western world. In the period since the Second World War, there has been a whole series of debates and controversies about the economic dimensions of development theory and practice but these can be summarized in ten basic questions that will be used to structure discussion in the rest of this chapter.

First, how does growth happen and what are its major drivers? Trying to understand the origins of growth is perhaps the most basic question of all, and one which absorbs the constant attention of the poorer countries. For some, it is simply a matter of following the right policy recipe – managing exchange rates, labour costs, inflation, investment and the like. But, others suggest, this economic formula will only work in the presence of a number of other key conditions. Human capital must be available in adequate amounts and with the required skills. Appropriate governance structures must be in place to regulate the actions of individuals and companies, and to avoid problems of corruption or exploitation. Political systems must be robust enough to avoid disputes over access to resources or the various benefits of development boiling over into destructive conflicts. This in turn raises the issue of whether it is possible simply to put in place one kind of economic system, such as liberal democracy, and then expect all other positive outcomes to flow automatically, or whether the various societal domains are much more discrete.

Second, is growth an easy process or does it require much effort and sacrifice? It has been suggested that with the removal of some of the 'unnatural' constraints on development, for example old corrupt elites or inward-looking governments, growth will occur spontaneously and naturally without the need for any further inputs. But other practitioners contend that in fact growth is difficult and only achieved at a great price. There are many false starts and wrong turns, and all the required conditions and inputs must be available at just the right time and place.

Third, in the generation of growth what are the roles of the market and of the state? If growth is seen as easy and natural, this usually rests on the assumption that market forces can be effective almost single-handedly: some basic regulation may be necessary but government involvement should be kept to a minimum. The extreme opposite of this view is represented by the now largely discredited centrally planned economies of the Soviet era, but many more moderate commentators have suggested that what is needed in the stimulation and management of growth is a creative and mutually supportive partnership between the state and the market, and this was the basis of the Asian economic miracle. This debate has been given added impetus after the onset of the global financial crisis (GFC), and one key argument presented here is that the state is once again recognized as being central to all parts of the growth process and of the broader development agenda (Tanzi 2011; Mazzucato 2013).

Fourth, what are the appropriate roles of the state and the private sector? Similarly, it has been contended that while the private sector can contribute a great deal to the generation of growth, governments are needed to guarantee the availability of certain key elements such as political stability, education and effective infrastructure. Governments can also provide financial incentives and facilitate co-operation between private and public institutions.

Fifth, how can processes of structural change be managed, and how can costs be ameliorated? Development does not involve a single period of transformation but is a continual process of change and renewal. Structural change of this kind is always contested, and while society as a whole may benefit in the long run some groups may have to bear great costs and hardship. This raises issues of how such intensely political processes are to be managed effectively, and how the costs as well as the benefits are to be apportioned.

Sixth, how can technology be generated, absorbed and used? Most theorists now recognize that growth processes, especially since the industrial revolution, have been partly driven by technological progress, and in the modern world the competitive position of all nations depends on their ability to generate or gain access to appropriate technologies. Even in advanced economies, this often requires creative alliances between universities, private companies and government research institutes but for less developed countries the tasks involved are even more fraught. This is particularly so in the early stages of development, when educated personnel are usually scarce, and in the difficult transition from simple, labour-intensive activities to more demanding higher-value industries. Countries such as China are now investing massively in upgrades of their technological base and this is creating problems for smaller nations with more limited financial resources.

Seventh, what is the role and rationale for foreign trade and investment? Much economic theory has been developed to support the notion that free trade is of benefit to all nations at every stage of development and will result in optimal efficiency in the use of scarce resources. However, in practice most countries have used various kinds of tariffs, quotas or other restrictions to benefit their own producers and such issues still make it difficult to move further with international agreements under the World Trade Organization. At various times, theories have been put forward in favour of certain kinds of restraints on foreign investment and access to particular markets until local industries have had time to establish themselves.

Eighth, what is the role of foreign aid? One of the enduring problems of development is to explain how countries can make the initial move to a higher level of growth, after which the process may become self-sustaining. Many writers have suggested that foreign aid can provide such an impetus, and allow the construction of essential infrastructure, educational facilities and the like. Indeed, much of the practice of non-government development agencies as well as large official programmes of assistance is based on such a proposition. However, aid, if not carefully targeted, can crowd out national enterprises and stifle local initiative.

Ninth, what is the role of international co-operation and of international organizations and networks? Many of the same questions about aid apply equally to the activities of international organizations such as the World Bank and the various regional development banks. There has also been fierce controversy about the role of the International Monetary Fund (IMF) in supplying policy advice to national governments, especially in times of economic crisis.

Tenth, is economic development easier or more difficult in the current era of globalization? There is no doubt that the international economic and political environment facing developing countries now is very different from that prevailing when, for example, the original 'Tigers' of Asia began their spectacular transformation. However, there is little agreement about whether in fact it is now easier or more difficult to begin the development transition. The rules of world trade have made illegal many of the strategies used by the developed as well as the Asian countries to achieve their rise, but it could be argued that, given the massive availability of foreign direct investment, development is now easier to achieve if the right policies are followed.

In this short chapter, it is impossible to go into details in an area that is so broad and to do full justice to all of the debates that have raged over the centuries; however, the aim is to at least introduce some of the most influential schools of thought on these key questions. In the later part of the chapter there is also a consideration of one of the key development issues of our age: the complex interrelationships at the international, national and more local scales between economic growth and inequality. Is inequality an inescapable result of processes of growth, especially in the earlier stages of the process? Has globalization resulted in an intensification of tendencies towards larger gaps between the rich and the poor? If large numbers of poor people can be lifted out of poverty, does it matter if at the same time the gaps between rich and poor are becoming larger? Is there evidence that growth rates can be maximized if in fact policies to minimize inequalities are pursued at the same time, which is a common interpretation of recent experiences in East Asia? Given the momentous shockwaves flowing from the GFC do our ideas and policy prescriptions need to be re-evaluated? These are policy issues that many analysts have also suggested are central to issues of political and social stability, and to the whole question of motivation and mass mobilization.

The main drivers of growth: competing schools of thought

The Classical and Neoclassical school

As was noted in Chapter 2, this set of theories has been clearly dominant both in the academic literature and in the policy formulations of the key international institutions, and has been so since at least the eighteenth century. The Europe that the major classical theorists knew was only just emerging from a past in which rapid economic growth had not been the norm, and one in which there was a delicate balance between population and resources. In such an environment the logical assumption was that population growth would depend upon the availability of those commodities necessary to support life, and food in particular, and that in any period of growth there was a constant race between the growth of population and the increased availability of those things needed to support life. Thomas Malthus made this constant battle between population and resource availability central to his arguments, believing that the geometric increases in population were bound in time to dwarf any gains that might be made through techno-logical development.

For these classical thinkers – such as Adam Smith and John Stuart Mill – the output that could be achieved from any economy was dependent upon the supply of labour, the total stock of capital, the size of available land and other natural resources, and the level of technol-ogy that could be applied to the productive process. However, a signifi-cant increase in the supply of land, which was by far the most important resource at the time, was seen as out of the question. This was also an age of relative capital scarcity, which was crucial since the rate of tech-nological progress was dependent upon the availability of new capital sources. The creation of new investment capital was directly dependent on the rate of profit, which was in turn related to the supply of labour and the level of technology available in the production process. As wage levels and household incomes increased, more food and better housing could be obtained, and this generally meant that more infant children survived to adulthood and were able to enter the growing labour force.

As will be obvious, there is a good deal of circularity in this argument: the total system grows through circular and cumulative causation – each success leads to a further round of expansion. But by the same logic any failure or contraction is successively spread and magnified throughout the system. While the supply of all factors of production was limited and finite, the one element that was perhaps most open to change was the supply of capital for investment, and this was depend-ent in large part on the rate of saving that could be achieved. But all of these early theorists had a view that at some time in the future a mature and essentially stationary economy was inevitable, albeit at a relatively high level of prosperity: none of these theorists was able to foretell the impact of the riches that became available for the New World and later from the numerous colonies that were acquired by the dominant powers.

Another common observation on the classical school is that since these writers lived in economies that were still predominantly agrarian, their arguments were built around a single sector that had the supply of land at its centre. However, as has been pointed out by some later reviewers (for example, Benjamin Higgins 1958), Malthus was some-thing of an exception in this regard. He noted that as development pro-ceeds there is an accompanying process of structural change, resulting in a diminished share of total output coming from the agricultural sec-tor. Thus he foreshadowed much later analysis that would assume a dual or multi-sector economy in which the structure and dynamics of each sector were rather different. He also argued that increasing returns to scale were a particular characteristic of the emerging industrial sector, and this has important implications for the usual classical assumptions about the inevitability of stagnation in mature economies.

It is likely that all classical theorists were well aware of the role of the entrepreneur in stimulating investment and technological progress, but this ingredient was not really introduced as a major element. However, it was taken up as a key explanation for progress by Joseph Schumpeter (1934), who saw growth not as a process of the steady accumulation of resources, labour and investment but as essentially unstable and episodic. He was of course the product of the twentieth century and not surprisingly saw the world in rather different terms from his classical forebears. Successful economies are those that are able to encourage and reward innovative contributors, and this will necessitate the emergence of a national income distribution that provides incentives for this creative class.

After the Second World War, as problems of post-conflict reconstruction and the development of the former colonies came to the fore, there emerged renewed interest in theories of growth. This can now been seen as the birth of modern growth theory which has been dominated by neoclassical thought, firmly grounded in the assumptions and methods of the classical thinkers but attempting to reflect the new realities of the world which these theories sought to explain. This group of theorists agreed on a wide range of issues but controversies existed about a number of key questions. One debate concerned the assumption of constant returns to scale that was inherited from the classical school. Many neoclassical theorists have been happy to retain this assumption, while others maintained that in the modern economy, as the size of production units increases there are often extra efficiencies in output. Secondly, some have argued that the growth of a number of key factors of production is exogenously determined, while others have suggested that most of these processes are endogenous to the system. Some economists, following Schumpeter, believed that technological development is the result of outside forces – particularly investment in education and the ability of the social and political system to generate creative entrepreneurs – while others have stressed that technological progress is largely internal to the economy mostly driven by 'learning by doing'. The general tendency in modern growth theory is to rely more and more on endogenous models, based largely on the ideologically driven assumption that the neoclassical economy is a self-contained and self-sufficient system. A third issue relates to the role and origins of human capital growth, which has been central to the debates about the East Asian growth model.

It is generally recognized that the neoclassical school was heralded in by Robert Solow (1956) through the formalization of his growth model, which assumed that in a competitive capitalist economy there are constant returns to scale and diminishing returns to all factors of production. Both labour and technology are exogenously determined and grow at a constant rate. Crucially, with these assumptions the economy converges to an equilibrium. Much later theorizing derives from this model, although some of the assumptions, and hence the convergence on equilibrium, have been questioned.

But in this period there also emerged a range of theorists that began to add a much greater level of sophistication to the debate. Many researchers had high expectations, or perhaps unrealistic hopes, of just what ought to be explained by these economic theories and felt compromised by the fact that in a number of areas key factors were determined externally to the models. Secondly, the expected convergence of incomes between countries did not seem to be happening. Thirdly, it was clear that many of the limits on the expansion of crucial factors of production that had been assumed by the classical theorists could no longer be justified. Importantly, the growth of the labour supply was accelerating rapidly as new medical services became available. Fourthly, the rapid technological advances that had been generated by both world wars and had revolutionized factory production in particular meant that technological change needed a much more central place in any explanation of growth. Finally, empirical evidence was also supplying ample examples to challenge the assumptions of constant returns to scale.

In the 1940s and 1950s, three particularly interesting theorists attempted to deal with these criticisms. Rosenstein-Rodan (1943) looked at the question of increasing returns to scale, arguing that these resulted from technical progress within the factory system and that enhanced labour productivity was derived from new methods of industrial training and from the creation of social overhead capital. He was a champion of what has become known as the theory of the 'big push', arguing that a minimum quantum of investment was necessary to kickstart growth, something that could not be achieved by small increments of finance. Also important was Nurkse's (1952) work on why income disparities between countries persisted, and in particular why capital did not flow at this time from rich, high-wage countries to poorer nations. His argument was that in poor countries, beset by vicious cycles of low productivity and small markets, investment levels were depressed. Equally influential has been Arthur Lewis's (1954) seminal work on the influence of surplus labour on patterns of economic development. He portrayed underdeveloped economies as essentially dual in nature, consisting of a small modern industrial sector and a large subsistence sector with extensive disguised unemployment. The existence of this pool of surplus labour should facilitate the expansion of the modern sector, which could draw in large amounts of cheap labour without causing wage increases. These were all important contributions, and Ros (2005), for example, has argued that these ideas were far more relevant to the real world situation that was emerging than much of the later theorizing.

So far I have concentrated on theories that attempted to account for growth within single countries but in fact international trade and investment have become increasingly important in the global economy and hence have also attracted a great deal of attention. Adam Smith is recognized as the creator of the concept of absolute advantage, according to which nations should concentrate on the production of goods in which they hold some kind of cost advantage. But it was Ricardo who extended this argument to include the case for specialization in national exports that had such an advantage, and who argued that partner nations in trade would all benefit from this kind of exchange. This has been the basis of much work within mainstream economics which has attempted to provide ever more technically sophisticated support for this basic proposition. However, a number of strong criticisms, or at least qualifications, of this unreserved support for the benefits of international trade, and, in particular, increasingly free trade, have emerged (see, for example, Dutt 2005; U. Patnaik 2005).

The neoliberal revolution

The rise to power of President Ronald Reagan in the United States and Prime Minister Margaret Thatcher in Britain heralded a move to a new form of economic orthodoxy that traced its heritage to some aspects of neoclassical economics, and also some elements of classical liberalism, but was essentially a new school of thought in its own right (Harvey 2005; Peck 2010; Mirowski 2013). As in classical and neoclassical economics, the mechanism of the market is at the very centre of neoliberal thought, but here it is ascribed almost supernatural powers as a perfect conveyor of information on all manner of phenomena. Its infinitely complex and always accurate structure makes it impossible for the human brain to comprehend, and mere mortals can do no more than attempt to respond to its signals and reap the benefits that this will confer. Success in the market is the ultimate goal of all entrepreneurs, and this achievement is sufficient to validate companies and provide the perfect seal of moral approval. Thus monopolistic companies that are successful in the market cannot be treated with suspicion, as they were in classical economic theory. Markets that develop any imperfections or inefficiencies can be relied on to be self-regulating as well as all-knowing: any problems that arise as a result of market activities can always be solved through further market innovations. However, this worship of the powers of the market is certainly not synonymous with laissez-faire: markets need to be constructed, maintained and defended partly by an active state apparatus. Thus neoliberals do not advocate the abolition of the state, but rather would restrict its role to this essential support for structures firmly centred on the market.

As in classical liberalism, notions of freedom are also at the centre of neoliberal thought, although Friedrich Hayek (1960) – one of the key figures in the foundation of this school of thought – was at pains to point out that liberty and democracy were not the same thing, and the differences between the two concepts have been the subject of much controversy. Hayek was particularly worried about the limitations placed on the freedom of individual action by any tyranny exerted by the majority of the population. This position highlights one of the paradoxes that writers on neoliberalism have spent much time considering – the seeming compatibility of neoliberal economic prescriptions with a variety of political systems quite different from those found in the US, United Kingdom or Australia, ranging from President Pinochet's Chile to the authoritarian rule by the Communist Party in China.

It is important to note, given the furious debate about inequalities in income that is currently taking place, that neoliberals see no problems with such extreme levels of polarization: in fact they see this as an essential element of their ideal market system and a key driver of progress. The rich are central contributors to the ideal society, and the rest of the population should look up to them and seek to emulate their success.

Marxist and neo-Marxist theories

Mainstream economic theory, and the policies derived from it, has always been seen by its adherents as being equally applicable to all nations regardless of their different histories or institutional systems – what has now become known as a 'one size fits all' approach. By contrast Marx first put forward a complex set of theories to explain the dynamics of capitalist economies, and then postulated a set of relationships between those nations that had made the transition to capitalism and the rest of the world.

Marx's theories, set out particularly in the first volume of *Das Kapital* and with Frederick Engels in *The Communist Manifesto,* are simultaneously explanations of developments in the spheres of economics, politics and social life, but it is the particular economic basis of the capitalist system that underpins everything. While all societies must enable the life of their citizens to continue through the production of food and other material needs, capitalism is unique in that all production is geared to the market exchange of commodities. The 'true' value of these commodities consists of the amount of human labour that has been devoted to their production but the capitalist is able to sell his products at a higher price, the exchange value. Wages must be paid by the owner to the workers to at least allow them to stay alive and reproduce the next generation of labour but wages are not set at a level equal to the exchange value of the goods produced. The difference is the surplus value, the basis of profits for the capitalist class. The capitalist system is inherently competitive and over time individual companies are faced with the problem of declining profits. This is partly overcome by the even greater exploitation of workers through the imposition of longer working hours or lower wages, and the existence of a 'reserve army' of the unemployed ensures that this has to be accepted by workers. There is also strong pressure to introduce new technologies.

At the social and political levels of analysis, Marx subscribed to a basic notion of historical materialism; people make and remake their lives through their productive activities, and it is the economic basis of society that produces a particular cultural superstructure. Crucially, workers within the capitalist system are alienated from the products of their labour, since the labour process is increasingly controlled by others, and consists of repetitive and specialized tasks within a complex division of labour. Thus there is none of the satisfaction of producing the complete and finished articles that was available to the earlier craft workers. Workers are also degraded through ever increasing levels of exploitation and hence are more alienated from each other as well as from the capitalist class (Hobsbawm 1998; Stedman Jones 2002; Wheen 2006).

Marx has been called the first real development economist in that he studies both development *under* capitalism and the development *of* capitalism (P. Patnaik 2005). Marx was very concerned with the historical origins of capitalism, and the particular (or perhaps unique) juxtaposition of forces that allowed it to emerge in Europe, processes that involved momentous struggles. The gradual expansion of commodity production resulted in the weakening of merchant capital, but rather more was needed to really allow capitalism to flourish, and the question of other key factors in this issue of transition has fuelled much debate. A related question that Marx addressed concerned the lack of a similar capitalist revolution in countries such as India and China that had been rather richer than Europe until quite recently but were now rapidly falling behind. His response to this issue was to put forward the concept of the 'Asiatic mode of production'. Village subsistence economies were both unlikely and unable to move towards a capitalist mode of production, and the class of nobles that extracted surplus from village production used this wealth for conspicuous consumption rather than for the initiation of more productive economic systems. Marx's key contribution, though, was to put together the historical issues of the transition to capitalism in Europe with the question of why the rest of the world was falling behind into a single overarching process of capitalist dynamics. Basic here was the concept of *primary accumulation,* which provided the means for the transition to capitalism and heralded in the system of labour essential for the new economy. Also crucial was the inevitable movement towards the *centralization of capital.* Processes of primary accumulation were facilitated by the extraction of surplus from the rest of the world and this process became ever more efficient and exploitative through the centralization of capital into ever larger companies – insights that many claim make Marx still the most convincing analyst of contemporary globalization.

These ideas have been built on by a range of theorists and political activists that have become known as the neo-Marxists. Perhaps most influential, and this includes policy-making in some countries down to the present, has been the emergence of the Latin American school of dependency theorists, a movement that has already been introduced in Chapter 2. But it is important to look at the economic underpinnings of this kind of theorizing and assess its historical accuracy and usefulness in policy terms.

Within these broad neo-Marxist schools' viewpoints it is important to distinguish between *structuralist* and *dependency* approaches. Influenced by Keynesianism as well as by Marx, the structuralists saw the dual North–South division as crucial both at the international and national levels (Saad-Filho 2005). Markets are often very poor at dealing with the priorities for change in such a situation and there is a strong case for government intervention. Structuralists argue that free trade and the international division of labour work systematically in favour of the rich countries and against the developing world, because of the long-term deterioration in the terms of trade for the products coming from the developing world. The only way out of this structural imbalance is for developing countries to undertake their own independent programmes of industrialization. But there are severe problems associated with local industrial growth: the private sector is often weak and savings rates often low and hence strong government intervention is again essential.

As we have already seen, the dependency theorists went much further in their critique of economic orthodoxy, arguing that the West had become rich initially through the exploitation of the periphery, thereby facilitating the process of primary accumulation, and that this transfer of surplus value from the poor to the rich continued in the current phase of the centralization of capital. Thus the dependency theorists were pessimistic about the strategies proposed by the structuralists, including the creation of national manufacturing capacity. Nothing short of a fundamental recasting of international economic and political relations within a socialist model would have any real impact on the lives of the world's poor.

The Asian model of development

The Asian model revolves around much more than a set of economic concepts and policies. It has grown from the very political and social foundations of some very distinctive societies, but in terms of the economics of the Asian model, it is the role of the state that has given rise to most controversy. The theory of the developmental state has drawn on a number of important strands of economic thought that highlight the key roles that governments may play (Chang 1999). Rosenstein-Rodan's theory of the 'big push' was one such key foundation as was Alexander Gerschenkron's (1962) work on late industrialization in which he affirmed that, as global production increases and hence the minimum scale of efficient output is raised, so the size of investments must also increase markedly, and only through state involvement can nations seek to join the club of industrialized powers. In Japan, more recently in South Korea, Taiwan and Singapore, and later still in China, the role of the government has certainly been central. Governments had clear and detailed strategic plans for the development of their economies and indeed their wider societies. Key industries were identified, protected and supported until they were strong enough to be competitive in world markets. Extremely large investments were made in physical infrastructure, such as ports, roads and telecommunications systems, and in social infrastructure, especially education. In most cases, competition within key sectors was carefully managed and emerging 'national champions' were often given a monopoly position. Trade union activity and hence wage increases were carefully controlled in the name of maintaining export competitiveness, for it was the emphasis on exports of manufactured products that was also a very distinctive component of the Asian model. At the same time, the lack of market discipline within most individual industrial sectors was replaced by strong government supervision (Amsden 1989, 2001; Woo Jung-en 1991).

Two relatively recent developments have now brought the Asian model into a rather different perspective. The onset of the Asian financial crisis in 1997 was seen by some as completely discrediting this form of development theory and policy; however, more recent developments in the region, and some new interpretations, have forced us to rethink many of these hasty judgements. Secondly, the rise of China and its continued dramatic growth have also redirected our attention to theoretical and practical approaches coming out of Asia that are both plausible and effective, both within their own terms and as models for other developing countries.

The seemingly inexorable rise of China is particularly significant but can it be considered as part of the tradition of the Asian development model? Many commentators from the orthodox economic school have argued that China's success has been grounded on its abandonment of its old communist agenda in favour of a capitalist system, but this would appear to be a gross oversimplification. Liew (2005) has argued that history, geography and institutional structure are all important in the choice of paths to development, and in particular the role of the Chinese Communist Party – albeit undergoing constant reform in the post-Mao period – has been central. The party has been able to reinvent itself and hold its monopoly position over power, and the market has been used as a tool of state power rather than as a replacement for it. Similarly, Baek (2005) has argued that China has adopted many features of the earlier East Asian developmental model, maintaining strong control over the financial system, supporting a large number of state-owned enterprises and fostering a range of national heavy industries.

The challenge of the GFC

The onset of the GFC has challenged many aspects of the conventional wisdom on the initiation of growth processes and, importantly, on the ways in which sustained progress can be maintained in the face of potential instability. The crisis and its implications are discussed in detail in Chapter 4, but here we consider some of the most important implications of this turbulent period, which at the time of writing is still reverberating through the global system. Of the myriad impacts, perhaps four are most important and likely to be long lasting in their influence: the need to rethink some of our key theoretical assumptions on economic growth processes; the return of the state as a central actor in the initiation and maintenance of global and national growth; an acceleration in the rise of Asian nations, and China in particular, as key players in the global economic, political and strategic systems; and the stagnation of the West and the concomitant rise in the relative importance of some of the developing economies.

As has already been noted in Chapter 2, a key impact of the GFC has been to call into question the supposed 'magic' of the market. Markets, which in the theories of many neoliberal writers had been assumed to be infallible, self-correcting and self-regulating guides to current and future values as well as future risks, were shown to be in fact unstable and unreliable, prone to both mass panic and hysteria. Critiques of markets and their operations have, since the GFC, come from a variety of directions. Historical analysis has shown that over a long period, beginning with a number of crisis periods in the nineteenth century, markets have failed at crucial times, plunging national economies and the global system into serious recessions (Krugman 2008; Ahamed 2009; Fox 2009; Shiller 2009; Cassidy 2010). High-level mathematical analysis, using fractal techniques, has also shown that markets are much more random and unpredictable than most commentators had believed (Mandelbrot and Hudson 2004). Much attention has also focused on risk and debt, and the ways in which these can build up to dangerous levels and threaten the whole global economy (Reinhart and Rogoff 2009; Roubini and Mihm 2010; Das 2011).

In the developed world the massive intervention by governments to prop up their financial systems and protect jobs – not always successfully – raised fundamental questions about relations between the state and the market. How long should such intervention continue, and to what extent should taxpayers be protected from future crises of this kind by improved regulation of the economy? Also basic is the question of in whose interests is the state intervening – a question that could equally be posed in the developing world. Duménil and Lévy (2011), for example, argue that we should not be surprised that the state would intervene on behalf of the ruling elites, and we should not expect any long-term change to come from such intervention, but other writers have taken a quite different view. In the developing world the role of the state that had been so downplayed in recent years especially by the key international organizations is now being reconsidered. Mazzucato (2013) has presented detailed evidence to show that in industrial countries such as the US, contrary to widely held perceptions, important technological advances have not been the work of talented and innovative individuals but have resulted from the work of government-funded laboratories. Semi-conductors, touch screens and the Internet itself have all been the work of this 'entrepreneurial state', with the private sector only coming in when governments had funded the risky part of all such developments and shown what was possible. She also suggests that in the developing world the state can play a similar catalytic role, and has highlighted in particular the successes of the Brazilian development bank BNDES.

As we have seen, state intervention was a key element in the Asian development model, and the enormous attention given to the rise of Asia since the onset of the GFC has included a renewed interest in the Asian model including the potential for interventionist state action in a number of new areas. China now has a much greater influence in Africa, Latin America and a number of other developing regions and this is obviously giving much greater emphasis to Chinese approaches to development. At the same time, the stagnation that characterized the US economy for so long and that is currently afflicting the economies of much of Europe has reduced the attractiveness of these models for developing countries. A number of developing economies, notably the so-called BRICS (Brazil, Russia, India, China and South Africa), are becoming much more important both economically and as models. The decline in the power of the US suggests that the unipolar moment that occurred immediately after the end of the Cold War is being replaced by a multi-polar system, and as we have seen in Chapter 2 some commentators are speculating that this may mean the end of the whole 'development agenda'. It is to these kinds of policy debates that we now turn.

Policies to stimulate growth

Many of the theories considered in the first part of this chapter, and in particular the orthodox theories, did not emerge in response to the problems of the poorer countries. Rather, they related explicitly to the explanation of growth in the already developed economies. It was assumed rather that these emerging economies would simply follow the same development paths as the now rich countries had done earlier. Thus, for much of the period after the Second World War, the new Bretton Woods institutions, and notably the World Bank, followed what might be called 'common sense' modernization strategies that attempted to reproduce the Western experience of growth. The particular emphasis was on the provision of infrastructure – roads, railways, ports, airports, dams and the like – that would facilitate development. In a few nations, socialist or neo-Marxist solutions were attempted but the triumph of the neoliberal agenda in the West encouraged the more widespread application of mainstream policy prescriptions. At the same time, the reaction in some quarters to the globalization experience and the related re-emergence of theories of imperialism and exploitation has also put some poorer countries at the forefront of a new kind of struggle. The example of rapid growth in Asia is also being seen by some as providing a justification for a new kind of policy direction. Thus, development theory and its policy recommendations have moved from being regarded as a marginal and exotic backwater to the very centre of intellectual ferment, and the impact of the GFC has significantly intensified this trend.

Orthodox policies and the Washington Consensus

In 1994, John Williamson wrote a landmark paper in which he set out what seemed to be the generally agreed policy framework within the Washington development institutions. His particular focus was on Latin America but his formula was rapidly applied to the rest of the developing world. The Consensus, which distilled the economic orthodoxy of the day, was based around the three pillars of macroeconomic discipline, microeconomic liberalization and globalization, and involved ten policy reforms, or 'Ten Commandments':

1. *Fiscal discipline with small budget deficits.* Macroeconomic stability is essential for continued growth, with low inflation a key component, but this can be undermined by large budget deficits.

2. *Avoidance of investment in sectors that offer low returns but that are politically sensitive or controlled by key pressure groups.* Government expenditure in particular needs to be carefully planned and controlled.

3. *Broaden the tax base and cut marginal tax rates.* Tax systems need to provide adequate incentives as well as sufficient revenue.

4. *Financial liberalization is essential.* The supply of credit, the setting of interest rates and similar financial decisions are more appropriately determined by the markets than by the government.

5. *A unified exchange rate should be set at a level that induces export growth.* Exports are central to inducing wider growth processes and non-traditional exports in particular need to be encouraged.

6. *Trade restrictions should all be rapidly replaced by tariffs and these should be progressively reduced.* Quantitative restrictions on trade give windfall profits to privileged importers, while tariffs, which instead channel this revenue to the government, can be gradually whittled away.

7. *Barriers to foreign direct investment (FDI) should be removed.* FDI is more stable than either portfolio capital or bank loans and should be encouraged.

8. *State-owned enterprises should be privatized.* This would raise the efficiency and the profitability of these industries.

9. *Regulations that impede the entry of new firms or that restrict competition should be removed.* This allows the economy to become more competitive and protects consumers.

10. *Individual property rights should be protected by the legal system.* Such rights should also be extended to the informal sector.

(adapted from Williamson 1994: 26–8)

In his later writings, Williamson has examined many of the criticisms that have been made of this kind of policy framework (Williamson and Mahar 1998; Kuczynski and Williamson 2003; Williamson 2004). He maintains that the agenda has generally stood the test of time quite well and the major recommendations remain valid. However, from the outset he acknowledges that the name Washington Consensus is guaranteed to evoke in many quarters strong emotions of resentment against US arrogance, interventionism and even imperialism. He also argues that some policies that have generally become associated with the Washington Consensus were not part of his original formulation. He draws a clear distinction between his proposed set of reforms, which are firmly within the *neoclassical* tradition, and the newer *neoliberal* doctrines. He stresses that his original formulation did not advocate minimalist government, the slashing of government services, supply-side economics, monetarism nor the rejection of income redistribution as an assault on property rights and a serious disincentive to both companies and employees. He also stresses, in the light of the 1997 Asian crisis, that the premature deregulation of the capital account can have disastrous results unless a sufficiently strong and regulated financial and banking system has been developed; hence the sequencing of reforms needs serious attention (Stiglitz 2002).

Over the years since Williamson's original formulation, and partly in response to a number of criticisms, there has emerged an 'Augmented

Washington Consensus', which concerns itself particularly with issues of governance (Beeson and Islam 2005). Targets include central bank independence and inflation targeting, public sector reform, the creation of more flexible labour markets, adherence to World Trade Organization (WTO) standards and other benchmarks for the business and financial sectors, strengthening financial systems and governance, pursuit of democratic reforms, and the enunciation of poverty reduction strategies.

But a much more fundamental critique of the Washington Consensus has been undertaken by Stiglitz (2006). He has argued that the whole process has been a failure and that a 'Post-Washington Consensus Consensus' has begun to emerge. Most basic of all, he suggests, is the failure of theoretical and policy analysis to understand the economic structures of developing countries, and to recognize that there are fundamental differences between individual nations: one size does not fit all. Markets alone cannot produce outcomes that are either efficient or just, especially in an environment of rapidly changing technology. All societies seeking growth need to spread the risk associated with innovation and investment and must take care of the concurrent improvement of educational systems, physical infrastructure and the like. International institutions have created unfair rules in global relations and have foisted deeply flawed policy prescriptions on developing countries, he insists. Only national governments can play the indispensable regulating, co-ordinating and distributive roles, and these national policy-makers need to be closely involved in negotiations at the international level: more successful development strategies cannot be arrived at within Washington alone. Crucially, it is increasingly recognized that the 'one size fits all' certainties of the Washington Consensus are counter-productive and need to be replaced by strategies that acknowledge local conditions and priorities, and national and regional governments are best placed to design such initiatives (McKay 2013).

Challenges to economic orthodoxy: Marxist policies revived

In spite of the some of the more triumphalist predictions made at the time of the downfall of the Soviet Union, Marxist modes of analysis have undergone something of a revival in recent years. Several commentators have suggested that the power of the US is now on the wane and that the 'unipolar moment', that period of unchallenged power that the US enjoyed after the end of the Cold War, is over (Wallerstein 2006). Problems with the US budget and balance of payments situations, the resultant blow-out in international borrowings by Washington and the inherent instability in the global system that this creates may hint at the unravelling of US hegemony (Arrighi 2005). However, other Marxists have argued that such an analysis underestimates the control that the US now has over the global financial system, and this is central to understanding the dynamics of continued US imperialism.

Panitch and Gindin (2005, 2012) suggest that under the guise of globalization what we have seen is the imposition of a new capitalist, imperialist empire based on four principles. Firstly, the former fragmentation into national units has been replaced by a seamless, global capitalism. Secondly, the US has assumed responsibility for the creation and management of this system. Thirdly, the US has actively structured and limited the options of elites based in other states. Finally, international financial institutions have been essential for the mediation and structuring of this new global system. This has elicited some resistance, especially in the developing world, since this integration blocks the emergence of any real kind of coherent national development.

This kind of analysis has also been undertaken by David Harvey (2003), who has similarly argued that a new kind of imperialism is emerging, and has been taken a stage further in response to the GFC (Harvey 2010). The driver of these changes has been the crisis of over-accumulation that has plagued capitalism since the 1970s. In response, new markets and production capacity have emerged around the world but this also involves the creation of intense international competition. This is inherently unstable and involves frequent upheavals and crises, as in Asia in 1997. Threatened in the realm of production by new competitors in Asia, even though much of this has derived from the investments by US-based multinationals, the US has moved to assert its dominance through the financial system, backed by its unchallenged military superiority. But it is far from certain that this financial control can last for ever. The massive savings and investments coming out of Asia, many of them now allowing East Asian countries to control key assets in the US, may in fact herald a change in the balance of power.

In terms of policies, the re-emergence of radical political and economic initiatives in Latin America is based largely on resentment at what is seen as a new kind of US imperialism. However, the policies themselves appear to have changed little from the economic nationalism promulgated by the dependency school in the 1960s. There has not yet been a real attempt by Marxist scholars to spell out the policy options that are available based on their detailed analyses – but this problem of moving from theory to workable practice has always been one of the weaknesses of this school of thought. The most promising direction at the moment seems to involve something of a convergence between Marxist and East Asian approaches exemplified through the rapid emergence of China, which at least in theory remains a communist state.

Challenges to economic orthodoxy: The Beijing Consensus

The term 'Beijing Consensus' has been around since at least the mid-1980s, but it was popularized in a paper by Joshua Cooper Ramo (2004) and since then has taken on a variety of economic and political connotations. In his formulation, Ramo argued that the rise of China is achieving nothing less than the reshaping and reordering of the international system through the introduction of 'a new physics of development and power' (p. 2). This promises to other nations not only new and effective development policies but also ways to achieve true independence and freedom of action within a new international order, and is therefore a replacement of the highly prescriptive Washington Consensus. It is based around three key 'theorems', he suggests:

- rather than assuming that developing nations must start with simple and often outdated technologies and then graduate to more leading-edge approaches, it urges the immediate adoption of the most modern innovations 'to create change that moves faster than the problems that change creates' (p. 12);
- in periods of rapid change, it is impossible to control everything from the top. Sustainability and equality are central to new policy directions, so that income growth and quality of life are maintained, and social disruption and instability are minimized;
- self-determination must be maintained through the creation of the leverage necessary to resist any hegemonic powers that might seek to dominate the nation.

In terms of economic policy, we have seen that China has already adopted many of the tenets of the Asian development model as it emerged in countries like Japan, Korea and Taiwan, and all three of those nations have a significant stake in the current Chinese economy, tending to maintain and reinforce many of these methods and approaches. Such economic models are now being transferred into Africa and Latin America as China quickly expands its influence there. While China's search for reliable supplies of resources is certainly seen for what it is, a number of writers have seen evidence that Africa is being transformed in a very positive way that contrasts with earlier periods of Western involvement. The terms of trade for commodity producers have improved markedly while investment in infrastructure and in social services has also been vastly increased (Friedman 2009).

But it is in the political and security domains that the particular attraction of the Beijing Consensus rests. Beijing now offers a rallying point for all those who oppose what they see as a US-oriented project of imperialism, as well as the exploitation that goes hand in hand with the policy prescriptions of international organizations such as the IMF and the WTO. Certainly a number of commentators in the West have expressed some alarm about the growing popularity of the Beijing Consensus in many developing countries. Chief among these is Stefan Halper (2010: x) who fears that:

> China's governing model is more appealing to the developing world and some of the middle-sized powers than America's market-democratic model. Given a choice between market democracy and its freedoms and market authoritarianism and its high growth, stability, improved living standards, and limits on expression – a majority in the developing world and in many middle-sized, non-Western powers prefer the authoritarian model.

As such, this approach encourages the use of state power to achieve key national goals and this includes the continued use of methods that the rich countries were able to adopt during the earlier phases of their rise but which they now seek to deny to poorer nations now seeking a development transition of their own. In what is now a very influential book in much of the developing world, Ha-Joon Chang (2002) argues that it is a tragic mistake for richer countries to attempt to deny developing countries the right to adopt policies and institutions that are most appropriate to their needs and their current stages of growth, and more recently (Chang 2007b 2010) has made a broader attack on the ways in which the rich nations control the development and globalization agendas. Robert Wade, in looking at the legacy of his own important book on the role of the state in Taiwan's development (Wade 1990) makes similar points. While governments in rich countries are allowed much flexibility in setting policies aimed at upgrading those industries most crucial for their stage of growth, WTO regulations severely restrict such intervention in industries that are important for nations in transition to industrialization. This seems designed to ensure that already wealthy countries will not be challenged while underdeveloped countries will remain trapped in poverty. It is to this kind of perceived unfairness in the current global system that the Beijing Consensus has a particular political resonance (Wade 2004).

We must be careful of course to try to separate out the impact of the intellectual arguments that have surrounded the success of East Asia as a whole from the narrower appeal of China's foreign policy agenda. China is now heavily involved in trying to further its own economic prospects through the signing of large resource deals with a range of countries around the world but at the same time it has launched what has been called a 'charm offensive' to further its general influence in the world. In Africa, for example, a World Bank Report has argued that economic growth in East Asia generally, and in China in particular, offers the continent its own 'Silk Road' (Broadman 2007).

Two kinds of criticism have emerged of these initiatives from Beijing. The orthodox economic response has of course been to question the wisdom of adhering to the East Asian-style industrial policies. For example, Noland and Pack (2003) argue that growth in Asia was the result of good macroeconomic management and the contribution of industrial policies was minor or even negative. Hence the case for other countries following such policies is weak and, under current rules governing world trade, may be illegal. Other critics have pointed to Chinese support for African regimes with somewhat questionable human rights records, suggesting that principles of non-interference in the internal affairs of others may not be justified in such circumstances.

There is also the question about the role, if any, of industrial policy and government initiatives as countries attempt to move up the value-added chain into more technologically advanced forms of production. Emphasis on technology is one of the key elements of the Beijing Consensus, and certainly Chinese planners express concern that China must take care not to be trapped in the role of a low-cost, low-technology producer. The difficulties that both Korea and Taiwan have experienced – and indeed are still suffering – as they attempt to consolidate such a transition to high-technology status and escape the *middle-income trap* serves as an important object lesson in the immediate region (Bulman, Eden and Nguyen 2014).

A great deal has been written about the next stage of East Asia's growth, especially in the light of the Asian crisis of 1997 (for example, Gill and Kharas 2007; Gill, Huang and Kharas 2007). While much of this work has echoed the assumptions of the dominant economic orthodoxy, there is an increasing number of voices coming out of Asia itself suggesting a return to some of the ideas of the developmental state, albeit in a significantly modified form (for example, Park 2003; Chang 2007a, b). Such writers argue that a significant state role is still needed to accomplish some of the key tasks that will be necessary for a successful transition to a new kind of economy: co-ordination and planning for complex new situations, development of innovative vision, building of new institutions of various kinds and the management of the conflicts that are bound to accompany such profound societal changes (Chang 1999). Globalization does not reduce the need for state action, rather there needs to be redefinition of the key tasks that must now be undertaken to control and mould these forces to meet national needs through the management of currency appreciation, investment flows and industrial restructuring (Weiss 2003).

Growth and development in a globalizing world: towards a new paradigm?

By way of conclusion, it is essential to consider the prospects for growth and development in the current environment and ask whether it is now easier or more difficult for nations to be successful in making a transition to a more prosperous future. Central here is the question of whether the processes of globalization are relatively stable or not – and the impact of the GFC has raised serious doubts here – as well as the issues of whether income inequalities have risen or fallen in recent years, and how the various mechanisms of globalization are linked to particular outcomes.

Growth and inequality

There is now a very large literature on the question of the relationships between globalization and income inequalities at various scales of analysis; however, in this very acrimonious debate there is still little agreement. Supporters of globalization such as Dollar and Kraay (2002) and Bhagwati (2004) have asserted that global inequalities have in fact decreased markedly, while writers such as Stiglitz (2006) and Galbraith and Berner (2001) come to the opposite conclusion. In part, these differences reflect problems of data but there is also a question of the appropriate scale and focus of analysis. It has been argued that China and India are so large that their recent success provides bias at the global level, while for much of Africa and Latin America, for example, the picture is much less encouraging. In addition, Garrett (2004) has suggested that while in aggregate terms the poorer countries, again India and China in particular, may have done well from globalization, and there has also been rapid growth in most rich countries, there is a real problem for middle-income countries.

There is also a question of what measures of inequality are appropriate for such an analysis. Most writers have focused on absolute measures of poverty and on the number of people living below some key threshold level of poverty. Bhagwati (2004) has stressed that in China poverty declined from 28 per cent of the population in 1978 to 9 per cent in 1998. However, others have underlined the importance of measures of relative poverty. While many people now have higher incomes, they feel left behind because of the more rapid progress of others, and of the elites in particular. Several years ago, Denis Goulet (1971) introduced the concept of the 'shock of underdevelopment'. The poor may have always been with us but in an age of mass communications they are now made painfully aware of their poverty on a daily basis, and in particular they measure their own disadvantage relative to the rich people they now see on television and in films.

Also important here is the question of changes in income inequalities between countries as against within individual nations. Both are significant but in political terms resentment against fellow citizens seen as being unfairly advantaged may be more potent, and may even threaten the stability of globalization itself. In this area the data on inequalities seem unambiguous: a clear result of the neoliberal revolution has been the dramatic polarization of incomes and wealth to the benefit of the top 1 per cent, so it is hardly surprising that there has been an outpouring of new studies on this phenomenon and its economic, political and social consequences (see, for example Freeland 2012; Stiglitz 2013; UNCTAD 2013; Piketty 2014), and this has produced an array of startling statistics. The top 0.1 per cent of earners in the US, for example, now have incomes 220 times larger than the average of the bottom 90 per cent, while the top 1 per cent possess some 30 per cent of the nation's total wealth. It is hardly surprising, then, that the World Economic Forum has identified this polarization trend as the major problem facing the world in 2015, and one that can potentially have dramatic political consequences (World Economic Forum, 2014). Several writers have noted the similarities between this modern era and the wild, unfettered period of capitalist expansion in the later years of the nineteenth century – but this time the outcomes are global. In the rapidly growing economies of China and India, where neoliberal economic policies sit within two quite different political systems, growing gaps in income and wealth are also very marked: by some measures China is now a more unequal society than the US.

Five interrelated factors are generally seen as being behind the intense polarization now taking place: the almost universal imposition of the neoliberal paradigm, markets and how they work (or do not work), technological developments, the nature of a rapidly expanding financial sector, and the particular form of globalization that has resulted from these processes. Much of the debate in this area has centred on the industrial countries, and in particular the US. Stiglitz (2013) has argued that one result of rising inequality has been the dampening of economic growth, and he also suggests that inequality was a major factor in explaining the onset and nature of the GFC. Inequality, he suggests, is the result of how markets work in particular situations, shaped as they are by institutional structures, regulation (or lack of it) and more general political processes. Markets are not the impartial processes portrayed by many proponents of neoliberal theory but are subject to manipulation and capture by elites for their own benefit. Concentration of ownership in many industries has limited competition, and control over new technologies has bestowed monopoly powers in a number of markets, especially in the newer high technology sectors. The growth of the financial sector and in particular the development of derivatives and other forms of financial instruments has generated massive profits, with extremely large bonuses going to certain employees. Indeed, the new wealth being generated in the finance industry, benefiting both shareholders and some staff, has been a major factor in widening income disparities. Since the GFC the massive government bailouts for banks have imposed most costs on taxpayers while bank executives have continued to receive their generous bonuses and this has further widened income disparities.

In the developing world some of the arguments have been very similar, but the emphasis has been rather different. Within development theory there has been a long history of interest in how income gaps grow or narrow at different stages of development and the extent to which different levels of disparities have an impact on growth rates. What has been generally accepted is that in the early stages of growth – as activities in a few regions expand and agricultural areas are left behind – income gaps will widen significantly, but as growth proceeds and a large number of farmers leave for the cities incomes in these backward areas will eventually catch up, at least to some extent. This general relationship, known as the Kuznets Curve, has been widely validated in the past but there is now some evidence that in recent years such convergence has not taken place. In some developing countries, and in particular those rich in resources at a time when commodity prices have been at record levels, the state has frequently been captured – sometimes literally after insurrection or civil war – by an elite which ensures that all economic and social policies reward a small group at the expense of the many. Thus there has been renewed interest in what is known as the 'resources curse' or the 'Dutch disease' (McKay 2012). In other nations without this kind of takeover of the government a range of neoliberal policies has produced many of the same results. Particularly important has been, according to a recent report by UNCTAD (2013), the introduction of 'flexible' labour market policies. Minimum wage provisions have been removed, along with many other elements of social protection and safety nets. At the same time the outsourcing of many simple, labour-intensive manufacturing activities to developing countries, along with the transfer of basic technologies, has provided significant profits but given strong policy advice from international institutions for new manufacturing nations to ensure that their labour costs are kept low and competitive, workers have not shared in the large rewards that have accrued to owners and a small group of managers. Even if labour costs are kept down, many such aspiring manufacturing nations have not been able to move up the value added chain and hence have not been able to create significant numbers of better paid jobs. Also, many governments have not made the investments in basic health and education services that are essential for more broad-based and long-term development, while in other cases the structural adjustment loans imposed by the IMF have actually forced governments to reduce spending in such areas. The result has been that disparities have continued to grow, and some groups – notably women – have remained trapped in low paid jobs.

Two major regions stand out from these general trends. In many parts of Asia investment in education has been massive, funded by income from a rapidly expanding manufacturing sector. This in turn has provided skilled graduates for continual economic upgrading, but also vital here has been the use of various industrial policies many of which have been directly contrary to neoliberal tenets. The result has been a dramatic increase in average incomes. But even here severe disparities persist in some countries. The Chinese government, for example, has been very aware of the social and political instability that might result from these differences and has proposed a number of policy initiatives. In Latin America, which for many years suffered from huge income disparities, there has also been a narrowing of such gaps in the period since around 2003, but this has also been the direct result of rolling back many of the earlier policies based around the Washington Consensus.

While there is general agreement that income disparities have been increasing, there is much debate about the growth implications. On the one hand it can be argued that unequal distribution fosters social instability that can have disastrous consequences, and certainly in many countries the high incomes accruing to small elites have resulted in conspicuous consumption, fuelling resentment and doing nothing to increase productive investment. If the bulk of the population have only low incomes aggregate demand will remain suppressed, also giving poor incentives for investment. On the other hand it has been argued that a certain income gap is necessary to encourage hard work, personal investment in education and other measures designed to maximize future earnings. However, empirical evidence suggests that incentives can be effective at levels far below those found in many countries at the moment without risking the social instability that many now fear (World Bank 2006b).

One important element in the East Asian model, particularly in the early years, was its strong element of egalitarianism. This goes back to a rather different tradition of economic thought in East Asia. The Confucian heritage stressed the societal goals of universal order and harmony and gave particular emphasis to the obligations of rulers towards the welfare of their subjects. In Japan, a dominant school of economic thought emerged which stressed the need for 'administering the nation and relieving the suffering of the people' (Morris-Suzuki 1989). It is also significant that in China today a great deal of emphasis is being placed on the need to rectify, in the name of both equity and political stability, the great imbalances that now exist between the prosperous coastal regions and the much more backward inland areas (Shirk 2007).

In a major survey of this evidence, Kaplinsky (2005) puts forward what is perhaps the most persuasive conclusion. The experience of globalization has been extremely mixed, with some winners and many losers. Companies seeking new opportunities in developing countries are very discerning about the particular advantages of each location, hence some are chosen but many are not. Poverty then is not simple lagged effect, with all nations being able to eventually share in global prosperity. Indeed the emergence of even a small number of large-scale producers like China would result in massive saturation of world markets. Also, some locations that have advantages at some time may also be abandoned later in favour of new opportunities. Thus, development is a highly complex and situational process, and this has important policy implications.

Implications of globalization for growth theories and policies

Out of this somewhat inconclusive picture that has emerged from the literature on the relationships between globalization and income inequalities it is possible to discern some new trends that perhaps offer hope that a new paradigm may be emerging that can deliver more constructive directions for development policy. Most basically, the challenge that the GFC has posed to the dominant neoliberal model has allowed the emergence of new directions and the rediscovery of some older neglected ones.

One important earlier theorist whose reputation has now been spectacularly revived is Karl Polanyi, whose major work *The Great Transformation* (Polanyi 1944/2001) is now being championed by those who, especially since the GFC, have sought to discredit the whole neoliberal enterprise. Polanyi rejected the idea that an economy consists of blindly rational economic actors simply responding in an unthinking way to price signals from the all-encompassing market. Rather, all economies are *embedded* in wider political, social and cultural systems made up of institutions with unique and historically conditioned characteristics. Markets certainly have their place and can play a useful if limited role, but a completely self-regulating market is neither possible nor desirable, since this would require the transformation of both humans and the environment into pure commodities, thus ensuring the destruction of both. For Polanyi the great transformation that he was celebrating was not so much the historical movement towards capitalism but the overturning of the unregulated free-market system of the late nineteenth century and its replacement by the New Deal and a range of economic systems based on Keynesian macroeconomics that emerged after the Second World War. When he died, in 1964, Polanyi must have been convinced that ideologies favouring unrestrained free markets had been consigned to history. It is hardly surprising then that Polanyi has been rediscovered as a trenchant critic of contemporary neoliberalism (see, for example, Peck 2013; Block and Somers 2014; Dale 2010; Harvey Ramlogan and Randles 2014). Polanyi's daughter Kari Polanyi Levitt (2013) has focused particularly on the continuing relevance of her father's thought to the Global South, with particular reference to structural continuity and economic dependence in the capitalist world system and the onset of the GFC as a direct result of the transition from mercantilism to neoliberalism in the developing world.

In Chapter 2 we referred to the emergence from the World Bank of some new perspectives on the economics of development, and indeed on the basic goals to which policies in this area should be directed. In a series of publications, Justin Yifu Lin, who was the Bank's chief economist from 2008 until 2012, has outlined some of his thinking on both the targets that need to be identified and the means that can be utilized for achieving them, and in particular has derived some key lessons from China's recent development experience (Lin 2009, 2012a, 2012b, 2013). Lin studied in the Department of Economics at the University of Chicago, one of the intellectual hubs of neoliberal thought, but in his more recent work he has broadened his analysis in several important ways. Whereas the emphasis in neoliberalism is on the efficient allocation of resources via free markets, Lin places great emphasis on continued industrial upgrading and structural change as the key to successful development strategies, and concedes that governments as well as the private sector have a key role to play in these processes; however, he stresses that governments should play only a facilitating role for the private sector. Also, care must be taken to evaluate the precise comparative advantage that each nation has at a particular point in its development, and while some small deviation from the dictates of endowments of factors of production can be justified, any significant attempt to short-circuit a gradual process of upgrading will involve unacceptable costs. Thus, while Lin has moved his position, he is still some way from accepting the role of the developmental state that can defy comparative advantage on the way to rapid industrial upgrading – a position that has been taken by a number of commentators on how Asia was able to achieve such phenomenal success in its development (for example, Amsden 1989; Chang 2006). Even so, the position of the World Bank on a whole range of issues is now rather different from what it was until quite recently.

One crucial area in which the Bank's new priorities have become manifest is in the emphasis on job creation as perhaps the central concern of development policy. In its World Development Report for 2013 (World Bank 2012) it was argued that real development essentially happens through jobs. Most people attain their income through paid employment, but more than that they define their role in society through their careers, and social stability is largely dependent on an adequate supply of good jobs. Thus, governments need to approach development policies through a lens of job creation. Certainly the task ahead is enormous. It is estimated that in the shadow of the GFC some 200 million people wordwide are unemployed, including 75 million under the age of 25. Increasingly these unemployed or under-employed people are congregating in the burgeoning cities of the developing world, where youth unemployment is of particular concern. Echoing Lin, it is argued by the World Bank that role of government should be to create the conditions conducive for the private sector to expand employment. Important here are:

- *Guaranteeing the fundamentals* – especially macroeconomic stability, the rule of law, the creation of human capital, the supply of adequate financial resources, improved infrastructure, and good nutrition and health of the labour force.

- *Labour policies* – designed to avoid undue distortions of the labour market through over-regulation but at the same time providing protection for vulnerable workers and allowing all employees to voice their concerns.
- *Priorities* – recognizing that some jobs are more important for development than others and that 'good' jobs need to be given priority. This may demand selective interventions tailored to the local context.

The question of job creation brings us back to the crucial question of whether growth is now easier to attain for latecomers. On the one hand, the success of a number of Asian countries, China and India in particular, is seen by many as a shining example of just what is now possible. The process of 'industrial learning' that, as we have seen, has been central to Asian growth, and the flood of foreign direct investment in the region, has certainly had a major impact but outside Asia the picture may not be quite so rosy. Worse still, the growth of China may be making it even more difficult for other countries to compete for both markets and foreign investment.

There is also the issue of countries that have achieved some development being able to make the major transition to higher value-added kinds of production. This brings them much more into competition with the already developed countries and has been the subject of much debate in the context of the rules governing world trade. This is particularly significant in the case of China, which if it can successfully make such a transition could serve as a major market for a whole new generation of low-cost producers of simple industrial goods.

If Kaplinsky (2005) is right, some nations may be able to use their special locational advantages to attract international or local capital but what is clear at the moment is that most countries in the developing world now see themselves as trapped by a global system that is stacked against them and is generating increasing levels of inequality. This is a very dangerous situation that is threatening the very future of globalization itself. Similarly, Niall Ferguson (2005) has argued that the current situation – characterized by imperial overreach, rivalries between major powers, unstable alliances, rogue regimes and increased terrorism – is ominously like the situation before the First World War when globalization also crumbled, with disastrous results. As we will explore in Chapter 4 the GFC has brought such issues into sharp relief and raised the additional question of the ways in which inequalities at various geographical scales contribute to the high levels in system instability that we are now experiencing.

Chapter 4

Continuing Crises: The Developing World and the Global Financial Crisis

John McKay

The impact of the Global Financial Crisis (GFC), and its continuing aftershocks right down to the present have intensified our interest in systemic breakdowns of this kind and heightened debate about their causes, impacts and the most appropriate ways to deal with them. Crises of this dimension, or those as serious as the Asian crisis of 1997–8, are very traumatic events in their own right, resulting in losses of jobs, income and assets that affect wide sections of the community, and with ramifications that can often be seen for decades afterwards, made much worse in many countries by the absence of any kind of social safety net. In the case of many African countries, which have been in seemingly permanent crisis for some three decades, the impacts are catastrophic. In most cases these events also lead to a rethinking of ideas on economic systems, how they operate and to whose advantage. The Great Depression of the late 1920s and early 1930s heralded such a fundamental rethink, largely as an outcome of the work of John Maynard Keynes, resulting in the creation of the whole new sub-discipline of macroeconomics. But the GFC, in spite of its scale, seems to have been rather different. Certainly there has been an outpouring of new literature, and in some important quarters our thinking has been revolutionized, but as was noted in Chapter 3 key aspects of the neoliberal paradigm have been left surprisingly intact as the dominant ideas in economic and political practice. Similarly, the influence of key alliances between the business sector, networks of think tanks and practising neoclassical economists have lost little of their influence. In this chapter I review some of the new thinking that has emerged on the nature and causes of economic crises, but also seek to understand why these new ideas have so far not been able to dislodge neoliberalism from its dominant position. However, on a more positive note, I ask whether the discipline of development economics, which as we also saw earlier was side-lined by the universalizing position of neoliberalism, may in fact now be given new life resulting from a more strident rejection of neoliberalism in the developing world.

Global and regional crises in historical context: learning the lessons

The renewed interest in the longer-term historical evidence on crises at the global level and in various countries and regions is not just about learning the lessons of previous crises to avoid or at least minimize the impact of new ones, important as this is. Far from being isolated, such events can be seen as causally related: each crisis sheds yet more light on the structure and dynamics of the global system of development, illustrating how the various parts of the whole are related and interact with each other, and how the resolution of each new event helps set the scene for the next convulsion. Paul Krugman (2008) has called this kind of study *depression economics*, a field that many misguided economists thought had been long consigned to the footnotes of economic history. Seen from this perspective, the Asian financial crisis of 1997–8 was not just an event confined to one region as the result of local errors but essentially one of the harbingers of the GFC, a theme to which we will return later in this chapter.

Most attention has focused on the Great Depression of the 1930s and the contrasts or commonalities with the experiences of the 1980s, 1990s and now of course the GFC. But there has also been a return to the historical analysis of several periods of upheaval during the nineteenth century, and some important reinterpretations of earlier evidence (see, for example, Fishlow 1985; Ghosh 2001; Kindleberger and Aliber 2005). It is no accident that most interest has been generated by those crises that have threatened to have serious impacts on the West: if a crisis is no longer just out there in Africa or wherever, even if troubling images appear nightly on the world's television screens, it is much less disturbing than one that threatens to strike also at the rich nations.

But this intense level of enquiry, resulting now in a very large literature, has failed to yield any consensus on the predominant causes of these crises. The conventional view, enshrined in the Washington Consensus and its later manifestations (see Chapter 3), stresses that crises are essentially caused by internal weaknesses of policy, failures to implement the optimal mix of measures that include trade and financial liberalization, privatization of government-owned assets, tight monetary and fiscal settings, and the general strengthening of market-based systems throughout the economy. But this dominant paradigm has received much criticism from a number of directions. Several commentators have criticized the exclusive concentration on the internal causes of crisis, arguing that external factors are often just as important and in many instances paramount. The structure of the international financial system itself, the activities of hedge funds and other new financial instruments, the policies of the international agencies such as the International Monetary Fund (IMF), the policies of stronger Western countries (especially the United States) and the activities of multinational corporations have all been cited here. But more fundamentally, a number of writers have argued that crisis is the direct and inevitable result of the ways in which various regions have been incorporated into the global capitalist system. The precise details vary from region to region, and many forces are specific to particular historical periods but, as we shall see in relation to Africa, Asia and Latin America, crises have been explained as the result of long-term structural factors rather than specific and internal policy failings (see, for example, Frank 1980; Arrighi 2002; Akyeampong et al. 2014). Those writers who have emphasized the external or global causes of crisis have paid particular attention to the restructuring of international financial institutions and of the basic architecture of the global economy. The IMF has been criticized for being too concerned with the need to pay back loans owed to international lenders, often with dire consequences for the welfare of local residents. As we shall see, the IMF has also been criticized for its failure to learn the lessons of the Great Depression of the 1930s. It is now accepted that the policies put in place initially to deal with the Great Depression were entirely inappropriate and in fact made matters even worse. Yet it was just such contractionary policies that were imposed on Asian countries in 1997 when what was needed was a strong stimulus to encourage growth, and industrial expansion in particular (Stiglitz 2002; Blyth 2013).

How has the risk of crisis increased in recent years?

Even well before the onset of the GFC, a number of analysts were suggesting that the risk of crisis was significantly greater than it had been some decades ago. Attention has been focused particularly on the changing volume and nature of international financial flows, the progressive removal of state regulations controlling such flows, and the ways in which the introduction of these new financial systems has been supported by alliances between some governments in the developed world and the emerging financial industry.

There is no doubt that the volume of international financial flows has increased dramatically since the 1970s. In earlier periods, the amount of money flowing between two countries was made up of two components: first, payments for goods traded, and second, investments and loans from one country to another. Both of these flows continue to be important, and both have grown dramatically in recent years; however, in terms of sheer volumes of finance, these items have been overwhelmed by new components, especially speculative capital. Daily turnover in the world's currency markets just prior to the GFC was around $1.2 trillion, with much of this activity speculative in nature, but the fastest growing part of the financial sector in recent years has been derivatives, financial instruments often of a complex nature derived from a more basic financial instrument, and this was estimated to be worth $600 billion per day in 2008. These amounts dwarf the value of world trade, global investment flows and indeed the size of even the largest foreign exchange reserves. Even so, investment flows of various kinds are increasing very rapidly. Total cross-border capital flows – made up of equity and debt security purchases, international lending and deposits and foreign direct investment – stood in 2007 at $6.4 trillion per year, and were growing much more rapidly than global GDP (IMF 2007). In part, this reflected the growth of assets under management by pension funds, hedge funds and the like: total funds in this area are now around $76 trillion. But it is now accepted that perhaps 95 per cent of the capital moving across borders is speculative in nature, and financial authorities even in the largest and richest countries are very limited in their power to act in the national interest against such speculators. Significantly, as Panitch and Gindin (2012) have chronicled in great detail, these innovations in the global financial systems were introduced as a direct result of the rise of neoliberal thought.

A carefully researched critique of this new world of speculation has been developed by Susan Strange (1986, 1998). She has coined the term *casino capitalism* to describe this new phase in the global economy but she has more recently argued that things have moved on so fast since her original book was published that it is now better to talk about *mad money*. This frenetic movement of capital has a clear logic, she argues, but it is simply the logic of short-term profit, with no thought of the consequences for nations or communities. More recently Satyajit Das (2011) has coined the term *extreme money* to describe the even more frenetic pace of change in the financial world immediately preceding the recent (and ongoing) crisis.

Several factors have given rise to this new situation, but a notable element is the rapid growth in the amount of money available on world financial markets. This increased liquidity began in the early 1970s when rapid rises in the world price of oil flooded the markets with *petrodollars* seeking profitable investments. This source of money was quickly supplemented in August 1971 when President Nixon, in an attempt to solve the problems that the US government had in financing the Vietnam War, unilaterally abrogated the Bretton Woods system, refusing to allow the continued exchange of US dollars for US gold reserves. Still more money became available on financial markets in the 1970s and 1980s as a result of rapid industrial development in East Asia; only a small fraction of these funds could be absorbed into traditional channels. Thus the second factor in the development of this new economy has been the rapid emergence of new financial instruments and, equally importantly, the reform of existing government regulations to allow them to flourish. Existing banks were progressively freed from many of the limitations that had previously restricted their activities and even more important was the emergence of a new range of non-bank financial institutions. At the same time, foreign exchange rates were progressively deregulated, allowing markets rather than governments to set these rates. But for these new financial products to work more effectively and speedily, new technologies were needed for the instantaneous transfer of funds across the globe, and these were soon available thanks to advances in computer and satellite systems. However one vital piece was still missing: a push strong enough to overcome the reluctance of some governments to give up the national controls that still existed in many economies, and which were seen by many officials (correctly as it turned out) as necessary for continued stability in the financial sector. This final impetus was provided by the emerging alliance between the US government and the dominant players on Wall Street. The US government used extremely tough measures to ensure that even the most reluctant governments were persuaded to deregulate their systems, and in particular remove any restrictions on inflows of capital.

While all of these changes have been taking place in the financial system, there have also been important developments in the more traditional sectors, now frequently called the *real economy* – a telling comment on the nature of much financial activity! In spite of continuing protectionist policies in the European Union and the US, restrictions on world trade through tariffs and other means have been progressively reduced through a series of agreements negotiated within the General Agreement on Tariffs and Trade (GATT), which, soon after the conclusion of the Uruguay Round in 1993 became known as the World Trade Organization (WTO). This is one factor in the rapid growth of world trade, which since 1945 has expanded some twelvefold, compared with a fivefold increase in global output. But this increase in trade also reflects a growing internationalization of production through expanded foreign investment, especially by large, multinational corporations, a process that began on a large scale in the 1970s. At this time, profit levels for the large corporations of the developed world were being hit by a combination of three factors. First, the shocks to the international finance system provided by the Vietnam War and the dramatic increases in the world price of oil in 1972–3 and 1979 pushed up cost structures for many companies and resulted in strong inflationary pressures in many countries. Secondly, the 1970s were also a period of rapid wage increases in much of the developed world, with serious consequences for inflation and production costs. Thirdly, the global recession triggered by the oil price increases resulted in a significant and extended drop in demand for many industrial products. The total impact of these pressures saw a serious crisis in profitability for many companies, resulting in strenuous attempts to cut costs. The strategy favoured by some corporations was to move production offshore to cheaper locations, saving particularly on labour costs. But for this to be successful, several new features had to be in place. Global production networks can only work effectively if cheap and efficient transport is available. This was provided by the complex of innovations that has become known as the containerization revolution. A global network of production also requires an efficient and reliable means for monitoring, controlling and co-ordinating production and quality levels. This also became available through rapid advances in computer and satellite technology. Perhaps most important of all, the institutional basis had to be available in the new host countries to ensure that investment could be made on favourable terms. An increasing number of national governments, especially in Asia, were willing to provide such a favourable environment for foreign investment as part of their emerging strategies of export-oriented industrialization. This movement towards international production has continued to the present, resulting in a rapid growth in the levels of foreign direct investment (FDI).

Arguably the rapid increases in FDI flows heralded a new period in the nature of global financial flows. Eichengreen and Fishlow (1998) have contrasted this new era with earlier episodes on the basis of the dominant form or origin of financial flows, recognizing three distinct periods and modes of investment:

1. *The era of bond finance.* This was a long period of distinctive international financial flows originating in the nineteenth century and consisting of loans guaranteed by government, municipal or

private organizations. Strong bond markets emerged in London, Paris, Berlin and Amsterdam to service the emerging capital markets particularly in the US, Canada, Australia, Latin America and Russia, with much of this investment in infrastructure projects. A number of changes took place in this system in the early part of the twentieth century: the US emerged as an exporter of capital rather than an importer and by the 1920s a number of financial intermediaries emerged, notably investment trusts. The nature of the projects being financed and the countries of destination also changed, widening to include some much more risky markets. The system received a fatal blow in the global Depression of the 1930s, with many countries defaulting on their debts.

2. *The era of bank finance.* The late 1960s and early 1970s saw a period of rapid increase in liquidity, resulting from increases in oil prices, and the emergence of new financial instruments, supported by a new consensus on the need for financial reform and liberalization. At the same time new financial markets emerged, notably the Eurodollar market, and these pursued new investment destinations in the developing world. Large investment flows took place initially to Latin America, but then to East Asia and Africa. When the burden of this debt became too much and when it became clear that a substantial proportion of the money had been invested in unproductive projects – what Susan George (1998) has called castles in the sand – the result was the crisis of third-world debt, beginning with the Mexican default of 1982, that is still with us.

3. *The era of equity finance.* This period has been characterized by an emphasis on investment in shares in companies around the world, and Eichengreen and Fishlow date this phase from the end of the 1980s. By then, there had been significant changes in the financial regulatory systems of many countries, and pension funds and insurance companies emerged as major investors. By 1990, lending to Latin America was greater than at the peak of the previous period, and flows to Asia were also very large. In 1994 Mexico was again in trouble but this was passed off as a local effect attributable to particular national circumstances. The money kept flowing, encouraged by low interest rates in the United States and much of the developed world. Financial flows to Asia were enormous in the mid-1990s but a rapid loss of investor confidence, beginning in Thailand in the middle of 1997, heralded the onset of the Asian financial crisis.

More recently, and especially in the period following Asia's strong recovery from its own period of crisis and the dramatic rise of China,

Asian investors in particular have purchased very large quantities of US government bonds, financing the considerable budget and balance of payments deficits. Continued high levels of savings in Asia have allowed the build-up of massive debts in the US, resulting in some alarm about these serious global imbalances (Eichengreen 2007; Pettis 2013). In the period just before the GFC economists were divided about how damaging these might be in the longer run, but this factor is now part of the debate about the causes of the crisis and what needs to be done to prevent a recurrence.

Seeking to understand the causes of crises: the return of Marx, Keynes and Minsky

One of the results of the GFC, as has been underlined in earlier chapters, is that the conventional wisdom about growth and development have been seriously challenged, really for the first time in several decades, even if these new ideas have not been able themselves to become dominant. One area in which the old certainties have certainly been thrown into doubt is in the theoretical approaches to an understanding of the ways in which crises originate and are propagated, and this in turn has significant implications for our understanding of the appropriate policy responses. Here we consider the new relevance of several theorists that had been largely ignored for many years and evaluate the strengths of their approaches to the current situations. In particular we look briefly at the theoretical positions of Karl Marx, John Maynard Keynes and Hyman Minsky, all of whom have returned to prominence since the onset of the GFC.

Marx (1818–83) first became interested in the phenomenon of crisis at the time of what became known as 'the great crisis of 1857–8' triggered by the failure of the Ohio Life Insurance Company in New York, and incorporated some of his ideas in the *Grundrisse* notebooks, laying the foundations of a more ambitious search in his later work for a general theory of crises within capitalism. Basically, Marx concluded that the periodic crises were the result of problems in the sphere of production: capitalism's unrelenting drive for accumulation resulted in regular periods of overproduction and hence a falling rate of profit. This could only be resolved by the liquidation of some of this surplus production capacity, and the jobs associated with it, until a new level of output was reached that could be sold. Thus crises were the necessary and regular mechanisms of adjustment, albeit resulting in a great deal of pain to both capital and labour.

The GFC has revived interest in the Marxist concept of overproduction as the basic cause of periodic crises, and particularly important here has been the work of Robert Brenner. He has shown that the average rate of profit of corporations in developed countries has suffered a steady decline since the early 1970s (Brenner 2006). Intense competition between advanced nations, advances in manufacturing technologies and the emergence of a range of new industrial nations – particularly in East Asia – dramatically increased total output and put downward pressure on prices and hence levels of profit. A number of other Marxist scholars have questioned aspects of the theoretical basis of Brenner's work (for example Smith 2010), but there has been widespread support for the general thrust of the argument. More recently Brenner and others have re-evaluated the theory of overproduction in the light of the onset of the GFC, taking the crisis as a vindication of their approach.

But other Marxists have seen the growth of the financial services industry in a somewhat different light. Peter Gowan (1999) argued that the twin developments of neoliberalism within the US and globalization at the international level were used by vested interests, supported by the US government, to create what he called the 'Dollar–Wall Street Regime' – a potent economic tool to advance US national interests. Political and even military pressures have been used to maintain or impose local regimes willing to go along with this emerging institutional structure. These arrangements are presented as logical or even inevitable concomitants of economic and technological change but are in reality politically motivated and are extremely destabilizing. This instability is felt most in the vulnerable and sensitive poorer economies that are incorporated into the global financial structures, but it also produces damaging cycles of boom and bust in the advanced capitalist economies. Building on these kinds of observations Duménil and Lévy (2011) have argued that the GFC was not the result of overcapacity but of the inherent instability of the global financial system. Neoliberalism, they argue, was introduced by the ruling elites after the 1970s to recapture the income share that had been lost during the earlier period of redistributive and progressive policies introduced after the Second World War. New financial instruments and what became known as 'structured finance' created extreme levels of household debt in the US itself. Much of this debt was securitized and sold to foreign investors, while at the same time new derivatives markets and myriad new forms of risky financial instruments were launched at the global level. The results were dramatic. In the period leading up to the Second World War the incomes of the top 1 per cent of US households accounted for some 13 per cent of total income of all households, but declined to 9 per cent by the 1970s. The introduction of the range of policies that became known as neoliberalism reversed this decline, and by 2007 the pre-war share of total income had been restored, but this frantic dash to acquire high levels of income through financial services expansion created instability, culminating in the major crash in 2007–8.

One more general feature of the debate that has emerged after the GFC has been the resurgence of Marxist-inspired theoretical analysis, and the best of this work has involved a carefully considered review of the whole opus of Marxist research on the causes of crisis. Particularly useful here is the thoughtful review by Panitch and Gindin (2010) of the strands of critical analysis that have developed in this area since the original contribution by Marx himself in the 1850s. They make three key points:

- Crises are historically specific, therefore any analysis must be based on a thorough understanding of the conditions of accumulation and the general economic environment – profits, wages, the structure of trade, availability of credit, the dynamics of class structures and the dynamics of class–state relations.
- This form of contingency analysis must also be extended to explanations of the duration of particular periods of crises and the ways in which these are resolved.
- It is also crucial to understand how the resolution of one crisis leads to the emergence of new systems and relationships, and how these set the scene for the next crisis.

They illustrate such a mode of analysis by presenting their summary of how the GFC happened, building on an earlier but more detailed statement (Panitch et al. 2008). The nature of capitalism had been progressively transformed throughout the period since Marx was writing: competitive capitalism had given way to monopoly capitalism, and this in turn had been replaced by 'financialized' capitalism. High levels of leverage and risk taking were encouraged, leading to ever greater dangers of instability, which in turn spawned new kinds of hedging and risk spreading. The state became even more important as the final guarantor of the system, but while this was essential for the confidence of the financial markets it also invited 'moral hazard' and encouraged the emergence of speculative bubbles. Mortgage finance, especially in the US, became a key element of financial expansion, encouraged by government subsidies of various kinds designed to integrate the working class still further into the system and provide a political buffer – through constant expectations of increasing house prices – against any feelings of resentment at the stagnant or declining levels of real incomes resulting from the neoliberal policies adopted by successive administrations. Household debt, encouraged by these expectations of expanding equity in real estate, also fuelled consumer demand and hence the manufacturing sector. It was this house of cards that came crashing down in 2007–8.

Just as the work of Marx has been revived and to some extent reinterpreted in the light of more recent developments, there has been renewed interest in the theories of John Maynard Keynes (1883–1946), whose ideas were originally formulated in response to the Great Depression of the 1920s and 1930s. In his *General Theory of Employment, Interest and Money*, published in 1936, Keynes contradicted all the tenets of classical economic thought. Contrary to the prevailing assumption that markets and investors had perfect access to information and were thus able to evaluate any future risk, Keynes argued that uncertainty and responses to unknowable risk were at the heart of the economic behaviour of both investors and consumers. Future expectations were generally based not on rational calculation or on Adam Smith's 'invisible hand' but on conventions, stories, rumours and a strong element of crowd behaviour, amplifying both booms and busts. Crucially, Keynes argued, when aggregate demand collapses at the onset of a downturn the response of businesses is not to reduce prices – as the economic theory of the time postulated – but to slash output and hence employment, leading to a further reduction in demand and a spiral down into deeper crisis. The only effective policy response here is for governments to stimulate demand through making money available to investors as cheaply as possible and by undertaking capital works of various kinds, generating budget deficits for a time if necessary.

Robert Skidelsky, who through his monumental three-volume biography as well as many other writings has done more than anyone to argue for the continued relevance of Keynes, has interpreted the GFC in the light of what Keynes believed or would have argued in the current environment (Skidelsky 2009). At the onset of the GFC, most mainstream economists believed that economic actors possessed enough knowledge and information to make rational decisions based on accurate prediction of the risks involved. This so-called 'efficient market theory' has in Skidelsky's opinion been completely discredited by recent events, and yet a surprising number of economists still seem to hold to this irrational faith. While the onset of the GFC resulted in massive Keynesian-style government spending, Keynes himself argued that the role of government should not be confined to providing stimulus to demand at times of crisis but in enacting policies designed to maintain full employment at all times, and to minimize the chances of recurrent crises. Above all, Keynes was passionate about big moral issues such as the aims and limits of economic growth, and in the aftermath of the GFC, many of the more thoughtful economic analysts now urge a return to the macroeconomics of Keynes (for example Taylor 2010) and a greater emphasis on the big issues that are central to this book, notably development and income inequalities.

A more recent contribution to the theory of crises has been made by Hyman Minsky (1919–96), a researcher who was generally ignored during his lifetime but who is now central to the discussion of how to manage the post-GFC world. Minsky claimed that his major inspiration was the work of Keynes, but in fact many of his key concepts differ markedly from that earlier model. Minsky, writing much later than Keynes, placed the financial system at the centre of his concepts of economic dynamics and crisis. Keynes believed that the financial system could amplify movements towards crisis, but for Minsky finance was the major cause of instability. Modern capitalist economies, he argued, have an inbuilt tendency to create speculative booms – what he calls a dynamic of *upward instability* resulting in *system fragility*. During periods of relative stability and prosperity, there is a tendency for entrepreneurs to feel confident enough to take on higher and higher levels of risk. Systems of *hedging*, under which debt servicing costs are more than covered by expected revenue flows, may be replaced by *speculative financing* systems which rely on windfall profits for the refinancing of debt, and these in turn may be transformed into some kind of Ponzi scheme in which there must be constant borrowing in order to service existing debt costs. If enough businesses increase their risks in this way the result is an extremely high level of *system instability*. At this stage even a relatively trivial random shock will be enough to trigger a crisis – no major exogenous event is necessary. This is what has become known as a *Minsky moment*, and a number of writers have interpreted the onset of the GFC in just this way.

But even though Minsky was writing much closer to our own time than the two earlier theorists there are strong suspicions that the structure of the financial system has been transformed sufficiently to confound a number of Minsky's observations on both the causes of crisis and the policy tools needed to deal with such instability. Dymski (2010), while acknowledging that the GFC has shown the main contours of Minsky's analysis to be profoundly correct suggests that the stubborn refusal of the US economy to respond to government stimulus measures is the result of recent changes in the financial sector that

Minsky could not foresee, especially the changing roles of banks and other financial institutions (see also Das 2006).

The work of these three thinkers – Marx, Keynes and Minsky – could all be classified as theories that are fundamentally critical of existing systems, hence it is hardly surprising that supporters of the status quo have preferred proposals that favour some degree of modest reform, or even what Robert Wade (2008) has called 'incremental muddling through'. At one extreme, some commentators have argued that while instability may be inherent in modern capitalism the returns in terms of high growth rates during periods of prosperity are so much greater than under any other system that the costs from relatively infrequent bouts of crisis can be absorbed fairly easily and should simply be endured. At the other end of the spectrum there have been suggestions for quite serious reform, particularly in the regulation of the increasingly dominant financial system. This follows the logic of Keynes and assumes a key role for government in the ongoing prevention of future depressions. Much of this work has also involved the systematic study of various bouts of recession or crisis, particularly since the Great Depressions of the 1930s, drawing common and ongoing lessons and highlighting the ways in which the risks of instability have increased over the years.

Other explanations for the GFC and ideas to prevent a recurrence

As was noted in Chapters 2 and 3, the recent history of development thought has been dominated by faith in the market as the most effective allocation mechanism for resources of all kinds in every conceivable situation, but this blind faith in the superiority of market mechanisms has been perhaps the most obvious casualty of the GFC. Even if many economists and policy-makers still cling to this article of faith the old certainty has gone, and other quite different possibilities are at least being considered. A whole series of new studies have emerged on why market mechanisms are prone to fail, and much attention has been given to the psychology of markets that is at the heart of many of these problems.

Market mechanisms are of course based in part on the assumption of rational individuals armed with clear ideas on their desires and preferences, as well as perfect information about both the present and the future, but in practice few if any of these prerequisites exist. After reviewing the experience of a whole range of bubbles and crashes – starting with the Dutch Tulip Bulb Bubble of 1636 – Kindleberger and Aliber (2005) come down very firmly in favour of the Minsky model as the best explanation of what can go wrong in market operations. In particular they point to the key question of the availability of credit: when optimism is high and a bubble is building, credit is more easily available and hence the level of mania is exacerbated, while when a crisis hits, credit is cut off even for viable borrowers and the crash intensifies. This view has been strongly supported by Reinhart and Rogoff (2009) with massive amounts of data from a whole range of crises over some eight centuries. Not only are highly indebted companies and national economies highly vulnerable, but policy-makers and entrepreneurs refuse to believe the lessons of the past, arguing that this time things are different and all the old problems have been solved! As John Cassidy (2010) and Justin Fox (2009) have both stressed, most mainstream economists have chosen to ignore the growing body of research on the psychology of economic behaviour and hence the degree of irrationality in markets, preferring instead to believe that the economy – especially in the US – was a self-correcting mechanism that would quickly shrug off the impact of any speculative bubble and bust. This was certainly the view of Alan Greenspan, the former Chairman of the US Federal Reserve, but in a speech in 1996 he did warn about the possible emergence of 'irrational exuberance' in markets – and after the GFC this phrase has become his most famous utterance (Shiller 2009). However, few if any monetary authorities have yet to repudiate the theory of the self-regulating market, or put in place any coherent policies or regulatory systems to counteract these tendencies.

The GFC also ignited widespread criticism of the behaviour of the banks and other financial institutions, and in particular the excessively high salaries and bonuses paid to staff even during times when the industry was suffering gigantic losses and was relying on government bail-out packages to stay afloat. But again, while various politicians have railed against these excessive remunerations there seems to be little appetite to take any firm measures. There is a general acceptance that greedy and unscrupulous bankers should bear much of the blame for the GFC – and such finger pointing goes back to the Great Depression of the 1930s. But in this blame game it is also clear that the financial institutions have simply been taking advantage of a lack of government regulation in the whole area. This is not just a matter of unreasonable executive salaries, but of government complicity in the development of a culture of risk taking, excessive borrowing and highly leveraged investment. Central here was the repeal by the Clinton Administration of the Glass–Steagall Act of 1933 which had ensured the separation of investment banks from deposit-taking banking institutions. Paul Mason (2009) argues that this measure confirmed what had been happening in the financial industry for a number of years, culminating in the birth of modern investment banking, which had the appearance of being all-powerful – or so it seemed in the heady days just before 2007. The 'off balance sheet decade', in which innovative ways to hide the debt being accrued by clients were invented, saw the development of the 'shadow banking system' designed to circumvent the regulations under the Basel II agreement, and in particular the need for companies to maintain adequate capital cushions.

In part this dilution of regulatory oversight reflected an alliance between government and the finance industry in the US in particular, or at least a dangerous belief that what was good for Wall Street was in the interest of the nation, but there was also a dangerous lack of understanding of the processes at work in this new environment and of the risks that were created. This represented a dangerous failure of understanding and theoretical sophistication by the bulk of the economics profession (see, for example, Mattick 2011). The role of central bankers in the disastrous handling of the Great Depression ought to have been a warning, as Ahamed (2009) has argued, but history has not been part of the education of most students of this field in recent years (Mirowski 2013).

Much pain has been inflicted on the populations of many countries, both in the developed and developing worlds, by the zealous implementation of policies of austerity, and again this suggests a complete lack of understanding of the history of the Great Depression of the 1930s (Blyth 2013). There is now strong evidence to suggest that such measures are completely counterproductive, driving down employment and wages and therefore aggregate demand. The current focus on job creation and the expansion of the incomes of all sections of the population rather than of a small privileged few surely offers a much better way forward (McKay 2014). At the time of writing there is much debate about the levels of debt in Greece in particular, but also in Spain and Portugal. A new Greek government was elected on an anti-austerity platform but the implementation of these promises is proving to be difficult. The former Greek Minister of Finance, Yanis Varoufakis, has written a great deal about the impacts of the neoliberal agenda and its role in generating the GFC (for example, Varoufakis 2011; Varoufakis, Halevi and Theocarakis 2011) and is a prolific commentator on the current state of the global economy.

Criticisms of regulatory systems and policy frameworks at the national level have been matched by questions at the international level, targeting in particular key global organizations such as the IMF and the World Bank. It was these institutions that were intimately involved in the propagation of the Washington Consensus that has been so attacked, both before and after the GFC. The role of the IMF, an institution that many commentators believed was being marginalized before the GFC, has now come to the fore, but questions are being asked about the role of a 'lender of last resort' both in terms of how the GFC could have been managed better and in the avoidance of future crises. A lender of last resort is needed at the national level, and as we have seen in many countries during and since the GFC this has been essentially the role of the national government, shoring up the economic system, preventing further panic and providing credit in the absence of paralysed private sector institutions. But such mechanisms are also needed at the international level, serving many similar functions, and this theme will be taken up later in this chapter.

The GFC has also highlighted a widespread failure to understand the broader context in which economic processes have been taking place and the serious consequences that can ensue. Particularly important in the field of international development are the implications of inequality at various geographical scales, and the consequent emergence of serious global imbalances (Piketty 2014). In the industrial countries serious and expanding income disparities have been a clear consequence of neoliberal policies – indeed, as we have seen, the restoration of income shares for the top 1 per cent of the population has been viewed by some commentators as the real reason why such policies were initiated. For the bulk of the population, incomes have stagnated or even declined, hence the political necessity to expand credit facilities and make home ownership more accessible through the dilution of mortgage lending criteria which, as we have also seen, were at the core of the GFC. A recent Organisation for Economic Co-operation and Development (OECD) report has highlighted the patterns of inequality, which increased in the period of growth leading up to the GFC and have intensified since then. Crucially, this represents a serious drag on future growth at all levels (OECD 2015). At the international level, many nations – and particularly those in East Asia – have seen the promotion of high levels of exports to the developed nations as the best way of increasing national income in a global system characterized by large inequalities in wealth and power. Often this *Asian development model* has also contained incentives to encourage high levels of household savings that can be invested in national development projects. The result has been the accumulation of large pools of finance, including significant amounts of foreign exchange, in a number of countries. A prime example here is China, which by mid-2014 held reserves of US$4,056 billion. Some of this – along with similar reserves from other countries in East Asia and the Middle East – has been invested in US securities of various kinds, essentially funding much of the large borrowings of the US government as well as its corporations and private citizens. Asia's frugality has supported Western debt-driven excess. For the late developers, such as South Korea, Taiwan and China, the best strategy – as Rajan (2010) has noted – was clear: export to grow, use cheap labour resources to start the process, and gradually move up the technology ladder as capital stocks and human resources improve. Yet it is these imbalances in the global economy – caused by high levels of debt and huge trade and budget deficits in the West and equally large foreign exchange reserves, savings and trade surpluses in some key developing economies – that are seen by many as the fundamental cause of the GFC (see, for example, Eichengreen 2007; Roubini and Mihm 2010; Pettis 2013). This theme is explored in more detail in the next section, which examines the role of Asia in the GFC and the implications of the crisis for the future of this dynamic region.

Asia and the global financial crisis

We have already seen in Chapter 2 that the dramatic rates of growth achieved in a number of East Asian countries from the 1960s onwards posed a major challenge to analysts of the processes of development, and opinions varied widely as to the basic causes of this economic success. Similarly, the catastrophic crisis that hit the region in 1997 also gave rise to widely varying theories about the causes and implications of these events. Some commentators have argued that the causes of the Asian crisis were basically *internal* and resulted from the growing contradictions and inefficiencies that had emerged within the economic and political systems of these countries. Their policy response called for fundamental reforms of corporate governance, economic policy-making, the political systems and the relationships between the government and the private sector. By contrast, other researchers have suggested that, while there were certainly some internal shortcomings, the basic causes of the crisis were *external*, relating particularly to the problems in the structure of the international financial system. Their policy responses centred on the need for a new architecture of regulations governing these global flows of funds. The GFC has now given much support to this latter view, suggesting that the Asian crisis was simply part of a series of warning tremors before the full force of the shock waves hit in 2007. But one clear result is that after the GFC Asia's role in the global economy – already growing rapidly before 2007 – has been greatly enhanced, and this is in large part the result of the ways in which Asia responded to its own earlier crisis.

The onset of the Asian crisis is usually dated to July 1997 when in response to intense pressure from international markets the currencies of Thailand and Indonesia were floated in quick succession, leading to massive devaluations that were interpreted by international investors as a warning signal about the economic vulnerability of the whole region. Before the end of the year, the contagion of crisis had also spread to South Korea and there were fears that the country would default on the payment of its international loans. In December, the South Korean government was forced to call on the IMF for assistance and the largest ever emergency loan of US$58.3 billion was put in place. Similar, but smaller, loans were also obtained by Thailand and Indonesia. A number of other countries in the region were also affected by the crisis, notably Malaysia, but their governments did not find it necessary to seek IMF assistance. The impact on the most affected countries was catastrophic. The Indonesian economy declined by at least 14 per cent in 1998 and by some estimates inflation was running at 60 per cent. Both Thailand and Korea experienced declines of around 6 per cent, closely followed by Malaysia at 5.1 per cent. Unemployment became a serious problem throughout the region, resulting in marked increases in poverty levels. In the midst of the crisis, Korea managed to hold a presidential election, with a relatively smooth transition to the new government of President Kim Dae-Jung, but in Indonesia there was widespread political unrest, culminating in the overthrow of President Suharto.

Given the magnitude and importance of these events, it is hardly surprising that the Asian crisis has generated an enormous literature from a wide variety of disciplinary, theoretical and ideological perspectives (see, for example, Jomo 1998; Agenor et al. 1999; Jackson 1999; Pempel 1999; Haggard 2000; Woo et al. 2000; Stiglitz and Yusuf 2001; Chang 2007a). However, there is a wide divergence of opinion on the basic causes of the catastrophe, its policy implications and the appropriateness of the conventional management measures invoked by the IMF.

As was noted above, one major school of thought has paid particular attention to the internal causes of the crisis, stressing failures of macroeconomic policy and corporate governance. Much of this literature was unashamedly triumphalist, proclaiming that the Asian model, which had for many years been touted by some as more effective than the orthodox neoclassical paradigm, did not work after all. The aspects of policy failure that have been stressed by different authors and with relation to specific countries include: prudential regulation, and in particular the monitoring of the banking sector; corporate governance, and especially the assessment and management of risk; the management of exchange rates; the encouragement of too close relations between government and the private sector, leading to cronyism and corruption; an inadequate emphasis on technological upgrading and other means of increasing productivity; and an inappropriate willingness to bail out companies that are in trouble, rather than allowing inefficient firms to fail and thus encourage others to lift their performance levels.

These attempts to place responsibility for the Asian crisis squarely on the policy failures of the governments involved have been countered by a number of authors who have instead pointed to failures in the international system. Most influential among these is Joseph Stiglitz, a former Chief Economist at the World Bank and Chair of President Clinton's Council of Economic Advisors. He has given detailed evidence on US economic policies in Korea, arguing that these were central to the onset of the crisis (Stiglitz 2002). As early as 1993, there were discussions within the US government about ways of opening up the lucrative Korean market to a variety of US companies. In particular, Wall Street was keen to see the liberalization of the Korean capital market to allow greater foreign penetration. A number of critics urged caution, arguing that this action was premature and needed to wait until the necessary legal and regulatory frameworks had been developed in Korea, otherwise there was danger of serious instability. However, local US interests prevailed and Korea was pressured to undertake rapid deregulation. The result was a very rapid inflow of capital for a time but when the panic of 1997 set in there was an equally dramatic reversal. The fragile financial system could not cope and this premature liberalization of the capital account is regarded by Stiglitz as the single most important cause of the crisis.

Whatever the truth of these allegations, they were certainly believed by large segments of the population in many Asian countries. Many Korean businessmen, for example, have privately expressed their anger at the pressures on them to sell their companies, which they worked hard to establish, to American companies for what they regard as ridiculously low prices immediately after the crisis. The consequence has been the development of what Higgott (2000) has called the politics of resentment, widespread anti-American and anti-IMF feeling in the region. One result has been a concerted attempt by Asian governments to build stronger financial defences around the region, to work more closely together and to develop a strong regional financial body to reduce any possible future dependence on the IMF. This is the logic of a number of initiatives, such as the agreement in Chiang Mai to establish a regional monetary agreement, moves to strengthen Asian co-operation through the ASEAN Plus Three system and discussions about the establishment of an Asian Monetary Fund (Frost 2008). In 2014, China also championed a move to create and Asian Infrastructure Bank. Asian countries have also been very much to the fore in discussions about reform of the architecture of the international financial system, to provide greater protection to nations from the impact of speculation and unchecked money flows of the kind that destabilized Asia in 1997 (Eichengreen 1999). Above all, many Asian nations sought to insulate their economies by amassing massive foreign exchange reserves, acquired through aggressive export promotion efforts, and as we have already seen this resulted in the emergence of serious global imbalances that many have seen as a major contributor to the onset of the GFC.

Several commentators have argued that what has in fact emerged in much of East Asia is a bitter ideological and policy struggle between the neoliberal school and a more nationalistic group that stresses the need to return to some of the core values of the Asian model, albeit with some modification. Influenced by the international financial institutions and a number of Western governments, the reformers in countries such as Korea urged the complete restructuring of the entire political and economic system in line with neoliberal doctrine. But it is far from clear that such an outcome has been achieved, although there have been some reforms to be sure. In a volume edited by MacIntyre, Pempel and Ravenhill (2008) to mark the tenth anniversary of the crisis four major arguments are advanced about change in Asia since 1997:

- The desire to protect the region from any recurrence of the disaster of a decade earlier had forced significant changes to the political economy of the region. In particular, new initiatives on regional co-operation, banking regulation and social safety nets. Yet a number of other predicted policy changes, for example in the area of exchange rate management, had not eventuated. There had been an overall lack of uniformity in response to the crisis – rather, each country adopted its own approach, and even those countries not greatly affected by the crisis adopted important reforms.
- The long-standing Asian focus on achieving equity along with growth was generally reaffirmed; however, in some countries income disparities continued to widen.
- The crisis gave weight to critics of the old government-led model of development, and encouraged greater market liberalization.
- The response at the regional level was also very strong, resulting in important measures for financial co-operation and the creation of

safeguards – such as currency swaps and the creation of a regional bond market – to insulate the region from future crises. As a result Asia is now a much more coherent and institutionalized region.

But some critics have taken issue with some key elements of this assessment, particularly in relation to national reforms and the role of the state. There have been reforms, but also some reversals of earlier policy initiatives, and the existing domestic policy and economic regimes are, in the views of many, substantially intact (Beeson and Islam 2005; Hundt 2005; Robison and Hewison 2005). Even in the countries most directly affected by the crisis there has not been the wholesale movement to neoliberal approaches that many had predicted. The actions of the IMF and a number of Western governments in the immediate aftermath of the crisis continue to be seen by many in Asia as an attempt to impose neoliberal prescriptions on an unwilling region that had its own ways of stimulating growth (Klein 2007). Wade (2004) has argued that in many cases Asian countries have deliberately tried to give the impression of going along with IMF prescriptions but in fact they have returned to many of the policies that had been dismantled during the 1990s. There has been a return to the practices of the developmental state but often – with WTO rules and norms in mind – 'below the radar'. There was a widespread feeling in much of Asia that the 1997 crisis was the result not of internal shortcomings but of a premature liberalization of the financial system, largely in response to intense pressure from Western governments. This explanation has been given added weight by the GFC, and many Asian commentators are urging their governments – and those of the developing world more generally – to eschew such early liberalization and avoid the impacts of financial shocks originating in the West (Wade 2009; Stiglitz 2010).

The experience of the last decade has shown that development policy is not just a technical matter, but is highly political and therefore contested. In many cases political elites have simply used the new situation to their continued advantage. Importantly, the state has also used new opportunities to re-invent and re-legitimize itself, and is arguably as influential in the economy as it ever was.

Of crucial importance in this debate is the question of China and the precise model it has used to generate its spectacular growth. Can it be considered as part of the tradition of the Asian development model? Many commentators from the orthodox economic school have argued that China's success has been grounded in its abandonment of its old Communist agenda in favour of a capitalist system, but this would appear to be a gross oversimplification. Here again opinions are sharply divided. Wang Hui (2009), for example, has argued that China's history of revolution and its more recent phases of development are all part of single discourse of modernity, and calls for an entirely new model. By contrast, Huang (2008) argues that from the 1980s onwards the state-controlled sector based in the urban areas has become dominant, stifling progress in the more entrepreneurial rural areas. However, there seems to be strong support for the notion that China is basically following the lead of Asia's earlier developers such as Korea. Liew (2005) has argued that history, geography and institutional structure are all important in the choice of paths to development, and in particular the role of the Chinese Communist Party – albeit undergoing constant reform in the post-Mao period – has been central. The party has been able to reinvent itself and hold its monopoly over power, and the market has been used as a tool of state power rather than as a replacement for it (see also McGregor 2010). Similarly, Baek (2005) has argued that the state has continued to maintain strong control over the financial system, gives strong support to a large number of state-owned enterprises, has fostered a range of national heavy industries, and has based its growth on the fostering of both export competitiveness and of domestic savings – all familiar features of earlier growth strategies in East Asia.

In one key respect, though, the Asian model – particularly in the form that emerged after the Asian crisis – is being modified. In response to the evidence that global imbalances were a contributing factor in the GFC there has been much pressure on China to put more emphasis on its domestic economy rather than a single-minded search for higher export levels (Rajan 2010; Pei 2011). Political pressures have also emerged within China for such a move, with many commentators warning of the dangers of continued income inequalities between regions and also calling for more attention to improving standards of living and thus increasing internal consumption. The Chinese leadership has signalled its willingness to enhance the domestic economy and local demand, with some particular attention to the problems of many rural areas, and this should also increase the imports of foreign goods – a trend that will increase as the Chinese economy matures.

In Chapter 3 we have discussed the so-called Beijing Consensus and how this model is now being exported to much of the developing world. Indeed, the greatly enhanced role of both China and India in the global economy is one of the lasting impacts of the GFC, although the trends were clearly apparent in the preceding years, and as is explored in the next two sections of this chapter this is having a profound impact on processes of development in both Africa and Latin America.

Africa and the global financial crisis

In spite of some recent successes in some countries, sub-Saharan Africa is still clearly the most impoverished region of the world, and many statistics could be cited to illustrate different facets of this unfortunate condition. In 2013 annual per capita income was $1,615, only half that of the poorest parts of South Asia and less than one-seventh that of Latin America. Average life expectancy is only 50 years, again the lowest in the world, and the region also has the highest rate of infant mortality. Two million children die annually before their first birthdays: infant mortality rates have risen to 107 per 1,000 compared with 69 in South Asia. Some 70 per cent of the world's HIV/AIDS cases are in Africa. Around 40 per cent of the population lacks access to safe water and 33 per cent have no access to health services (Mills, 2010). The Ebola outbreak in West Africa in 2014–15 of course brought these problems once again to international attention.

This is certainly a crisis but, unlike for example the Asian financial crisis, this is not a short event with a quick onset and a relatively rapid recovery. This has been a long, slow deterioration, especially since the 1970s: in more than half the continent the average person is poorer than in 1970 (Moss 2007). The causes are complex and multifaceted, embedded in pre-colonial, colonial and post-colonial history and in the cultural history of Africa's diverse population. Space only allows us here to consider just some of the most important factors involved, and examine the ways in which the continent was affected by the GFC.

Arrighi (2002) and others have argued that one of the most important causes of the African tragedy is the form in which Africa has been incorporated into the global economic and political system. By the time of European colonization in the late nineteenth century, Africa had already been devastated by several centuries of Arab and European slave trading from the region and this was exacerbated by decades of further exploitation. Many of the African states that achieved independence in the 1960s had very arbitrary boundaries, cutting through many major ethnic groups, and many had difficult geographies because of their size, shape, harsh terrain, poor climates or very uneven population distributions (Herbst 2000). The fragmented nature of many African societies and political systems, and the very old tribal antagonisms that existed between a number of groups, worked against the consolidation of state power and authority in many of these new countries. The result was a large number of weak, poorly organized or even dysfunctional states. Few if any states were able to mobilize the resources needed to compete in the new, globalizing economy that emerged from the late 1970s onwards.

Many were in fact faced with civil wars, insurrections or armed conflicts over access to scarce resources. Recently, Africa has suffered from a large number of internal conflicts, certainly more than any other region, and by 2014 the number of refugees fleeing their own countries had reached 3.4 million, with a further 5.4 million being internally displaced.

A lack of adequate human resources has been a particular problem for the continent. To make matters worse, Africa has suffered from a serious flight of skilled people in recent years. It is estimated that 60,000 doctors, engineers and university staff left Africa between 1985 and 1990 and this exodus has continued at a rate of 20,000 per year since then (Mills 2002, 2010). Add to this the impact of a range of debilitating diseases and the extent of Africa's problem of skills and labour becomes very clear.

A further basic problem facing Africa has been its clear marginalization in the global system that has emerged since the late 1970s, and especially since the end of the Cold War. During the Cold War, a number of debilitating wars by proxy were fought in Africa by the superpowers but few if any economic benefits were received. Since the early 1990s, Africa has been largely seen as irrelevant in global economic, strategic and political terms. The continent now accounts for less than 1 per cent of annual global financial flows. By 2001, sub-Saharan Africa accounted for a total FDI stock of only US$116 billion, compared with US$1,243 billion in East and South East Asia (UNCTAD 2002). China alone now attracts more than 10 times as much FDI per year as the whole of Africa. International investors see Africa as poor, politically unstable, lacking in human resources and with inadequate infrastructure. There are also few domestic sources of investment, given the low level of average incomes, and as a proportion of wealth or exports African countries remain among the most heavily indebted in the world. Savings rates in Africa are the lowest in the world, less than half of those found in Asia, and some 40 per cent of all the domestic wealth that does exist is held outside the continent. Arrighi (2002) has argued that, as a result, Africa has always been very dependent on foreign capital but this turned away from the continent in the drastic restructuring of the global economy that took place in the 1980s.

Partly as the result of the failure to create productive export industries capable of generating significant export earnings, Africa has been unable to make any headway in paying off the debt that has been accumulated over previous decades, but particularly since the 1970s. In 1999, Africa's debt was estimated to be some $201 billion. In many African countries, external debt became larger than total GDP and in some cases debt servicing requirements in terms of interest repayments alone far exceed total export revenues (Gibb et al. 2002). A debate continues over the question of how the international community should respond to the continuing burden of debt in poor countries, many of them in Africa. One influential group has lobbied for the forgiveness of debt under the banner of the loose alliance called Jubilee 2000. In 1996, the World Bank created its Highly Indebted Poor Countries (HIPC) Debt Initiative to allow poor countries to break free from these past debts. By 1999, $3.4 billion had been set aside for debt relief, but Jubilee 2000 has consistently argued that much more needs to be done. In 2005, the largest donors agreed to give further debt relief, with up to 100 per cent reduction in some countries, although some campaigners have urged wider coverage for the programme (Moss 2007). Critics of debt relief, on the other hand, have argued that there is no point in cancelling debts until there is tangible evidence of real reform in Africa, otherwise yet more external assistance will be wasted (Easterly 2001). These problems are exacerbated, Moss (2007) contends, by a largely ineffectual aid industry that is confused and fragmented: the aid agencies are becoming part of the problem rather than offering a solution.

Poor economic performance and poor quality leadership and governance are widespread problems, but as Clapham, Herbst and Mills (2006) point out, the record has been particularly bad in Africa's large nations such as Nigeria and the Democratic Republic of the Congo. In East Asia, some large nations, Japan and more recently China, have provided real leadership for their regions but in Africa it is really only the smaller states such as Botswana and Mauritius that have had any real success, and this has had limited spillover effects.

Given this multitude of problems, what are the prospects for reform and reconstruction? There have been many grand plans for African reconstruction in the past, including a series of studies by the World Bank (1981a; 1984a; 1986), the Lagos Plan of Action produced by the Organization of African Unity (1981), and the United Nations *Plan of Action for African Economic Recovery and Development, 1986–1990* (United Nations 1985). The actual impact of these ambitious programmes has been very disappointing.

But many commentators in Africa suggest that globalization, if handled well, can provide a new way out for the continent. In particular, the rise of India and China and the increased prices being offered for the minerals and other resources with which Africa is well endowed may offer a way forward. Asia offers both large markets and growing industries that can absorb not just traditional exports like cotton but also food and consumer goods. Tourism from Asia can also be a key earner of foreign exchange. Thus, while Africa may have been marginalized by the West, Asia can be the new Silk Road (Broadman 2007). Critics have questioned whether China's exploitation of Africa's resources will be any more benign than was the earlier colonial rape of Africa, pointing out that almost all Chinese investment has been in resources, and oil in particular, often in countries like Sudan that have questionable development credentials. However, others have suggested that if handled carefully China and India can help the continent to higher levels of growth: it is for Africa to make decisions and plan for its own future (Winters and Yusuf 2007). An optimistic view has been presented by Friedman (2009) who argues that China is already in the process of transforming parts of Africa, not just by increasing demands for resources but by exporting entrepreneurial methods and more general Asian dynamism, and incorporating Africa into Asian industrialization. This view been supported by Gonzalez-Vicente (2011) who argues that China's demand for minerals from both Africa and Latin America has vastly improved the position of resource-rich countries, giving them more choice of investors and development opportunities as well as improving their terms of trade. China's method of operation, it is argued, is fundamentally different from earlier Western investors and the results can be much more positive and less exploitative. But China's 'hands off' approach to local political regimes means that there are dangers in some situations of enhancing the power of regimes that are certainly anti-development: there is a need for local communities to be more active in making sure that they are involved in determining their own futures.

Optimistic forecasts for Africa's future have been based around two particular opportunities. Africa's enormous reserves of energy and mineral resources have been in great demand on the international market, resulting in greatly enhanced revenues for some governments, although the recent fall in the prices of many minerals has dampened some of this hopeful expectation. The productive investment of these financial flows, if managed properly, can still provide a catalyst for development (McKay 2012; World Bank 2014c). Similarly, as labour costs in East Asia rise large numbers of more routine jobs in the manufacturing sector are being exported to other regions, and there may be opportunities for Africa to attract some of this new industrial employment (United Nations Economic Commission for Africa 2014).

The theme of Africa needing to take hold of its own destiny is now a common refrain among commentators from all parts of the continent. Governance and leadership problems and issues of ethnic and religious conflict have dogged the region and can only be solved by the African nations themselves. This has become even more urgent since an implicit bargain has been struck between Africa and the major economic powers: Africa will reform itself in return for significantly increased assistance of various kinds. It was self-help and African internal reform that was central to the launch of the New Partnership for African Development (NEPAD). This is a joint initiative of the African leaders themselves, but it has been endorsed by a meeting of the World Economic Forum in Durban in June 2002 and by a meeting of the G8 in Canada later in the same month. In July, also in South Africa, the African Union was launched, replacing the old Organization of African Unity, and this was partly meant to symbolize a new and united beginning to co-operation in the region in support of NEPAD.

The aim of NEPAD is to put an end to poverty in Africa, reduce its marginalization in the world economy and forge a more equal relationship with the developed countries. A primary target is a growth rate of at least 7 per cent but in order to achieve this there must be peace, good governance and effective policy-making on the continent. It is still perhaps too early to judge how effective this new initiative will be, and some community groups have already denounced NEPAD as a sell-out to foreign interests, but many commentators see this as one last chance to bring some hope to the people of Africa after decades of devastation and poverty. The next decade will be a crucial one.

Latin America and the global financial crisis

The situation in Latin America is in some ways a combination of the deep-seated and extended structural crisis described for Africa and the shorter but very dramatic shock that affected Asia in 1997. The problem for Latin America is that, while its structural problems are not as severe as those in Africa, they are still very serious and the financial crises that have afflicted the region have been both regular and very deep.

We have already seen in Chapter 2 that a number of scholars from Latin America have been influential in the initiation of new ideas in development thinking, especially in exploring the ways in which the region has been adversely affected by outside exploitation. One of the most influential of these thinkers in recent years has been Fernando Henrique Cardoso, who in a widely quoted book (Cardoso and Faletto 1979) argued that the association of national and international capital could never lead Brazil to the goal of independent industrial development: rather it would deepen existing inequalities and result in a loss of control over national development. There was some excitement in the development profession, then, when Cardoso was elected President of Brazil in 1994. The result, however, was a disaster for the Brazilian people (Rocha 2002). Instead of following his own warnings about the dangers of unequal alliances with foreign capital, Cardoso argued that the last decade of the twentieth century had seen the unprecedented growth of capital and its availability, something not foreseen by earlier theorists. Countries such as Brazil could gain great benefit from being one of the major destinations of these capital flows. Thus, he embarked on a reform programme very much along the lines of those advocated by the IMF. The capital account was liberalized, earlier protectionist barriers were removed and state enterprises were privatized. In order to attract more foreign capital, interest rates were increased to the highest levels in the world. After some early good results, the long-term impact was just as Cardoso had predicted in his earlier book. Locally owned industries collapsed under the pressures of high interest rates and increased foreign competition and, as the economic indicators started to deteriorate, still higher interest levels had to be imposed. But in the end this did not prevent a serious flight of foreign capital. Unemployment levels increased and income inequality became worse than ever. It was not surprising, then, that in the presidential election following the end of Cardoso's term in 2002 the left-wing opposition candidate Luiz Inacio Lula da Silva should gain such a clear victory. But US fears about a turn to the Left did not eventuate. Lula softened many of his earlier views and adopted a moderate reformist agenda. This has attracted some criticism from more radical groups but Brazil has gradually gained the confidence of the international financial community, and by the end of his term in office Lula was hailed as driving the transformation of Brazil into a future global economic giant. Growth has been healthy, with particular progress in agriculture, although there have been many fears expressed about the impact of government development policies, especially in the Amazon region.

But all of this is not to deny that there have been some serious internal problems in Latin America as well. As we saw in Chapter 2, a number of studies have compared the growth experience of Asia and Latin America and attempted to explain why Asia has been so much more successful. The most commonly cited explanation is the difference in the behaviour of the governments and the elites in the two regions and, as in the case of Africa, we come back to the question of *state capacity* as a key variable in successful development strategies.

As in Africa, a number of Latin American countries are pinning many of their hopes on future export growth derived from increased Asian, and particularly Chinese, demand. Resource-rich countries such as

Brazil and Chile have signed several agreements with China and the Chinese leadership has certainly extended its charm offensive to this region. Gonzalez-Vicente (2011) has suggested that Latin America has fared rather better than Africa in its dealings with China because its generally more democratic regimes have been able to turn increased export earnings into development gains for the wider population.

Even before the onset of the GFC, economic policies in much of Latin America were undergoing significant changes. In Venezuela, Bolivia and Ecuador left-wing governments have moved away from the orthodox, market-oriented development programmes promulgated by the IMF, but the more social democratic administrations of Brazil, Uruguay, Chile and Paraguay have re-emphasized the role of the state in economic management and in development policy. The major reason, as Ocampo (2010) and others have pointed out, was frustration with the widening income disparities that seemed to be the inevitable result of market reforms, and the increased role of the state at a global level that has resulted from the policy responses to the GFC has intensified this shift. In much of the region there has been more emphasis on Keynesian countercyclical macroeconomic management and concern with more interventionist development strategies to improve equity, encourage new export opportunities, diversify export markets, enhance domestic savings rates, foster local technologies and boost regional integration (Rojas-Suarez 2010). Latin American countries are also becoming more global in their approaches to economic and foreign policies: as we have argued one major impact of the GFC has been to speed up the transition to a multipolar world, and Latin America is now becoming far more vocal on the wider stage. Brazil has been one of the leading developing countries demanding a new trade deal for the poorer countries as part of the WTO Doha Development Round. Brazil, India and China now form a formidable group working to remove restrictions on access for agricultural products from the developing world into the rich markets and to have US and European agricultural subsidies wound back.

The GFC and the future of globalization and North–South relations

The main argument presented in this chapter has been that most profound changes, including those in the economic domain, occur as the result of crisis events of one kind or another – high-impact, low-probability occurrences that are now being recognized in the literature as *Black Swans* (Taleb 2010). We have seen that Minsky and others have argued that such dramatic crises are more likely following periods of relative stability, and so it was with the GFC. However, as has also been noted in Chapter 3, neoliberalism has remained remarkably intact as the dominant development paradigm both in terms of the alliance of big business, some key think tanks and research institutes as well as with some compliant governments (Crouch 2011) and in the realm of dominant ideas (Mirowski 2013).

However, as has become clear from our short reviews of the recent development experiences in Asia, Africa and Latin America criticisms of neoliberalism have been much more strident in the developing world after the GFC than in the industrial countries. As a result many of the ideas central to development economics that had been displaced by the neoliberal revolution have now come back into favour, supported by what appears to have been a significant movement in opinion within the World Bank. Thus, it may be that the real challenge to neoliberalism may come from the developing world through a renewed criticism of dominant Western ideas from the development studies community. Even though neoliberal ideas have penetrated into most parts of the world there are still important elements of most developing economies that still operate in a non-capitalist manner. Here there survive important elements of earlier systems based on communal and co-operative obligations, and these would seem to have something in common with the forms of 'collaborative production' that Paul Mason (2015) sees as now emerging in developed counties to replace a failed neoliberal project with something he calls *Postcapitalism*. This is an interesting and even exhilarating possibility and one that has the potential to renew the relevance of the entire field as we seek a better understanding of the world that is emerging from the ruins resulting from the GFC.

Chapter 5

Politics and Governance

Damien Kingsbury

Many developing countries commonly appear to be beset by problems of corruption, limited accountability, poor governance and limited political representation. They often have only occasional and poor engagement with notions of democracy and with a propensity to various degrees of failure of state institutions. To some extent, this perception is based on a history of failure of developing countries to consistently conform to a modernist Western model of political processes, the value of which has been the subject of lively debate. To a considerable degree, too, many of these features are some of the defining characteristics of a developing country, particularly one that has not progressed in its overall development.

More specifically, however, developing countries have each faced a range of economic, social and institutional challenges, some of which have been, or are in the process of being, successfully overcome and many of which have not. Those unresolved challenges can be both a product of, and lead to, the undermining of political stability. Within this framework and recognizing that individual countries face specific historic problems, there are elements of consistency between the issues they have faced which allows a general analysis of development politics that can be applied when understanding specific case studies.

This chapter sets out the main features of politics in developing countries, indicating how the relationships between these elements form a complex interweaving of factors that preclude providing simple answers to their multi-faceted problems. It begins with identifying how the origins of developing countries through colonialism and post-colonialism shaped their experiences, and then considers the successes and failures of post-colonial political identity, the politicization of militaries, tensions between economics and politics, regime change and issues in democratization and authoritarian government. It concludes by addressing issues of governance, the relationship between the state and society and how these may play out in regime

138

change, and what has often been put as the normative imperative of democratization.

This chapter is based on the idea that 'development', which proposes processes by which people can improve their lives, is in large part shaped by political and social freedoms and accountabilities. The idea of development has traditionally been focused on economic development or improvement in the material welfare of people. Some commentators, notably politicians in developing countries, have even argued that economic or material development should take precedence over political development and that political development should be put on hold to ensure that fragile or conflicted political environments do not hinder the efficiencies of organization necessary to lift poor countries out of poverty. In some cases, this position has also been allied with the view that political development, especially if that means democracy and civil and political rights, is a foreign imposition, does not necessarily accord with pre-existing cultural or political values, and may constitute a form of imperialism.

Related to the view that economic development should take precedence over political development – that people will be unconcerned about politics if they do not have enough to eat – is the view that higher levels of material development are necessary to sustain higher levels of political development.

This argument, often put by more authoritarian governments in favour of political closure, is, following the 'developmental' model, that if people lack food security or they are illiterate, they will not only be less concerned about politics but less able to meaningfully participate in a given political process, or what has been termed by some as 'rice before rights' or the 'full bellies thesis' (see Howard 1983). A countervailing view is that if people have the opportunity to freely express themselves, and to hold their politicians accountable, they are more likely to be able to ensure there is adequate distribution of food and other available material goods, including education (see Sen 1999a).

A countervailing view is that if people have the opportunity to freely express themselves, and to hold their politicians accountable, they are more likely to be able to ensure there is adequate distribution of food and other available material goods, including education (see Sen 1999a). This then raises the fundamental question of whether it is economics that drives politics, or politics that drives economics, or what has been referred to as the debate about the competition between structure and agency. These issues will be discussed within the context of contemporary theory on wider interpretations of governance and evolving political practice.

The origins of developing countries

Most of the world's developing countries came into existence in the period following the Second World War, in which struggles for liberation that had begun to find their voice in the 1920s and 1930s became more compelling in the post-war era. Even those states that were not formally colonies, such as Thailand, were often defined by aspects of the colonial experience, not least in terms of their borders and the status of their external relations. The major exception to the post-war experience of decolonization was in Latin America, which had largely shed the imposition of colonialism in the early nineteenth century. But even its subsequent experiences tended to reflect the broadly shared experiences of later post-colonial states.

There have been two defining qualities of developing countries that derive from their post-colonial status. The first is that the successor states have almost all been based upon prior colonial boundaries, usually reflecting colonial convenience rather than prior ethno-linguistic unity. This is based on the principle of *uti possidetis*, or that which is possessed at the time of independence. 'Based on the maxim of Roman law, the doctrine of *uti possidetis ita possidetis* (as you possess, so you possess), treats the acquisition of a state's territory as a given, with no territorial adjustments allowable without the consent of the currently occupying parties' (Mahmud 2011: 60). There have been exceptions to the application of this principle, in the case of India and Pakistan, and French Indo-China, for example, but it has otherwise been overwhelmingly applied and has thus created inherent problems with a disjuncture between the conception of 'nation' and the heterogeneity of the state.

The second quality is that most developing states came to independence through a military struggle, with military forces and ideology subsequently coming to play a major and often self-defining role in the orientation of the state.

Having achieved independence, many developing countries have frequently failed to sustain the sense of unity of purpose that liberation helped engender, and have also not sustained their often-claimed commitment to either a generalized sense of freedom or a representative, accountable and participatory political process. The aspirations often associated with independence – that independence will address the problems that beset the colonized territory – have commonly exceeded the capacity of the newly formed state to deliver. Indeed, such aspirations were often confronted by reduced state capacity as a result of war and the loss of colonial expertise, organization and capital. Expectations of improvement in the lives of the people concerned not only went beyond that which the colonial power was able to provide, but were further out of touch with the reduced post-colonial environment (Chandler 2010: 170).

The gap between post-colonial expectation and the (lack of) capacity to fulfil them invariably produced political tensions (Jefferess 2008: 163). In multi-ethnic post-colonial societies and in particular within the context of post-independence material scarcity, there has been a tendency for political leaders to reward their political supporters at the expense of other groups (Grawert 2009: 138). This form of patron–client relations has often been based along specific ethno-linguistic lines, although exceptions arose where patron–client groups form around other areas of geographic or, more commonly, economic, interest. That is, where the bonds of a united struggle against colonialism may form an initial sense of unity, this unity was often not maintained in the post-colonial era.

In an open or plural political environment, such as post-colonial democracy, this lack of unity has in some cases manifested as political opposition and dissent. In cases where governments have little initial capacity, they may struggle to maintain organizational control and consequently had a tendency to close political space and thus revert to forms of authoritarianism, often employing repressive colonial-era legislation (see Collier 2009: 173–6, 186 on the relationship between state capacity and post-colonial democracies). In cases where such governments have derived from a military or revolutionary background that reflected a high degree of non-consultative hierarchical organization, such organization is reflected in the political style and orientation of the new government.

Political identity

Independence movements in colonial territories were frequently accompanied by a rise in the assertion of a nationalist identity, usually cohering around their opposition to the colonial authority. But because most colonies were constructed according to geographic convenience rather than along ethnic lines, they usually included distinct tribal or ethnic groups, many of which traditionally had ambivalent or even hostile relations. Moreover, it was a common practice for colonial powers to employ one ethnic group in a position of advantage over others, as a mechanism for recruiting ethnic groups in support of the colonial enterprise (e.g. see Horowitz 1985: 527). In some cases, post-colonial states succeeded in developing a sense of relatively coherent national identity but in others attempts to compel loyalty to the national project failed, especially where some ethnic groups felt discriminated against on the grounds of their ethnic identity and where the 'civic guarantee' of equal inclusion failed to apply. This was particularly so where a specific ethnic group with a grievance within a reasonably geographically coherent area did not acknowledge the legitimacy of an administration from a separate location or over the claimed area, or where that sense of legitimacy was never adequately established or was lost, illustrated by separatist movements that affect or have affected many developing countries.

Ethnically heterogeneous post-colonial states in particular have tended to exhibit vertical or regionally based group tendencies, where they are constructed from multiple pre-existing and self-identifying communities and where the civic function of the state, in which all citizens are treated as equal, is weak. Given that most post-colonial countries are 'ethnically diverse' (Collier 1998) and often have weak civic institutions, there is a tendency for such states to coalesce along ethnic rather than civic lines. In this, it is assumed that ethnically diverse states that have weak civic structures will necessarily employ a higher degree of compulsion in order to maintain state control. Conversely, ethnically diverse states that have stronger civic structures will have a greater proportion of voluntary inclusion in the state.

Given that many developing post-colonial states have weak civic institutions – variable institutional capacity being a characteristic of the development process – few such multi-ethnic societies have made a fully successful transition to becoming voluntary states in which an overwhelming majority of their members freely choose to be citizens. Commonly, there has been an element of compulsion in accordance with an overt 'nation-building' project. Where this nation-building project has been predicated upon a higher degree of compulsion, it has tended to produce a reaction or to exacerbate existing tendencies, often by way of assertion of an alternative or separate identity. In the former case, where the distinction is between the ruling elite and the ruled, this can lead to 'horizontal' social divisions or class-based dissent, including 'classes' characterized by political dispossession. In the latter case, the distinction is between ethnic groups, or 'vertical' distinction (Eriksen 2002: ch. 3). This then raises two questions: what it is that constitutes a nation, and how claims to nation can be assessed.

National identity as the basis for the assertion of nationalist claims can be characterized in two broad streams. The most common and primordial quality of national identity is based on ethnicity (Smith 1986: 22–46). As Anderson (1991) has noted, a common language is the principal mediator through which individuals may not know each other but may actually or potentially communicate across distance and hence perceive themselves as having a common interest.[1] This language can be commonly shared as the first quality of group formation, in that it was already spoken by the constituent members of the political group. In many developing countries, however, the state language is often not the first language of its citizens but may have been developed to help create a sense of common communication and hence identity. So, too, have countries commonly emphasized elements of their history to help form a common political bond. However, basing the national project solely on an ascribed history or culture, i.e. what it means to be of a particular nationality, without extending that to include wider civic values, raises the prospect of reifying a mythical 'glorious past' (see Smith 1986: 174–208). In reifying itself, ethnicity becomes inwardly focused, exclusivist and reactionary, which can lead to political division and conflict both with external nations (e.g. the Khmers and the Vietnamese in 1978) and within the state between constituent ethnic groups.

The territorial reach of nations has, however, historically shifted, especially prior to the advent of modern state sovereignty (the Westphalian system of fixed borders), when populations were often fluid. These shifts were still underway when colonial powers cemented what were subsequently to become state borders.

The second defining quality for a more modernist, less ethnically prescriptive national identity is based on shared cultural or plural civil values (see Miller 1993, 1995, see also Smith 1998: 210–13). Shared plural, civic values correspond to a more voluntary, inclusive, participatory and open political society (for example, liberal democracy), usually based on an equally and consistently applied rule of law. An important element of this is common civic identity, manifested as political participation. However, such participation can be fairly directly challenged by power-holders.

However, where national bonds are historically weak in relation to the state and civic bonds are not evident, states tend to compel membership of a 'national' community following, rather than preceding, the creation of the state. Compelling membership of ethnic minorities to be members of states include most post-colonial or developing states. Such compulsion tends to preclude civic values, in which the state rules by (often relatively arbitrary and frequently oppressive) law, thus denying justice. This could be seen to be the case in the Arab states that consequently faced popular uprisings in 2010–11. By contrast, voluntary nationalism, in which members freely embrace their agreed commonality, appears to provide a more stable basis for social equality of difference under rule of law (see Seymour 2000; Habermas 2001a, 2001b).

While many developing countries were historically divided and few could be said to have existed as nations prior to independence, through the commonality of the struggle and, usually, the contiguity of the land, many did increasingly form strong national identities in direct response to the real or perceived depredations of the colonial experience and in particular wars of liberation. This further quality of defence, or security, in nation formation parallels and overlaps with Hobsbawm (2004: ch. 4) and Gellner's views on the role of industrialization in nation formation. In this respect, the principles of defence (or a militant independence movement) require similar organizational structures to an industrial environment, with clear lines of management and control and the standardization of communication (especially language) and worker/soldier practices. The importance of shared liberation struggles or mutual defence cannot be overstated. Where outsiders may argue that a 'nation' has not historically existed, given a common cause and organization it can come into being relatively quickly and with a high degree of both coherence and commitment in cases of mutual preservation.

The state and the nation

Many post-colonial states have been based on colonies that did not necessary reflect the unity or distinction of pre-existing ethnic identities, but, claiming the principle of *uti possidietus* or full possession of prior claimed territory (ICJ 1986: 554), often had difficulty in establishing a non-ethnic (i.e. civic) form of national identity (Hasani 2003). As a result, there have been numerous claims to separate national identity which have led to competition between the self-identifying nation as a bonded political group and many post-colonial states (see Griffiths 2003).

The state, in a contemporary sense, refers to a specific and delineated area (Smith 1986b: 235) in which a government exercises (or claims to exercise) political and judicial authority and claims a monopoly over the legitimate use of force up to the extent of its borders. Within a given territory, the state can be identified by the presence and activities of its institutions, which define its functional capacity (Evans 1995, see also Krader 1976: 13). While a state claims authority within its borders, along with a monopoly on the use of force, it normatively does this on behalf of its citizens, as a manifestation of their political will. This implies a social contract between the state and its citizens, in which the state can expect, and compel, a duty to comply. In return, citizens can expect that the state will reflect and represent their interests. In reality, however, many developing countries have only incomplete control of their territory or their institutions do not always function, much less function well, up to the extent of their territorial borders. Moreover, such social contracts that exist between developing states and their citizens have been frequently undermined, compromised or arbitrarily changed to suit the needs and interests of ruling elites. In enforcing their will, particularly in relation to violent opposition, political elites in developing countries have resorted to using militaries for domestic purposes.

Militaries in politics

One of the most significant problems that have beset developing countries has been the involvement of the military in civilian politics, in some cases disproportionately influencing government and in others taking control of the government. There have been too many military coups to give even a sample, but all have reflected and contributed to a high degree of political instability.

While almost all countries agree that they require the presence of a military, Desch (1999) has argued that civilian authority over militaries works best where a state faces high external threats and low internal threats. Civilian control of the military works worst, according to Desch, where a state faces high internal threats, such as separatism or revolutionary movements, and low external threats. In those conditions, the military is more likely to see itself as a political actor or as the protector of the state, often justified by the role played by militaries (or their precursor guerrilla organizations) in independence movements. In conditions of high internal and external threats or low internal and external threats, Desch suggests that civilian control over the military sits between the two extremes. In developed countries, however, the tendency has been for low internal and external threats to equate to greater civilian control over the military (see Lasswell 1941, see also Dains 2004). Militaries in developing countries also appear to have interpreted as an internal 'threat' a perceived or actual lack of competence by civilian leaders.

Huntington (1957) argued that the most effective method of asserting civilian control over the military is to professionalize them, but that this capacity to professionalize the military is often not present in developing countries and in particular where the state is unable to meet the full costs of the military, and hence militaries engage with private businesses outside civilian control, meaning they are less accountable to civilian governments.

Notably, too, when military organizations do influence or exercise political authority, they are by definition hierarchical, closed and relatively authoritarian (see Huntington 1957). This is especially the case where the military derives its ethos from revolutionary idealism, in which its role in the securing of independence is usually only the first step on the road to a wider social transformation.

Where society is otherwise initially disorganized or where alternative legitimate sources of power have not yet become established, or where the post-independence development project either heads towards failure or actually fails (e.g. Afghanistan, Somalia, Sudan), military control is regarded by power-holders as necessary to maintain state organization or, in some cases, cohesion. This then has the capacity to devolve into a situation where the newly independent authority may lose legitimacy through its exclusive, non-participatory and non-representative system of organization, or where it compels often geographically and ethnically specific reluctant citizens to remain within the state. Again, a significant element of this tendency towards political closure in the face of state incapacity set against growing frustration and disappointment came to characterize many new developing country governments, when tensions between increasing political closure on one hand and growing frustration on the other spilled over into violence. Governments moved to assert their authority, as was again demonstrated in many Arab states in 2011, but a breakdown of state institutions in a number of instances led instead to near state collapse, in some cases resulting in the even stronger assertion of the status quo, in others a generalized chaos and dysfunction but, very often, eventually in regime change (e.g. Egypt, Tunisia, Libya).

Democracy, democratization and regime change

In the period since the end of the Cold War, there has been an upsurge in the number of states around the world that define themselves as 'democracies'. This is in part due to the electoral processes employed in a number of former Soviet states and the turn towards electoral processes in formerly authoritarian client states that have since lost the patronage of one or other of the two former superpowers. However, not all regime change has been democratic, democratic change is not inevitable and it is possible for democracies to revert to other, less- or non-democratic forms of political organization. Further, what is claimed to be 'democratic' may not be that, or it may be a procedural democracy, employing a relatively free electoral contest but failing to provide a range of more substantive democratic qualities such as the separation of powers between government institutions, equitable and consistent rule of law, civil and political rights such as freedom of speech and assembly, or the opportunity to fully participate in the political process (see Schumpeter 1976; Dahl 1986; Burton et al. 1992: 1; Grugel 2002: 6).

In debates about democracy and democratization, Fukuyama (among others) argues that there is only one final form of democracy – liberal democracy associated with free-market economics (Fukuyama 1992). Such 'democratic absolutism' has frequently run contrary to the political experience or preferences of developing countries, even where they accept a substantive democratic model, for example, with a higher degree of economic intervention. As a result, there has been considerable debate over the value and appropriateness of a 'one size fits all' democracy, not least in developing country contexts.

There are, in theory, over 500 types of democracy (Collier and Levitsky 1996) – many more than there are democratic governments. Within these definitional criteria there are basic political model distinctions such as presidential as opposed to parliamentary models, centralized versus federal and so on. These are not democratic criteria as such, but rather different types of democracy, each of which has systemic advantages and disadvantages. The main distinctions between democratic types are around the ways and extent to which they meet some or all of conventional democratic criteria. That is, the principal distinction is between whether the democracy in question is a minimalist or proceduralist model, or maximalist and substantive, and how these qualities are manifested.

A procedural democracy is understood to hold reasonably regular elections which are more or less free and fair. A substantive democracy holds regular, free and fair elections, has state institutions capable of instituting government policies which are accountable and under government control, has a strong and active civil society and is one in which law is equally and consistently applied and in which there are no meaningful challengers to the democratic process (Collier and Levitsky 1996: 10).

Despite Collier and Levitsky's argument for acknowledging 'diminished sub-types of democracy' (Collier and Levitsky 2009), it could also be suggested that there is a democratic 'cut-off point', less than which is not actually 'democracy' but a different political form that also shares some democratic attributes. An 'expanded procedural minimum' model is equivalent as a democratic cut-off point in most Western democracies. This definition includes ('reasonably') competitive elections devoid of ('massive') fraud, with universal ('broad') suffrage, basic civil liberties such as freedom of speech, assembly and association, and an elected government with effective power to govern ('institutional capacity').

There have also been objections to democracy, which have frequently been adopted by non-democratic governments to rationalize their political structure and orientation. Pre-democratic governments such as monarchies have generally been opposed to democracy on the grounds that it stands in opposition to hereditary right to rule. Authoritarian governments also argue that democracy promotes social division and short-term interests over long-term planning (e.g. see Hoppe 2001; Kaplan 2005). In some cases, they also argue that democracy can imply a tyranny of the majority. Communist governments have argued, too, that democracy is a subterfuge for capitalist control of society and that the only political choices are those between parties or individuals representing versions of exploitative capitalism.

There has been a long-expressed view that notions of democracy are culturally specific and are not transferrable to non-Western societies (e.g. see Zakaria 1994). 'With few exceptions, democracy has not brought good government to new developing countries ... What Asians value may not necessarily be what Americans or Europeans value', K. W. Lee said by way of defending what were claimed to be 'Confucian values' (Address to Asahi Forum, 20 November 1992). Similarly, Halper has argued that democracy is a dead idea and that China's authoritarian model will come to dominate the twenty-first century (Halper 2010).

Related to the view that economic development should take precedence over political development is the view that higher levels of material development are necessary to sustain higher levels of political development. Consistent with these views, particularly up to the 1990s, was the argument that suggested that developing countries could not 'afford' liberal government and that only strong government could deliver desired development outcomes. This argument was particularly strong in East Asia and was justified by citing the examples of the 'Asian Tiger' economies of South Korea, Taiwan, Hong Kong and Singapore, none of which enjoyed liberal government during the period of their economic development (though each of which enjoyed specific opportunities that assisted their economic development). Each of these East Asian states was described as a 'developmental state', referring to relatively high levels of state autonomy from vested interests as well as relatively high levels of intervention in economic planning, regulation and performance. While this model, originally based on the Japanese experience with its Ministry of International Trade and Industry (MITI) under the Liberal Democratic Party rule between 1955 and 2009 (with an 11-month interregnum in 1993–4), has tended to function in states with limited political plurality, political closure is not a prerequisite for relatively high levels of such intervention. To illustrate, there was a relatively high level of government intervention in the Swedish economy until the 1990s.

In cases where democracy is established, there can also be a democratic tension around the acceptance of a plurality of views, some of which might be antithetical to furthering such openness (e.g. majority imposition, or voting to end voting) and which may set up points of conflict within a society still struggling to come to grips with low levels of institutional and organizational capacity. Many developing countries have difficulty in overcoming these tensions and may sometimes slip into chaos, often ended when the military or another authoritarian party imposes its own undemocratic will. This then raises the issue of regime change, which in developing country contexts may be towards, or, more likely, away from, open, plural political models.

Regime change

The issue of regime change is critical in the process of political development and is often at the point at which options for democratic openings occur (e.g. the 'Revolutions of 1989' in which a number of Soviet bloc states adopted democratic practices). By regime change, what is meant is a fundamental shift of political values, and is more commonly not via an orderly handing over of government within an established and agreed political framework (with the exceptions to this general trend among some former Soviet bloc states). Regime change usually follows a period of rising political tension and its common feature is political instability in the period leading up to, surrounding and following such change. As a consequence, regime change can be accompanied by political violence, especially between groups representing the status quo and aspirants for change.

Regime change that is internally driven tends to reflect a failure of the existing system to either fulfil the basic requirements of a key social sector or sectors, such as rural or urban workers, the middle class, business owners, traditional oligarchs or the military. This failure to satisfy such sectoral interests may reflect a basic ideological position that predisposes the government to ignore or oppose particular interests. Alternatively, it may also reflect a government's incapacity to function in favour of its preferred interest sector, such as where the government becomes excessively corrupt, factionalized or otherwise unable to exercise authority, or where its key institutions cease to meaningfully function. In this respect, regime change is most commonly a consequence of horizontal, interest-based political change (class or social group-based revolutions). A government either tends to represent one horizontal group by replacing another, or a horizontal group or coalition of groups replace their own, failed government. Regime change is rarely vertical because vertical divisions that are so strong as to successfully challenge a government tend to want to establish a separate state. Vertical regime change may, however, occur in tribal societies, such as Afghanistan or Rwanda, where the government tended to reflect the assertion of specific tribal interests within the state.

The period of regime change is the point at which there is greatest political flux and hence both opportunity and threat. Where there is opportunity, it is usually associated with the end of a chaotic or dysfunctional regime. Sometimes, however, this change may be away from plural government towards a more closed or authoritarian political model. Even where new forms of government may have the external characteristics of democracy (such as in the Philippines in 1986 or Indonesia in 1998), there may be partially or completely hidden components that fundamentally compromise the capacity of the general population to meaningfully participate in political affairs or to be genuinely represented (see O'Donnell 1996 for discussion on this broader topic). That is, where regime change is towards democracy, it may be procedural, or less than procedural, rather than substantive.

Beyond this, regime change is not by definition towards a normatively more desirable or participatory outcome. Although the tendency towards the end of the twentieth and early twenty-first centuries has been for regime change to move away from authoritarian models, it can also impose non-democratic or authoritarian rule. As discussed, regime change can be from or to any other particular regime type. O'Donnell and Schmitter (1986) identify eight basic political model types, each characterizing degrees of democracy and liberalism. At the most authoritarian end of their scale, O'Donnell and Schmitter identify autocracy, or 'dictadura', as constituting low democratic capacity and low levels of liberalization, moving to or from a plebiscitary autocracy usually via a coup or revolution. Graduating towards a medium level of liberalization while retaining low levels of democratization is characterized as liberalized autocracy, or 'dictablanda', which might reflect a number of authoritarian but not dictatorial regimes (such as Singapore). Instituting limited political democracy with medium liberalization, or 'democradura', opens the next political category, representing less authoritarian but still restrictive regimes, such as in Malaysia and perhaps the democratizing states of sub-Saharan Africa. States moving towards popular democracy, representing high democratization with low liberalization might be characterized by India or Sri Lanka before the effective limitation of the latter's political space after 2005.

O'Donnell and Schmitter's next category of political democracy, reflecting higher democratization and greater liberalization, appears to correspond to a number of Western or Organisation of Economic Cooperation and Development (OECD) states but is not commonly reflected in developing countries' political systems. The use of the term polyarchy to describe this category has been further developed by Dahl's inclusion of the following attributes: elected officials, free and fair elections, inclusive suffrage, the right to run for office, freedom of expression, alternative information and associational autonomy (Dahl 1989: 221). Related to the form of polyarchy that is reflected in the political status of many OECD countries is the category of social democracy, implying higher democratization and high liberalization.

Assuming that authoritarianism and its variants have a negative normative value, this implies that the opposite has a positive normative value. Although perhaps reflecting the era in which it was written, O'Donnell and Schmitter's assessment of normatively positive politics contrast with even then more libertarian economic views. In this respect, they equate higher democratization and highest liberalization to welfare democracy (presumably of the type then found in Scandinavia and to a lesser extent Australia, New Zealand and the UK) and to socialist democracy (O'Donnell and Schmitter 1986: 13) (although it is unclear where a genuine socialist democracy has actually existed).

Due to conflicting interests, much regime change will be opposed, and transitions especially from authoritarian to democratic models require a shift in the allegiance of the military. The military itself will therefore often be politicized and divided between those who support regime change and those who oppose it. O'Donnell and Schmitter (1986: 15–17) characterize such military factions as 'hardliners' and 'softliners'. As these terms imply, hardliners oppose change, while softliners facilitate change, usually cautiously. Examples of successfully facilitated change by military softliners who have taken advantage of 'the military moment' (1986: 39) include Portugal and Greece in 1974, the Philippines in 1986 and Indonesia in 1998, although there are also numerous examples in Latin America. Moreover, limited liberalization away from a direct military rule while retaining a capacity for existing elite control or liberalization without introducing democracy may also be facilitated by such a softline military approach (for example, the removal of direct military rule in Indonesia 1986–8 and relative liberalization without democratization in 1991). Softliners, however, sometimes overestimate their popular support, and may engender a backlash that sets back movement towards liberalization (O'Donnell and Schmitter 1986: 58). For example, in Indonesia, the resignation of President Suharto in 1998 following a shift by a majority in the military towards a 'softline' position was in turn followed by a conservative or hardline backlash in which Suharto's immediate successor, President Habibie, quickly failed in his bid to be elected to that position with his liberal successor, Andurrahman Wahid, being ousted halfway through his own presidential term. Softliners also encountered a backlash in the initial military-led steps of Portugal's 'Carnation Revolution' in 1974, and during Turkey's return to electoral politics in 1983.

As Dahl noted, a state is unlikely to quickly develop a democratic political system if it has had little or no experience of public contestation and competition, and lacks a tradition of tolerance towards political opposition (Dahl 1971: 208). That is, regime change in such a state is at least as likely to default to an alternative authoritarian government, or to partially do so. Similarly, although cautioning against political expectations arising out of such structural preconditions, Di Palma noted that economic instability, a hegemonic nationalist culture and the absence of a strong, independent middle class all impede transition from an authoritarian political model towards one that is more democratic (Di Palma 1991: 3).

There is debate in development politics over whether there is a structural or causal link between economic and political development. One view has it that societies need to reach a certain level of economic development before they can enjoy a similar level of political development (e.g. see Acemoglu and Robinson 2006: ch. 3). A competing view posits that a higher level of political development is possible without related economic development. This specific debate reflects a broader 'structure–agency' debate, in which there are competing views over whether material circumstances shape development outcomes or whether there is scope for human 'agency' or choice to determine how societies organize themselves.

In considering transitions from authoritarian to democratic models, there are a range of conditions that might be claimed to be essential for successful regime change. As noted by Dahl, these include control of the military and police by elected civilian officials; democratic beliefs and culture (Dahl 1989: 111) and no strong interference by foreign powers that are hostile to democracy (for example, the USSR in Eastern bloc countries). Further, Dahl identified conditions that were not absolutely necessary, but which were favourable for the establishment of democracy, including a modern market economy and society, and weak sub-cultural pluralism (or lack of opportunity for inter-ethnic conflict) (Dahl 2000: 147, see also Dahl 1989: ch. 8).

In what Dahl has referred to 'the democratic bargain' of trust, fairness and compromise (1970), this pact normatively corresponds to a type of social contract.

The evolution of political forms from absolute autocratic rule towards civil government that encourages political participation, representation and accountability, requires a type of social contract between citizens and its government. Under absolute rule, a completely sovereign monarch or tyrant is not party to any contract but rules with unlimited authority. Under this form of government there is no neutral authority to decide disputes between the ruler and the citizen. Under the 'social contract' model, however, the government accedes authority to the population, mediated by an independent authority (for example, an independent judiciary) in return for right to rule. This occurs on a sliding scale of a balance of authority until it is agreed that authority is ultimately vested in the citizens, is only held by the political leader or government on behalf of the citizens and is able to be rescinded by the citizens in an agreed and orderly manner (that is, through regular elections).

In this, it is important that elites who intend to continue or expand their political rule are able to satisfy, or be seen to address, most outstanding demands while at the same time avoiding the strongest dissatisfactions from manifesting into collective action. As O'Donnell and Schmitter note, and which appears to be borne out by experience, transitional regimes from authoritarianism tend to be smoother and more successful if they promote essentially conservative political outcomes, as this is seen as less threatening to out-going authoritarian elites. Democratic 'idealists', usually on the left and centre-left, are only given the opportunity to engage in transitional processes if elite survivors from the previous regime are willing to negotiate a mutually satisfactory set of rules of the new game (O'Donnell and Schmitter 1986: 70). Where such negotiations fail, more active, usually leftist or strongly liberal-reformist, political actors may be rapidly marginalized, as occurred in post-1986 Philippines and post-1998 Indonesia. In the latter case, those demanding total reform of the political system were quickly marginalized, resulting in the fragmentation of the reform movement (comprising in particular students, civil society and humanitarian non-governmental organizations (NGOs) and coalitions). Of particular transitional note, however, was the role played by military 'softliner', Susilo Bambang Yudhoyono, first as the leader of the reform faction of the Indonesian military in the early 1990s, following from dissent towards the then president, and then as a political actor and finally as president himself. Yet he was also victim to a conservative coalition, with his second and final term in office (2009–14) being noted for inaction. In the case of the

Philippines, public protest against then President Marcos and the blatant falsification of election results, backed by sections of the military, led to his ousting and replacement by his electoral opponent, Corazon Aquino, the widow of Marcos's murdered former opponent, Senator Benigno Aquino. While Corazon Aquino came to power on the back of a popular protest movement (often referred to unreflectively as 'people power'), she in fact ushered in elite rule mirroring that of the oligarchic pre-dictatorship era. Under Aquino, the Philippines' elite structurally excluded genuine open participation in politics, despite it formally being an open electoral contest. One interesting aspect of regime transitions is the role played by external events. Although there are numerous exceptions, it appears that critical political shifts most often occur at times of pronounced social, economic and/or political dislocation. A range of pre-existing tensions or pressures must already exist in order to capitalize on the subsequent rupture, but the rupture itself appears to act as a catalyst for regime change. By way of illustration, the Russian Revolution took place after Russia's disastrous involvement in the Great War. China's nationalist revolution was precipitated by colonial domination and its communist revolution came in response to Japanese occupation, while Portugal sloughed off dictatorship in the wake of failed colonialism and economic collapse. Similarly, Nicaragua deposed its dictatorship after a destructive earthquake, the Philippines and Indonesia removed dictators following the Asian economic crisis, Greece after the Turkish invasion of Cyprus and Argentina removed its military junta following its defeat in the Falklands War. In the two latter cases, democracy was achieved by stalemate and lack of consensus rather than by prior unity and consensus (see O'Donnell and Schmitter, 1986: 72). Indeed, virtually the whole post-Second World War decolonization period could be attributed, to a greater or lesser extent, to the direct and indirect economic, military and political effects of the war.

Transitions born of crisis are, of course, not consistent in their outcomes, illustrated by the shifting contest between democracy and authoritarianism throughout Latin America and in countries such as Thailand and in much of sub-Saharan Africa. There are even cases of voluntary political redundancy, such as in Spain after Franco's death, although this too might be seen as a political 'shock'. In some cases, the 'shock' itself, though, is little more than an excuse to exercise an overdue necessity, where an ossified regime is aware of its redundancy yet still requires an excuse to dignify and hence ease its own departure.

As noted, not all regime changes are towards democracy. Some changes may be partial (for example, the Philippines post-1986, Indonesia post-1998) or lead to conflict (such as Cambodia 1975–98).

Others simply revert from one type of authoritarianism to another, as has often been the case in sub-Saharan Africa. These different experiences of regime change invariably reflect competing views of what constitutes political progress: what is to some fairness is to others interference, what to some is freedom is to others disorder depending, as discussed earlier, on how one views the basic concepts of freedom and equality.

The state, society and democratization

Reflecting on the relationship between the state and society within the context of degrees of freedom, Stepan noted the putative if changing focus of the state from economic to political development:

> The assumptions of modernization theory that liberal democratic regimes would be inexorably produced by the process of industrialization was replaced by a new preoccupation with the ways in which the state apparatus might become a central instrument for both the repression of subordinate classes and the reorientation of the process of industrial development.   (Stepan 1985: 317)

The development of 'bureaucratic authoritarian regimes' that are associated with, if not necessarily responsible for, economic development (seen as industrialization) in a number of developing states, noted above as 'developmental states', has also fragmented and inhibited potential political opposition. The rise in the relative authority of formal or recognized state institutions, and the non-negotiable imposition of their development programmes, has diminished other political institutions including both the formal pluralist institution of 'opposition' and the capacity of civil society (Stepan 1985: 317). This in turn comes back to attempts to delegitimize political alternatives, and, in particular, those that are necessary for a successful plural polity but which have an imposed reduced capacity that in turn delegitimizes them.

If there is a differentiation between early and more recent approaches to institutions, it is in understanding institutions as not being just organizations of people with particular roles, but sets of rules or codes of behaviour that can include, for example, respect for the rule of law, notions of equality and tolerance of or respect for alternative views (e.g. see Hall and Taylor 1996). The key distinctions here are between formal and informal rules or codes of behaviour, with greater emphasis being placed on important informal rules that nonetheless effectively play a formal role in political society. An example of an informal rule that might be considered critical is the opportunity for the creation and maintenance of civil society organizations which have a central role in the open political function of developing states. The 'rules' by which such groups organize themselves are one way in which they constitute institutions, but the fact of their existence and their shifting social and political roles have also become institutionalized. That is, there is an expectation that such organizations will exist in a developing country, will be acknowledged as existing and will from time to time contribute to public debate and decision-making.

In circumstances where legitimacy implies consent to rule it is normative, in that it reflects a social value judgement about whether or not a ruler or government has the 'right' to occupy that political position. This in turn opens up questions of moral authority and the extent of correspondence between such matters and between ruler and ruled. Positive legitimacy implies explicit agreement about the circumstances that confer legitimacy, such as compliance with the equal and consistent rule of law and the correspondence between the action of the ruler and such compliance. That is to say, legitimacy of rule derives from a sense of justice in social and political relations; where a sense of justice prevails, the social and political circumstances may be regarded as legitimate.

The relationship between civil society and government has been proposed as an indicator of the democratic health of the state, with the varying capacities of each institution being a key determinant. Stepan posits four sets of relationships between the state and civil society, which are characterized as the following:

1. Growth of state power and diminution of civil society power, which often occurs during the closure of political space by governments in developing countries.

2. Decline of state power and growth of civil society power, which is unusual in developing countries.

3. Growth of both state and civil society, which is again unusual in developing countries but may occur in democratic transitions.

4. Decline of both state and civil society (but with option of civil society growth outside the state), which tends to reflect failed state status.   (Stepan 1985: 318)

Stepan was primarily concerned with the growth of state power in developing countries at the expense of civil society, or the imposition of bureaucratic authoritarianism with a parallel reduction in the capacity of non-state actors to compete with state power. While Stepan focused on Latin America, this situation could also characterize 'strong states' such as China, Vietnam or Syria in which an independent civil society is relatively weak. In the transitional phase away from bureaucratic authoritarianism, state power declines and civil society strengthens as a consequence of the opening of greater political space (for example, as military domination declined in Thailand). Civil society may also increase in its own right and therefore act as a contributor to declining state power (for example, Poland). Growth of both state and civil society power can be seen either in competition or as providing a balance for each other. With the former, the instability that derives from competition is unable to be sustained, and tends to either degenerate into internal conflict or the state or civil society fails to sustain its position and hence declines in power relative to the other. More positively, however, state power can be defined not only as bureaucratic authoritarianism (negative state power) but also as benign state capacity or an ability to resist the influence of vested interests (positive power). In such cases, where there is strong civil society and strong positive state power, the two are likely to interact together to increase their respective capacities. Perhaps the best examples of this can be seen in the Scandinavian states and to a lesser extent in other plural democracies.

In cases where both state and civil society power decline, however, there is the possibility of state failure or reversion to pre-modern methods of state organization (ASC et al. 2003: 4), as neither institutional segment is available to compensate for the weakness of the other. Such a power vacuum often draws external actors into the collapsed political space. This could be seen in the case of Iraq during the insurgency against US intervention from 2003, where US intervention created the power vacuum and then led to the necessity of its continuing, if increasingly troubled, presence. Similarly, the political space collapsed in Afghanistan prior to the rise of the Taliban, and in East Timor from late April 2006 (see also FfP 2006). In studying the reduced autonomy of the Brazilian state in the early 1980s, Stepan noted the view of executive branch leaders that only the reduction of state autonomy relative to civil society through a process of liberalization could rein in the state's security apparatus. That is, if the state was weaker relative to civil society, then its institutional components would also be relatively weaker, including those that political leaders viewed as rather more malignant.

State institutions

The role of institutions has been identified by the World Bank, among others, as being central to the success or failure of development projects, particularly in their larger and more bureaucratic sense. That is, the capacity of states to make use of aid, to deliver its benefits and to sustain the process of development generally is seen by the World Bank, and many others, to be vested in the institutions of the state. This thesis was first developed by Huntington (1968) and later addressed by Fukuyama (2004).

After his earlier foray into determinist normative claims of the inevitability of democracy and free-market capitalism in developing countries, Fukuyama appeared to recognize that liberal democratic capitalist outcomes in developing societies was not necessarily a given. Responding to his own country's assertion of military power, Fukuyama recognized two sets of closely related problems. The first was that the US had intervened in the affairs of other states (most notably, Panama, Lebanon, Somalia, Afghanistan and Iraq) with the explicit intention of ending non-democratic regimes and in most cases, at least rhetorically, ending support for terrorist organizations and those countries' related military capacities (for example, 'weapons of mass destruction'). Such intervention was justified on the positive grounds that it was intended to bring democracy to these countries. However, local populations did not automatically see the benefits of a 'democratic' system of government when it appeared to be imposed and represented an alien ideology. More to the point, it was difficult to establish a democratic framework in states that did not enjoy the range of institutions that allowed democracy to exist, much less flourish. It was the lack of such institutions that was in most cases responsible for allowing particular states to degenerate to the point where they were unable to prevent, or allowed the existence of, terrorist organizations.

The second problem was a failure of state institutions more generally that provided fertile ground for the establishment of organizations that might be seen as antithetical to political development, e.g. the Taliban in Afghanistan, the Islamic Courts Union in Somalia. Beyond this, the lack of capacity or performance of state institutions was widely and increasingly seen as a key reason why such states remained mired in underdevelopment. This shift to an institution focus began in organizations such as the World Bank following the collapse of the Soviet Union and the shift from communitarian–bureaucratic systems of government (that is, 'communism') in a number of eastern European states towards a more free-market liberal democracy. The initial impediment in these regime transitions was a lack of institutional capacity. This was mirrored in the parallel transitions from authoritarian forms of government towards more open and, for a while at least, increasingly democratic forms in developing countries such as the Philippines, Thailand, Indonesia, Argentina, Nicaragua and Chile.

Governance

Along with normative claims to democratic principles, the issue of 'governance' has become central to developing countries in the period since the end of the Cold War. No longer able to rely on the support of patron states under which there were few respected rules in exchange for strategic loyalty, developing countries have had to begin to order themselves in ways that conform to international standards. Reflecting donor countries' ideological shift away from government-centred approaches to development while at the same time recognizing the limitations of neoliberalism, at the peak of the Clinton–Blair political dominance the World Bank and UNDP opted for a 'third way', reflected in a 'semantic shift' (Mazower 2012: 369) towards good 'governance'.

As Mazower has noted, the business school model of 'corporate governance' adapted to development needs included a sense of social and environmental responsibility, along with poor – and usually large – government being regarded as the chief impediment to development (Mazower 2012: 369–70).

Having first arisen in public development discourse in the early 1990s, a 'Commission on Global Governance' was established in 1992 and its first report, *Our Global Neighborhood*, published in 1995. According to Mazower, a 'governance' approach reflected 'a creed justifying far-reaching interventions in the public administration, law, and political systems of countries around the world' (2012: 370). UNESCAP identified good governance, in a more benign way, as accountable, transparent, responsive, equitable and inclusive, effective and efficient, following the rule of law, participatory and consensus oriented (UNESCAP 2011). Each of these criteria accords with other general definitions, apart from that of being 'consensus oriented'. While consensus can be an important tool for resolving conflict and ensuring that no parties' fundamental interests are neglected, in traditional or developing societies it can also be used to impose the will of more powerful (and often self-interested) figures and may disempower the legitimate claims of less powerful groups. Moreover, consensus and rule of law do not sit easily together, especially where disputes arise over issues of law and equity.

Ideas of governance are closely related to institutional development, in particular regarding the capacity and probity of state institutions to undertake the functions that are allocated to them (World Bank 2011). In particular, the World Bank sees good governance linked to its anti-corruption activities as being important to its focus on alleviating poverty. The World Bank's Worldwide Governance Indicators (WGIs) project identifies aggregate and individual governance indicators for

213 economies over the period 1996–2009. Within the WGIs, the World Bank identifies six dimensions of governance, including 'Voice and Accountability', 'Political Stability and Absence of Violence', 'Government Effectiveness', 'Regulatory Quality', 'Rule of Law' and 'Control of Corruption'. Importantly, each of these criteria link with the others in constructing a political environment in which citizens (and investors) can expect a high degree of consistency in the political and economic environment, in which there are now off-budget 'surprises' and which provide mechanisms for accountability in cases where government institutions do not function appropriate to their brief.

The Asian Development Bank identifies a similar (but far from identical) set of criteria for 'governance', including accountability, predictability, participation and transparency. Its work in the governance field has been primarily in strengthening accountability institutions, including audit agencies, anti-corruption commissions and the judiciary. It notes that 'strengthening the rule of law ... is crucial to encourage private sector investment and combat corruption' (ADB 2011). The ADB's criteria for governance differs in detail from those of the World Bank, but its basic goal of ensuring a safe, legal and consistent political and economic environment is consistent with that of the World Bank.

Notably, while both the World Bank and the ADB recognize there need to be different approaches to ensuring good governance in specific societies, both are equally focused on combatting corruption in government institutions and agencies as a primary means of ensuring the best possible environment for economic development. Increasingly, however, equal and consistent application of rule of law and ensuring a government that is open and responsive to citizens' needs, along with the other key qualities of good governance, are seen not just in instrumentalist terms of helping to ensure economic development. Like political development more generally, they are increasingly seen as a political good in their own right.

Conclusion

No two developing countries have identical political histories, systems or processes, but many do share some of a range of characteristics that help to explain why they often reflect particular outcomes that often appear to meet less than a normative standard: the way in which most developing countries have come into being, being physically shaped by their colonial experience, informed by their experience of colonialism and the wars that were often fought to end it. Having started from a low level of development in terms of economic and organizational capacity, many new states have subsequently slipped further, engendering disappointment and disenchantment with the independence process and tensions over the allocation of scarce resources. Very often, where different ethnic groups have been brought together in one state as a consequence of prior colonial incorporation, such tensions can take on a tribal or 'nationalist' hue and, in cases where the ethnic group has a specific territory, can lead to claims for separatism. These types of situations can become particularly problematic where states have limited capacity or skills to deal with such problems and, often through a military acculturation, respond with repressive measures, leading to a diminution of the legitimacy of the state.

Such states may liberalize over time, especially in light of a lack of support from other, more powerful states that might have had an interest in maintaining particular regimes. In some instances, popular revolts (e.g. the Philippines, Thailand, the Arab states) or the internal collapse of a prior regime (Indonesia) may also lead to democratic change. Too often, however, regime change is not permanent or even long-standing and collapses of government, coups and so on frequently lead to a cycle of authoritarian or military government, a process of liberalization and then a return to authoritarianism and so on.

One of the main problems that arises from such political instability and the lack of representative government and accountability that usually accompanies it is that the mechanisms of government intended to ensure good governance are rarely in place. As a result, the overall development project tends to struggle under a burden of corruption, inefficiency and sectional self-interest. This then feeds into a sense of disillusionment with and the illegitimacy of the state, which leads to the predictable government response and the cycle referred to above. This is not the only reason why so many developing countries have failed to break out of the cycle of poverty, mismanagement and poor government, in some cases for over 60 years. But it has been and remains a common and significant contributing factor in the failure of the development process for many countries.

Note

1. Anderson's principal reference was to the use of print technology in the dispersal and standardization of language, but the principle of a common language applies regardless of the mechanism of its dispersal.

Chapter 6

Aid and Development

Janet Hunt

This chapter considers the various ideas about development that have shaped international development assistance over 60 years. It looks at the various motives for co-operation and assesses the current state and role of development co-operation in light of globalization and significant progress in reducing poverty in developing countries. It also considers the role that development co-operation has played towards the Millennium Development Goals and what future aid will play in a very changed development environment relative to other sources of finance.

The purpose of aid

Since the Second World War there has been a broad understanding among developed countries that in order for the world to become a moderately equitable place, or at least to alleviate some of the worst suffering, there needs to be some form of international assistance. For some developed countries, this follows a perceived sense of responsibility following the process of decolonization. For others, it is intended to assist less developed states to reduce the probability of their further decline and potential for instability. Many donors also provide aid to enhance their own economic, political and strategic interests, through encouraging their exports, or shaping the economic policies or political persuasion of recipient countries and 'stabilizing' other states. The alternative term 'development co-operation' perhaps captures some of these mutual benefits which have often been influential in the nature and direction of aid.

Historical background

Although some official development assistance (ODA) began earlier (Rist 1997), after the Second World War the formation of the United

162

Nations and its specialized agencies, and the establishment of the International Bank for Reconstruction and Development (IBRD) and International Monetary Fund (IMF) signalled the creation of a global system of development co-operation. The initial role of the IBRD, now better known as the World Bank, was to raise capital for the reconstruction of Europe and Japan, while the IMF was to promote international monetary stability. (Hellinger, Hellinger and O'Regan 1988: 14; Ryrie 1995: 4–5).

The idea that there could be a concerted international effort to address poverty and underdevelopment is attributed to President Truman's inauguration speech (Rist 1997: 71). US bilateral assistance began in 1948, with the Marshall Plan to assist with Western European reconstruction in the face of advancing communism in Eastern Europe; soon foreign economic aid was integrated with military aid to meet Cold War objectives (Zimmerman 1993: 8). The late 1940s and the 1950s was a period of optimism, in which people believed that it was indeed possible to eradicate hunger and misery resulting from underdevelopment, perhaps within a decade (Hoffman 1997). The underlying theory was that growth in developing countries would create development, and this would be achieved through large investments of capital, coupled with technical expertise. The emphasis was on modernization and industrialization, using surplus labour from rural areas to achieve import substitution (Tarp 2000: 19–23). Keynesian economic theory emphasized government investment, adding further intellectual support for the value of providing foreign aid.

European aid programmes developed strongly in the 1960s as European countries recovered from war and were in a position to join the effort to assist the developing world. In particular, as decolonization of Asia and Africa proceeded, former colonial powers, such as France and Britain, launched major development assistance programmes to their former colonies.

Although the Organisation for Economic Co-operation and Development (OECD, i.e. 'developed') countries account for by far the largest proportion of aid, it is important to recognize that non-OECD countries are involved too. For much of the Cold War period, the USSR and its Warsaw Pact allies accounted for almost 10 per cent of aid (Manning 2006: 372). This was directed to Eastern European reconstruction and other Cold War 'fronts', notably in Asia and parts of Africa. China assisted African countries such as Tanzania and Somalia from the 1960s onwards (Nayyar 1977; Klare and Anderson 1996; Manning 2006). Following the end of the Cold War, Russia and some other Eastern bloc countries themselves became recipients of OECD aid.

In the period surrounding the oil boom of the early 1970s, Arab countries also provided assistance to developing countries. Indeed, in 1978, aid from OPEC countries reached a peak of 30 per cent of global aid (Manning 2006: 373), though it subsequently declined. Today these countries remain active again, along with other so-called 'emerging donors', countries such as Turkey, Mexico, Korea and Brazil, along with China, India and Russia that actually continue long-standing roles (Manning 2006; Kharas 2009; Kragelund 2008; World Bank 2010a).

What is new today about these emerging non-Development Assistance Committee (DAC) donors is the scale and assertiveness of their efforts and the competition they are bringing into the aid system (Woods 2008). Some 30 or more such countries now provide about 10 per cent of aid (Paulo and Reisen 2010; Kim and Lee 2013) with some already equalling or surpassing the smaller DAC donors in the amounts of aid they provide. Indeed aid from Arab countries, especially Saudi Arabia, Kuwait and the United Arab Emirates, averaged 1.5 per cent of their gross national income in the period 1973–2008, more than double the UN target and five times the average of DAC countries (World Bank 2010a). The combined contribution of 'ODA-like' flows from Brazil, South Africa, China and India exceeded $3.7 billion in 2011 (Hudson Institute 2013: 5).

There is considerable debate about whether non-DAC aid is more tied to procurement of goods and services in the donor country than in the case of DAC countries, and the extent to which it is complemented by trade and investment or provided for political reasons (Chun, Munyi and Lee 2010; Overseas Development Institute 2010; Paulo and Reisen 2010). The strength of many southern donors is that they now share their own experiences of development and the lessons they draw from that with other developing countries (Kim and Lee 2013).

The origins of non-government aid preceded these government initiatives and can be traced to between the First and Second World Wars; although it should be recognized that the Red Cross had already been established as early as 1863 (Stubbings 1992: 5), while 'proto-aid' charitable organizations, notably Christian missions, existed prior to that. As Smillie notes (1995: 37–9), Save the Children began to help child victims of the First World War. Foster Parents Plan (now Plan International) was a response to children affected by the Spanish Civil War. Oxfam began to provide famine relief to victims of the Greek civil war in 1942; CARE sent food parcels from the USA to Europe in 1946; and World Vision began to assist victims of the Korean War. These are among the major international non-governmental organizations (NGOs) today.

The role of the private sector in development co-operation has become a major trend since the 1990s. Today, philanthropy accounts for almost US$56 billion annually (Kharas 2012). Major philanthropic foundations such as the Open Society Institute and the Bill and Melinda Gates Foundation are big players. The Gates Foundation now disburses some $4 billion per year, making it larger than some 11 official donors in 2011. Private contributions from individuals and corporations in the 'emerging donor' countries are also growing (Hudson Institute 2013). Online philanthropy, through websites such as Global Giving and Kiva, links individual donors directly to projects in developing countries (Desai and Kharas 2010: 1113).

The second avenue for the private sector which has grown since the mid-2000s is through public–private partnerships with official donors, particularly in areas such as health, economic infrastructure and agriculture (Tomlinson 2012: 146). The decline in aid budgets and the significance of the remaining development challenges may be reasons for this trend.

Most significant, however, is the fact that in 2011 flows of private capital from developed to developing countries amounted to US$322 billion dwarfing aid flows (Hudson Institute 2013: 5). And emerging economies China, India, Brazil, and South Africa 'accounted for $103 billion in total private financial flows to the developing world, compared with $577 billion from the twenty-three donor country members of the Organization for Economic Cooperation and Development (OECD)' (Philanthropy News Digest 2013).

How much aid, to whom?

In the early years of aid, it was thought that 6 per cent economic growth was needed in developing countries to address poverty. The necessary capital investment to gain this level of growth, it was suggested, would require 0.7 per cent of the GNP of the developed nations (Jolly 1999: 36–7). This is the origin of the target for aid set in 1970, still current today, more honoured in the breach than in its realization. Only five of the 25 member countries of the OECD Development Assistance Committee – Denmark, Netherlands, Sweden, Norway and Luxembourg – have consistently met the 0.7 per cent target, with the UK reaching it in 2013, and Netherlands just missing it that year (OECD 2013a: 172; OECD 2014).

Historically, the pattern of aid growth has always been uneven (Tarp 2000: 85; German and Randel 2002: 145; Padilla and Tomlinson 2006: 3). After initial growth during the 1970s, between the early 1980s and the late 1990s aid levels fell steadily (German and Randel 2002: 149) despite rapidly growing per capita wealth in OECD countries in that period (Padilla and Tomlinson 2006: 4). Following UN member states' commitment to the Millennium Development Goals in Year 2000, and various related agreements (Tomlinson 2010: 157; Nunnenkamp and Thiele 2013), total ODA experienced an 'unprecedented increase', and 'grew by 63 percent during 2000–2010' (United Nations Economic and Social Council 2012: 12) to US$128.5 billion, or an average of 0.32 GNI. Since 2011, the impact of the global financial crisis and the Eurozone crisis saw aid fall but it recovered somewhat in 2013 to return to 0.3 per cent of GNI for OECD countries, almost $135 billion in total (OECD 2014a). However, heavy cuts to aid for least developed countries in 2011 and 2012 signal a trend which may increase as more aid in the form of 'soft loans'[1] goes to middle income countries (United Nations 2013b: 53).

While US aid was significant in the early decades, by 1980 the European countries were providing double the US contribution (Ryrie 1995: 10). In dollar terms the US, the UK, Germany, France and Japan now contribute the largest amounts of bilateral aid. Despite their large volumes of aid, the contribution of the US and Japan as a percentage of their GNI is small (Davies and la O' 2013; OECD 2014a) and since 2000, European Union members of the DAC have contributed between 50 per cent and 60 per cent of global ODA (European Report on Development 2013: 46; OECD 2013a: 172).

In efforts to bring greater focus onto the quality and direction, not simply the volume, of aid over the years, two indicators have been used. One relates to the proportion of aid going to least developed countries (LLDC) and less developed countries (LDC) in response to concerns that too much was going to middle-income countries, the other to the proportion of aid being spent on basic social services (BSS), such as health services, education, potable water and sanitation (Jolly 1999), which were each below 2 per cent of aid (Randel and German 1997) and have grown a little since (OECD 2013a: 268).

Most recently, attention has switched to the extent to which aid is being directed towards achieving the Millennium Development Goals, a set of eight goals with clear targets and measurable indicators, agreed at the UN Millennium Summit in September 2000, which to some extent address the above concerns in a new guise. In this case, more serious measurement and reporting regimes have been instituted (United Nations 2006b). A further measure of aid quality introduced by NGOs in 2010 is the calculation of 'real aid'. 'Real aid' discounts three areas of expenditure DAC donors are allowed to count as part of their ODA: debt cancellation; the costs of supporting developing country refugees for their first year as residents of donor countries; and the estimated costs of educational infrastructure for developing country students studying in donor countries. NGOs argue that these cannot be viewed as legitimate aid expenditures (Tomlinson 2010: 152–6).

The geographical distribution of aid has changed significantly over the decades. These shifts reflect the changing dynamics of development, as Asian countries like India and China make gains in poverty reduction while high levels of poverty persist in Africa. In 1961, almost a quarter of all aid went to the Middle East and North Africa, 20 per cent to South Asia and less than 10 per cent to sub-Saharan Africa (Ryrie 1995: 12). By 2011, 38 per cent of ODA went to Africa, 27 per cent to Asia, 8 per cent to the Americas and the rest to other regions (OECD Development Aid at a Glance 2013: 3). There has also been a marked rise in the share of ODA going to least developed and low income countries (LDCs and LICs) since 2005, from 31 per cent in 2005 to 49 per cent in 2011, and a corresponding fall in aid to middle income countries (MICs) from 61 per cent to 43 per cent, although this trend may not continue (United Nations Economic and Social Council 2012: 13; OECD Development Aid at a Glance 2013: 2).

Shifts have also occurred in the sectoral distribution of aid. In the early period there was a very strong emphasis on economic

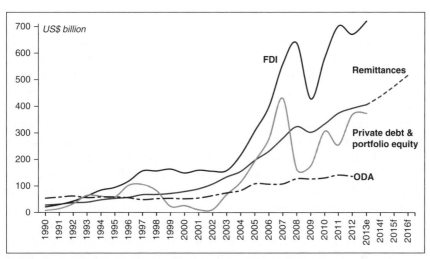

Source: The World Bank, *Migration and Development Brief* 22, 11 April 2014, p. 3.

Figure 6.1   *Aid in relation to other external finance and remittances to developing countries*

infrastructure development, but the largest allocation is now to social infrastructure (over 40 per cent) (OECD 2014b). Over the decade from 2000, some $69 billion of new bilateral aid was spent on debt relief (Tomlinson 2012: 124) and an increased amount of aid, averaging around 8 per cent annually, is now spent on emergency humanitarian assistance. ODA provided to and through NGOs has risen from less than 5 per cent of official development assistance in the mid-2000s to around 14 per cent since 2009 (OECD DAC 2006 and 2007, OECD 2013b: 5).

Currently around 60 per cent of aid is provided through bilateral channels; that is, directly from one country to another. The remainder, apart from the small but growing amount through NGOs, is provided through multilateral organizations, which include the various specialized UN agencies such as the World Food Programme, UNICEF and the United Nations Development Programme. The international financial institutions, especially the concessional arms of the World Bank and the various regional development banks, are also included. Some new multilateral funds, such as the Global Fund to fight AIDS, tuberculosis and malaria, have earned growing support (United Nations Economic and Social Council 2012: 12).

Aid from emerging donors is not included in the DAC calculations of ODA, and issues arise about the definitions and transparency of such aid; only some of these donors report their aid to the DAC (OECD 2013a). What is clear is that they tend to emphasize the productive sectors of the economy more than social sectors in their assistance (Kragelund 2008). But these 'rising powers' from the South are clearly becoming a much stronger force in development thinking, challenging the traditional approaches of OECD DAC donors, and strengthening South–South co-operation for development (Institute of Development Studies 2013).

However, beyond ODA and non-DAC aid from 'emerging donors', aid from all private sources (such as NGOs, religious groups and private philanthropy) is growing fast and attracting more scholarly attention (Kharas 2009, 2012; Hudson Institute 2010, 2013; Davis and Dadush 2010). Indeed, research is highlighting the overall fragmentation of aid, resulting from the new range of donors and the proliferation of institutions within donor countries that now provide aid.

Also attracting more attention is the development value of remittances sent by developing country workers overseas back to their home countries. These have grown rapidly to become the second largest source of private financial flows for developing countries (Hudson Institute 2013: 25). At $410 billion in 2013, they far exceed ODA.

The largest recipients are India, China, the Philippines, Mexico, Nigeria and Egypt but in a number of countries remittances, though smaller, may account for between 24 and 48 per cent of GDP. These include Tajikistan, Kyrgyz Republic, Lesotho, Nepal and Moldova (World Bank 2013). Whilst there has been some debate about their development value, Gupta et al. (2009) found that in Africa remittances contribute directly to poverty reduction and financial development. They also provide valuable foreign exchange. But Mughal (2013) cautions about the inflationary and other impacts remittances can have.

What has shaped levels and distribution of aid?

There can be no doubt that colonial histories, foreign policy and trade objectives have had a major influence on both the levels and distribution of aid. thereby reducing aid's effectiveness in poverty reduction (World Bank 2002c: 5; Human Rights Watch 2002). This has been particularly the case for the US and a number of larger aid donors (by volume) such as France. Tarp (2000) shows that aid from smaller countries, such as Sweden, has been better shaped by the needs of recipient countries than that of other, larger donors.

While Cold War objectives often shaped aid in the earlier years, since 9/11 new foreign policy objectives have asserted themselves in aid agendas – signalled in December 2001, when the USA pledged Pakistan over US$1 billion in debt forgiveness, investment, trade and refugee relief (Jefferys 2002: 3). This was clearly associated with the US government's 'war on terror' policy (Human Rights Watch 2002) and its need to maintain a close alliance with Pakistan because of its engagement in neighbouring Afghanistan. OECD countries have since seen development co-operation as a useful tool in their fight against terrorism. Following 2001, Afghanistan, Pakistan and Iraq received 17 per cent of all new aid committed from 2000 to 2008 (Tomlinson 2010: 123, 160), and Afghanistan remained the recipient of the largest amount of aid in 2011 (OECD Development Aid at a Glance 2013: 2).

A major commercial aspect of aid has been the fact that over decades much of it has been 'tied' to developed country providers. Such involvement of private sector companies based in donor countries increases costs to developing countries by up to 60 per cent (United Nations Economic and Social Council 2012: 17). Tying may require firms who manage projects to be registered in the donor country, procure commodities, such as food aid, from donor sources, and place donor country expatriates in developing countries as technical advisers or link tertiary education places to universities in donor countries (Simons et al. 1997: 130–3, 187; Randel, German and Ewing 2002: 14–15; Padilla and Tomlinson 2006: 14; OECD DAC 2007).

Overall, some progress has been made since 2000 in untying aid but 17 per cent of ODA remains tied (Clay, Geddes and Natali 2009; UN Economic and Social Council 2012: 17). Even when aid is untied it seems donor country-based companies still gain a high percentage of aid contracts (Tomlinson 2010: 176).

Aid has also been shaped by new agendas, and, since the 1990s, influenced by the view that it is only effective where 'good policies' are in place. This really means policies consistent with the so-called 'Washington Consensus', or the particular brand of neoliberalism being promoted by Anglophone countries in the donor community. At the same time, donor governments' commitment to the 1996 DAC goals and the Year 2000 MDGs (to halve the proportion of people living in poverty and their associated social goals) has influenced donors to re-assess where aid was going, what effect it was having and whether the goals could be reached. The focus turned to assisting those countries where poverty is significant but where 'good governance' policies were in place (Dollar and Levine 2006). Yet despite aid growth, there was initially not a real shift to the MDG sectors of education, health, food security and poverty reduction; rather foreign policy and debt reduction drove the direction of new aid spending. However, the focus on MDGs has gradually improved (Tomlinson 2012: 125).

What has aid been like?

Though the goals of aid have remained much the same, the ways donors aim to achieve them have altered considerably over the years, with project aid the favoured early approach and an array of other mechanisms, among them technical assistance, NGOs and emergency assistance subsequently utilized (Mosley and Eeckhout 2000: 131).

In the early 1970s the 'basic needs' approach extended the 'development project' into new areas, such as agricultural development, health and education. A trend towards large 'integrated rural development projects' greatly increased the complexity of development tasks. The weaknesses and problems that such projects faced led to greater focus on government policy environments as a key factor in successful development.

At the end of the 1970s, Keynesian economic policies gave way to neoclassicism and a focus on macroeconomics. Then the debt defaults and economic recession at the beginning of the 1980s led to a major rethink in development circles. An aid mechanism was needed which could quickly help stabilize the economies of deeply indebted poor countries, where private sector investment had dried up. Thus began lending and balance of payments support that was predicated on IMF-directed 'structural adjustment' programmes, requiring recipient countries to liberalize and deregulate their economies. By the mid-1990s, the World Bank had also moved towards emphasizing structural adjustment packages, which became 'about a third of World Bank lending and just under 20 per cent of the bilateral aid budgets of the OECD countries' (Mosley and Eeckhout 2000: 136–7); many countries were still experiencing those processes in 2010.

Though countries undergoing structural adjustment found that their export trade improved, investment deteriorated, poverty increased as services reduced and the impacts on growth were unconvincing (Moseley and Eeckhout 2000: 136–9). Many developing countries became more vulnerable to negative influences on the trading environment and in a bid to compete, developing countries tended to bargain each other downwards, which had a negative impact on levels and distribution of income (Morrissey 2000).

Thus the next phase was to shift to other mechanisms, notably through the private sector and, on a much smaller scale, through NGOs. For example, there were significant increases in World Bank funds to the International Finance Corporation which supports private sector development in the developing world (Ryrie 1995: 121–61). The OECD emphasizes that, in general, 'countries which have used market opportunities and developed dynamic private sectors have fared better than those that have not' (OECD 1989: 78–9). It urged donor governments to assist developing countries to meet the preconditions for developing a vibrant private sector (OECD 1989). The abolition of monopolies, strengthening competition, an appropriate regulatory environment, efficient banking, transport and communication facilities were among these requirements which aid began to address.

While donor countries are changing the mechanisms through which aid is provided to try to make it more effective, the problem of 'donor proliferation' remains significant (Acharya, de Lima and Moore 2004; Frot and Santiso 2010; AusAID 2010a). Fengler and Kharas observe that 'growth in aid agencies has proceeded as fast as growth in aid dollars' (2010: 6). They have documented 233 multilateral aid agencies and 56 donor governments with official aid agencies, some with several agencies which are involved in development programmes. Add to this a vast array of private funding agencies and the complexity of the aid system becomes apparent.

In light of this, a renewed emphasis on greater donor co-ordination and support for developing country planning has flowed from earlier initiatives by the World Bank to promote the Comprehensive Development Frameworks (CDFs) and Poverty Reduction Strategy Plans (PRSPs) at national level. These frameworks were intended to be participatory exercises to assist governments to focus on policies and programmes to reduce poverty. Their success appears to have been limited, due in part at least to a failure to appreciate the political power dynamics operating in recipient countries (Booth 2011). It is within this context that greater support for SWAPs and budget support emerged. Sector-wide approaches (SWAPs) enabled donor funds to be co-ordinated and integrated into developing country sectoral budgets (e.g. health). However, the weakness of donor co-ordination and the extent of donor intervention means that such strategies have been far from ideal in giving recipient governments a greater chance to drive development (Randel, German and Ewing 2002: 17; Cassity 2010).

The 2005 *Paris Declaration on Aid Effectiveness*, developed through the OECD DAC, aimed to further reform aid management. Its key principles were: developing country ownership of development policies, strategies and co-ordination; alignment of donor aid flows with national development strategies, with a single related framework of conditions or success indicators; greater harmonization of donor approaches to aid management; a focus on results; and mutual accountability for development performance. The *Accra Agenda for Action* adopted in 2008 extends the attempt to improve aid, through commitments relating to predictability of aid, use of country rather than donor systems as a first option for aid delivery, changing conditionality away from donor prescriptions to recipient country development objectives, and further untying of aid (OECD DCD-DAC n.d.). The most recent in this series of processes for improving aid effectiveness was the Busan High Level Forum held in South Korea in 2011. Much more inclusive of new donors and civil society, this meeting turned its focus to the broader question of *development* effectiveness, seeing aid effectiveness as merely one component of this wider goal. The meeting recognized that development occurs through a complex mix of FDI, remittances, domestic resources and private loans as well as aid. It urged that aid should play a catalytic role rather than be the major source of development finance. Nevertheless, it added to the Paris principles new principles of 'inclusive partnership' and 'transparency', and emphasized the need for coherence between aid and other policies such as trade and migration if development outcomes are to be achieved (Kim and Lee 2013; 4HLF 2011).

However, aid 'fragmentation' remains a major problem, with a number of obvious costs (Frot and Santiso 2010). Cambodia receives over 400 donor missions each year 'and government officials report spending 50 percent of their time meeting and reporting to donors' (Fengler and Kharas 2010: 15). And while the number of aid projects has dramatically increased, their average size has significantly reduced (Fengler and Kharas 2010; Frot and Santiso 2010).

Volatility of aid levels is a further problem particularly in countries in which political and security considerations play a large part in donor aid flows (Fengler and Kharas 2010: 17–19) or when 'the number of donors to a country is small, and the aid budget is heavily concentrated within the forms of aid which are "reactive" to the recipient country's predicament, such as food aid, emergency aid, and program budget support aid' (Bulír, Gelb, and Mosley 2008: 2046). Strategies which reduce aid fragmentation and volatility, while retaining some flexibility are seen as important for effective aid, along with approaches which align better with developing country budgets and priorities (Moon and Mills 2010).

While these aid effectiveness initiatives have been underway, the number and scale of natural disasters and complex humanitarian emergencies drove a considerable expansion of emergency relief funding during the 1990s and the 2000s. The Asian tsunami in 2005 (Global Humanitarian Initiative 2010; OECD Development Aid at a Glance 2013: 2) and the enormous Syrian crisis as well as major disasters in the Philippines in 2012 and 2013 and chronic situations in Somalia, Sudan and South Sudan have driven these increases (Global Humanitarian Assistance 2013: 8, 15). OECD aid for emergencies, around US$1 billion in 1990 (German and Randel 2002: 151) had reached some US$12 billion by 2008, or 12 per cent of all aid (excluding debt relief); it had dropped back to around 8 per cent of ODA by 2012 (Global Humanitarian Initiative 2010: 5, Global Humanitarian Assistance 2013). However, as Jefferys (2002: 2) shows, emergency humanitarian aid is rarely dispersed according to need; rather it depends on the geopolitical interests of donors and, often as a result, the media profile of particular humanitarian situations. For example, the enormous response to the 2005 Asian tsunami which led to US$7,100 being available for every person affected contrasts starkly with the US$3 per head available for those affected by the Bangladesh floods of the same year (Tsunami Evaluation Coalition 2006).

Many of the recipient countries of humanitarian assistance are conflict-affected states, and the ability of local and international humanitarian players to provide aid 'in a neutral, impartial and independent way' (DARA 2010: 9) and maintain humanitarian space in such locations has become more difficult as military forces have become more involved in aid activities (Global Humanitarian Initiative 2010: 9). The increasing politicization and 'securitization' (i.e. the use of aid to assure donor security) of aid risks distorting aid agendas and priorities and challenging humanitarian workers' ability to meet the needs of affected populations (Collinson, Elhawary and Muggah 2010; DARA 2010; Global Humanitarian Initiative 2010; Hameiri 2008; Jacoby and James 2010; Save the Children 2010).

Other major changes in aid in more recent decades have reflected greater attention to social and environmental aspects of development. The struggle for aid to address gender equity has been a long, hard one (see Chapter 10) and the translation of gender policies into effective practice is difficult. Official donors have also adopted NGO language about participation, empowerment and community development, but rarely has the full import of these approaches been implemented. Genuinely inclusive and participatory aid requires major shifts in processes, attitudes and behaviours to really transform power relationships at organizational and interpersonal levels (Groves and Hinton 2004; Hickey and Mohan 2005). Efforts to bring a rights-based approach to development co-operation have struggled to gain legitimacy and enjoy practical application. In addition, changing global circumstances have brought a range of other aid agendas to attention, among them preventing the devastating spread of HIV/AIDS, combating the trafficking of people and promoting drug control through support for farmers to convert from growing opium to other crops.

Another area in which it has been difficult to make progress is the environmental sustainability of aid efforts, despite the attention brought to these issues since the Rio Earth Summit in 1990. Climate change funding has been growing, however, with total OECD bilateral aid for climate change amounting to 16 per cent of total ODA between 2010 and 2012. The impact of climate change, particularly on agricultural and food production, and the likelihood of more frequent extreme weather events in developing countries, has renewed attention to the link between environmental factors and development. In particular, debate is around how climate change mitigation and adaptation measures should be financed and what the balance should be between these two objectives (Ayers and Huq 2009; Macintosh 2010; Porter et al. 2008; Tomlinson 2010, OECD 2014c). To date, the Global Environment Facility (GEF) and the World Bank through its Clean Energy Investment Framework (CEIF) (Porter et al 2008: 13–14), have been important multilateral funds. However, the Bank has been roundly criticized as its funding for renewable energy and energy-efficiency projects pales to insignificance in the face of its continuing funding for power generation projects through fossil fuel development and large dams (Porter et al. 2008: 17).

A further initiative is the UN's Collaborative Programme on Reducing Emissions from Deforestation and Forest Degradation in Developing Countries (UN-REDD). This is a carbon-offset scheme whereby carbon emitters (whether corporations or governments) purchase carbon credits generated through the maintenance of carbon-storing forests in developing countries (Considine 2010: 1). However, many risks have been highlighted which could jeopardize the extent to which such a scheme (or similar others) would significantly reduce deforestation or degradation and associated carbon emissions (Macintosh 2010). Furthermore, there is concern that climate change expenditure does not divert ODA away from other important development priorities facing poor people who are not responsible for greenhouse gas emissions (Tomlinson 2010: 172–5).

How effective has aid been?

Clearly the stated purposes of aid are related to economic growth, the reduction of poverty and the alleviation of suffering. Aid is thus, correctly, assessed against such criteria. Certainly the number of people living in poverty has dropped considerably over the last three decades, and a significant number of previously poor countries have experienced such growth (UNDP 2013; Kharas 2012) that they are now classified as middle income countries, often no longer recipients of aid; but we cannot attribute this to aid alone. Over the years, aid's success may not have been optimal, partly because aid has been badly distorted by other agendas. Despite this, Alvi and Senbeta conclude that aid has had a 'significant poverty-reducing effect' (2012: 1).

One approach to assessing the effectiveness of aid is to examine evaluations of aid programmes. The World Bank published a review of evaluations of development assistance in 1995 that drew five conclusions about the conditions that were necessary to make aid effective. These included ownership by the government and participation of affected people; 'good governance'; sound policies and good public sector management; close co-ordination by donors; and donors' own practices focusing less on inputs and more on effects of development (World Bank 1995).

The emphasis on sound policies reinforced a continuing focus on conditionalities associated with World Bank and IMF loans provided for debt relief programmes. Such numerous conditionalities attracted considerable criticism. Notably, many related to controversial privatizations of essential services, such as energy or water supply; trade liberalization measures; and various measures unrelated to poverty reduction priorities (Kovach and Lansman 2006).

Much of the debate about the effectiveness of aid has been at a macro level, focused on the extent to which aid has contributed to growth in developing countries. A 1997 Burnside and Dollar study was particularly influential in donor circles. It concluded that 'aid has a positive impact on growth in a good policy environment' (cited in Hansen and Tarp 2000: 116). This fed into the World Bank's own study authored by Dollar, *Assessing Aid,* in 1998. Such work shaped a great deal of aid thinking since the late 1990s in that a strong emphasis was placed on countries having sound policies in place (later greater attention was paid to institutions rather than policies) and aid was directed where such conditions existed (Battaile 2002: 2–3). However, other work challenged Dollar and Burnside's argument, suggesting that where aid was not excessively high in relation to GDP, it had a good effect on growth even when policies were poor (Hadjimichael 1996, Hansen and Tarp 2000: 45, 118).

Similarly, McGillivray et al. (2006), reviewing 50 years of studies of aid effectiveness, found that, in the absence of aid, growth would be lower but they found no consistency in the results about the policy contexts in which aid works. However, there appears to be some evidence that there can be decreasing returns to higher levels of aid within countries, that relatively stable levels of aid, rather than volatility, increase effectiveness; that aid has greater impact on growth in countries outside the tropical zones, and that aid is only effective when the country is politically stable and its benefits are greater if a country is more democratic. McGillivray et al. also note that the evidence suggests 'that aid clearly worked at the micro level' (2006: 1045) in contrast to the debate about its macro outcomes.

The neoliberal policies associated with reducing the scope of the state and enhancing the scope of the market have now been re-assessed. Empirical evidence demonstrated that during the period of neoliberalism overall economic growth had been slower than in earlier decades, the gap between the rich and poor countries widened and Africa in particular, which had been the subject of many of the 'Washington Consensus' prescriptions, performed poorly. East Asian countries, on the other hand, did well but their success, initially used to bolster arguments in favour of export-led growth, was reinterpreted to recognize that interventionist policies and appropriate mix of state and market mechanisms had led to their achievements (Onis and Senses 2005).

The emerging 'Post-Washington Consensus' articulated by Onis and Senses (2005), and supported by economists such as Joseph Stiglitz

(2002), suggests that actions by states can improve the functioning of the market, but at the same time the market can improve the functioning of states. The key point is that it is competition between public and private services, rather than privatization itself, which may drive efficiencies. Other important roles for the state include investment in education and infrastructure, support for dissemination of new technologies, and pro-poor interventions (Onis and Senses 2005: 274–5). Thus recent thinking about development focuses on the performance of both the state and market simultaneously, 'institution-building and democratic governance' and 'the importance of additional policies to deal with key social problems such as pervasive unemployment, poverty and inequality' (Onis and Senses 2005: 277). Indeed, Booth's research tracking development of Asian and African countries over 50 years highlights the importance of policies: the more successful Asian countries had all 'adopted policies which combined (i) macro-economic balance, (ii) rural-biased public investment and (iii) economic freedom for smallholders', whereas none of the African countries had done so (Booth 2011: s8). In particular Booth highlights the importance of agricultural policies, a point emphasized as far back as the late 1970s.

One of the most recent consequences of the intense debate about the effectiveness of aid and accountability of donors is the call for greater transparency about where aid goes and what it does. An aid transparency index ranked 67 donors for the transparency of the information about their aid, with four ranked as 'very good' and 23 as 'very poor' in 2013 (Publish What You Fund 2013). Another response, particularly among civil society organizations, has been the development of charters and standards, initially for humanitarian response, but now covering development work too (The Sphere Project 2004; INGO Accountability Charter 2006; HAP International 2008). However, as Eyben (2008) points out, it is important to reflect on the *processes* of mutual accountability, address the power imbalances and engage in relational dialogue which respects diversity of views and allows for adaptive learning if aid is to become more effective. Indeed Ramalingham (2013) argues that linear models on which aid has historically been designed need to be abandoned, as social and economic change is not linear. Rather we should better appreciate open, dynamic, non-linear systems. Aid design needs to allow for learning and adaptation, so that change emerges through self-organization and the interactions of a multitude of different agents. Our emphasis should thus be on social relations and networks that will foster emergent change. Leach et al. (2007) and Hummelbrunner and Jones (2013) indicate how this might be undertaken in a range of development contexts.

Criticisms of aid

Yet, even as calls for an emphasis on poverty reduction and recognition of the failings of the Washington Consensus gained some traction, criticisms remained about the power inequalities implicit in the aid system, and indeed in the wider global political and economic arrangements which keep poor countries poor.

For example, NGOs argued that as a result of the 'Post-Washington Consensus', the 'governance' agenda was being distorted to allow the powerful international financial institutions further opportunities to impose their policy agendas on developing countries, creating unrealistic and non-democratic demands on them for major public sector reform (Randel, German and Ewing 2004). NGOs argued for a greater focus on democratic accountability mechanisms and a human-rights based approach to development to enable poor people to act as citizens, rather than be the objects of externally imposed policy prescriptions.

Non-government organizations had earlier made concerted criticisms of a number of major aid projects, specifically those supported by the World Bank and/or the Asian Development Bank with major environmental and social effects. These campaigns led in turn to a range of demands for changes in World Bank *policies* in areas such as information disclosure, resettlement, indigenous peoples and the environment (Fox and Brown 1998; Rumansara 1998; Siwakoti 2002).

Of course aid has always had its critics; some focus on aid as a concept which distracts from other more significant reforms needed or which fails overall to deliver its claimed benefits, others on the failings of specific projects or types of aid. Quite early on, the basic human needs approach to aid was criticized for being an attempt to thwart developing country efforts to push for a new international economic order (Galtung 1997). Others asserted that development assistance was simply a new form of post-colonial control and imperialism (Weissman et al. 1975: 13), a view echoed by NGOs more recently who argued that the conditionalities increasingly associated with aid enabled donors to exert power over developing countries (Randel, German and Ewing 2002). The contrasts between the policies developing country governments were forced to pursue and those enjoyed by developed countries is the ultimate hypocrisy which NGOs decried: 'southern governments are forced to privatise and liberalise, while OECD restrictive practices, tariff and non-tariff barriers cost developing countries US$160 billion a year' (Randel, German and Ewing 2002: 5).

Hancock (1989) also criticizes official development assistance as a concept. He argues that the bureaucratic institutions that manage aid are secretive, bloated and self-serving. He is particularly critical of a host of failed and unsustainable projects which have often left governments indebted while donor country private corporations responsible for the project implementation walk away with handsome profits. Easterly reinforced arguments made earlier by Bauer (1993) that aid is no solution to raising living standards in developing countries. He argues that the problems are frequently to do with poor governance and politics, which aid cannot resolve (Easterly 2006). McGillivray et al.'s research (2006) suggests that aid has indeed contributed to growth and reducing poverty, but where politics leads to instability Bauer may be right. However Easterly's renewed critique is that despite claims that aid is supporting development of democracies, in fact since 1972, on his calculations, around a third of all aid has consistently gone to dictatorships. Whilst the end of the Cold War was expected to change this practice, Easterly argues that the 'war on terror' now helps explain its persistence, particularly in relation to Central Asia and Ethiopia (Easterly 2010). Moyo (2009) goes further to assert that because of its many problems, aid to Africa should cease and African governments should instead raise development funds from international capital markets.

Aid in an era of globalization

An original purpose of ODA was to supply capital to the developing world but since 1990 private international finance to developing countries has increased dramatically, from US$44.4 billion to around $700 billion per year, six times greater than current aid flows. As globalization proceeded, the question emerging was, 'What specific role would development assistance play in a world in which private financial flows were increasing so rapidly?' Most foreign investment was initially directed to around a dozen countries in East Asia and Latin America, notably China, with very little flowing to the LLDCs. However, since 2010 this is changing: Africa is receiving strong investment in natural resources. Cambodia, the Democratic Republic of Congo, Liberia, Mauritania, Mozambique and Uganda all had significant foreign direct investment increases in 2012, and for the first time ever developing countries received more than half of all foreign direct investment (UNCTAD 2013). But private investment has its dangers. In 1997, the financial collapse in East Asia which reverberated through Thailand, South Korea and Indonesia in particular illustrated the risks of rapid withdrawal of speculative capital and the collapse of a country's currency. Private capital sources significantly reduced after the 2007–8 global financial crisis (GFC) (Chibba 2011) and again in 2012, although in the latter case flows to developing countries were sustained while those to developed countries dropped sharply.

As noted, some three trillion dollars is traded daily on global foreign exchange markets (Seguino 2010: 190). Rapid movement of speculative capital leads to great volatility and instability in financial markets and has the capacity to suddenly plunge millions of people into poverty. So, while flows of private finance have contributed to the development of a number of nations, the problem with these flows from a human development perspective is their size and volatility and their capacity to undo development gains virtually overnight.

Of course the failure of regulation to keep pace with the high-risk new financial instruments being utilized in the financial powerhouses of the world led to the GFC in 2007–8. This crisis had considerable impacts for the developing world, coming as it did hot on the heels of a food crisis and energy crisis. The World Bank estimated that these crises pushed some 64 million people back into extreme poverty and the depth of poverty people were experiencing was also worsening (World Bank 2010a: viii; United Nations 2010b: 7). Over a billion people were food insecure according to the Food and Agriculture Organization (FAO) as a result of falling agricultural production, population increases and higher food prices; these combined with higher energy prices were creating stresses for poor people in developing countries even before the financial crisis took effect. The impacts of the GFC on developing countries were varied, through a reduction in private capital flows, particularly to emerging economies, reduced trade and lower prices, and in some cases reduced remittances (Griffith-Jones and Ocampo 2009). The type of effects varied significantly from country to country. For example, remittances to Bolivia fell 8 per cent in 2009 whereas those to Bangladesh continued to grow, albeit more slowly than before; oil exports from Sudan more than halved in 2009 compared to the previous year; Cambodia lost a third of its garment employment (te Velde 2010: vi-vii). Longer term effects of these multiple crises and the subsequent Eurozone crisis remain, although somewhat tempered by the rise of the emerging economies and their engagements with lower income countries (Griffith-Jones and Ocampo 2009).

Of course much of the theory of globalization has rested on the promotion of trade as a driver of economic growth. (Oxfam 2002). Yet trade theory is not being borne out in practice for much of the developing world, as poor people, far from benefiting from global trade expansion, are losing out. And trade restrictive practices by the developed world are frustrating developing countries' aspirations. Oxfam estimates that the total cost to developing countries of all export restrictive practices is over US$100 billion annually.

Trade liberalization has proceeded in a highly asymmetric manner. Many developing countries have been forced to liberalize, but developed countries continue to block equitable access to their markets for developing country produce. Key trade-related agreements on investments (TRIMS), services (GATS) and intellectual property rights (TRIPS) negotiated since the 1990s make illegal many of the industrial development policies used by the successful East Asian countries, which favoured national firms, and thus entrench current global wealth hierarchies (Wade 2003). The Doha Round of the World Trade Organization (WTO) negotiations, which started in 2001 and was intended as a 'development round' to assist developing countries, had until 2013 failed to reach any agreement which could address these problems. In December 2013 the WTO finally agreed some 'trade facilitation' measures by 'cutting red tape in customs procedures' which is estimated to boost annual trade by over $400 billion. However, other important agenda items such as agricultural subsidies and trade in environmental goods and services remain to be negotiated (The Economist 2013).

One consequence of globalization has been the use of aid to boost the private sector, and support the financial sector and trade liberalization policy generally (Kragh et al. 2000). Morrissey (2000: 375–91) notes that aid can be used to assist countries as they liberalize trade, or to support the development and necessary infrastructure for regional trade agreements. Kovsted says that aid is also now being used to strengthen the financial sectors of developing countries 'against excessive volatility' (Kovsted 2000: 333). Interestingly, a popular form of support has been for micro-finance institutions that meet donor interests in stimulating markets and assisting the poor simultaneously.

Both trade and private sector investment in developing countries may have superseded official development assistance in total volume but official development assistance is still required by poorer countries, even as more rapidly growing countries such as China, India, Brazil, South Africa and others assert themselves as significant players in the global economy. In particular, China is on track to become the largest economy in the world within a decade, although that does not imply that poverty, especially in its more remote areas, will have been eliminated. The challenge of the considerable poverty remaining in MICs suggests that in future concessional loans, rather than grants, may be the preferred aid strategy and greater attention will need to be paid within countries to inclusive growth and social protection policies.

It is also arguable that widening inequality and the stresses and strains of globalization have contributed to the number of intra-state conflicts in the 1990s. Gates et al. (2012) have calculated the enormous development impacts of conflict, which Collier et al. describe as 'development in reverse' (Collier et al. 2003: 13). Apart from the effect on economic growth, Gates et al. establish that: 'Conflict has clear detrimental effects on the reduction of poverty and hunger, on primary education, on the reduction of child mortality, and on access to potable water' (Gates et al. 2012: 1713). This issue has come to the fore in the context of a very changed aid environment – the global 'war on terror'. And notwithstanding the broader impact of the combined food, energy and financial crises of the late 2000s, and the Eurozone crisis of 2011–12, the use of aid in conflict or post-conflict, 'fragile state' environments is a key focus.

Conflict and state-building

The role of aid in 'fragile', 'failing' or 'failed' states, or in conflict and post-conflict environments, took on new urgency after 2001 when the South was rendered 'as a source of international crime, terrorism, and conflict that contributed to global instability' (Howell 2006: 123). Fear that failed states would be havens for terrorists galvanized donor countries, and provided a perceived legitimacy for more aggressive intervention (for example in Afghanistan and Iraq) (Duffield 2005; Natsios 2006; Hameiri 2008). Of course, the use of aid in conflict settings is not new but the scale and frequency of aid operations in association with UN-led peacekeeping has changed, and appears likely to persist in the future. Over 1.5 billion people live in fragile states and some 30 per cent of all ODA is spent in them, although how it is spent is the subject of some debate.

Many aid organizations have worked hard to ensure that the victims of conflict are assisted in ways that avoid fuelling violence through a deeper appreciation of the dynamics of conflict (Anderson 1999). Apart from the obvious role of aid in assisting refugees and displaced people affected by conflict, aid is being used in the transition to peace and democracy, for example in supporting peace talks and monitoring peace agreements, the establishment or re-establishment of the state institutions, macroeconomic assistance, the conduct of elections, supporting justice systems, landmine awareness and clearance and the restoration of livelihoods in the longer term. The complexities of providing aid in these contexts should not be underestimated, particularly where political instability persists, power shifts constantly at many levels, and the legitimacy of aid-dependent governments is challenged (Suhrke 2006).

These issues have generated considerable research and debate about strategies donors can use in situations where states are 'fragile', 'failing' or 'collapsed', terms which often obscure more than they reveal about the causes and possible solutions, and the complex processes of state formation and capacity development involved (Milliken and Krause 2002; Fritz and Menocal 2006; Nelson 2006; Rosser 2006). Post-conflict and fragile states have organized themselves into the G7+ grouping, to share experiences and discuss with donors the particular strategies necessary to strengthen them. Above all, the G7+ group emphasizes the importance of country-led development and country ownership (International Dialogue on Peacebuilding and Statebuilding, n.d., 2010).

A clearer picture is developing about the relationship between nation-building (the development of citizenship identity among a population), state-building (establishing the formal institutional structures of a state) and peace-building (building mechanisms and processes for resolving violent conflicts, engaging in reconciliation and establishing lasting peace). Lessons from research on aid for peace-building emphasize that understanding the politics matters, while not allowing aid to be politically driven. Research also stresses the need to maintain good development principles, build state capacity (including extending the reach of government to the rural areas), engage for the long term and invest considerable resources. The need to deal with the causes of conflict and conflict players is also evident (Fritz and Cammack 2006).

However, not all writers believe this rational approach will succeed. Duffield (2002) draws attention to the huge growth in the 'shadow economies' – the informal sector and the illegal cross-border networks and flows of cheap goods: entire parallel systems to the formal economy, officially unregulated but controlled by powerful players. This shadow economic network sustains warring parties in conflict zones, enabling them to conduct modern warfare. These networks and flows have also sustained people, provided them with essential goods, food, medicines and consumer items unobtainable or unaffordable through other channels. Liberal globalization, he argues, has created the spaces within which these shadow systems have flourished. Such systems, he argues, 'resist liberal norms and values' (Duffield 2002: 1059). Duffield sees the aid system, with its own public–private networks of practice, as a new approach to imposing a 'will to govern' over these 'borderlands' as part of a wider security system; for him, the rediscovery of 'development' as the solution to these borderland 'crises' fails to recognize the reality that an alternative modernity is being practised within them, one that challenges liberal systems.

Of course the contribution of aid to peace-building, however successful or otherwise it might be, is but one use of aid as a 'public good'.

A global 'public good' may be considered any issue which has trans-boundary benefits, or addresses trans-boundary problems. Among the most obvious are global challenges like climate change, deforestation, trans-boundary pollution, the spread of disease, especially HIV/AIDS, drug trade and people trafficking, and reducing population growth (Kaul 1999).

Already a significant proportion of development assistance is being spent on these types of activity. As Hopkins (2000: 436) points out, many of these global public goods initiatives provide some global regulation in the face of market failure and thus present an alternative to the neoliberal paradigm. They also, however, reflect the use of aid for purposes of self-interest to developed countries thereby increasing political support for aid. There are difficult tensions between maintaining the focus of aid on poverty reduction and building political constituencies in the developed countries for increased aid budgets. The 'global public goods' use of aid clearly creates the risk of pursuing multiple objectives that cannot all be met and which may even conflict at times.

From the Millennium Development Goals to the Sustainable Development Goals

While security concerns may have driven increases in aid in the first decade of the twenty-first century, and indeed may shape to a large degree where that aid goes, there are competing frameworks which provide an important official agenda for aid.

In the 1990s, a series of United Nations World Conferences on aspects of social development defined a set of goals for governments to achieve. This led to the adoption by the United Nations at its Millennium Summit in Year 2000 of eight Millennium Development Goals (MDGs). Significantly the MDGs included commitments by developed countries in areas such as aid, trade and debt relief, and they were backed up by a series of concrete indicators for each goal. The most recent UN reports on progress indicate that two targets were reached five years ahead of schedule – halving the proportion of people living in extreme poverty and providing more people with access to improved drinking water, while others, such as the target to reduce malnourishment, would only be reached by 2015 with urgent action. But some are far from being met, among them the primary education and maternal mortality targets (UN 2013b, 2014). Nevertheless, the World Bank projected that, 'by 2015, about 970 million people will still be living on less than $1.25 a day in countries classified as low- or middle-income in 1990.' (UN 2013b: 7). Progress has been very uneven, with much of the poverty reduction in China, while the absolute number of poor people grew in sub-Saharan Africa between 1990 and 2010 even though the rate of poverty fell and despite huge progress in some African countries towards many of the MDGs (Fukuda-Parr et al. 2013). The one MDG which showed little progress was MDG 8 concerning developed country commitments on aid and trade, although debt relief has improved.

Kabeer (2006) highlights the real challenge of meeting the MDG targets in relation to what she terms 'durable inequalities'; these result from various group identities or categorizations such as caste, ethnicity, indigeneity, or other 'devalued identities' or spatial disadvantages. The High-Level Panel established to recommend a development agenda post-2015 has taken this challenge to heart, and urges that by 2030 extreme poverty should be eradicated and the world should 'leave no-one behind' (UN 2013a: 7). The debate since 2013 has been about the post-2015 development agenda, and in particular how the international momentum can be maintained and considerably strengthened, aligned with the agenda emanating from the Rio+20 Conference towards sustainable development, and how peace-building can also be central (UN 2013a); furthermore there has been strong emphasis on greater participation of poor people, civil society and developing countries themselves in framing the goals and the processes of achieving them, on economic aspects of development and on viewing the achievement of goals more holistically, rather than in isolation from each other (Manning et al. 2013).

The 17 Sustainable Development Goals adopted by the UN General Assembly in September 2015, with their 169 specific targets, offer a new broader agenda that encompasses economic and social development, environmental sustainability and peace (United Nations 2015b). They come into effect in January 2016, are ambitiously meant to be achieved by 2030 and are intended to apply universally, that is to *all* countries. There is a strong emphasis on reducing inequality and ending discrimination within countries with perhaps less emphasis on inequality between them. Much will depend on implementation (Melamed 2015), and as Nicolai et al. (2015) have demonstrated, current rates of progress will not suffice if the targets are to be met. Much greater effort is needed, and yet if the rates of progress achieved by the top achieving countries over the last 15 years were attained by others, the goals are not impossible to reach. Financing will, however, be a key issue. Development co-operation funds alone will not suffice, and the agenda assumes partnerships with the private sector in particular as well as with civil society. How this financing will be achieved, and how much this will further stimulate the privatization of services remains to be seen (Muchhala and Sengupta 2015). Certainly countries will need to prioritize targets consistent with their contexts (Samman 2015), and no doubt better data, including disaggregated data that can assess progress on 'leaving no-one behind', will be essential (Wheeler 2015).

Importantly, the MDG targets caused donors to focus more closely on the quality and effectiveness of aid, and particularly its impact on poverty reduction (Simons et al. 1997; DFID 1997, 2000 and 2010; Ministerial Review Team 2001). The debate about poverty was further stimulated by the publication of Jeffrey Sachs's book *The End of Poverty* (2005). Sachs, an economist formerly associated with orthodox structural adjustment policies, argued that ending poverty is possible with the right investments in a range of capitals which the extreme poor usually lack (human, business, infrastructural, natural, public institutional and knowledge capital). Sachs has been criticized for simply repackaging modernization, uncritically urging the deeper integration of peripheral countries into the highly unequal global marketplace, downplaying the historically important role of states in development and failing to address ecological and other critiques (Sneyd 2006). His work certainly ignores the development critiques of other 'post-development' writers such as Escobar or Shiva (Pieterse 1998).

However, attention to 'pro-poor' or 'inclusive growth' within a modernization paradigm has certainly increased in the early twenty-first century. This type of economic growth is attained within a policy context which favours the poor and marginalized, rather than one in which growth increases relative inequality (World Bank PovertyNet 2006; World Bank 2006c; Roberts and Cave 2010; United Nations 2010b).

In the early 2000s, in the context of financing the MDGs, there was growing interest in 'innovative sources of finance' to supplement the contributions of ODA. A number of ideas were proposed, some of which could have dual benefits. These include global environmental taxes; a small tax on air travel; the financial transaction tax (also known as the Robin Hood tax) – a very small tax on all foreign exchange transactions; creation by the IMF of Special Drawing Rights, with contributions by donor countries; an International Finance Facility with funds from capital markets; increased private contributions through NGOs and private foundations; a global lottery or global prize bond; and facilitating increased remittances from emigrants to developing countries (HM Treasury 2004 and 2006; Atkinson 2006).

Whilst some of these proposals appear not to have progressed since then, others have. Most movement has been in remittances, as we have already seen, and philanthropic contributions from OECD donor countries reached an estimated \$58.9 billion in 2011. Private donations from emerging economies such as India, South Africa and Brazil appear to be another new phenomenon (Hudson Institute 2013). Financing for health aid now involves a range of innovative measures (Sandor, Scott and Benn 2009) and an air ticket levy scheme started in 2006 has contributed one billion US dollars for programmes relating to AIDS, tuberculosis and malaria (Sandor, Scott and Benn 2009:1; UNITAID 2012: 16–17). Norway is also contributing to this fund through a carbon levy. A very small financial transactions tax, already adopted in France in late 2012 with 10 per cent of the revenue going to development, is being levied by ten additional countries in the European Union in 2014, although it is not yet clear whether the revenues will be applied to development. It also seems likely that Germany will adopt such a tax, but opposition in Europe remains vocal (Griffith-Jones 2013). Some point out that that illegal money flows, or capital flight, from developing countries amount to US\$641–979 billion per year, or roughly ten times ODA, so measures to prevent such losses would be extremely valuable. The Norwegian government has begun research to address this (Boyce 2002; Government Commission on Capital Flight from Poor Countries 2009: 11).

The future of aid for development

The world in which aid is now delivered is a very different one to the period when aid began. We have seen many previously poor countries (e.g. South Korea, Nigeria, Indonesia, India) graduate to middle-income status or higher, often becoming donors themselves. In the 2000s, 27 countries graduated to middle-income status, according to World Bank classifications (Sumner 2010: 9–10), and around three-quarters of the world's poorest people now live in these countries (Sumner 2012). The 39 LICs are now home to just a quarter of the poorest people (Sumner 2010: 2). Thus thinking about poverty reduction needs to take account of this significant shift, and the focus has to move from countries to people. According to Sumner, around 23 per cent of the poor live in fragile states (both LICs and MICs), hence aid will inevitably continue to be important in such contexts. However, whether aid is the solution to poverty in MICs remains an open question, for as Sumner notes, 'one overall read of the data is that poverty is increasingly turning from an international to a national distribution issue, and that governance and domestic taxation and redistribution policies are becoming more important than ODA' (Sumner 2012: 875).

Related to this question of distribution is concern about rising global and national inequality. Watkins points out that the strong growth in Africa has not generated the gains in poverty reduction that could have been achieved were inequality not rising. He argues that 'Without rising inequality, economic growth could have lifted another 700,000 people out of poverty in Tanzania' (Watkins 2013: 3). Thus the distribution and quality of growth matters, and is a matter for policy attention. The predominance of private sector financing in development now may mean that such finance is directed less directly to poverty reduction, and more to broader growth, particularly through investments in infrastructure and resource industries. Remittances may also be less directed to poverty than to where opportunities for migration exist (Kharas 2012).

One clear direction for the future is greater South–South co-operation, which offers a different model of development co-operation from that preferred by DAC donors. Some suggest that the new model represents a shift to 'horizontal' partnerships of greater equality and mutual benefit, whereas the DAC model is characterized as consisting of more 'vertical partnerships' with their various conditions and requirements. As Gore suggests (2013: 774), these characterizations may be caricatures since recent policy shifts in some DAC donors led by conservative governments, particularly the non-European members such as Canada, New Zealand and Australia, seem to indicate a move towards a greater focus on economic co-operation for mutual benefit, and in all cases aid is shaped to at least some degree by the geo-political interests of the donor.

Aid will also be used strategically to secure access to or control of scarce natural resources as pressures on soil, land, water and marine life and forestry resources increase over the next decades. It is likely that the future will see a significant increase in conflict over the control and management of such natural resources. The role of emerging donors such as China is particularly relevant in this regard. Moore and Unsworth note that, 'The Chinese make it very clear that they want access to oil, other commodities, and markets for manufactured products' (Moore and Unsworth 2006: 711), while studiously avoiding any conditionalities or concerns about governance common to Western donors. This of course is no different to Japan's similar interest in assisting countries which can supply its raw materials. Although some legitimate concern may exist about the potential of emerging donors like China to undermine some of the well-developed DAC system principles, in many ways emerging donors are no different from DAC donors in linking their own foreign policy and trade interests to their aid programmes; Western concerns about China's role in Africa seem somewhat overstated (Kragelund 2008; Tan-Mullins, Mohan and

Power 2010) but the significance is that China is a non-OECD player that, along with India and a number of other developing countries, such as Brazil, is gaining considerable international clout. This is changing power balances in the aid system.

A continuing emphasis will be on transparency and effectiveness of aid and accountability for outcomes to the poor; there is also likely to be a more vigorous debate about the other conditions necessary, beyond aid, if the global Sustainable Development Goals are to be achieved. Pressure will continue to mount for faster and more meaningful action on trade, particularly market access for agricultural goods to Europe and the USA, without the large concessions in other areas (such as services) that the developed world is demanding of the LICs. But aid, debt and trade cannot be viewed in isolation from other signals the world sends to the warlords and dictators of the poorest, most conflict-ridden states. The secretive nature of huge deals that international resource companies strike with government elites around oil, minerals and other resources encourages corruption and enables governments to avoid accountability to their people. The demand from the West for narcotics fuels an illegal trade which also promotes corruption and violence, the consequences of which have been all too evident in countries such as Afghanistan and Myanmar. The proliferation of arms, many of which are manufactured in the developed world, fuels deadly conflicts in the South which impede development (Moore and Unsworth 2006). These wider interconnections between the rich and poor worlds need to be exposed and resolved. For example, the trade in 'conflict diamonds' and the role of trade in other minerals (such as cassiterite) and cocoa in fuelling conflict have been highlighted (Grant and Taylor 2004; Global Witness 2007; Schure 2010). Aid alone will never solve these sources of poverty, corruption and violence; only concerted and comprehensive approaches that challenge powerful forces in the developed as well as the developing world can ultimately address them.

Note

1. 'Soft' loans are loans with very low, non-commercial interest rates and are considered to be eligible as ODA.

Chapter 7

Defining and Measuring Poverty

Matthew Clarke

Introduction

Poverty and development are intrinsically linked. Indeed, it is through the process of development that poverty is reduced. Development seeks to improve the lives of the poor which are characterized by premature death, preventable illnesses, limited access to clean water and sanitation, economic insecurity and (often) illiteracy. Those who are interested in ending poverty and improving the lives of the poor must therefore be primarily interested in good development outcomes.

Poverty can be assessed in a number of ways. The most common is using income as a measure of poverty. Under this approach, it is estimated that 600 million people live in poverty on less than US$1.25 per day. However, this is not the only way to understand poverty. It is possible to define – and therefore measure – poverty in a variety of ways. This chapter will begin, therefore, with a review of how poverty is defined and describe the movement from the long-held approach of it being solely a function of income to its more recent multidimensional understanding best encapsulated by the Millennium Development Goals. An assessment of the recent changes in poverty will then be undertaken utilizing various poverty measures and data.

Defining poverty?

To better implement development interventions, it is necessary to define poverty. 'Clarification of how poverty is defined is extremely important, as different definitions imply the use of different indicators for measurement; they may lead to the identification of different individuals and groups as poor and require different policies for poverty reduction' (Ruggeri Laderchi et al. 2006: 19). Thus, before we can eradicate poverty we clearly need to know what it is we are ending and who is experiencing it as only then can we determine what sort of development interventions will be most appropriate.

As already demonstrated, the most common conceptualization of poverty is the lack of financial resources – in other words, how much money you have. If we determine that having greater than US$1.25 a day is sufficient to meet basic needs, then the world has 600 million people who do not have enough money and thus live in poverty. But there are other ways to define poverty (Ruggeri Laderchi et al. 2006). In addition to this common monetary approach, poverty can be understood in terms of capabilities, inequality and social exclusion, and participation.

Depending on which approach is used, those who are identified will differ, as will their number and most certainly so too will the development implementations needed to eradicate their poverty. It is useful to briefly discuss each approach before discussing some pertinent issues in greater detail.

Monetary poverty

Defining poverty as a lack of income is intuitively attractive. From our own personal experience, we know that money affords us the freedom to purchase both our basic needs and our desired luxuries (whether they are good for us or bad for us). In economic jargon, we increase our utility or happiness when we consume more by the simple fact that purchasing a particular commodity reveals our belief that this commodity will increase our utility (if the commodity will not make us happy, why purchase it?). Thus the more we purchase, the greater our utility or well-being. As a human characteristic is holding unlimited desires, increasing income therefore increases our ability to maximize our utility (i.e., purchase additional goods and services). Alternatively, having less money reduces our ability to consume and this lowers our utility. At the extreme, having income below a certain level means that even the basic needs (food, shelter and clothing) cannot be adequately met and an individual can be said to be experiencing poverty.

As stated, this approach to poverty is the most widely accepted within the development and economic literature. Other than its intuitive attractiveness, discussed above, this is largely due to its long-standing application, dating back as it does to the earliest work on poverty in England during the nineteenth century (see Booth 1887; Rowntree 1902). This approach is still being used as is evidenced by the 2015 headline target of the Millennium Development Goals to *reduce by half the proportion of people living on less than a dollar a day*. The basic approach to eradicating poverty is simply to increase people's income. If poverty is defined as living on less than US$1.25, then increasing income above this figure will lift an individual out of poverty.

Capabilities approach

The second approach is a more recent understanding of poverty though it has ancient roots in Aristotle and more recently in Ruskin (1862), writing in the mid-nineteenth century. Poverty in this sense is the absence of well-being. Well-being is not simply the measurement of economic possessions but the capability of utilizing them in an appropriate manner. Amartya Sen (1984, 1985a, 1987a, 1987b, 1993) provides the modern understanding and argues that well-being is not measured by the possession of a commodity, nor the utility of the commodity, but rather by what the person actually does with the commodity. Individuals who have low levels of functionings and capabilities can be said to be living in poverty.

For example, it has been found that resources are not related strongly to functionings and therefore the attainment of a high quality of life (functioning) is not dependent on high levels of material standard of living (resources) (Lovell et al. 1993). The key is the efficiency with which people use their resources (Denison 1971). Thus, efficiency or skills or social habit allow 'people with relatively low levels of resources to lead a relatively high quality of life, and vice-versa' (Travers and Richardson 1993: 48). Other issues, such as personal circumstances (including health), the environment, social climate and social state, are all contingencies that 'can lead to variation in the "conversion" of income into the capability to live a minimally acceptable life' (Sen 1999b: 360). Exactly what is a minimally acceptable life has not been adequately defined. Such an approach also allows great cross-cultural applicability in societies where monetary income is less important.

However, moving from theory to a practical application has proven difficult. In terms of empirical application, the Multi-dimensional Poverty Index (MPI) estimated by the UNDP is increasingly being applied. As with the Human Development Index (HDI), the MPI is a composite indicator made up of three dimensions: (1) education; (2) health; and (3) a living condition. More specifically it calculates the percentage of households that experience overlapping deprivations in three dimensions. These dimensions are represented by ten indicators. Education is measured by years of schooling and school attendance. Health is assessed by child mortality and nutrition, while living conditions are a combination of access to an electricity type of cooking fuel, type of flooring, access to and type of sanitation, access to and quality of water supply and assets of the household.

Policies to increase capabilities (and thus reduce poverty) would include focusing on improving people's ability to function and achieve success in life. This includes improving literacy levels and health as well as facilitating people to participate in the formal economy.

Inequality and social exclusion

Inequality is a further important aspect of poverty. The level of inequality within a society provides insights into the level of development experienced by that society including developed countries (see Piketty 2014; Stiglitz 2013). Income equality explores issues of distribution and access hidden within other discussions of poverty, such as the focus on average income or income per capita. It is possible that whilst average income, for example, is of a reasonable level a high level of disparity exists within that country due to the unequal distribution of that income. In the extreme instance, it is possible for a country of 100 people to have an average income of $1 (meaning that the total income for the whole country is also $100) but for 99 people to have zero income and the last person to have the full $100. Under these circumstances, understanding poverty requires understanding the divide between poor and non-poor.

The divide between poor and non-poor can be understood in both absolute and relative terms. The absolute gap is concerned with the actual circumstances of the poor and is best encapsulated by discussing monetary poverty. This gap is between these circumstances and what they require to achieve basic survival. Do they have enough income? Do they have enough freedom? Do they have enough access to a functioning environment? If the poor do not have 'enough', they can be said to be living in absolute poverty. The relative gap is concerned with the actual circumstances of the poor when compared with the actual circumstances of the non-poor. This gap is concerned with inequality. How much less income do the poor have than the non-poor? How much less freedom do the poor have than the non-poor? How much less access to a functioning environment do the poor have than the non-poor? If the poor have significantly less than the non-poor, a situation of inequality exists and there is relative poverty.

Within developing countries, greater emphasis is (rightly) placed on absolute poverty. In developed countries, whilst instances of absolute poverty may occur, greater emphasis is placed on relative poverty – or income inequality. For any number of reasons, there are individuals within wealthy countries that, when compared to the wider population, are excluded from experiencing the average standard of living enjoyed by the majority of that country. While they may not be considered poor when compared to those in developing countries, they are considered poor when compared to their own compatriots. Thus, this relative poverty (or income inequality) is often termed *social exclusion.*

As relativity is central to this conceptualization of poverty, empirical measurement is largely based on which experiences characterize the normal society and that which those who are excluded cannot experience. As such, those who do not have access to the Internet, enjoy a foreign holiday every two years, own a car (or the resources to own a car), have the ability to access $5,000 credit with a week's notice, etc. may be considered as being socially excluded. Such measures must naturally be constantly updated. For example, perhaps 30 years ago, the social expectation might be owning an electric fridge or having a black-and-white television, etc. As the quality of life increases in wealthy countries, so too do the expectations of what is required to be fully participating within that society. Interestingly, this is not a new idea at all and can be seen in the writings of Adam Smith, who noted the need for a day-labourer to wear a linen shirt so as not to be ashamed when in public. Determining levels of social exclusion therefore requires subjective estimates of what is required to participate in society and then (typically) household surveys to determine who is deprived of participation.

Participatory approaches

Thus far, the different concepts of poverty discussed have been determined by those other than the 'poor'. It indeed seems incongruent that, whilst the revealed preference approach (discussed above) gives primacy to the individual to determine what best enhances their own utility, such primacy is withheld when determining what poverty actually is.

Non-government organizations (NGOs) and community-based organizations (CBOs) have long understood the importance (if not necessity) of having communities participate and lead the development process. Such participation can be time-consuming and difficult to manage but sustainable outcomes require community ownership of any interventions if they are to have any lasting impact. This is because communities are experts on their own circumstances. By and large, communities know (with perhaps some guidance or facilitation) their strengths, weaknesses, resources and needs. Likewise, they are also very knowledgeable around issues of poverty. Utilizing this knowledge can provide useful insights into who the poor are and what they identify as their needs and desires for the future.

The largest international survey of this kind was undertaken by the World Bank in the late 1990s. In *Voices of the Poor,* over 40,000 people were interviewed in nearly 50 countries. Five key characteristics of poverty were found:

> First, poverty is multidimensional. Second, households are crumbling under the stresses of poverty. Third, the state has been largely ineffective in reaching the poor. Fourth, the role of NGOs in the lives of the poor is limited, and thus the poor depend primarily on their own informal networks. Finally, the social fabric, poor people's only 'insurance', is unravelling.   (Narayan-Parker and Patel 2000: 7)

Such insights would be unlikely under the previous approaches discussed because of the silence of the poor themselves within this analysis. There is great value therefore in including the poor in defining and measuring poverty. Indeed, when poverty is discussed with the poor, the actual term 'poverty' is sometimes considered inappropriate. For example, many Pacific countries prefer the term 'hardship' to poverty. Social networks often prevent hunger and outright destitution that are often associated with the term 'poverty' (IMF 2005). 'There is a social understanding in this community: nobody goes short of food; there's always somewhere to stay; the old and young are looked after; and the mentally ill, the disabled and the chronically sick are looked after' (Webber 1985: 45). Thus, the nature of poverty in the Pacific often relates to a lack of access to basic services and a lack of income-earning opportunities rather than outright destitution (AusAID 2006).

The input this participation has had on policy, though, is less clear. Whether the international finance institutions or national governments have incorporated the understandings that grew from this participatory approach is yet to be seen.

Summary of different approaches

Defining poverty is contentious. Having diverse understandings of poverty is more than semantics because it has a practical effect. If we are interested in ending poverty, we must initiate policies that will directly and positively impact on those experiencing it. This can only be done if we can measure poverty, yet measuring poverty can only occur if it is clearly defined. Thus the different definitions and approaches discussed above will result in different measures, individuals and groups being identified as living in poverty and different policies and remedies being proposed and implemented.

Each approach has its own strengths and weaknesses. The monetary approach is intuitive and easy to measure but very narrow. Policy outcomes are focused on the formal economy but this may overlook those whose participation in the formal economy is limited for any number of reasons. The capabilities approach presents a multidimensional view of poverty but there is ambiguity about exactly how to apply it empirically. The policy outcomes cut across economic, social and political spheres but, with limited resources (as a consequence of these countries being poor), the impact of such policies may be limited. Inequality provides a further level of understanding poverty but is limited to focusing on monetary measures of income. Social exclusion is more relevant to wealthier countries than developing countries. While offering flexibility, its subjective nature also hinders a policy focus. Policies that do emerge often focus on redistribution more than on wealth creation. The final approach allows the voices of those we are concerned with – the poor themselves – to be heard. But the analysis and policy reaction still lie with the experts or non-poor and thus control at this important point is removed from the poor.

Measuring poverty

Having decided how to define poverty, it is then necessary to measure it empirically before any poverty reduction strategies can be implemented. Understanding who is experiencing poverty and the extent and depth of that poverty will inform anti-poverty policies. This knowledge will ensure that the correct programmes are designed and the correct people are targeted. Measuring poverty, however, is not without difficulties. There are both technical challenges and data constraints that must be addressed.

While each of the approaches to poverty discussed above are valid, discussion on measurement issues here will focus on the most common – assessment of money, capability and inequality. Social exclusion is less relevant for developing countries and the participatory approach has not been widely adopted by the international agencies (despite the World Bank's *Voices of the Poor* report).

Assessing monetary poverty

If poverty is to be defined as a level of income necessary to provide for certain basic necessities required for living, it is obvious that the primary data need to concern household income. Interestingly though, the

World Bank prefers to use expenditure (on consumption) data rather than income data. First, expenditure on consumption more closely relates to having enough to meet basic needs as income itself is only the means of allowing consumption (income, for instance, doesn't necessarily consider access to or availability of goods and services). Secondly, consumption is more constant over time whereas income can vary seasonally or during times of harvest failure, for example. Even if income moves up and down, expenditure on consumption will remain fairly level as households either save excess income during boom times or access credit during bust times. Finally, expenditure on consumption is more accurately measured. Data collected through household surveys have shown that there is often a significant discrepancy between estimates of incomes and estimates of expenditure on consumption.

This data is usually collected from household surveys. Lengthy questionnaires focus on a number of areas but of most importance for measuring monetary poverty is total expenditure on consumption. Often these are divided into major categories composed of food and non-food items, for example:

- food
- housing
- household operation
- clothing and footwear
- transport
- tobacco and alcohol
- payment of debt
- miscellaneous goods and services.

These data are then contrasted with data collected on income, including:

- annual wage/salary income
- annual income from self-employment and related business activities
- annual income from previous job
- annual income from services
- annual income from benefits
- annual income from home production
- annual income from cash gifts
- annual income from goods received
- annual income from gambling
- annual income from rent
- annual loan income
- annual income from other sources.

Data collection is a technical (and thus expensive) exercise. Often developing countries have neither the capacity nor the resources to undertake such surveys. Lengthy periods between data collection are not uncommon within poorer countries and this constrains analysis and thus policy formulation and implementation (such data constraints will be discussed in greater detail in the next section).

Having obtained reasonable data on consumption expenditure (and income), it is possible to then estimate poverty. There are a number of ways this can be done. The first step is to define the poverty line. This is an (arbitrary) estimate of what is required for an individual to meet the most basic of necessities. It can be estimated as 50 per cent of the country's average income, or it might be an estimate of the income required to purchase the minimum calorific requirements to survive, or it simply might be a common dollar amount for all countries, such as US$1.25 a day. Having nominated the poverty line, estimates of the experiences of poverty can be made.

The most straightforward estimate is the *headcount index*. Having determined the poverty line and now knowing the different expenditure (income) levels of the population, it is a simple exercise to simply rank those expenditure (income) levels from highest to lowest and count the number of people whose expenditure (income) falls below the nominated poverty line. The headcount index is simply the number of people whose income/expenditure is below the nominated poverty line compared to the whole population. This describes the number of people within the population experiencing poverty. Thus, it possible to say 20 per cent or 30 per cent and so on of the population are below the poverty line. This can be tracked over time to determine whether the incidence of poverty is increasing or decreasing. An interesting consideration of this though is the impact of poverty when the poverty line is increased. While US$1.25 has been used as a global benchmark for some time, it is now being argued that this should be increased to US$1.75 to take into account rising costs of living. If this increase does take place, the number of people living in poverty globally increases from 600 million to nearly 900 million. This revised figure would suggest that the Millennium Development Goal of halving the proportion living in absolute poverty by 2015 has not been achieved.

Regardless of the actual figure selected to represent the poverty line, the headcount index does not provide any indication of the depth of poverty: that is, how far below the poverty line the poor are. To determine this shortfall, it is necessary to subtract the income of each individual living in poverty from the poverty line and then add all these together. This sum is then divided by the poverty line and divided again by the total population. The result of this mathematical exercise is the total income shortfall or *total poverty gap*. This is also known as the Foster–Greer–Thorbecke poverty measure (Foster et al. 1984). Knowing the poverty gap is useful as it provides information on how much extra expenditure (income) is required to lift people out of poverty.

A third poverty line measure (related to the poverty gap) is *poverty severity,* which also considers inequality amongst the poor. This exercise is the same as the poverty gap, except that once the difference between the poverty line and the income of the poor has been divided by the poverty line, this result is multiplied by itself (or squared) before it is aggregated and divided by the total population. Intuitively it makes sense that the expenditure (income) distribution is uneven throughout all levels of society and so there will be inequality even amongst those below the poverty line. This measure considers this inequality and provides information, therefore, on not only the number of people below the poverty line and by what amount they are below it but also the distribution of incomes of those below it.

These three different measures provide different descriptions of the incidence of poverty and thus provide different priorities for policymakers and practitioners interested in reducing poverty. Consideration to three aspects should be given when planning poverty reduction strategies as different interventions will impact on different groups and affect future measures of poverty in different ways.

Assessing poverty of capability

If poverty is to be considered more multidimensional than a narrowly focused monetary approach, it follows that its measurement must also consider a wider range of indicators. As discussed, for instance, the MPI has quickly become the most widely applied approach to measuring poverty and is based on three dimensions represented by ten indicators.

> The key value-added of a rigorously implemented multidimensional poverty index is that it conveys additional information not captured in single-dimensional measures on the joint distribution of disadvantage and the composition of poverty among different multiply deprived groups. It also provides a consistent account of the overall change in multidimensional poverty across time and space. To argue this is not to suggest that single-dimensional measures be abandoned; it is to suggest that they be supplemented.   (Alkire 2011: 4)

The MPI is calculated using the following formula:

$$\text{MPI} = H \times A$$

where *H* is the headcount or the percentage of people who are identified as multidimensionally poor and *A* (intensity) is the percentage of dimensions in which the average poor person is deprived. A household is deemed poor if they are deprived in at least 33 per cent of the weighted indicators.

In multidimensional as in unidimensional poverty, *H* (the headcount) is familiar, intuitive and easy to communicate. It can be compared directly with an income poverty headcount, or with the incidence of deprivations in another indicator, and also compared across time. *A* (intensity) reflects the extent of simultaneous deprivations poor people experience.

There are also limited policy implications flowing from the MPI as any concerted efforts to reduce it must be focused on its component indicators only. Whilst there are undoubtedly benefits to this, it does narrow the policy targets and moves this approach away from a multi-dimensional concept, as is its intent.

Assessing poverty through inequality

Assessing inequality is generally limited to assessing income. There has been substantial debate within the development economic literature regarding income inequality. Initially, it was considered that increasing inequality was linked to economic growth and, as economic growth occurred, income inequality would increase. At a certain point, though, this increase would cease and inequality would fall. The implication for poverty reduction is that nations would have to expect relative poverty to initially increase (as income inequality increased) following periods of economic expansion prior to this very same economic expansion bringing about poverty reduction. Thus, economic growth would cause relative poverty to increase in the short term, but assist it to fall in the long term. This phenomenon was termed 'the inverted-U curve of income inequality' as this described the shape of a graph plotting income inequality over time (see Kuznets 1955). Since this was first posited (and supported by numerous empirical studies), it has been found to be incorrect with little evidence to support changes in income inequality associated with economic growth (see Deininger and Squire 1998). For those interested in reducing poverty, such a finding is of use because it means that economic growth can be pursued as a tool for reducing poverty without any expected short-term worsening of inequality. The explanation as to how empirical 'proof' could change over time is due to the quality of the data available to test this theory. Kuznets (and others) had very limited inequality data 60 years ago and that which did exist was unreliable. Only recently has more reliable income inequality data become available.

There are three approaches commonly used to assess income inequality: size distributions, Lorenz curves and Gini coefficients. Within the size distribution approach, income data are arranged in ascending order, from least amount of income to greatest amount of income. This ordering can then be divided into different groups, the most common being quintiles or deciles. Each quintile represents 20 per cent of the population and each decile represents 10 per cent of the population. Ratios between different groups can then be made. A common ratio, the Kuznets ratio, compares the income earned by the top 20 per cent of the population to the bottom 40 per cent of the population.

The Lorenz curve plots similar information within a graph (see Figure 7.1). The number of the individuals is plotted on the horizontal axis while the percentage share of total income is plotted against the vertical axis. Importantly though, both are plotted in cumulative measures. This curve is contrasted to a 45° line originating from where the horizontal and vertical axis meet. This straight line represents a perfectly equal distribution of income. Along this line, for example, 1 per cent of the population earn 1 per cent of total income, 2 per cent of the population earn 2 per cent of total income, right through to the final point plotted which represents 100 per cent of the population earning 100 per cent of total income. The greater the 'bow' between the 45° line and the distribution curve, the greater the inequality.

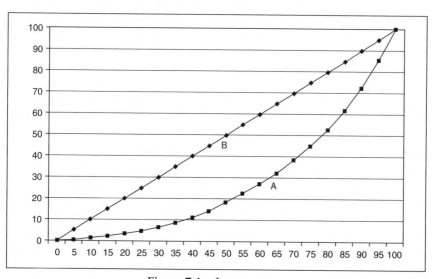

Figure 7.1   *Lorenz curve*

The Gini coefficient is an estimation of the ratio of the area between the two lines (the 45° line and the distribution curve (B) and the area lying underneath the 45° line (A). A high Gini coefficient indicates a high level of inequality within that country. Conversely, a low Gini coefficient indicates a low level of inequality. The Gini coefficient is a useful measure of inequality as changes within it can be more easily tracked over time – compared to shifts in the Lorenz curve.

The recent experience of poverty

Ending poverty is an endeavour that the international community is intent on achieving. This is evidenced by the universal adoption of the Millennium Development Goals and the United Nation's Decade(s) for the Eradication of Poverty (1997–2006 and 2008–17). Perhaps most importantly the issue of poverty and its eradication has assumed and sustained a prominence that will assist in increasing the visibility of the poor. This section will review poverty levels and trends focusing on the monetary, capabilities and inequality approaches to poverty.

Monetary approach

The first MDG is to *eradicate extreme poverty and hunger*. Success against this Goal is to be assessed against the target of *reducing by half the proportion of people living on less than a dollar a day by 2015*. At the global level, it is probable that this target will be achieved but, when considered at the national level, there are many countries that will fail to achieve this target. While current data is scarce, taking the most recent household survey data for 119 countries (which account for 95 per cent of the developing world's population), Chandy and Gertz (2011) used historical and forecast estimates of consumption growth per capita to estimate poverty levels. Their results suggest that global poverty – using the monetary approach based on $1.25 per day – would have fallen from more than 1.3 billion people in 2005 to less than then 600 million by 2015.

While poverty remains clearly a South Asian and sub-Saharan-African phenomenon, unlike in past decades when poverty reduced in one region but grew in another region, poverty reduction in the first decade of the twenty-first century occurred across all regions. This is particularly good news for sub-Saharan Africa as, for the first time, its poverty rate has fallen below 50 per cent and was projected to fall below 40 per cent by 2015. However, as poverty is falling more quickly elsewhere, the percentage of the world's poor living in Africa will actually increase from nearly 30 per cent to 60 per cent. Poverty in this sense will therefore be seen increasingly as an African problem. While in the past India had the largest number of the world's poor, it is expected that this dubious honour will fall to Nigeria.

It is of course the world's two populous nations, though, that have driven down the global poverty trends. China and India have been responsible for 75 per cent of the fall in people living in poverty across the globe. More than 350 million Indians have been lifted out of poverty over the past decade and China may effectively eliminate its own absolute poverty by 2015.

The robustness of this poverty reduction is an important concern. While it is undoubtedly positive that people are being lifted out of poverty, it is also important that this improvement is not subject to shocks. In this regard, it is interesting to consider the 2008 global food crisis and the 2007–8 global financial crisis. Both these economic shocks had dramatic consequences around the world.

A lack of affordable food affects every aspect of a country's development. Rising costs of food undermine the purchasing power of poor people and exacerbate the tragedy that is global hunger and malnutrition. It fuels civil unrest and further limits access to basic human rights. Food prices increased dramatically in the first half of 2008, resulting in a global food crisis. While price increases differed between countries, the price of many food staples, such as rice, corn and maize, more than doubled in a matter of months. The consequences of these price increases were immediate. The global food crisis created a host of humanitarian, human rights, socio-economic, environmental, developmental, political and security-related challenges. Approximately 100 million people fell below the poverty line as a direct result of these price increases (Ivanic and Martin 2008). Food riots erupted in many cities and regional centres in all parts of the world as people protested and sought support from their governments.

Further exacerbating the global food crisis was the global financial crisis (GFC). The major impact of the GFC has been a contraction of economic activity worldwide. Indeed, in the latter half of 2008, global economic growth fell sharply, with major developed countries falling into recession. The GFC led to falling asset values, reduced consumer demand and credit constraints in a reinforcing cycle of ongoing economic uncertainty. Many developed countries, including the UK, US, the Eurozone and Japan entered into recession over this period. Moreover, the contraction of global economic activity also directly affected the world's poor, with the World Bank (2010a) estimating 64 million people falling back under the poverty line.

While both these events directly resulted in some gains in poverty reduction being lost, it is important to note that they have not had lasting consequences for overall poverty reduction trends. They do make clear, though, that poverty as defined and measured through the monetary approach does suffer a weakness of not adequately taking into account the vulnerability of people who are 'just' above the poverty line falling 'back' because of external economic shocks.

Capabilities approach

If poverty is considered more multidimensional than that assessed within the monetary approach, it follows necessarily that the indicators of this concept must also be multidimensional. Empirical measures of the capabilities approach are less common in the literature

However, it is the MPI that is perhaps the most widely operationalized measure of this capabilities-based approach to poverty. The 2013 MPI has been estimated for 104 countries with a total population that equates to 78 per cent of the global population. However, the data requirements needed, as limited as they are, render any analysis of changes in this measure over time extremely difficult. For example, data to estimate the 2013 MPI was based on a range of surveys that occurred between 2002 and 2011. Thus some of the data being included in this composite indicator is more than a decade old. This makes it very difficult to not only compare countries' performance but to also assess improvements (or deteriorations) over time. This is one of the weaknesses of this approach. The heavy data requirements that are frequently unable to be met with recent data from developing countries often make the robustness of the resultant index somewhat questionable. That said, it is clear that the African continent is home to more countries with higher levels of poverty measured by the MPI than any other region.

Inequality approach

Due to the nature of data required to estimate the Gini coefficient (i.e. individual or household income levels normally collected through household surveys), aggregated regional estimates of inequality are of limited value. Therefore, it is difficult to determine whether income inequality for one region or another has increased or decreased over time. It is preferable to undertake this analysis on a country-by-country basis. The World Institute of Development Economic Research located within the United Nations University has the most comprehensive dataset on income inequality. As with other measures of poverty, time lags in collecting primary data and estimation mean that the most recent data can be more than five years out of date.

There is a distinct lack of accurate and comparable data on inequality for most developing nations. This makes it difficult to track movements of inequality over time or compare inequality meaningfully between countries.

Summary

It may be said that there is a poverty of data around poverty. It is very difficult to develop appropriate poverty interventions when basic data, such as the number of people living on less than a dollar a day, do not exist. Of course, the collection of data is an expensive exercise and removes potential resources from actual poverty alleviation programmes. However, such expenditure can be justified in terms of monitoring and evaluation. Ending poverty requires knowledge of the past as well as of current situations in order to determine what interventions are needed and whether these interventions have been successful.

Conclusion

Ending poverty is clearly not an easy task. Indeed, that the international community can only seek to reduce by *half* the proportion of people living on less than a dollar a day suggests that complete eradication is perhaps impossible. If this MDG target is achieved, more than 600 million people will still be in poverty and a further billion more living just above this level of miserable existence.

How then to proceed? Poverty is experienced by individuals. While countries may be considered poor (or wealthy), it is women, men and children who experience the harsh realities of poverty. Interventions intended to reduce poverty must be cognisant that the primary target must be individuals. However, that is not to say that all policies must be micro in nature. Pro-poor activities can be micro or macro in nature. It is therefore valuable to seek to increase foreign investment, increase trade and undertake infrastructure projects as these activities can also improve the lives of the poor by providing greater employment opportunities and access to markets. Any success in ending poverty is thus predicated on benefits flowing primarily to the poor.

Regardless of how it is conceptualized, the reality of poverty should not be romanticized. It is harsh and inhumane. Children die unnecessarily, hunger is constant and basic needs go unmet. Those experiencing poverty lack freedom to determine their own lives and once in poverty it is often difficult for them to escape. If poverty is to end, it will require co-operation and goodwill at the international, national and local level. The international community has pledged to reduce poverty by half before 2015. Indeed, all regions have made improvements, though the driving force behind the significant reduction in global poverty levels is largely through the achievements in China and India. Sufficient resources exist at the international level to end poverty if wealthy countries meet their commitments of providing just under 1 per cent of their GNP in overseas aid.

Interventions to end poverty rely on understanding the experience of poverty. It must be defined and measured before appropriate interventions can be planned and implemented. It is precisely poverty's overwhelming nature that requires every effort to be made in order to eradicate it.

Chapter 8

Community Development

Damien Kingsbury

Development is intended to improve the lives of people so there is, then, a strong and logical case for development starting with people. Community development focuses on development projects as they directly relate to and include the participation of local, usually rural or small urban, communities. In particular, it addresses issues that are of immediate concern to those communities that are intended to have the capacity to produce continuing localized results. It also reflects the notion that development, broadly conceived, is about the enhancement of the potential of people to emancipate themselves (see Sen 1999a). That is, it is intended to give them greater capacity to exercise control over their own lives (see Tesoriero 2010: 65). This is usually referred to as 'empowerment'.

This 'empowerment' approach to development 'places the emphasis on autonomy in the decision-making of territorially organized communities, local self-reliance, direct and inclusive (participatory) democracy, and experiential social learning' (Friedman 1992: vii). However, like many other good ideas that have been encapsulated in a single word or phrase, 'empowerment' has been used so widely and by so many people and organizations for so many different purposes that it has started to lose meaning: '[I]n some countries, governments talk glibly of empowerment of the poor in their development plans, having stripped the term of any real meaning' (Gardner and Lewis 1996: 118).

As will be discussed in this chapter, one cannot 'empower' another; 'empowerment' must come from within. This chapter addresses some of the main issues in community development, looking at both the strengths and weaknesses of attempts to assist communities to empower themselves. The experience of community development has in many cases been positive but, as with the rest of the development process, it has not been immune to problems.

Like all ideas about development, what community development, or empowerment, means is contested, reflecting the range of interests that come into play when theory meets practice. There are two primary foci for community development, the first being encapsulated in the idea that it is about development of and for the 'community', or what has been referred to as 'community driven development' (CDD) (see World Bank 2014a), and the second is about development via community decision-making processes or participation (e.g. see Nelson and Wright 1995). The 'community', in this instance, is usually defined as the local group or otherwise small groups of people, usually living in relative isolation, that are characterized by face-to-face relationships. In this, the 'community' size is determined by the needs of co-operation and either consensus or an agreed regulated process of decision-making. On this basis, the size of a viable community can vary from place to place, and is not able to be universally determined (Hodge 1970: 68). As a consequence, community development programmes must involve a capacity for modification according to local circumstances, according to locally determined criteria of what constitutes the community, and to suit local needs. What should be noted is that 'internal' approaches to community development reflect a fundamental reorientation of development towards a grass-roots or localized process and outcomes, usually implying local participation in the process.

> Community participation serves immediate instrumental goals such as the identification of felt needs as well as the mobilization of local resources. But it also promotes broader social development ideals: by participating fully in decision-making for social development, ordinary people experience fulfilment which contributes to a heightened sense of community and a strengthening of community bonds. (Midgley 1986: 9)

This is in contrast to external, macro-level or infrastructure development projects that only indirectly affect people at the local level, and in which local communities have very little, if any, say, usually little or no participation, and almost always no control.

Bottom-up versus top-down

Community development processes have been shown, in a number of cases, to produce real, tangible and appropriate benefits for local people, as well as providing a greater sense of self-worth and empowerment. Such forms of development also work within and help preserve aspects of local culture that give meaning to community life and which assist in maintaining and enhancing the social cohesion that is necessary when engaging in a process of change.

While large-scale and state-originated development projects can address macroeconomic or infrastructure requirements that can determine the parameters for more localized development, it is common for such 'top-down' projects and decision-making to fail to deliver tangible benefits to many people, including the most marginalized. Many large-scale projects not only fail but are not designed to meet the needs and preferences of people at the local level, are often not based on local experience and are frequently unsustainable once the aid provider has left. State-run projects may similarly have a focus which is not intended for the communities most directly affected. The adoption of 'bottom-up' or 'flat' local decision-making structures is thus seen as more responsive in addressing local needs. According to the World Bank:

> [E]conomic growth is necessary but by no means sufficient to achieve widespread poverty reduction in the world. The [World Development] Report [on Poverty] lists three essential pillars – opportunity, security, and empowerment – to achieve a significant rate of sustained poverty reduction amongst the poorest population groups. By the same token, the recently released book on *The Quality of Growth*, published by the World Bank Institute, also clearly demonstrates the shift from a predominantly 'economic growth' development model to an approach in which the development of human and socio-cultural capital is deemed a sine qua non for achievement of balanced and sustainable development ... [I]n countries with a relatively low level of inequality and a medium level of economic growth, the chances for large-scale poverty reduction are considerably greater than in countries with high economic growth and high levels of income inequality.   (World Bank 2001a; see also World Bank 2002a)

While local empowerment is important, not all decisions taken at a local level are appropriate. Some decisions are based in a sense of desperation and are, hence, very short-term or immediately focused, with little or no focus on longer-term sustainability. Other decisions can be based on a limited understanding of opportunities or of the consequence of such decisions, for example, taking out small loans which meet immediate needs but create longer-term debt problems. In yet other circumstances, traditional or recently established elites who retain power or influence in local settings take or limit decisions, often in their own interests or, again, with a limited understanding of options or outcomes. Within many traditional societies, hierarchical power structures often removed from ordinary people not just the power to make larger decisions about their collective lives but constructed a social psychology of deference towards power-holders. The issue of social power is a complex one and can be inconsistent across political and cultural contexts, despite what might otherwise be seen as commonalities of interest in particular strata of society and very often the common material conditions applying to particular circumstances. As Weitz notes: 'when involving entire communities in development, the social planner must be capable of using existing social relations advantageously'. That is, a failure to recognize and sensitively employ traditional leaders and others can lead to development project failure (Weitz 1986: 167; see also Warren 1993).

However, CDD is intended to overcome many of these and other shortcomings, by developing and enhancing local empowerment, participatory governance, demand responsiveness, administrative autonomy, greater downward accountability and enhanced local capacity.

> Experience has shown that when given clear explanations of the process, access to information and appropriate capacity and financial support, poor men and women can effectively organize to identify community priorities and address local problems by working in partnership with local governments and other supportive institutions.   (World Bank 2014a)

External involvement

Assuming that local decision-making is most likely to produce results sensitive to local needs and desires, such decision-making may still require assistance, advice or information available primarily from external sources, e.g. the state or multilateral institutions such as the World Bank. However, outside aid providers can (sometimes unwittingly) shape local agendas or inappropriately insert themselves into local decision-making processes in ways that may not be sustainable and that may destabilize local social relations. The role of the development worker is thus among the most difficult issues in community development, especially when it is focused on empowerment. In simple terms, while a situation might require the intervention of an external agent to facilitate circumstances that allow change, that external intervention by definition must, at some stage, precede empowerment, and may displace it. Based on the assumption that if communities could change themselves they would have done so, though it is desirable it is a rare and extraordinarily sensitive community development project that is able to allow local people to lead.

In all discussion about community development, it must be noted that external factors, from the environment to government to broad material and economic conditions, will have a constraining influence on what is or is not achievable within a local context. According to Friedman: 'local action is severely constrained by global economic forces, structures of unequal wealth, and hostile class alliances' (1992: xii). If development is to look to communities as the source of change, they must also seek to transform social power into political power and engage in national and international issues (Friedman 1992: xii).

Yet, as noted, in helping to create an environment in which people can make decisions for themselves, decisions are often made for them. The first decision is whether or not the community in question wishes for such intervention in their lives. Further interventions tend to flow from that, including decisions about what aspects of community development are or should be available, what the priorities for community development are, the nature of local social and hierarchical relations and decision-making, and so on. This is especially the case if there is an explicit assumption on the part of development planners that there should be co-ordination between local and wider development goals (Weitz 1986: 79), which is common to much development planning. This is despite acknowledging the necessity of recognizing the 'needs, beliefs and abilities of traditional peoples' (Weitz 1986: 78). However, as Freire (1985) noted: 'Attempting to liberate the oppressed without their reflective participation in the act of liberation is to treat them as objects which must be saved from a burning building, it is to lead them into the populist pitfall and transform them into masses which can be manipulated.'

In this, Freire implicitly opposed such populist manipulation and made it his project to assist with the creation of conditions that would allow people to 'liberate' themselves. Korten also notes that it is not really possible for one person to 'empower' another. People can only empower themselves (1989: 118–19).

Oliver recognized the potential conflict between the ideas of development planners and local people when he noted that it should be 'the first task of a voluntary organization ... to encourage the people to speak up when aid projects go wrong' (Oliver 1983: 137). Weitz similarly noted that there needed to be an active 'feedback relationship' to allow constant revision of local development projects to fully take into account field realities (Weitz 1986: 174). In this, Weitz and Oliver were primarily referring to covering up aid programmes that were failing or that had failed in order to save official embarrassment, but still allowing for such failure to be repeated. Similarly, Jain, Krishnamurthy and

Tripathi suggest that 'the basic reason for the failure of rural development and poverty alleviation programmes is the exclusion of the people from participation in the development process and the abandonment of the institutions of democratic decentralization and the related electoral process' (Jain, Krishnamurthy and Tripathi 1985: 15). Democratic decentralization, in this context, means 'recognizing multiple centres of power' (sometimes referred to as 'Public Interest Partnerships'), which assist in ensuring accountability, transparency, participation, equity, predictability and efficiency. In this sense, what is broadly referred to as governance becomes essential, reflecting the authenticity of local electoral democracy. In simple terms, 'good governance is good for development' (Gonzalez, Lauder and Melles 2000: 165).

However, the principle of appropriate development programmes and the necessity for vocal local input remains valid. Weitz (1986: 174) similarly noted that there needed to be a bottom-up 'feedback relationship' to allow constant revision so that programmes could conform to local realities.

Background to community development

Ideas about community development were first commonly propagated in the early 1970s, following what was widely seen as the failure of the 'decade of development' of the 1960s in which decolonization did not automatically result in development and in which explicitly modernist or industrial policies were mistakenly regarded as the universal path to 'take-off'. What occurred instead, in many developing countries, was a mixture of semi-development, development experiencing losses and then gains in succession, or just simple underdevelopment, in which a number of countries increasingly went backwards. The overall result, at a time when the West remained optimistic, was an overall decline in developing countries and especially amongst the majority poor of developing countries. As Mortimer noted, this was in large part due to the blind faith held by Western planners in the value of modernization and, consequently, in the lack of value accorded to 'peasants' (Mortimer 1984: ch. 3).

In response to continuing and increasing poverty in developing countries, then later as president of the World Bank, Robert McNamara outlined the basic needs, or 'redistribution with growth' approach to development, which focused development on local initiatives. McNamara's then groundbreaking view was that poverty alleviation for the world's poorest 40 per cent was of primary importance, although this should not be undertaken in ways that would damage prospects for economic growth (UNICEF 1996: ch. 3). In this, McNamara was influenced by the 'peripheral' work of NGOs, and thinking such as that expounded by British economist E. F. Schumacher in his seminal work *Small Is Beautiful*, which turned away from large-scale industrialization and macroeconomics towards more appropriate medium levels of technology and local economics.

Yet, while this shift in focus was important, the origins of community development can be traced to some of the first thinking about development as a part of the process of decolonization, pre-dating the optimistic and sometimes grandiose ideas of the 1960s. The original United Nations position on community development, for instance, was that it 'is a technique for improving the levels of living, particularly in underdeveloped areas, community development being interpreted as a process creating conditions of economic and social progress for the whole community with its active participation and the fullest possible reliance upon the community's initiative' (UN 1958: 21).

Participatory democracy

One of the major criticisms of democratic processes has been that, through increasingly centralized representative processes, it has become too distant from the people being represented. Participatory democracy implies the greater direct participation of political constituents in political decision-making processes. Most common methods of participatory democracy are direct democracy, in which constituents vote directly on matters that affect them, primarily through local power structures or heavily decentralized political models. The advantage of this approach is the greater access to decision-making processes and potentially greater legitimacy of political outcomes. However, such systems do have limited application in large, complex societies that require broad decision-making affecting large populations. There are also questions around the extent to which voters might be familiar with the detail of all of the subjects they might be required to decide on, as well as the potential for short-term or narrowly focused decisions which could have longer-term or wider negative consequences.

One increasingly popular mechanism developed to address the sense of distance in political decision-making, and which has also been applied in limited ways in non-democratic states such as China and Laos, has been that of 'deliberative democracy', sometimes also referred to as 'discursive democracy'. This model of decision-making combines elements of representative as well as direct democratic processes, with constituent members of a political group (e.g. village, town) discussing political decisions or laws with representatives and having a consensus view of their deliberations reflected in political action. An alternative to this approach is deliberative polling, in which participants do not meet directly. The deliberative democracy model was initially developed in the 1980s but has since seen widespread theoretical adoption and, in some cases, practical use (e.g. see discussion by He 2010 of its application in China).

The principal benefit of deliberative democracy is intended to be, through being able to trace their origins, as with other participatory forms, an increased sense of legitimacy in political decisions. There is also a sense in which, through widespread consultation, there is a higher degree of impartiality, rationalism and knowledge of relevant facts in decision-making (Bessette 1994). Some negative consequences of this process, however, include the argument that the process inhibits rather than helps rational decision-making, that it is ideologically biased in favour of liberalism and republican models over parliamentary ones, that, like other participatory methods, it can too readily reflect self-interest and that it promotes a division between the state and society (see Blattberg 2003).

Given that decisions on spending usually limited income is key in political processes, participatory budgeting is a key element of participatory democracy. This process usually involves the public identification of spending needs, their prioritization, the public decision-making process and, finally, its implementation via public officials. While this process can have some of the shortcomings of more general participatory decision-making, it does increase equity and the transparency and accountability of financial decision-making. In Porto Alegre, Brazil, since 1989 this process has led to direct improvements in water and sanitation and access to public education (Lewit 2002). Since this beginning, the process has spread elsewhere in Latin America, to Asia, Europe and North America. Despite positive outcomes, the actual rate of participation in the process has been proportionately low, with some 50,000 people in Porto Alegre participating from a population of 1.5 million. Further, some experiences have shown that participation rates decline after initial needs have been met. The process has, however, increased in popularity and provided a real mechanism for addressing needs as understood at the community level.

Education as development

There is widespread agreement within the development community generally and among community development planners in particular that education creates the best conditions for empowerment and community development. In particular, literacy programmes are widely seen as both an instrumental good, in that they can produce measurable benefits and create opportunities for material improvement in the lives of people, and as a good in themselves, in creating choices for decision-making that might not have previously existed.

Even though the use of education was an early approach to community development, its history dates back even further, being first conceived of by the British Colonial Office in the 1920s, although it was not applied in Africa until the 1940s. Ghana launched its first mass literacy and education campaign in 1951, which was soon after adopted by the nearby French colonies (Manghezi 1976: 41). In this, community development was seen as 'a vehicle for progressive evolution of the peoples to self-government in the context of social and economic change' (Manghezi 1976: 39–40). The idea of community development was not well developed initially, although even at this stage it was recognized that education was a critical component which found translation as the opening of 'development area schools' and similar projects (Manghezi 1976: 41). The movement did, however, find some parallel in Mahatma Gandhi's *swaraj* (self-rule) or stateless community movement, increasingly including passive resistance and non-co-operation, initially developed in South Africa before being imported to India as the basis for the claim to independence. As then, newly post-colonial African states sought to create new development models and the central role of education was given a new lease of life under Tanzania's 'Ujamaa Villages' programme in the 1960s.

The idea of empowerment, in this context, is reflected in the ideas of Paulo Freire (1976, 1985), based on the need to develop people's abilities to understand, question and resist the circumstances that keep them in poverty. Freire promoted not just the idea of the necessity of education as a model for empowerment, but also that the spread of such education should itself be an act of empowerment ('all teach, all learn', understood as Freire's 'dialogic method' 1976: ch. 4), critically engaging with and hence changing the lived experiences of the participants (also see Kincheloe and Horn 2007). In this, education generally, and literacy in particular, are seen as critical criteria for individual and group development (see also Rensberg 1980). Freire's critique was essentially derived from a 'bottom-up' perspective of social and economic relations and was predicated upon the idea of reflection (via education) leading to action (praxis) (Freire 1985: ch. 3). Perhaps the biggest difference between Freire's revolutionary pedagogy and the role of education in more contemporary community development is that the latter is based upon a more localized and, hence, contained basis, and that it seeks to allow its recipients to participate in wider economic and political spheres rather than to overthrow them.

Freire's work can, nonetheless, be understood as a basic principle of 'capacity-building', in which local communities not only have opportunities to make decisions but have developed an enhanced capacity to be able to do so. Discussion about capacity-building has been a significant feature of development discourse since the mid-1990s, yet there are few clear definitions about its meaning. One interpretation has capacity-building as equivalent to developing social capital (CVCB 2007), while others have it as the development of practical skills. According to the United Nations Development Programme (UNDP), capacity-building is 'the creation of an enabling environment with appropriate policy and legal frameworks, institutional development, including community participation (of women in particular), human resources development and strengthening of managerial systems' (cited in Global Development Research Center, n.d.). Walker, in whose work this definition is also cited, adds that the UNDP 'recognizes that capacity building is a long-term, continuing process, in which all stakeholders participate' (Walker 2007).

Of these attributes at a community level, literacy, as the most fundamental aspect of education, has thus remained a key issue in empowerment and participation of local communities. It remains both an obvious means to individual and local development and feeds in directly to the capacity of the state, via its constituents, to proactively to pursue its own wider development goals. Literacy can also be argued, as noted, to be an end in itself, in terms of enhancing the scope of individuals to participate in a literate world.

In a not dissimilar fashion, literacy has been cited as being useful to individuals as well as for 'development' in Bangladesh (although this nominally assumes the questionable distinction between the welfare of individuals and 'development'). A literacy programme was developed by the Friends in Village Development Bangladesh for landless men and women, which was based on small groups and was combined with organizational support, savings and credit schemes, technical assistance for income generation and the rebuilding of a sense of self-worth. 'Literacy is therefore linked to generating local group structures and capacity-building', not least of which is the capacity to participate in the development process (Gardner and Lewis 1996: 117). It is worth noting here that those developing countries that have performed best, such as the 'newly industrialized countries' of East Asia, invested heavily in education as a precondition for their growth. In particular, the centrality of education to Confucian thinking resulted in massive investment in education in Singapore, Taiwan and South Korea, in each case with dramatic results.

While literacy has been identified by most governments of developing countries as a – probably *the* – critical development issue, it has not been free of problems, both internally and externally. One of the internal problems with education campaigns is that they do not necessarily address the educational imbalance that can occur between people with and without power. That is, a person with power who is probably already literate may have their literacy enhanced, while an illiterate person may achieve only a basic level of literacy and, in terms of complex written information, still be at a significant disadvantage (especially if their literacy is tested, for example, via a contract or another complex device).

Significantly, almost one in seven of the world's population remains illiterate – they cannot read or write a simple sentence – with adults representing over 80 per cent of this group. Unsurprisingly, two-thirds of those who are illiterate are women (UNESCO 2013), indicating not just a gender preference in education but the continued structural disadvantage of many women in developing countries.

Literacy is also most useful when combined with other technical support or enhancement. From an external perspective, education campaigns have often been amongst the first to be affected by externally imposed 'structural adjustment' programmes in which government spending is cut to reduce public expenditure and debt. While cutting education spending can be seen as a 'soft' option for governments seeking to reduce expenditure in the face of an unsustainable burden of debt, it is very often recommended by external 'consultants' whose concerns are less for the welfare of ordinary people or, indeed, for enhancing the productive capacity of workers than they are for short-term macroeconomic outcomes. This disregard for the personal and social value of education very often reflects an unstated ideological bias against mass participation that is potentially occasioned by mass education.

Social distinction

Within any given social context of a local community in a developing country, there is likely to be a marked distinction between elites and others. That is, people with political or economic power (or other forms of social capital) will, in most cases, tend to be somewhat set apart from the vast majority who do not enjoy political or economic power, even though they will necessarily interact and may display elements of a type of social contract. In particular, what once might have been a simpler dichotomy has become complicated by shifting patterns of patronage, land ownership and employment. Traditional elites might operate as a hereditary or quasi-elected village or district head and enjoy certain privileges as a consequence. But there has also emerged a new category of political or administrative elites who owe their appointment to political associations or patronage that may be more connected to larger urban centres and modernist or quasi-modernist political formations such as political parties. Power-holders will almost always attempt, often vigorously, to retain or enhance their social, political and economic power (see Burkey 1988: 165).

Associated with such localized political clients or *apparatchiks* are lesser functionaries who may also obtain some personal benefit by way of political association, perhaps through their or their family members' appointment to jobs, business concessions, protections or favourable treatment – a set of practices known in Indonesia and Timor-Leste, for instance, by the acronym 'KKN' (*Korupsi, Kolusi dan Nepotisme*, or Corruption, Collusion and Nepotism). Shopkeepers and other small business owners might also be seen as falling into this category. In a critique on the value of encouraging small enterprise, Fromm and Maccoby noted that 'entrepreneurs do not solve the village's economic problems. They become middlemen, money lenders, and store keepers ... the result is to increase dependency and powerlessness of the landless' (Fromm and Maccoby 1970: 205, see also Chau, Goto and Kanbur 2009). In more traditional societies, such a localized sub-elite might occupy regularized positions within the community hierarchy, such as legal or religious adviser (often the same), or local constabulary or peacekeeper.

In contrast to localized elites and related sub-elites are 'urban masses' (town dwellers), migrant workers, and rural peasantry. Urban masses, or more commonly in a local context, town dwellers, are largely those people who function at the lower end of the cash economy, as employees, small stallholders, as the under-employed (e.g., those hawking minor trinkets, matches or newspapers, or voluntary traffic or parking attendants and so on) or as the unemployed. Town-dwelling unemployed may include victims of economic downturn or other reasons for loss of gainful employment, peasants who have lost their land, single parents (usually mothers), street children (functional orphans), the mentally and physically disabled and others who, for various reasons, have slipped through the usually threadbare social networks that help sustain people in difficult times.

Migrant workers often constitute a separate group of town dwellers, not necessarily being fixed to social networks, living in fringe communities (in both figurative and literal senses) outside local social and official support structures and not being a part of local decision-making processes. They may be structurally precluded from broad equality of access to material well-being, such as through lesser pay, access to potable water or electricity, education for their children, health care and so on. Migrant workers may also be employed on a seasonal basis, and either be transitory or unemployed during 'off' seasons. As a consequence, migrant workers are excluded from decision-making at a number of levels and there is often resistance to their incorporation into local decision-making processes.

Interactions between the various strata of society, and the subsequent capacity for or interest in power sharing, do find broad commonalities across the development context. But there are also regional differences, usually borne out of local experience over a long period. Illustrations of these differing contexts come from as far apart as Mexico and Indonesia. Within the rural Mexican context, the taking and giving of orders may be unpopular with peasants who are productive and who tend to hoard. Authority or 'leadership' suggests to them exploitative bosses, which has strong negative connotations and is therefore not popular. There is, in this, a lack of interest in forcing compliance on the part of others (Fromm and Maccoby 1970: 209). In such a respect, local organization requiring leadership can be difficult to obtain. In a different cultural context, there is a widespread view that village office should neither be coveted nor too highly rewarded. One consequence of this, though, is that 'villagers might content themselves with mediocre leadership for long periods without concerted attempts at replacement' (Warren 1993: 123).

Notions of authority and hierarchy vary from context to context, and the role of authority in local decision-making and how that is employed is not consistent. In some cases, authority is a capacity not to be trusted or to be used with caution. Warren noted that in Bali, members of the traditional aristocracy, civil servants and agents of political parties who were seen to have status, office or wealth (that is, traditional patrons) had difficulty in presenting their views publicly in what was seen to be a disinterested manner. Hence, orators without such *manjar* (significance), but who have influence based on personal qualities, including knowledge of local *adat* (customary law) and skills in public speaking, are often in as strong or a stronger position to persuade local people of the value of an idea.

As a consequence of this public distinction between formal and informal authority figures, a dual leadership pattern can emerge. However, within this, while the ideals of the group were supposed to predominate, formal or traditional decision-makers still exercise informal influence on orators. 'Although close association with patrons would compromise an orator's credibility, covert alliances develop and orators are able to use their skills to frame factional interests of powerful patrons in terms of principles acceptable in the public forum.' This presentation of a shadow leadership pattern, allied to formal and informal political arenas and codes of expression, shares certain features with Bloch's proposition (1975: 6, 12) that formalized rules and speech forms are essentially vehicles of traditional authority and established power relations. That is to say, even though this social environment might portray itself as formally egalitarian and moral, it actually remains hierarchical and instrumental (Warren 1993: 73). Deeply ingrained notions of structural hierarchy may thus mean it is difficult to achieve local development projects without the consent or participation of local authority figures, or that their involvement will more likely guarantee the success of a project.

Warren has noted that the Indonesian family planning project, which has been generally regarded as successful, achieved its greatest success on the island of Bali. This has been identified as being a direct consequence of what was called the *Sistem Banjar* (Neighbourhood Association System), in which the village community was a conduit for family planning. By way of illustration of its success, in 1985 Bali had the highest rate for use of contraceptives (74.5 per cent) in Indonesia, compared with the national 52.2 per cent average (Warren 1993: 217; Arifin 2010). This use of contraceptives was directly linked to the highest drop in the fertility rate, which declined by almost half. In order to achieve this level of contraception usage, heads of *banjar* (neighbourhood or hamlet associations) were sent to training seminars and liaised with district family planning field workers to provide information and contraceptives. *Banjar* heads were also responsible for registering eligible couples, compiling statistics on contraceptive use and motivating acceptance in communities (Warren 1993: 218). According to Warren, the *klian* (head) of Banjar Tegah said the contraceptive campaign 'would not ever have succeeded if it hadn't gone through the *banjar*. Before everyone was embarrassed to talk about such matters. Now it is normal. At each assembly meeting we discussed family planning until everyone understood sufficiently' (Warren 1993: 218). This conformed to Weitz's view that, 'when involving entire communities in development, the social planner must be capable of using existing social relations advantageously' (Weitz 1986: 167). However, this also reflected the broad interests, and reinforced the status, of the local elite.

Apart from local elite input, Warren said there was no difference in contraceptive use based on social or economic status, although there was variance between *banjar* (between 30 and 60 per cent acceptance) which correlated to the distance between *banjar* and the local family planning clinic (Warren 1993: 219) and between support or otherwise of *klian* for the programme (Warren 1993: 220). Proximity to both the source of the programme and the motivator for the programme was critical to the success of a local programme. Warren noted that while local leadership was important, and was influenced by proximity, discussion of leadership or local institutions also needed to take account of Balinese conceptions of the 'popular' which were unquestionably influenced by modern ideas about democracy as well as traditional practices and status orientation (Warren 1993: 123).

Social organization

Even in local projects, in which autonomy is meant to be paramount, there can continue to be a heavy reliance upon external agencies for assistance, in which case the local community provides only part of the total requirement to undertake a local project. One illustration of this, from Indonesia, is where local funding and communal labour (*gotong royong* – mutual help) supplemented a quarter of the cost of a local project established by the Public Works Department. Notably, two weeks' labour was provided by a local military unit under the *Angkatan Masuk Desa* (Army Enters Village) programme for local public works. This programme was developed in the mid-1980s as a means of bringing the army closer to the people, to enhance 'development' more generally but also to cement the military's role in the development process as well as to keep a watchful eye over potential dissidents and leftists.

Yet, even though this was a government-sponsored scheme and the military component was supposed to be paid for out of the military's own budget, the *klian banjar* was still required to make a 'donation' of a monetary 'gift' to the military commander as repayment for the assistance provided (Warren 1993: 225). In such instances, most of the 'gift' of cash would be kept by the local military commander, although a portion of it would be paid to his own superiors in his patron–client network, and a portion would be spent on or distributed to the soldiers who actually undertook the work to support their living conditions or as supplementary wages. In this way, the autonomy of village projects was still compromised by broader state projects, patron–client relations, and notions of hierarchy and authority, the unofficial but socially constructed reciprocal elements which most villagers found impossible to escape.

In relation to Indonesia's primary education campaign, begun in 1973, central government funding via sub-provincial districts allowed villages to sub-contract or manage construction of new schools themselves. This was regarded as:

> one of the most beneficial and least controversial development programmes, expanding rural employment while broadening educational opportunities. The effect of Inpres SD (the presidential decree that launched the programme) was to raise primary enrolment across Indonesia to a claimed 85 per cent by 1980 (the World Bank said enrolment was 78 per cent in 1984, indicating a tendency for the government to over-inflate its claims).   (Warren 1993: 215)

Because of the benefit to both local education and local employment, under this programme 'villages devoted considerable energy to this task.' A *klian* of one of the *banjar* in *Desa* (Village) Siang said: 'besides giving work here, the buildings are better. Why? Because they are ours. If they call in someone from outside, I wouldn't trust them' (Warren 1993: 215).

Even in what was widely considered to be a successful community development programme, there was still some disquiet with the reliance of the programme on outside sources. In this case it was due to corruption at the next level of government up from the village: 'leaders in Tarian and other *desa* expressed frustration at the substantial loss in real value of materials received for projects when delivery was managed through the *kabupaten*'. In this, some building materials were stolen, while others that had to be purchased through the sub-provincial district administration were overpriced (Warren 1993: 230). The role of the *klian banjar* also retained some capacity for capriciousness in development projects. In another village studied by Warren, which was built over the water of a bay, the village head dominated the use of the fresh water tank and left the other two unused tanks outside his home. Fresh water was supplied, at a high cost, by an enterprising Bugis merchant (Warren 1993: 229). However, despite such problems, and reflecting the balance in favour of meeting development objectives, *banjar* continued to be used to balance local decision-making and central needs and objectives.

Because of the 'balancing of central needs and objectives', while Indonesia's primary education and fertility reduction programmes both recorded a relatively high degree of success, there were also concerns about how genuinely independent much decision-making was. For example, while local communities and community leaders were co-opted into supporting government programmes, there was little community discretion about what programmes they might pursue. Further, the linkage between local implementation and higher-level involvement was frequently used as a means of exercising political surveillance and control over local communities. As a result, 'many critics of development ... view participation as a degraded term, which has only served to "soften" top-downism and has been successfully stripped of its previously radical connotations' (Gardner and Lewis 1996: 111).

Co-operatives

The world's single biggest traded crop is coffee (following oil as the world largest traded commodity) and it is the dominant export of non-oil-producing developing countries. Yet, apart from plantations, most coffee is grown and harvested by small landholders who are entirely at the economic mercy of local buyers who, in turn, sell to the world's trading houses. The price of coffee is set not at the point of sale of the original product but in the world's stock exchanges. However, given the vast gulf in the price between coffee as a globally traded commodity and the price paid at the farm gate, it is perhaps the ideal product for a co-operative venture. Collective bargaining power that can increase the growers' price for coffee can make a major difference to the income of coffee farmers, yet barely register on the global pricing radar.

As a long-standing but much debated area of economic community development, co-operatives were originally designed to pool the resources of a number of local people, including labour and machinery, into a common enterprise. Co-operatives continue to demonstrate their usefulness, especially in the areas of better buying and selling power, and in removing middlemen from such arrangements. Co-operatives can also allow a division (specialization) of labour which, in principle, should allow for greater efficiencies of production (Fromm and Maccoby 1970: 210–11). Weitz also recognized the benefits of co-operative arrangements, noting that they could make available technology and equipment too costly for individuals, transform small-scale farmers into significant economic blocs, that they made production more efficient and that they could expand opportunities to acquire new markets and suppliers (Weitz 1986: 163; Trewin 2004). However, Weitz also noted that expectations of what co-operatives could achieve were sometimes overstated and that expectations exceeded their capacity to deliver, especially in the shorter term. This, he said, needed to be clarified to co-operative participants to ensure that their expectations corresponded to an achievable reality and to preclude disappointments that could undermine the co-operative enterprise (Weitz 1986: 164).

Even with such clarification of the capacity of co-operatives to produce results, some members of co-operatives have also felt that their respective labour is not always adequately rewarded, especially for those who feel they contribute more but receive back a share based on the number of contributors but not the effort committed. This perceived or real reduction in incentive has led, in some instances, to a reduction in productivity, especially where co-operative members are rewarded at the same rate, regardless of how hard or otherwise they work. Compelled co-operative ventures, such as the '*Ujamaa* (socialist) villages' of Tanzania in 1973–6, were often resented and, constructed as 'collectivization'; co-operatives were a social and economic failure in China and Vietnam, with overall losses in farm productivity due to the loss of smallholder incentive. In other cases, however, such as Israel's *kibbutz*, co-operative/communal ventures have been far more successful, primarily due to their voluntarism rather than compulsion. And the traditional 'mutual assistance' of many village communities has worked as one model for co-operation, bringing with it a powerful cultural recognition of the need for village units to work cohesively at important times of the year. But especially as an imposed model of local economic organization, co-operatives have had a very mixed record of success. Where co-operatives or co-operative endeavours have a higher degree of voluntarism, they also have a much higher degree of relative success.

In comparing co-operatives in Maharashtra and Bihar in India, and in Bangladesh, Blair noted that the success or failure of co-operative enterprises resulted from a combination of factors. The success of a co-operative included having adequate infrastructure and hence access to loans and the co-operative's financial structure (including having a built-in repayment system for loans to avoid defaults). Issues of land tenure, the size of landholdings as an incentive or otherwise towards co-operative behaviour, social cohesion, political culture and, of course, competence all contributed to success or failure (Blair 1997). Jain, Krishnamurthy and Tripathi also noted the issue of landholding size as a factor in co-operative success, indicating that small farmers were more likely to want to be involved in co-operatives. They also noted that, regarding co-operative finance, there was 'no evidence to suggest default is more frequent among small farmers than among large farmers' (Jain, Krishnamurthy and Tripathi 1985: 57).

Expecting the unexpected

Anthropologists have noted that one of the most critical factors affecting development programmes, especially those that are located within and run by the local community, is the impact of development on local patterns of behaviour and economic, social and political relations. That is, development programmes that alter a local environment are not free from flow-on effects, nor are they free of importing external values (such as consumer materialism), despite the implied belief that all societies can potentially adapt with relatively little disruption to the development paradigm. In seeking the advantages of development and in focusing on its potential for positive contribution, there is frequently too little concern for potential negative consequences, meaning that 'unexpected' problems can and do arise, sometimes to the extent of derailing the development process. That is 'social change often entails costs that are neither expected nor planned for' (Appel 1990: 271).

In recognizing that there are impacts from the local development process that are often not planned for, Appel noted seven principles of social change within the development context. They are:

1. Every act of development or modernization necessarily involves an act of destruction.
2. The introduction of a new activity always displaces an indigenous activity.
3. The adaptive potential of a population is limited, and every act of change temporarily reduces this potential until such time as that change has been completely dealt with.
4. Given such reduction, each act of change has the potential to cause physiological, psychological, and/or behavioural impairment in the subject population (such as stress or 'social bereavement').
5. Modernization erodes support and maintenance mechanisms for managing social stress.
6. Change always produces psychological loss, as well as compensation for such loss.
7. Change threatens the nutritional status of a population, and there is often disruption to traditional nutrition patterns. (Appel 1990: 272, see also Price and Pittman 2014: 183).

In identifying these factors, Appel also notes that they are all exacerbated by the speed of change. That is, the speed of change might not just have a quantifiable impact – that twice the rate of change will

226 International Development

produce twice the potential problems – but the quality of the impact can increase disproportionately to the rate of change: twice the rate of change could lead to a greater multiplier of related problems (1990: 273). The encouragement given to a shift to cash cropping, for instance, can damage local ecology and lead to a loss of subsistence crops. The loss of access to locally sourced food can and often does have a direct impact on the nutritional status of local communities (Appel 1990: 273–4). Not only is the variety of nutritional sources not always available in a purely cash context within a local community at the lower end of the development scale but cash crops may be subject to total failure (mixed crops tend to be subject to partial failure), hence depriving the grower of access to any return. Further, the trajectory of prices for cash crops, on the whole, declined in real terms between the late 1970s and around 2006, with regular dips in pricing depending on the extent of oversupply and relative competition on global markets. This then reduced the potential income to subsistence crop growers until the more recent price increase and, hence, their capacity to secure adequate supplies of food. Even when the sale price of agricultural commodities increased, this was often at the wholesale and retail end of the market, with little of the benefit being passed on to growers. This then returns to the observations made by Weitz, Warren, Friedman and Oliver: that in any community development process, there needs to be primary recognition given to the knowledge, values, needs and desires of the local people, which is what, at base, community development is supposed to be about.

Community development at work: the East Timor experience

In assessing the practical potential for community development, a significant example has been East Timor's Community Empowerment and Local Governance Project (CEP), 2000–2006, which stands as a useful illustration of the benefits and problems of such an enterprise. The CEP in East Timor showed what was available through community development but it also pointed to some of the problems that continue to trouble local development projects. The CEP was a World Bank-funded project (or series of three iterations of the same project) intended to stimulate community-level development projects and to encourage democratization at a local level in a society that, prior to its commencement, apart from one violent and externally organized election, had never previously experienced the democratic process.[1]

The formative stages of the CEP came into being soon after the UN returned to East Timor in late September 1999, following the Indonesian army's 'scorched earth' policy in response to the UN-supervised ballot in which the East Timorese voted to separate from Indonesia. Already the equal poorest province in Indonesia, East Timor had more than 70 per cent of its buildings and infrastructure destroyed by the retreating Indonesian army and its militia proxies. Prior to the vote, East Timor had been under Indonesian occupation since late 1975, during which time there were limited attempts to introduce literacy and centrally planned development programmes, the latter mostly contributing to larger Indonesian-owned enterprises. After the first year of the incipient CEP, in November 2000, the US$21.5 million programme largely shifted from the control of foreign employees to an indigenous management team. From this time, the small management team in Dili supported 60 sub-district facilitators, more than 800 village facilitators, and one district project accountant and a district monitor in every district, all of whom were East Timorese.

Recognizing East Timor's history of not previously having experienced democratic decision-making, the key CEP objective was to introduce and establish transparent, democratic, and accountable local structures in rural areas to make decentralized decisions about development projects. While providing the opportunity for local communities to rehabilitate basic infrastructure and revive local economies, the local councils established under CEP were intended to be a vehicle for the local expression of development needs and desires, and for implementing projects. This was, at the time, regarded as a good example of 'bottom-up' development planning and as representing a new policy direction by the World Bank, which funded the project. The former UN Transitional Authority in East Timor head of District Administration, Jarat Chopra, described the CEP as 'an introduction to local democracy, as well as a functioning form of self-determination in the reconstruction process' (La'o Hamutuk 2000).

After its first 12 months, the CEP had funded over 600 sub-projects and supported the formation of 57 sub-district councils. More than 400 village development councils were founded in all districts, between them accounting for a total of 6,270 representative council members. One notable aspect of this programme was that the council positions were equally divided between men and women (TFET 2000; World Bank 2000). This was in contrast to East Timor's deeply entrenched culture of male domination. However, while this division of representation by sex was broadly regarded as appropriate (not least by many

East Timorese women), it was a very clear example of the imposition of external values on a sometimes reluctant indigenous society:

> In many ways, the CEP councils are creations of the 'international community' – albeit with the expressed support of the CNRT [Timorese National Resistance Council]. In this regard, they are not as legitimate and vibrant as socio-political structures that have emerged out of local, long-term processes. As the 'Joint Donor' report noted, '[A]t present the talent and energy at village level is more likely to be found around the chief and the old clandestine structures than within the council.' It is such structures that the report contends 'must be built upon if the country's urgent rural development problems are to be solved.' What the report calls their 'control mentality and gender bias,' however, run counter to international notions of democracy, as well as to the official positions of the CNRT. How the CEP will reconcile its praiseworthy principles with the need to respect indigenous beliefs, practices, and structures is an ongoing challenge. In this regard, working more closely with local and national organizations – such as East Timorese women's groups, for example – might go a long way toward realizing many of the CEP's goals.   (La'o Hamutuk 2000: 6)

As a result of the post-ballot destruction, local communities largely chose to invest CEP funds in rebuilding or repairing community and personal infrastructure. Some 43 per cent of funding was allocated for the construction of community meeting halls, a quarter for small roads linking up to larger ones and for the repair of agricultural infrastructure, 15 per cent for the restoration of household assets (such as pots, pans, plates, cups, and/or spoons shared by villagers) and productive equipment (such as simple, communally owned farm equipment, lathes, or saws), 10 per cent for repair of water supply infrastructure (wells and pipes), and 7 per cent for schools or clinics. 'Vulnerable groups' and others, such as orphans and widows, were targeted for CEP support, as were local NGOs and the development of community radio (La'o Hamutuk 2000; Estefa 2001). (It has been common experience in developing countries since the advent of transistorization that radios are the cheapest and most accessible form of mass communication.) As noted by a then senior CEP manager, Chris Dureau, reflecting on the programme a decade later, it was a priority for traumatized communities that had lost everything to re-establish a sense of normality, by replacing some of that which had been destroyed, rather than embark on what were perceived as ambitious small business projects.[2]

While the CEP was seen as relatively successful in introducing democratization to East Timor, and in improving the social, economic and political position of women, it also had some failures. The introduction of localized democratization necessarily led to tension with traditional power structures and, in cases where traditional leaders prevailed, it served to strengthen their political position as well as offering them the chance to exploit economic opportunities offered by the projects. Similarly, although the CEP served to strengthen and, in principle, democratize local decision-making, there was an initial lack of co-ordination between villages, and between villages and the district-level administrations. This was, in large part, resolved through the establishment of District Advisory Boards providing such linkages. The position of women in such CEPs was also less successful, with a continuing 'culture of silence' on the part of many women (and expected by many men), and otherwise a lack of active participation on the part of many women. Further, not all CEP elections were as democratic as intended, with some 30 per cent of elections undertaken by 'acclamation' of candidates who had been chosen by local leaders. Villagers were also frequently inactive, in part due to a lack of training, in part due to lack of reward and in part due to concern over introducing opportunism to impoverished environments. According to Dureau, the CEP's project of dispersing money to districts initially undermined democratic principles, mostly because the processes intended to ensure participation were in many cases short-circuited to ensure the efficient dispersal of funds (Dureau 2003).

On balance, however, the CEP was widely regarded as having achieved a number of its goals, not least of which was the locally directed repair of the physical fabric of East Timorese society, as well as wider social and government capacity building (World Bank 2006b). Between the CEP and externally supervised elections for the legislature and the presidency (and following the vote for independence), notions of participatory and representative democracy were overwhelmingly enthusiastically received, and were becoming ingrained into the thinking of many, perhaps most, local people as a desirable and legitimate means of decision-making. The biggest threat to this process related not to the success or otherwise of the CEP but to the broader economic conditions of the fledgling state, the social dislocation caused by unmet economic expectations and the continuing social trauma of a quarter century of mass brutalization. Set against this backdrop, the CEP functioned to restore or establish some order of normality and, broadly conceived, 'progress'. However, as a programme with a finite tenure for external funding, there was real concern about its viability after its external sources of funding ended. When that time came, the real test of the success of the programme was able to be measured. On balance, while the project did enhance the livelihoods of many in the shorter term, the original iteration left few lasting benefits.

The purpose of the CEP was to provide funding to communities for infrastructure and social activities. While the World Bank ran with the idea, the Asian Development Bank preferred an emphasis on governance. Communities that were funded tended to use the funds available to restore a sense of normality rather than thinking about long-term development strategies. It was initially a puzzle as to why communities opted for 'normalization' rather than development, but the pattern of recurrence showed that the message from communities in post-disaster or conflict places such as Aceh, Afghanistan, Laos, Bougainville and the Solomon Islands was that communities initially needed small-scale activities of limited duration. Efforts to establish 'proper' development activities in most cases were not successful. According to Dureau, 'We now know that in these situations the communities fall into the category of recovery rather than development' (personal communication 4 May 2011).

A decade on from the CEP, an evolved model is widely regarded to have generally worked well, if with some qualifications, and has become the benchmark model of community empowerment projects in a number of other countries. Indonesia followed with similar initiatives such as with the evolution of the National Program for Community Empowerment which became the Kecamatan Development Program, reflecting an increased menu of social activities and longer-term involvement consultation, and the Musrenbang (*Musyawarah Rencana Pembangunan* – Multi Stakeholder Consultation Forum for Development Planning). These programmes offered progress in community involvement in local decision-making, which led to the establishment of locally determined projects including new roads, potable water, irrigation, health clinics and schools (World Bank 2010b).[3] Similar projects were also developed in a number of other developing countries across Asia and Africa.

Local versus global

There is little doubt that the world is, in many ways, becoming a smaller, more connected and integrated place. Interestingly, however, while the world grows smaller, many local cultures are asserting themselves as an alternative to global standardization or homogenization.

This is nowhere more pronounced than in relation to states, many of which as developing countries have only made the transition to statehood in a qualified manner, perhaps reflecting their specific historical and material origins as colonies designed to suit imperial interests rather than local needs. The failure of many states to meet, or have the capacity to meet, the needs of many of their citizens, and the broad sweep of globalization, has meant that some communities have turned back to themselves for development, if in fact many of those ever ceased to do so. It is worth noting too, however, that globalization also offers the opportunity for increased networking among the marginalized and dispossessed, thereby helping to strengthen their respective positions. Like all such change, globalization can have positive as well as negative impacts, depending on which element is being referred to or how it is being employed (see Tesoriero 2010: 178).

For many in developing countries, what is called 'development' but which in other contexts might just be a simple, perhaps minor, improvement in standard of living, is the product of local conditions, effort, imagination and capacity. Governments can and do develop major infrastructure projects and sometimes these have a direct positive benefit on local people. But very often they do not and in too many cases the effects are deleterious, or are simply not sustained and, hence, become a larger economic burden. Yet, there is no quality of government that exceeds its desire to involve itself down to the most local level of its population, in part certainly to be able to claim some equality of care of its citizens but, almost as surely, to regulate and control them as well. It is at this point that there exists the juncture between state and local aspirations for development.

Similarly, there is little doubt that some local development projects have to fit into a wider development scheme. For example, and other than for initial educational purposes (learning how to learn is often done best in a 'home' language), it would be rather pointless developing a local educational facility if the language being taught was not consistent with a wider literacy programme: so too a road project, in which roads to a proposed bridge faced each other at points that did not correspond. Equally, however, the one-size-fits-all model of development can also fail to address specific local needs, impose inappropriate development and silence the voice of the local community. Even with the best of intentions, external authorities can only rarely presume to know how people think without actually asking them. Added to this are all the usual inefficiencies and disengagements of a larger hierarchical or bureaucratic structure, the continuation of patron–client relations, modified forms of economic status and deference, and the consequent potential for corruption and reduction of service at the final point of the process.

It is not accurate to say that all the problems of development decision-making can be resolved by devolving responsibility for such decisions to the local level. Even amongst local communities there are specific interests, conflicts and tensions and a lack of capacity that can and do derail local decision-making processes, or which default to traditional, often non-representative and usually exclusive power structures. There are also problems with awareness, education and technical competence. Yet, in acknowledging such issues, the legitimacy of direct representation in local decision-making remains valid, the sensitivity and awareness to local needs, concerns and values is most acute at the local level. So too is the capacity for inclusiveness in and, hence, ownership of the development process greatest at the local level. Development is not just about the accumulation of material resources but about the allocation of such resources. In societies that have less than perfectly representative political systems, the process that determines such allocation is most sensitive to local needs when decisions are taken at the local or community level.

Notes

1. Much of the information regarding East Timor is taken from the author's direct experience of regular visits since the country voted for independence in 1999.
2. Discussion with Chris Dureau, Baucau, Timor-Leste, April 2011.
3. The Kecamatan Development Program was run between 1998 and 2009 by the Ministry of Home Affairs in conjunction with the World Bank. Its key principles included being a decentralized, participatory and transparent programme in which residents could suggest their own local spending priorities. See www.worldbank.org/id/kdp (accessed 26 February 2016).

Chapter 9

Gender and Development

Janet Hunt

In the early post-war years, when the concept of 'development' evolved, issues of gender equity were not considered relevant to the economic development of Third World countries, and it took some time before that changed. Today, significant advances have been made in recognition of the importance of gender in development due to research and activism by feminist researchers and development workers. This is particularly true since the United Nations Decade for Women 1975–85, and the UN World Women's Conference in Beijing in 1995, both of which had considerable impact on development thinking. Yet following the impacts of debt and adjustment in the 1980s and 1990s and the multiple crises of finance, food and energy in the first decade of the twenty-first century, and despite a global commitment to the MDGs, the challenge of making development gender equitable remains significant.

Despite some progress in the last 25 years, gender inequality remains a feature of every region, though it is most pronounced in South Asia, sub-Saharan Africa and the Middle East. Women are under-represented in governmental decision-making in most countries, holding only about 22 per cent of all seats in the world's national parliaments.[1] Although women's formal labour force participation has increased in recent decades (before declining in some regions since the global financial crisis), we have not enjoyed equal wages or equal employment opportunities with men and we undertake a high proportion of the unpaid care work in society. And while 197 countries have now ratified the CEDAW (Convention on the Elimination of All Forms of Discrimination Against Women), women do not in practice enjoy the same legal rights as men in many countries. In particular women are discriminated against in areas relating to financial and economic resources, such as their right to land and property and their right to conduct business independently (UNDP 1995; UNIFEM 2000; World Bank 2001b; United Nations 2009, 2010). Thus women are more vulnerable to poverty than men, especially as a result of widowhood, separation or divorce, and the consequent loss of access to productive assets, although equating all female-headed households with poverty is oversimplistic, as Chant (2004, 2008, 2010b) emphasizes.

Sex and gender: what are we talking about?

In raising the issues of gender inequality, early writers focused on *women* in development. A shift in emphasis to *gender* in the last decade of the twentieth century signalled a change in perspective and approach. While women and men differ biologically – that is, their *sex* is different – the behaviour and socially learned characteristics associated with their maleness or femaleness is their *gender*. The learned behaviours and roles associated with being male and female may vary from culture to culture. For example, in one culture males take care of money. In another, it is the women who control the purse strings. Thus roles associated with each gender may vary from place to place, as well as over time. In the economic sphere, men and women often undertake different activities. Women may plant certain crops; men may plant others. Harvest work may be gender specific. In each setting, we have to be clear what the roles are and how they interrelate.

A study of rural households in Vietnam, for example (Kabeer and Anh 2000) noted that Vietnamese women have always been active traders unlike their counterparts in South Asia and the Middle East. By the late 1990s in Vietnam, some 90 per cent of men and women were involved in income-earning economic activities, but women were more likely than men to be found in 'catering, food and beverage manufacturing, wholesale and retail trade, and garment and leather industries. Men predominated (80 per cent) in storage and transport services, mining and fishing' (Kabeer and Anh 2000: 11). They also explored men and women's specific agricultural roles. Such detailed and localized analysis is required to identify gender roles and responsibilities, and thus to identify appropriate development strategies.

Early development workers, however, made false assumptions, that women's roles were largely as mothers and 'housewives' in the European sense. Their extremely significant *economic* roles in the household or as farmers were entirely overlooked. As early as 1929, Nigerian women were resisting their loss of land and their reduced status as farmers, as a result of colonists' efforts to 'modernize' agriculture (Boserup 1970; Mies 1986).

Thus early development projects neglected to understand the diverse roles women were playing in social and economic life. As a result, some projects made life worse for women, depriving them of land which was taken over for the development project's crops, denying them access to technical assistance, while providing resources, training and education and increased income to men, and often, unknowingly adding to women's work burden (Rogers 1980; Dey 1982).

Development activities for women were generally either mother–child health projects (generally with more focus on the child than the mother) or family planning projects to reduce population growth (Rogers 1980). Such projects did nothing to enhance women's status or promote their equality, although they may have been of some practical support.

Integrating women into development

Ester Boserup's seminal work, *Women's Role in Economic Development* (1970), challenged all this. The book documented different household and farming systems in Asia and Africa, pointing out that there were vast differences between the social and economic arrangements in the various household types, and in what she termed male and female farming systems. She observed that women played a very active role in agriculture in Africa, particularly in areas of extensive farming and shifting cultivation. In Asia, on the other hand, in intensive, settled agriculture where the plough was used, women took a far lesser role and their labour was replaced by male landless labourers. She drew attention to the significance of land tenure arrangements and stimulated a plethora of empirical research to explore these issues in many different contexts. Furthermore, she argued that women could play a much more active role in industrial development and the modern sector and that economic growth would be enhanced if this were encouraged. Her view was that, contrary to popular belief, women would not take jobs from men but would expand the available labour force and hence the opportunities for economic growth (Boserup 1970).

Boserup's work stimulated the emergence of the Women In Development (WID) movement (Moser 1993) which embraced modernization and argued that women should be 'integrated' into development. If there was to be economic growth, women were to contribute to it and get their fair share of its benefits: women's subsistence farming should be given access to credit and extension services equally with men; women should have equal access to educational opportunities to give them the opportunity to participate in the modern sector. The language of 'efficiency' was adopted by the WID advocates, to convince development planners to involve women in development. It was a language the latter understood, although it was clear they had little idea how to implement the approach (Rogers 1980; Moser 1993).

Early efforts to respond to WID advocates resulted in the establishment of women's projects and women's desks in development agencies, peripheral to the main development effort which simply remained unchanged. Thus projects for women were supported in areas such as 'home economics' and traditional crafts, as well as credit for income generation. The theory was that women's poverty resulted from their underdevelopment, and all that was required for development to occur was to increase their productivity through provision of credit (Moser 1991). Many of these programmes were poorly conceived with limited outcomes (Buvinic 1986).

The mainstream of development was barely touched. Even as late as 1995, a study of four major donors and two Southern aid-recipient countries found that donor agencies had avoided hard choices, 'creating underfunded mandates, adding a few projects to their existing portfolios, and supporting research, training and the development of operational tools and techniques' (Jahan 1995: 126). WID had become a technical fix, not an agency for empowering women and genuinely transforming development (Jahan 1995). The fundamentally gendered development theories on which the whole development 'project' rested were not up for question.

Women and development: a new critique

While modernization was being critiqued by the school of dependency theorists, feminists were developing their own Marxist-based critique of modernization. Marxist feminists saw that the accumulation of capital resulted not simply from the exploitation of 'peripheral' countries, but from the free subsidy of women's unpaid reproductive and subsistence labour. Maria Mies argued that capitalism could not spread without the subjugation and exploitation of women (Mies 1986). Her research found that, contrary to former belief that men were the preferred labour force, women were being employed in some key areas at lower wages and in poor conditions. She found that poorly paid 'compliant' women were the labour force of choice in many multinational companies, particularly in the electronics, textile and garment industries in free trade zones (FTZs), and in large commercial agricultural companies. Their work was seen as 'supplementary' to the male 'breadwinner' so they were typically paid only 50–70 per cent of male wages in FTZs, and their generally casual employment arrangements made them vulnerable (Mies 1986; Pyle and Dawson 1990; Pearson 2001). Women had indeed been integrated into development, but in such a way as to perpetuate inequality and their own subordination (Mies 1986: 114). The poor conditions under which many garment workers are still employed was highlighted to the world in 2013 when a Bangladesh garment factory collapsed, killing over 1,100 people, most of them women. Bangladesh's garment industry brings in some 80 per cent of its foreign exchange, with 5,000 factories in Dhaka alone, and 3.5 million workers employed. Yet garment workers may be required to work ten hours a day, seven days a week, in hazardous conditions. And while this industry may have provided poor rural women with some income in this and other poorer countries, such workers remain highly vulnerable to exploitation (Third World Network 2013).

Mies' work was published a year after the Nairobi Women's Conference to mark the end of the UN Decade for Women. At Nairobi, a new 'southern' women's network, 'DAWN' (Development Alternatives for Women in a New Era), also made a strong critique of current development approaches. Sen and Grown (1987) explain DAWN's view that implicit in many of the activities and discussions about women and development it is assumed that,

> women's main problem in the Third World has been insufficient participation in an otherwise benevolent process of growth and development. ... Our experiences now lead us to challenge this belief. ... Equality for women is impossible within the existing economic, political and cultural processes that reserve resources, power and control for small sections of people. But neither is development possible without greater equity for and participation by women. (Sen and Grown 1987: 11, 15)

Thus the DAWN women were also challenging the WID approach and its assumption that modernization just needed to incorporate women. They recognized that to challenge this development orthodoxy, women needed to be mobilized and empowered to realize a different development vision.

Gender and development

The focus on women's empowerment became one thread in the next phase of work to promote gender equity in development. But the main thrust was to shift attention from women themselves to the *relations between men and women* and particularly to analyse the unequal power relations between them at every level, from the household to the national economy. Gender workers recognized that all social, political and economic structures needed to be examined, with the intention of transforming development to become a more gender-equitable process (United Nations 1999). Development organizations adopted gender and development policies, guidelines and procedures in an attempt to achieve 'Gender Mainstreaming' across the institutions (Rathgeber 1990; Ostergaard 1992; Moser 1993).

An important contribution to the analytical work was made by Caroline Moser (Moser 1993). She distinguished between women's 'practical' and 'strategic' needs, and highlighted the interrelationships between women's different roles – reproductive, productive and community managing. Women's 'practical needs' were those which resulted from their current subordinated position and might include assistance in areas such as education, improved health care, agricultural advice, etc. But their strategic needs are those which might help to transform their situation. These might include legal reform to remove gender discrimination; an end to violence against women; and more politically active and better organized women. Such changes would contribute to an end to women's subordination. Moser challenged development programmes to address women's strategic gender needs, not just their practical ones. Her call for better understanding of women's triple roles would also help shape development programmes to avoid increasing women's workload, and focus on improving their lives.

At the same time feminist economists were trying to deal with economic models of the household which were still far from accurate. In general, development economists have treated the household as a single unit and much data collected at the household level is not gender disaggregated. Bina Agarwal (1997) developed a gendered 'bargaining model' of the household which explores how men and women interact within households to meet their subsistence needs, have access to necessary resources and frame the 'social norms' within which such bargaining takes place. In addition she outlines the external factors in the market, the community and the state, which shape the bargaining power available to different household members. Thus a woman's ability to bargain favourably to have equal access to resources for subsistence, such as land, may be affected by laws relating to inheritance, her access to government officials who deal with land registration matters, her educational level and legal literacy, the community's view about the legitimacy of her claim (whatever its legal merits) and her ability to support herself independent of counter-claimants (such as brothers or uncles) (Agarwal 1997: 14). Wiig found in Peru, for example, that gender-equitable land titling gave women greater say in decision-making in the household and community in particular in relation to land and agricultural matters (Wiig 2013). Greater attention is now being given to these institutional factors and societal gender norms that Agarwal also highlighted, indicating the power they have in shaping gender relations within the household (Mabsout and van Staveren 2010). Tripathy (2010), however, challenges Agarwal's model of the developing world's household as a site of conflict, arguing that families are also sites of co-operation. Rather, she says, we should understand that 'masculinity and femininity ... are not something which men or women have, but are constantly re-constructing themselves in a context of shifting priorities' (Tripathy 2010: 120). Whilst Tripathy may be right about the mutability of gender relations, nevertheless Agarwal's approach of detailed analysis of gender at the household level and its interaction with wider societal factors– which has been underlined by Mabsout and van Staveren's work – presents a challenge to development planners to check their assumptions, carry out their prior research and pay greater attention to the gendered effects of different policies and programmes. However, the real world may be more complex than our gender analysis models suggest and there is scope to develop approaches that will capture a less essentialized reality, recognize co-operation as well as conflict in gender relations, and take account of multiple sources of inequality (Woodford-Berger 2007).

Gender and adjustment

While efforts were under way to make development policies and programmes more gender sensitive, many countries were facing enormous problems of indebtedness. From the early 1980s, the Philippines, Mexico and many African countries were undergoing the rigours of structural adjustment. Governments had to reduce spending, currencies were devalued and there was a strong push to trade more and open the economies to foreign investment (Beneria 1999). In the name of 'economic efficiency', the policies shifted a considerable burden onto women to make up for the austerity measures which were imposed. At the household level, women's workloads increased as they struggled to provide for their families.

The effects on women of structural adjustment programmes have been well documented (see, for example, Commonwealth Expert Group 1989; Elson 1991; Sparr 1994; Beneria 1999; de Pauli 2000; Floro and

Schaeffer 2001). As formal sector employment shrank for both men and women, women increased their activity in the informal sector, working long hours in petty trading. Cutbacks in public expenditure on food subsidies, health care and education hit women too. As income fell, food prices rose for many staples, such as maize in Africa, rice in Asia, and oil and cooking fuel. Women were faced with trying to provide for their families on less. They extended their food growing to try to overcome the impact of reduced household income. Women's health suffered from reduced nutrition, cuts to health services, and increased cost of medicines. The introduction of user-pays fees in education often meant that the girl children of the family dropped out of school, leaving boys to continue (Sparr 1994).

Not all women were affected negatively. For example, in the Philippines there was a growth in urban industrial employment especially for young women, due to export promotion (Floro and Schaeffer 2001). Overall, though, it became widely recognized that the gender impacts of structural adjustment policies had been negative and overlooked and that women needed to focus on macroeconomic policies.

Gender and the environment

By the early 1990s, global attention shifted to the environment. Women have been intimately concerned with environmental problems in many parts of the world, often being the ones who felt the effects of environmental destruction most keenly. In Kenya, the Green Belt Movement, a national women's movement, has had a massive impact through its collection of indigenous seeds, development of tree nurseries and tree-planting programmes across the country (Rodda 1991). And in North India, the 'Chipko' movement of women made world news by hugging trees to stop them being felled (Shiva 1989).

At the Rio Earth Summit in 1992, women's advocacy led to recognition of women's role as environmental managers and gained government commitments for women to participate more in environmental decision-making. However, the central assumption of the final statement, that more economic growth was needed to provide the resources to solve the world's environment problems, was seen as an inherent contradiction by many feminists (Braidotti et al. 1997). Indeed, writers and activists such as Vandana Shiva saw this approach as nothing less than destructive maldevelopment.

Shiva's ecofeminist views derive from her experience working with Indian peasant women farmers coupled with her intellectual critique of

Western science. Shiva says that Western patriarchal science achieved dominance as a mode of thinking by: 'excluding other knowers and ways of knowing' (Shiva 1989: 22). Shiva contrasts this reductionist mode of thinking with the Indian cosmology which is holistic, creative, dynamic and integrated. The relational aspects of all parts of life and nature are understood. She contrasts the way women have tradition-ally managed food, water and forest resources in a sustainable manner, and how new approaches (e.g., the 'Green Revolution') have damaged the ecology and undermined women's traditional methods of nurturing their environment. For example, in Shiva's view, scientists and agricul-tural 'experts' who focused on increasing the output of one crop, such as sorghum, neglected to recognize that the traditional farming system was a complex and ecologically balanced one, with multiple produce that withstood drought conditions and provided good nutrition for growers' families. There was no miracle of high yields in the new sys-tem when the total production of the diverse old one was taken into account. In fact, the new varieties left people far more vulnerable to crop failure in drought conditions (Shiva 1989: 122–31).

Wee and Heyzer (1995) recognize that some women have benefited from prevailing patterns of growth but their concern, like Shiva's, is the depletion of the natural resource base on which rural women in particular, but in the end all of us, depend. They argue that what is required is that the many realities experienced by different people need to be reflected in development decision-making. The empowerment of poor women, so that their reality can count as much as anyone else's, is critical to a transformation of development. They suggest that the efforts to make visible (and to place a value on) women's unpaid work, and the hidden free subsidies which the natural environment provides to development, is an important part of the process of making alterna-tive realities visible.

In line with this, Marilyn Waring (1988) developed a pithy critique of the United Nations System of National Accounts (UNSNA), the sys-tem used by all countries to establish their economic results. As she so clearly demonstrated, women's unpaid work and the 'free' con-tribution of nature is never valued, and hence not recognized in the national accounts of nations. This results from a series of gender-blind bureaucratic definitions of what is measured which exclude a huge amount of women's reproductive work. If such services were pro-vided commercially – water and fuel purchased from utility companies, food bought in the market, meals purchased in a restaurant and child-care provided in a childcare centre – all this would be included in the national accounts. But when a woman provides it herself, she is deemed economically inactive! Despite detailed proposals about how women's work could be valued and counted for national statistics (Lewenhak 1992), no country has yet adopted such an approach, although some are developing 'satellite accounts' (United Nations 1995).

More recent debates about gender and the environment now relate to the gender-specific impacts of climate change and how to respond to them. The United Nations Framework Convention on Climate Change (UNFNCC) makes no reference to gender and women have been scarce in decision-making around this issue. Yet climate change has the potential to exacerbate gender inequalities, and increase women's work burden in a number of ways. For example increasing extreme weather events will impact women's agricultural activities, but their poor asset base and their difficulty in accessing credit may make climate change adaptation strategies difficult to implement; however there may be possibilities that climate change mitigation strategies, such as the introduction of bio-gas cookers, could benefit women (Demetriades and Esplen 2008; Oxfam and United Nations Vietnam 2009; Smyth 2009).

Postmodernism and difference

The postmodernist school of thought, which questions the 'grand theories' of the past and the idea that rational thinking and technological solutions will bring 'progress' to the world, reinforces Wee and Heyzer's view that what is needed to transform development is to open it up to different voices, different meaning systems and different realities.

Postmodernists draw attention to how the category 'woman' or 'man' is constructed, and how particular categories of women (poor women, Third World women, Asian women, Muslim women) are created, and by whom. Mohanty has been particularly critical of western feminists who have presented the 'third-world woman' as implicitly, if not explicitly, 'ignorant, poor, uneducated, tradition-bound, domestic, family-oriented, victimised, etc.' in contrast to Western women 'as educated, as modern, as having control over their own bodies and sexualities, and the freedom to make their own decisions' (Mohanty 1997: 80). Such categorization has colonialist overtones and is rejected by feminist writers from the developing world.

Parpart's 'feminist post-modern critique' of much development discourse highlights the significance of 'difference' in gender debates. As she explains, the practical implications of this critique are to get planners to take seriously the realities of women's lives, especially to explore different women's views about what changes they want from development: 'this approach to development recognizes the connection between knowledge, language and power, and seeks to understand local knowledge(s), both as sites of resistance and power' (Parpart 1995: 264).

It is this perspective that demonstrates the importance of women being organized, documenting their own lives from their own perspectives as subjects, not objects, of research (validating their own knowledge), and having a key role in development decision-making. This is particularly important for minority women, indigenous women, women who are old, or who have disabilities, or who may be particularly marginalized in development planning.

However, the global political climate of recent years, with its emphasis on 'identity politics', is at the same time a troubling development for women's rights and women's voices. Attacks on women's rights have 'resulted from the resurgence of religious identities that include the assertion of "traditional" gender roles and systems of authority' (Molyneux and Razavi 2005: 1000). Some women align themselves with such movements in the face of powerful actors – national or foreign – as part of a backlash against globalization and 'modernity', consumerism and excessive libertarianism. Women may wear the hijab, for example, as a deliberate act, to assert identity or to shield themselves from men. Feminists, particularly those in the Muslim world, have promoted alternative interpretations of religious texts which support gender equity to counter this trend but the political environment is not always safe for debate and dialogue of this nature. Development actors concerned to promote gender equity confront significant challenges in such contexts where power is held by fundamentalists of any religion, or where women and their identities become pawns in complex tribal, political and religious conflicts or global power plays (Hopkins and Patel 2006; Shepherd 2006; Kandiyoti 2007, 2011; Tadros 2011). Balchin (2010) however lays out many strategies which can be used to challenge any religious fundamentalisms which may oppress women, and both Kandiyoti and Marchand suggest ways to move beyond the binaries of religious/secular or Western/other to unpack 'actors, interests and practices' (Kandiyoti 2011:13). Unpacking gender relations in Bangladesh, Ahmed suggests that many Muslim women draw on feminist Muslim spirituality to help them improve their lives (Ahmed 2008), thus more nuanced understandings of Islam are required if gender equity is to be achieved in Muslim settings. Marchand (2009) seeks to explore the concept of the 'Global South' (which embraces poverty in developed as well as developing countries) and 'in between' sites such as trans-national migrant communities, to help rethink the sharp distinction between First and Third Worlds embedded in development discourse.

Such approaches have also led to an exploration of 'masculinities' in development (Bannon and Correia 2006). An important issue to explore is how men contribute to reproducing inequalities in gender relations, and how they can help transform the situation (Greig et al. 2000). There are complex issues involved, as men all benefit from their gender privilege in relation to women, but recent work is suggesting that, as some men's traditional roles disappear or change following economic restructuring, they are left with very low self-esteem which manifests itself through descent into alcoholism and increased violence and abuse towards women (Snyder and Tadesse 1997; Narayan et al. 2000; Silberschmidt 2001). Their definitions of 'masculinity' appear to be challenged by their new circumstances.

Other writers recognize that men themselves are caught within the dominant definitions of masculinity and argue that it is in many men's interests to promote different masculinities and challenge the domi-nant gender norms which constrain them (Ruxton 2004; Karkara et al. 2005; Esplen 2006; Ahmed 2008). Some guidance and tools for explor-ing such opportunities are now available (Greig and Edström 2012; ILO 2013; Otieno 2014). From a development perspective, it seems critical to engage with men, particularly young men, if gender inequali-ties are to be reduced. Issues such as HIV/AIDS, reproductive health and violence against women cannot be resolved unless dominant men are engaged and change their behaviours towards women as well as towards marginalized men. Various strategies and programmes are now underway which encourage men to play positive roles in sexual relationships, fathering and family care, and in preventing violence and conflict; successful approaches draw on men's sense of responsibility, their power to contribute to change for the better, and are built on posi-tive behaviours rather than attributing blame (Ruxton 2004; Esplen 2006). Other strategies emphasize the costs and stresses on men of stereotyped gender expectations whereby they are expected, for exam-ple, to provide for their families and undertake dangerous or very long hours of work in order to do so (ILO 2013).

Most recently, the very binary of male/female is being challenged, with gender identity being seen as far more complex and fluid. Development and human rights issues facing lesbian, gay, bisexual, transgender and intersex (LGBTI) people have come to the fore, in part due to the HIV/AIDS epidemic, and due to changing social norms in many, though not all, countries. Boyce and Coyle (2013) explored issues facing LGBTI people in Nepal, where a relatively permissive legal system co-exists with a more ambivalent societal milieu where such people experience prejudice and marginalization. Edström, Das and Dolan (2014) argue that patriarchy and the way power relations between different gender identities are structured and maintained should be the focus of future research. They highlight areas which have been neglected, such as dealing with institutionalized violence, men and domestic work, and men who have sex with men.

Overall, the lesson from postmodern thinkers is that rather than focusing on predefined categories such as male/female, ethnic or not, Western/non-Western or any other binary, we should focus on the processes which produce these identities and categories and understand the interplay for these identities in human lives. We should be asking who creates them, how they are used, and whose interests they advance.

Community development approaches

Since the 1990s, approaches to development have been inclined to be more participative and inclusive than in the past but we have to ask what happens in gender terms when participative methodologies are used. It is not at all clear that gender equity will result from more community participation, particularly unless special measures are put in place to give voice to the views of women, especially those more marginal in the community (Gujit and Shah 1998).

Community participation approaches can easily lead to a false consensus being derived from the views of those with power and influence in a community while issues which it is difficult for women to raise are neglected. An obvious example would be domestic violence, which is unlikely to be raised using the methodologies of mapping, village transects and other visual tools, nor while the perpetrators are present (Gujit and Shah 1998; Cornwall 2001). Separate opportunities for women to participate are necessary but in some parts of the world not always easy to arrange where women are secluded or accompanied by male relatives wherever they go.

At the same time, one cannot assume that women's interests will always compete with men's, or that all women will have an investment in changing the status quo. Women in positions of privilege may well resist change designed to benefit poorer women (Cornwall 2001). Facilitators of community participation approaches need to be sensitive to gender and power dynamics within a community and have strategies to address them.

Too often, culture and tradition has been used to prevent women overcoming discrimination and enjoying basic human rights. It is easy for men to suggest that feminist ideas from the West are being brought into a developing country in a colonial manner. However, everywhere there are local women struggling for women's rights – whether this be to prevent violence against women, female genital mutilation and so-called honour killings, or to achieve equality under the law, adequate sexual and reproductive health care, protection of their environments or adequate income. In a globalized world they are likely to have information from women elsewhere that may help or inspire them but their efforts are grounded in their own experience and reality.

The concept of women's empowerment is itself a complex one (Rowlands 1998). Naila Kabeer (1999, 2005) sees empowerment as about the 'ability to make choices' in the face of genuine alternatives which women themselves can recognize. Often power may be unquestioned, for example by women who accept violence against them or less access to food than men as 'normal'. Alternatively, as Sharp et al. (2003) illustrate in relation to Bedouin women, women may enter a 'patriarchal bargain' with men, operating within certain constraints in order to receive protections, and perhaps not distinguishing their interests as separate from those of their families. Unless women can choose to challenge such power relations, Kabeer argues, they cannot be said to be empowered. Van Staveren (2013: 109) quotes Narayan's 2005 definition of empowerment:

> Empowerment is the expansion of assets and capabilities of poor people to participate in, negotiate with, influence, control, and hold accountable institutions that affect their lives.

Van Staveren goes on to say:

> Although there are some differences, the literature tends to agree that women's empowerment is a process involving agency (referred to in the definition above with wordings like 'negotiate', 'influence', and 'control'), access to resources (or assets) and institutions, which together affect how women are able to improve their well-being absolutely and, more importantly, relative to men. (Van Staveren 2013: 109)

Van Staveren argues that all three elements (agency, institutions and resources) are interrelated and necessary for women to achieve empowerment. Her research found that access to resources is important for women's empowerment but constraining institutions may limit the extent to which women can transform their resources into well-being benefits and empowerment. This indicates that focus must remain on these institutions – both formal and informal. Kabeer, while focusing more on 'agency', comes to similar conclusions about where attention should be placed. She differentiates between agency which helps women carry out their existing roles more effectively (passive agency) and that which helps them address the patriarchal constraints they experience (transformative agency). It is the latter, she says, which is truly empowering (Kabeer 2005: 15).

However, in the development world, the concept of empowerment has been interpreted largely to mean economic empowerment of individual women through credit programmes, yet evidence that engaging women in such market activities empowers them is scarce (Oxaal and Baden 1997; Pearson 2007); some would go even further to argue that such programmes exemplify a wider trend of disciplining women into neoliberalism (Marchand 2009: 928). A more recent trend is the emphasis on women and entrepreneurship in the context of greater priority being given to private sector development by donors (Wu 2013), although a more complex understanding of empowerment including women's agency, the institutional environment and social accountability networks, as well as assets, income and return on investment is recommended for measuring women's economic empowerment (Wu 2013).

The need for such a comprehensive approach to empowerment is very evident. For example, having a gender equality clause in a constitution will have little if any practical effect on the ground if it is not developed into specific laws in areas such as discrimination in employment, land inheritance, access to services and prevention of violence against women. Furthermore, such laws are of little practical use if women are unaware of them or if it is difficult, or impossible, to get them enforced. Thus top-down strategies must be complemented (if not preceded) by community-level strategies which might have real benefits for women. For example, the use of community-shaming strategies may be of more practical use to prevent men being violent to women than distant laws in a country where the legal system is weak and obtaining justice is expensive.

For example in Afghanistan, the January 2004 constitutional guarantee of women's equality means little in a dangerous security environment, where livelihoods are precarious and much of the economy is criminalized. Furthermore, as Kandiyoti illustrates, 'the issue of women's rights continues to occupy a highly politicised and sensitive place in the struggles between contending political factions in Afghanistan'

(Kandiyoti 2005: vii) and such rights may be sacrificed in political settlements which privilege other interests and priorities (Kandiyoti 2007). Women's vulnerability is affected by complex intersecting historical and current factors, despite the very courageous leadership some women have displayed.

Gender and globalization: the way ahead

Whilst a shift to a more gender-sensitive participatory and community-oriented approach to development is welcome, the major trends of globalization may have far wider gender effects that might dwarf any positive impacts. Globalization of economies cannot be separated from globalization of political ideas and movements; as Heinonen says, 'globalization creates uniformity, but it has also created resistance to uniformity,' as culture, religion and gendered identities of women and men are mobilized to express local identities of resistance (Heinonen 2006). Ideas about gender equality can nevertheless spread more rapidly with wider access to global communications, and gender roles and norms may be influenced by global ideas.

Economic globalization over recent decades has involved 'liberalization' of trade and deregulation of markets, and an emphasis on privatization; this includes the deregulation of the financial sector. The role of the state in economic affairs has inevitably been reduced. A further aspect of globalization is the increased mobility of labour and the gendered flows of migration and the impacts these generate. However, the structure of national economies and women's location within them, as well as state policies, affect the extent to which impacts of globalization are differentiated by gender (UN 2010).

Research on the gender effects of trade liberalization indicates complex findings, mainly because the gender impacts vary according to a range of factors, particularly women's role in the export sectors of specific national economies. For example, 'trade expansion exacerbates gender disparities in agricultural-based African economies and reduces them in manufacturing-based economies like Honduras' (Bussolo and De Hoyos 2009: 18).

The interaction of gender inequality and trade can also have diverse effects on different women *within* a nation. In Mexico, trade liberalization stimulated a huge rise in jobs for women but most were in food processing (tortilla making) and pay dropped significantly (Cardero 2000). Women also increased their employment in agriculture, but their piece-work hours in the agricultural export sector lengthened (Fontana et al. 1998). Jobs in the textile and apparel industries increased but women's proportion of those jobs reduced, and they were overwhelmingly represented in the low-skilled, low-paid positions. Men were three times more likely to be in technical or managerial positions. Many of the new jobs for women were in small enterprises where conditions are poor (Cardero 2000). In South Africa trade liberalization favoured urban and male-headed households in relation to rural and female-headed households (Cockburn et al. 2007) while in three different African countries it widened the gender gap in wages (Cockburn et al. 2008).

Overall, factors such as 'gendered patterns of rights in resources, female labour force participation rates, education levels and gaps by gender and patterns of labour market discrimination and segregation, as well as sociocultural environments' affect impacts of trade liberalization in diverse contexts (Fontana et al. 1998: 2). And the effects on gendered poverty may be threefold: 'changes in employment structures and wages; changes in prices and their impact on consumption patterns; and changes in financing for social expenditure' (ODI 2008: 2) as government income may reduce due to tariff reductions.

In the early years of trade liberalization attention was primarily on the impact on female workers in the manufacturing industries, but since 2000 the focus is shifting to women in the services sector, as automation is displacing women in manufacturing. But the services require different, higher-level skills, including computer, English language and related skills for data entry and call centre work. In some places, though not all, the gender wage gap has reduced in the export sector of economies, perhaps in part driven by this shift in the nature of employment (World Bank 2012). As the World Bank notes, 'Gender equality appears to be higher in countries with larger export shares in female intensive goods and vice versa' (World Bank 2012), a point supported by Chen et al. (2013) in relation to China. Various studies have demonstrated that the gender wage gap is reduced in export industries, particularly where physical strength is not a required labour attribute (Chen et al. 2013; Rendall 2013). Schober and Winter-Ebmer (2011) found that gender wage discrimination, rather than fostering export-oriented growth, tended to reduce it, although their findings are not universally accepted (Seguino 2011).

However, rather than trade expansion envisaged through trade liberalization, declining global trade due to the 2007–8 global financial crisis (GFC) also had gender-differentiated effects. These varied significantly according to pre-existing gender inequalities, gender segregation in the economy and each country's specific contexts and policies (Jones,

Harper et al. 2009; Elson 2010). Some of the most obvious were loss of employment in export sectors which generally employ large numbers of women (Raaber 2010). Poor and marginalized women have been particularly affected, and the financial crisis has exacerbated the pre-existing food and fuel crises. Women's informal sector work and unpaid caring work has expanded. Sadly, with families under greater stress, violence against women and children has also increased (AWID 2010; King and Sweetman 2010; Raaber 2010).

However, men have been affected more in some countries, as Razavi et al. explain (2012: xxv):

> [I]n Ukraine, where the metal processing export industries, which primarily employ men, were hit hard by the collapse in global demand, men's employment declined much more than women's. Conversely, higher proportions of women lost their jobs in Cambodia, Egypt, Mauritius, Morocco and the Philippines, largely because of job losses in the textile and clothing sectors, where women's employment is concentrated.

Before the GFC, financial liberalization was a macroeconomic area with little understood gender effects. Singh and Zammit (2000) had studied the gender implications of rapid movements of capital following the Asian financial crisis in 1997 and found that the effects were likely to be differentiated by gender, with women suffering more, particularly if the downturn was long and deep. Stotsky (2006) also drew attention to the gendered effects of exchange rate depreciations which may differ according to whether women are largely engaged in subsistence agriculture (in which case it may push costs up and have negative effects) or in export industries which may benefit from new jobs.

Overall, globalization has provided women with new opportunities, but it has also made them vulnerable to rapid global economic changes. Razavi et al. (2012: xix) summarize this situation well:

> Processes of globalization have coincided with women's increasing labour force participation, with empowering consequences for some. This increase is in part a result of the creation of new employment opportunities in production for export following the liberalization of international trade as part of the globalization agenda. However, the increasing participation of women in the labour force should not be read as a straightforward story of progress. Globalization policies have also produced adverse outcomes for significant numbers of women (and men). Crisis-induced disruptions to household income associated with financial liberalization, and

job losses linked to competition from cheap imports and public sector reforms are pushing many women into low-paid temporary, seasonal and casual employment. As informal workers, many women have limited access to social protection measures. ... Women continue to be primarily responsible for unpaid care and reproductive work, indispensable to the functioning of the 'productive economy', despite doing more hours of paid work.

In response to the GFC, feminists highlighted again the need for more women to be involved in macroeconomic decision-making (Seguino 2010) and for the recognition of care work. Feminists have urged a new approach to economics which recognizes the invisible 'care economy', and is based on human rights (Razavi 2009; Raaber 2010); they are promoting a 'social economy' designed to achieve an equitable distribution of well-being (Randriamaro 2010). Care work is often seen as a 'burden' to be reduced, rather than as a contributor to human well-being, and development agencies' focus on women's labour force participation and entrepreneurship implies that this work has greater value than care work (Eyben 2013). One aspect of globalization has been the growth in female migration and the global role of women in the care economy. The feminization of international migration, especially in the last 20 years, reflects this. Since 2006 almost half of all international migrants are women, often in low-paid, insecure employment in manufacturing, service industries and the care sector. This has led to recognition of a 'global care chain' as other women care for the migrant workers' children or family members left behind. Women tend to remit a greater proportion of their income to their home countries than men do, and in some cases, despite gender wage disparities, remit more in absolute terms than men (Benería et al. 2012).

In the short term, there are many policy prescriptions required to provide for greater economic security and gender equity (Seguino 2010), among them better social protection policies (King and Sweetman 2010: 12). As Kabeer notes, most workers in developing countries are found in 'part-time, irregular and unstable forms of work with little or no social protection' (Kabeer 2008: 15) and women are most numerous and vulnerable among them; hence social protection policies are needed which are designed with full appreciation of these gender issues. Cook and Pincus (2014) report on strengthening of social protection policies and approaches across South East Asia post the Asian financial crisis of 1997, but note that women who are not in the formal labour sector often miss out on social insurance and 'social protection programmes often reinforce traditional gender roles and can disadvantage women by imposing additional time burdens on them.' (p. 14). As Razavi et al.'s study concludes, 'the extent to which social protection mechanisms are inclusive of women depends on how they are designed, financed and implemented' (2012: 58), and economic policies need to take gender equality goals more seriously.

Gender and governance

At the global level, the system of human rights instruments and a range of 'soft law' agreements aim towards gender equity. The Convention for the Elimination of All Forms of Discrimination Against Women (CEDAW) and the Beijing Platform for Action are the key documents within this system. In contrast, the system of rules for trade and financial services overseen by the World Trade Organization has far more impact due to its tough penalty regime. This system operates without any serious consideration of gender equity concerns. This suggests a need for reform of global governance structures to bring these systems into alignment and to ensure the goals of both embrace gender equity.

However, to date, interest in 'governance' has been largely focused at a national level and has been largely gender blind. One valuable economic governance initiative is the concept of gender-responsive budgeting (GRB). As Budlender remarks, the budget 'is in many respects the single most important policy or law passed by any government, determining the resources to be allocated to its policies and programmes' (Budlender 2001: 323). In South Africa, for example, a Women's Budget Initiative was developed through a collaboration of women's NGOs, women researchers and women parliamentarians. Its success in generating a debate about budget impact on women, boosting funding allocations in some key areas for women and inspiring other African countries to undertake a similar exercise has been important. Budlender suggests that the greatest effect is opening up budget discussion, formerly the preserve of white, male businessmen, to women of all races across South Africa and bringing gender issues, including the unpaid work of women, into economic debates there. GRB ideas have spread rapidly, with diverse interpretations of the idea and variable results in countries as diverse as India and Timor-Leste; whilst not a panacea, GRB is one strategy to contribute to reducing women's poverty (Budlender 2009; Costa, Sharp and Elson 2009; Elson and Sharp 2010; Jhamb and Sinha 2010; Jhamb, Mishra & Sinha 2013).

The second area of governance is the public sector reform agenda which has been associated with the economic restructuring taking place in many countries. Public sectors have been 'downsized' and privatized with little consideration for the gender effects, both in terms of women's employment and the provision of essential social and other services. The privatization of water has been particularly contentious from a gender perspective, with evidence from a number of countries indicating negative impacts on women through high prices and reduced access, and low priority given to improving access to water in rural areas. (Brown 2010; Laurie 2011). A similar story of failure to improve the lives of the poorest women is true of electricity privatization, at least in sub-Saharan Africa (Bayliss and McKinley 2007). And the lack of publicly provided infrastructure and services in a range of areas increases women's unpaid work burden (Budlender 2008).

Legal reform, the third area, may include incorporation of the CEDAW provisions into national law and reform of laws to eliminate gender discrimination through the statutes but Das Pradhan (2000) points out that there are many difficulties associated with attaining gender inclusion in legal development programmes and projects. However, this aspect of the 'governance' agenda is potentially a very useful one.

Fourthly, civil society programmes may include support for women's organizations, especially those involved in promoting women's human rights and empowerment. Such funding initially grew, but it appears that funding to women's rights groups has reduced since 2010 (Sen 2013).

However, the general principles of governance agenda – especially transparency, accountability, efficiency, equity and participation – *in theory* should provide a useful set of principles on which gender advocates can base their case. But to do so, they need to challenge orthodox assumptions about these concepts. At what level and for whom is efficiency to be judged, for example, when it seems to mean shifting care and responsibility from the public sector increasingly to women at home and in the community (Chant 2007, 2010; Budlender 2008; Robinson 2010)?

There are particular challenges in places where governance has collapsed, or is being built anew after conflict, as women play numerous roles in conflict as well as disaster settings (Bouta and Frerks 2003). Most frequently, development agencies view and treat women as victims but at least greater attention is now being paid to gender issues, particularly violence and human rights abuses against women, in post-conflict development and emergency humanitarian work (OECD DAC 2010b). Less opportunity is given for them to play active roles in peacemaking and peace-building (Karam 2001; Borer 2009; AusAID 2010b), where there is considerable scope for improvement (UN Women 2012).

The adoption of UN Resolution 1325 on Women, Peace and Security in October 2000 has begun to generate some momentum through women's active advocacy (Security Council Report 2010).

Gender and the Millennium Development Goals

The Millennium Development Goals provided an agreed international framework for development co-operation from 2000 to 2015 that potentially provided an avenue to bring the two development strands together. The third goal specifically related to gender equality and the empowerment of women, and the fifth to reducing maternal mortality, while all other goals clearly required attention to gender matters, although this was not emphasized or adequately implemented (Johnsson-Latham 2010; Fukuda-Parr 2010). The gender equality goal was interpreted narrowly through indicators that focused only on equality in girls' primary and secondary education suggesting that if these were achieved, gender equality would exist in all areas of life. This limited approach to gender equality was roundly criticized by feminist groups around the world (Antrobus n.d.: 14–15; Rao and Kelleher 2005; UN Millennium Project 2005). Women's representation in parliaments was added in response to pressure but the other measures were ignored and in 2014, UN Women re-emphasized these broader concerns in their assessment of the MDGs:

> While the three indicators under Goal 3 reflect important dimensions of gender inequality, MDG 3 does not cover several critical issues such as women's disproportionate share of unpaid care work, women's unequal access to assets, violations of women's and girls' sexual and reproductive health and rights, their unequal participation in private and public decision-making beyond national parliaments and violence against women and girls.   (UN Women 2014: 4)

Nevertheless, there has been substantial progress towards the MDGs and the rather narrowly defined gender equity goal. UN Women's 2014 assessment of gender equity and the MDGs (for full details of the MDGs see Chapter 6) reveals that, overall, there remains a wide gender gap in employment:

> Due to pervasive occupational segregation, women are overrepresented in low paid jobs, have less access to social protection, and are paid on average less than men for work of equal value. Women's

employment opportunities are further limited by the disproportionate amounts of unpaid care work that they perform   (UN Women 2014: 2).

However, there have been significant gains in girls' participation in primary and secondary education, and globally, gender parity has now been achieved at the primary level. There remains a major inequality in women's parliamentary representation, and gender violence remains widespread. While maternal mortality rates have declined significantly (by 47 per cent) since 1990, globally hundreds of thousands of avoidable maternal deaths still occur, 80 per cent of which could be avoided with access to basic maternal health care services (UN Women 2014: 6). In another important health area, young women have a much higher risk of contracting HIV than young men. And though access to clean water and sanitation has increased over the 15-year period, the burden of collecting water daily still falls on women in over 70 per cent of households that still need to do this, and access to sanitation remains a major problem for millions of women around the world. UN Women note that 'progress on the MDG targets has been slowest in conflict-affected and fragile states, but these same countries have notably lagged on the gender-specific MDG areas' (UN Women 2014: 2).

The debate now has shifted to the post-2015 agenda, and the need to embed gender equality throughout any new global development agreement that is negotiated, and how that might best occur (OECD 2013a; Seguino 2013; Sen 2013). The High-Level Panel on the post-2015 development agenda that reported to the UN Secretary General in 2013 recommended a stand-alone gender equity goal: to 'empower girls and women and achieve gender equality', with very specific targets to eliminate violence, end child marriage, ensure women's rights to own and inherit property, sign a contract, register a business and open a bank account, and end discrimination in political, economic and public life (UN 2013a: 30). Gender and development advocates have articulated a wider range of targets with greater emphasis on sexual and health rights, paid and unpaid work, economic empowerment, decent work, decision-making influence across all spheres, access to land and other assets, the mainstreaming of gender-equality targets across the whole development agenda and the need for gender-disaggregated data. (New York Multi-stakeholder Roundtable 2013; Gender and Development Network 2014). One of the most important areas to include in any set of targets is a reduction in violence against women, especially women in conflict-affected and fragile states (UN Women 2012). While they have had some success, more remains to be done.

The focus on MDGs coincided with, and reinforced attention to, the strategy of mainstreaming gender, a concept which will be explored below. Both have also stimulated a proliferation of new work on improved measurements of multidimensional poverty and gender equity. Early work on measurement of gender disparity by the UN led to two measures: The Gender-related Development Index (GDI), which measured the impact of gender inequality on the Human Development Index (HDI) score for each country and the Gender Empowerment Measure (GEM) which attempts to measure women's economic and political participation as an indication of empowerment. Both were subject to much debate and subsequently various other measures have been developed and used, each with its own strengths and weaknesses as a measure of gender equality (Beneria and Permanyer 2010; Bessell 2010; Jones, Harper et al. 2010; Pogge 2010). In late 2010 the UNDP replaced the GDI and the GEM with the Gender Inequality Index (GII), which explores three dimensions of gender inequality: empowerment, economic activity and reproductive health (Gaye et al. 2010). The Social Institutions Gender Index (SIGI) takes a rather different approach as it measures social institutions rather than individual outcomes. It rates a country on a range of indicators relating to family code, civil liberties, physical integrity, son preference, and ownership rights. Thus, it brings into focus the social institutions within different nations that contribute to or constrain gender equity. (Drechsler and Jütting 2010; OECD DAC 2010a). In a similar vein, Harper et al. (2014) argue that social norms are a major barrier to transforming gender relations and that to foster genuinely transformative change requires a focus on discriminatory social norms. They urge the use of what they term 'transformative indicators' to encourage the kind of social change they seek. Thus while they also focus on many of the indicators already discussed, they urge attention to the measurement of social attitudes, for example towards violence against women, or the value of boy and girl children, and they usefully highlight data sources for their proposed measures.

One of the most significant challenges facing any measurement of inequality is the availability of comparable and reliable gender-disaggregated data across all countries, particularly on issues such as violence against women, unpaid care work, informal sector work, and participation in decision-making. Global measures therefore inevitably have to work with data currently available, while advocating for new data to be collected which will better indicate the diverse realities of women and men's lives. As Chant (2010a: 3) notes, there are growing concerns that a focus on women's employment and income in both policy and measures of gender equality does not fully reflect the areas in which change is required if women's well-being is to improve. She suggests that these less measured areas such as access to land, legal rights, time poverty and overwork, vulnerability to violence and power in decision-making may be more significant. One emerging tool is the Individual Deprivation Measure which attempts to overcome many of these limitations and would enable such gender-disaggregated data to be collected and analysed (Wisor et al. 2014).

Gender mainstreaming

Since 1995, gender mainstreaming has become the dominant policy approach in development agencies. In the late 1990s, the Commonwealth Secretariat suggested that gender 'is mainstreamed when the development process and frameworks are transformed in ways which ensure the participation and empowerment of women as well as men in all aspects of life and especially in decision-making structures' (Taylor 1999: 7).

To achieve gender equity it becomes essential to ensure genuine institutional commitment, resources and strategies for gender mainstreaming in all development institutions. This includes national development planning bodies, government departments, donor agencies and non-government agencies. But to date institutions have found gender mainstreaming difficult to achieve. Poor resourcing, inadequate staffing levels and insufficient expertise and lack of corporate leadership have dogged efforts to gain better gender policies and programmes in many development agencies (Randel, German and Ewing 1998; Bytown Consulting and CAC International 2008). Mainstreaming brings with it the risk of complacency, policy 'evaporation' and oblivion (Goertz and Sandler 2007); it may be treated as a technical issue without attention to its power dimensions; and the likelihood of its implementation appears to rest strongly on the extent to which gender equity 'fits' with the overall goal of a department or institution (Mukhopadhyay 2007; Subrahmanian 2007). Mainstreaming implies that gender is dealt with throughout an organization, but as Tiessen observes, rather than being everywhere, it ends up nowhere, because responsibility for ensuring that it is happening is too dispersed (Tiessen 2007). The expectations feminist advocates may have of bureaucracies as potential agents of social transformation is viewed by some as a result of poor theorizing about policy and its implementation (Goertz and Sandler 2007; Mukhopadhyay 2007; Standing 2007). Rather than seeing social change as the result of gender mainstreaming policy, these writers argue that policy-making and implementation is itself a politicized social process within gendered institutions. So the transformative potential of gender mainstreaming gets subverted through the institutional processes in which gender inequality is embedded; in essence, within institutions gender equality is being reproduced and contested in day-to-day interactions (Eerdewijk and Davids 2013; Parpart 2013). Some argue that trying to mainstream gender in the context of a violent and insecure world, with policy increasingly framed through a security lens, is contradictory, and that we need to deepen our understanding of women's responses to violent situations and masculinist hierarchies and foster human security (Leckie 2009).

Rao and Kelleher (2005), like Tiessen (2007), argue that genuine institutional transformation is what is required. The 'deep structures' of organizations, the 'taken-for-granted values, and ways of thinking and working that underlie decision-making and action' have to change (Rao and Kelleher 2005: 64). These include the cultural and accountability systems in which gender bias is embedded.

The changing nature of aid, following the Paris Declaration on Aid Effectiveness, may also make mainstreaming more difficult to achieve, notwithstanding the release of the OECD Development Assistance Committee's 'Guiding principles for aid effectiveness, gender equality and women's empowerment' (OECD DAC 2009). The overarching principles underlying these aid arrangements include greater developing country ownership of development and alignment of aid with national development strategies, greater harmonization of donor support and greater mutual accountability through managing for results. As UNIFEM[2] comments, women will not benefit unless gender equality is seen as 'a key component of poverty reduction and national development' (UNIFEM 2006: 3). Currently, there is usually limited priority given to gender equality in development plans and budgets, donors may struggle to harmonize around gender as a priority and the proposed results to be measured usually neglect gender equity. Ironically, measures to enhance aid effectiveness may fail to do so where gender is concerned.

There remains an urgent need to bring gender considerations into macroeconomic institutions, policies and programmes. Feminist economists have made important contributions to date (Benería 1995; Pearson 1995; Grown, Elson and Cagatay 2000) but few mainstream economists would argue that gender equity should be a deliberate goal of economic policy. They usually argue that it will result from greater economic growth (World Bank 2001b) and achieving that is their primary objective. However, a survey of research on gender and macroeconomics (Stotsky 2006) draws attention to the fact that, while this is true, gender *inequalities* also *reduce* economic growth. She urges recognition that 'systematic differences in the behavior [sic] of men and women may lead to different macroeconomic outcomes ... and different public choices with regard to the composition of expenditures' (Stotsky 2006: 48). Unless economic policies at all levels explicitly try to support gender equity, they may well undermine it (Molyneux and Razavi 2005). Overall, Kabeer and Natali (2013) found that while 'greater gender equality, particularly in education and employment, contributes to economic growth' there is 'much weaker and less consistent evidence for the reverse relationship relating to the impact of economic growth on gender equality' (pp. 34–5).

Finally, while development planners and economists pursue the development model which feminists like Wee and Heyzer, Shiva and the DAWN network roundly condemn as unsustainable and unjust, the question of the sustainability of the current development path refuses to go away. This is a critical question. How significant will it be to have gender equality on a development path which is utterly unsustainable?

Notes

1. http://www.ipu.org/wmn-e/world.htm.
2. UNIFEM was merged into a new agency 'UN Women' in 2010, bringing together a number of small agencies dealing with women's affairs within the UN.

Chapter 10

Environment and Development

Damien Kingsbury

It is an a priori observation to say that without the environment there can be no development. Any capacity to develop, no matter how it is defined, must occur within the physical context and ultimate limitations of the available material circumstances, the most basic of which is the earth, its waters and its atmosphere: land to grow food on, water to drink and air to breathe. The global rush to achieve and expand material development has been predicated on the capacity of the physical environment to support it. In some cases the environment has been despoiled and in others it is simply running out of resources. Care for the environment and its use in a sustainable and affordable manner, for present and future generations, are perhaps the most critical issues in the development process (UNEP 2015: xvii).

The rise in importance of the environment in developing countries has paralleled a growing awareness of such issues in developed countries and, hence, among many bilateral and multilateral aid agencies and aid organizations. While there has been much cross-communication on this issue, increasingly developing countries' awareness of environmental issues has also come from direct experience with environmental problems. The growth of industrialization, often quickly and with few, if any, environmental safeguards, and populations swelling on the back of the 'green revolution', has had a real and substantial impact on many developing countries.

In particular, arguably the world's most important and potentially most devastating environmental problem – global warming – is a direct result of global industrialization's emission of carbon dioxide and other 'greenhouse' gases into the atmosphere (Stern 2007). As well as carbon dioxide, greenhouse gases include methane, nitrous oxide, hydrofluorocarbons, perfluorocarbons and sulphur hexafluoride that also contribute directly to building a cloud of gases which trap heat, thus increasing global temperatures. This has a wide range of negative consequences, including destroying the atmosphere's ozone layer, which increases penetration of biologically harmful ultraviolet rays. As the 'Stern Report' noted, the economic impact of global warming alone could shrink the global economy by up to 20 per cent if not acted upon; such action would cost around 1 per cent of global GDP per year (Stern 2007: ch. 2). The Stern Report has since been supported by further evidence of global warming and its existing, as well as future, impact upon the planet and, hence, upon the capacity for development (see NASA 2015).

All industrialized and industrializing countries are responsible for greenhouse gas emission, including all developed countries as well as many developing countries. This indicates two related points; that environmental degradation does not recognize borders and is ultimately a global problem affecting all peoples, if in some cases disproportionately; and that all countries have a responsibility to actively reduce or eradicate environmentally unsustainable practices. The signing in 1998 of the Kyoto Protocol by 192 countries (the United States signed but did not ratify the agreement, and Australia signed in 2012) was recognition of both this impact and these countries' responsibility to address the problem, even if developing countries are largely exempted from the provisions of the protocols. Having noted that, reflecting a developing neoconservative economic agenda that has privileged economic growth over the environment, having signed the Kyoto Protocols Canada withdrew as a signatory in 2011. Doing so, it cited a lack of progress and an unwillingness to pay hefty penalties for failure to meet its emissions targets. Russia also abandoned its binding emissions targets for the second part of the agreement.

Yet set against such broad recognition, to date the development process's environmental record has been poor. Environmental degradation has continued at a pace that has had a major impact on the capacity of some societies to continue to function (e.g., South Korea, see Cho 1999), while establishing a global problem that may not be reversible. Similarly in China, its coal-fuelled rapid industrialization has led to among the world's worst air pollution along most of its eastern coast while substantially contributing to the wider global problem. In recognition of this, by 2013, China decided to develop alternatives to non-renewable energy production, especially the use of the heavily polluting brown coal, and led the world in terms of renewable energy production (Matthews and Tan 2014), in solar power (photovoltaic cells), wind power and hydroelectricity. Germany and South Korea have been following suit, especially in the development of solar power.

Although most developing countries have not yet reached such a devastating level of industrial development, the industrialization process has been causing the vast majority to show serious signs of failing to implement environmental safeguards, the rationale being that as developing countries they could not 'afford' such safeguards (to illustrate, under the Kyoto Protocol there are no binding emissions targets for developing countries). This environmental failure did not to begin to include over-logging and deforestation, land degradation and desertification, and run-off from herbicides, insecticides and human waste pollution that not only reduces supplies of potable (drinkable) water but also damages the wider environment.

Part of the reason for continued unsustainable ecological practices derives from there being little or no consensus about the range of meanings of sustainability or the terminology that is used to denote it. Moreover, since the release of the Brundtland Report in 1987, there has continued to be debate about what does or does not constitute sustainable practice and the range of or limitation on options about addressing environmental challenges.

In particular, there are extensive debates about whether there is a need for continued economic growth and over the lead times for introducing adequate and sustainable energy sources. This is set against further debates about population growth and what constitutes a sustainable population, how to best manage the environment not just for the present generations but for future generations, possible technological options for supporting population growth (or not, as the case may be), patterns of consumption and the culture of consumerism. One part of the debate around 'sustainable development' even suggests that the term is internally contradictory (e.g. see Ferry 2009), in that development by its nature consumes finite resources. Brundtland's classical definition of sustainable development meeting 'the needs of the present without compromising the ability of future generations to meet their own needs' (1987) is a case in point; it does not appear to be possible to meet present and future needs on the basis of existing and projected populations. Brundtland's own, more complete, definition was more sophisticated than this simple rebuttal might imply, and she acknowledged the range of competing and contradictory forces at play in the development process. There have also been criticisms of sustainable development on the basis of unknown or unintended consequences, particularly economic consequences.

Within the global environmental debate, there are serious questions about how long current development processes can continue before ecological systems collapse as, in some cases, they have already done or are starting to do so. Within the global warming debate, there is now widespread global acceptance, as indicated by the signing of the Kyoto Protocol, of the need to curb the emission of carbon dioxide and other greenhouse gases. There is also related concern about the effects of industrialization on global ecological systems. Environmental damage may occur in one country and be a consequence of that country's policies but environmental degradation, such as acid rain, does not respect arbitrary state divisions. Damage in one country can easily impact upon another country, or many countries, and widespread environmental collapse is no longer a matter of if, but when and where, should there not be a fundamental shift in development thinking, planning and implementation.

Global warming

Although recognized in some sectors as a major climatic issue for many years, the issue of global warming has only recently been taken seriously as the world's biggest environmental problem. That this phenomenon is happening is now accepted as scientific fact by the scientific societies and academies of science in all industrialized countries. In 2010 alone, of 74 countries measured, 21 recorded their highest ever temperatures, with a further 15 countries recording their highest temperature in the previous ten years.[1] Even the American Association of Petroleum Geologists, which has a vested interest in continuing fossil fuel production, has modified its position from rejecting the science to being noncommittal. According to the Stern Report, commissioned by the British government, global temperatures have already risen, if by a small margin, over the previous century, but are likely to rise between 2°C and 3°C, and with an even chance of rising by up to 5°C, over the next 50 years (Stern 2007; see also Hansen et al. 2006). The Intergovernmental Panel on Climate Change (IPCC) has predicted a slightly smaller rise in global temperatures, of 1.1 to 6.4°C, depending on greenhouse gas emission and climate sensitivity, between the start of the twentieth and end of the twenty-first centuries. As noted by the Labor Environment Action Network, total global carbon dioxide emissions increased by 70 per cent between 1970 and 2004 (see also Figure 10.1) and continued to rise at an increasing rate. The annual increase of total global carbon dioxide emissions jumped from an average 1.1 per cent over 1990–99 to more than 3 per cent between 2000 and 2004. This growth rate of emissions since 2000 has exceeded even the most pessimistic projections of the IPCC (LEAN 2011).

In short, global warming has already begun fundamentally to shift the balance of the planet's water, which has seen the biggest rise in temperatures, from reduced polar ice caps and lost permafrost to flooding

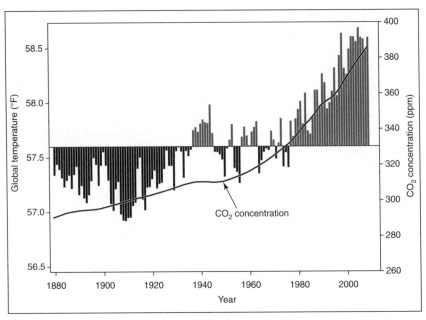

Source: National Climatic Data Center, US Department of Commerce.

Figure 10.1   *Global temperature and carbon dioxide presence*

of low-lying lands. This is expected to directly affect some 200 million people, to lead to increases in tropical areas as well as turning once fertile lands into arid areas, thus decreasing food production. It will alter the habitat and survivability of up to 40 per cent of the earth's species and generate unexpected and increasingly volatile weather 'events', including both extended drought and flood. As with other negative impacts, those people already living closest to absolute poverty and with little or no capacity to absorb such impact will be most affected by such change.

> The effect that increased droughts, extreme weather events, tropical storms and sea level rises will have on large parts of Africa, on many small island states and coastal zones will be inflicted in our lifetimes. In terms of aggregate world GDP, these short term effects may not be large. But for some of the world's poorest people, the consequences could be apocalyptic. In the long run climate change is a massive threat to human development and in some places it is already undermining the international community's efforts to reduce extreme poverty.   (UNDP 2008: 3)

The main approaches to limiting further climate change include greater restrictions on the production of carbon dioxide waste and tradable carbon emissions; the creation of a global carbon market, in which the production of carbon is taxed; further development and expansion of non-carbon sources of energy (such as hydro, solar and wind power); the preservation and expansion of 'carbon-sinks' – large forests such as those found in Brazil and Borneo and the creation of new forests; and a reduction of overall consumption. However, there remains considerable debate about how to resolve the global warming problem. Developing countries, such as China and India, have been exempted from the Kyoto Protocols, which has enhanced their industrial capacity in contrast to industrial countries that have committed to limiting greenhouse gas emissions. This has led the US to refuse to ratify the protocols on the grounds that it would unfairly limit its own economies. Having noted this, China has since committed to a programme that, by 2050, is intended to see coal-fired energy reduced to between 30 and 50 per cent of total energy production, with the remainder being produced from oil, natural gas and renewable energy sources (Weidou 2005, see also DRC 2014).

Population reduction

In terms of reducing overall consumption and assuming that people will not volunteer to significantly alter their consumption behaviour, one of the critical and most controversial issues in environmental development revolves around the capacity of the earth to sustain existing numbers of people. There are those who believe that the earth has greater capacity to sustain people than currently exists (Simon 1994) and those who believe that the earth is already being taxed up to or beyond its capacity (e.g., UNEP 1999; Varfolomeyev and Gurevich 2001).

Even where the earth has shown that it has a high carrying capacity, this is usually enhanced by the use of fertilizers, pesticides and high-energy transport, all of which add a cost that is not often factored into economic assessments (see Milbrath 1996: ch. 10). That is, the full cost of industrialization or other forms of production and energy consumption rarely accounts for 'off-book' expenses such as to the environment. For example, the use of agricultural pesticides can and often does enhance productivity but it also has implications for water quality (UNCSD 2002b), while transport and manufacturing costs rarely incorporate costs to the atmosphere. In this respect, the full cost of economic growth is usually greater than the simple single bottom-line formula used by most accountants in that it also uses 'public good' (clean air, water, habitat, other amenity) that is not properly, or often at all, costed. In particular, there is conflict over the notion of 'public' or shared resources, especially where this 'free' resource (e.g., water, air) is used excessively or unwisely and impacts on 'non-market' activities (Portney 1982: 4). In this sense, private markets may allocate resources inefficiently and the 'externalities' generated by private development may impact on a wider 'public good' (Portney 1982: 6). In one sense, the over-exploitation of some resources by some parts of the earth's population, or 'resource capture', produces a structural imbalance in access to resources (Homer-Dixon 1999: 15–19) and potential for conflict.

There are significant parts of the world that have a very limited carrying capacity and are vulnerable to degradation due to over-exploitation. These marginal areas, such as Africa's Sahel, are growing in size and their capacity to support life is reducing. And apart from the consumption of non-renewable resources, it would appear that at some point there must, logically, be a limit to the carrying capacity of the earth, regardless of how sensitively and wisely it is used.

There have been, as Homer-Dixon has noted (1999: 53) distinct physical trends in global change, and while these have occurred over varying timescales and in different locations, their effects have become increasingly global and interrelated. Homer-Dixon noted an interconnectivity between, for example, human population growth, rising energy consumption, global warming, ozone depletion, rising cropland scarcity, tropical deforestation, rising scarcity of free water, declining fish stocks and a more general loss of biodiversity (this has since been reconfirmed by a number of studies, not least by UNEP 2015 and NASA 2015).

In particular, the sheer increase in the global population, the consumption of natural resources implied by such growth and the human and industrial pollution that has been produced, is perhaps the single most important issue. Of the world's 7.3 billion people at 2015, around 6 billion live in developing countries and more than 4.5 billion live in rural areas (World Bank 2014b) and depend largely on agriculture for their income or subsistence. Korten notes that while the world's poor only add marginally to environmental degradation, if they were to achieve higher levels of development the already unsustainable consumption of natural resources would quickly move into the critical zone. Yet the alternative is to condemn the poor to underdevelopment in perpetuity (Korten 1989: 166). And there is also a view that suggests poverty actually increases environmental degradation through more desperate use of resources, such as forest depletion for fuel wood. The only way to raise global standards of living to a higher, more equitable level is to reduce global consumption, most readily through reducing the global population.

Assuming no change in behaviour away from a global tendency increasingly to consume natural resources or the adoption of less resource-reliant technologies, it would appear there needs to be a considerable reduction in the world's population in order to accommodate limited natural productive capacity and to find alternative and more sustainable finite natural resources. However, the only sign of absolute population reduction, apart from natural or human calamities, has been amongst the most developed societies. Many countries have reduced the rate at which they are increasing their population, leading to overall stable population growth in developed countries (World Bank 2014b). This implies that global society will have to develop significantly further before there is any in-built tendency towards population reduction and, frankly, all indicators are that there is not time for this 'natural' process to take place before environmental catastrophe. The argument that suggests there are limits to the earth's capacity to sustain an increasing population is sometimes referred to as Malthusianism, or neo-Malthusianism, a later version of which posited that as resources are finite, and larger families in any case contributed to poverty, birth control and subsequent population reduction were necessary conditions for sustainable development.

The world's total population was about 1.65 billion in 1900; by 2015 it had grown to 7.3 billion, representing a more than fourfold increase. The annual growth rate, while slowing since the late 1960s to just over 1 per cent in the early twenty-first century, had peaked at 88 million a year in 1989, reduced to around 74 million a year by 2003, went up to 75 million in 2006 but was expected to continue to decline to around 40 million over the coming four decades, to reach just over 9 billion people (USCB 2011). See Figure 10.2.

Added to this has been a massive shift in consumption patterns over the 100 years, currently doubling each 30 years, notably in industrialized countries but also in developing countries. The massive increase in hydrocarbon (oil and gas) consumption and its consequences for the environment (e.g. greenhouse effect, enhancing desertification), is one illustration of the shift in consumption (see Figure 10.3). 'Peak oil', in which the maximum rate of known oil reserves is reached, was thought to be 12.5 billion barrels per year in the year 2000, but was later revised to occur, or have occurred, around 2014–15. However, depending on viability, a shift towards the development of shale oil extraction may have deferred that date. This meant that while known and

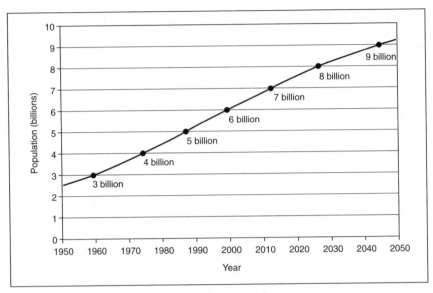

Source: USCB, *International Data Base*, December 2010 Update.

Figure 10.2   *World population, 1950–2050*

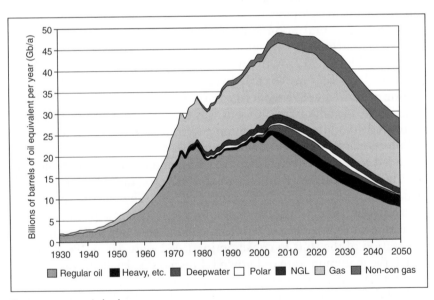

Source: www.aspo-ireland.org.

Figure 10.3   *Global oil and gas production profiles*

anticipated oil reserves would last until around 2060, accessing such oil will become increasingly difficult and hence more expensive, especially against increasing levels of consumption, thus pushing up the price of oil and oil-based products such as petrol (gasoline).

One short-term consequence of this 'peak oil' phenomenon was that oil companies were increasingly pushing to explore for oil in wilderness heritage sites, such as the Arctic region. Another was that they were attempting to cut exploration and production costs, leading to short cuts that resulted in environmentally damaging spills, for example in Nigeria, the Amazon basin and the Gulf of Mexico. Another, more positive, consequence was that, slowly, a number of oil-dependent companies were exploring alternative energy sources, if often in hybrid forms with oil-based energy. Similar to the global consumption of oil is the world's increasing demand for timber and timber products, including paper, which is leading to increased deforestation as well as forest reduction more quickly than forests can regenerate (Dangwal 2005; Tscharnthe et al. 2010).

The main criticism of neo-Malthusianism derives from governments and policy-makers who claim that large populations sustain markets that are necessary to increased growth, and are also capable of caring for increasingly larger older populations which are especially noticeable as a consequence of fertility 'booms' such as those following the Second World War and the 'Green Revolution'. Some governments also continue to argue that a large population is necessary for defence purposes, although the linkage between the two reflects a pre-modern view of strategic advantage. And apart from cultural traditions, in which larger families are regarded as a safeguard against abandonment in old age, some religions (such as Roman Catholicism) actively encourage propagation to increase the numbers of their followers. The rationalization of this position is that the earth is intended for the consumption of humanity, and that it has the capacity to sustain a much greater overall consumption. Many policy-makers (including the Catholic Church) also argue that the earth's problems less reflect overall consumption and more reflect the unequal distribution of consumption (see Homer-Dixon 1999: 35–7).

Having noted this, by the 1960s the governments of some of the more heavily populated countries decided that their population 'bomb' was already ticking and took steps to limit population growth (see Ehrlich 1969, for one of the first, most critical, though somewhat alarmist, discussions on the subject). The 1960s were critical in this respect, as not only had a number of countries recognized that there was about to be a major problem with excessive population but at the same time fertility rates were growing, to peak at 2.1 per cent a year between 1965 and 1970 (Homer-Dixon 1999: 13). Of the world's most fertile countries, as of 2014, the top 122 were all developing countries, with 29 of the top 33 countries located in Africa, with between just under five and just under seven live births per woman.

Asia, on the other hand, moved early to curb its own ballooning populations. By 1966, 12 of 22 Asian states had taken measures to curb fertility (Ness and Ando 1984: 18). The world's first, second and fourth most populous countries, China, India and Indonesia, remain three prominent examples of countries that have active population control policies and, while the heavy-handedness of these policies in India and particularly in China have given ammunition to the 'pro-fertility' lobby, they have served as recognition that population growth has costs as well as benefits. However, the success or otherwise of these programmes was less the issue than a recognition of the basic problem. And not all countries with large populations, high population densities or limited environmental capacities support the idea of limiting their populations.

Ness and Ando noted that contrasting with the Asian experience, only 4 of 26 Latin American countries, 3 of 40 African states and 3 of 18 Mediterranean states had adopted fertility control measures (1984: 19). This reflected the Asian lead in the fertility control field that was itself predicated on a public recognition that median and mean population densities were generally higher in Asian countries, and tended to be higher in other countries that also adopted fertility control programmes (Ness and Ando 1984: 22–3). The success of those programmes further reflected the actual strength of implementation of the programme (Ness and Ando 1984: 132–9). Not surprisingly, the timing of the move towards controlling fertility rates corresponded with more localized policy planning as a result of independence, rapidly increasing populations as a consequence of the 'Green Revolution', and access to new and more widely available methods of contraception.

Deforestation

The impact of population spread and consumption is perhaps most visible in terms of loss of forests and associated desertification. Along with, and related to, global warming, deforestation is equally the world's most significant environmental problem. Such deforestation has a number of implications, including soil erosion, land degradation (in particular degradation of arable farmland) and desertification, loss of habitat for various animal species and reduction in other biodiversity, the absorption of carbon dioxide (resulting in increased global warming) and a reduction in the production of oxygen, upon which all animal (and human) life depends (FAO 2001). Estimates vary but, at the current rate of deforestation, some of the world's major forests, such as those in Indonesia/Borneo, Papua New Guinea and the Amazon Basin, will be completely eradicated within 30 years, and possibly sooner. Chile, with approximately one-third of the world's temperate rainforest, at current rates of logging, could be completely deforested by 2022.

Brazil contains the world's single largest forest, in the Amazon Basin, but existing logging, which has been driven by the timber industry and new settlements and farmland, has depleted the forest at an unsustainable rate. Between 1978 and 1996, some 52 million hectares, or 12.5 per cent of the total forest, was cleared, representing a loss of around 2.9 million hectares a year. Logging, continuing at the rate of 13,000 hectares a day, or 4.75 million hectares a year, received renewed impetus at the beginning of the twenty-first century as Brazil struggled to meet external loan repayments. The president of the Amazon Working Group (representing some 350 regional non-governmental organizations (NGOs)), Claudionor Barbosa da Silva, said that 90 per cent of funding to Amazon conservation programmes had been cut to meet International Monetary Fund (IMF) loan schedules, along with two-thirds of rainforest protection capacity and demarcation of lands belonging to indigenous peoples. Austerity measures resulting from the IMF programme encouraged illegal logging of the forest (Knight and Aslam 2000). Other countries looking to address critical economic problems through increased excessive logging of old-growth forests included Russia and Indonesia, which, along with Brazil, were home to just under half of the world's old-growth rainforests. While the rate of Brazil's deforestation began to slow into the twenty-first century, it again jumped in 2014, up by 29 per cent, showing that while awareness of the negative impacts of deforestation had increased, it remained a tenacious environmental problem (Bevins 2014).

While environmental policies in Indonesia were always very poor, the decentralization of government following the end of the New Order in 1998 further impacted on the environment, in particular exacerbating the loss of Indonesia's tropical rainforests. Already very poor, local environmental protection has slid further, due to less central control over logging, short-term local government economic priorities and the decentralization of corruption. The annual deforestation rate between 1985 and 1997 was estimated to be 1.7 million hectares (Resosudarno 2002). Since 1998, that level has increased significantly. A 2007 UN report estimated that illegal logging in Kalimantan accounted for three-quarters of all logging in Indonesia, which made the single largest contribution to Indonesia becoming the third largest greenhouse gas emitter in the world. At recent rates of deforestation, Indonesia may lose 98 per cent of all its forests by 2020 (UNCTSD 2007).

In other areas in Kalimantan and in northern Sumatra, in the face of a larger economic collapse, illegal logging has increased dramatically, although local governments have turned less than a blind eye towards it, by taxing the logs that are illegally taken to continue to raise revenue: 'In the months of April, May and June 2000 alone, the district [of Kotawaringin] raised 24 billion rupiah by taxing illegal timber coming out of [East] Kotawaringin ... This initiative is effectively "legalizing" illegal timber' (Resosudarno 2002: 8). And, as Resosudarno notes, much illegal logging has taken place in protected and conservation areas (2002: 9–10). This type of experience is common in many developing countries, where forests have been seen as a resource with almost unlimited exploitable potential. In Kalimantan, as of 2014, deforestation continued apace, primarily to make way for monocultural palm oil plantations (Widoyoko 2014).

In some areas, it can be simple government policy that leads to excessive logging. In Myanmar, between 40 and 50 per cent of the state remained under forest cover by 1995. Between 1990 and 2005, the country lost 18 per cent of its forests (Htaw 2008). However, Myanmar's government, which retains a legal monopoly on logging, remained desperate for hard currency to finance its military following the long-term collapse of its economy. The international community condemned Myanmar's illegal but lucrative opium/heroin and amphetamine trade so, until it began to open up its economy in 2013, it increasingly turned to logging. At the same time, anti-government guerrilla groups also engaged in logging to support their campaigns while allowing corrupt Thai generals and Chinese and Thai businessmen also illegally to log or buy logs from across the border (KNG 2011). The situation with logging was eased somewhat as international investment sanctions were lifted in 2012–13 and foreign capital flowed into Myanmar.

Where once forests covered around 55 per cent of Thailand, they now cover around 5 per cent, with half of those remaining being held in reserves. Thailand, once a wood exporter, now imports timber and paper (similarly to Nigeria). In this, Thailand has been effectively logged out and further logging is now banned there (Gallasch 2001: 8–9, 11; see also Bryant in Hirsch and Warren 1998). Similarly, logging is also banned in Yunnan Province. China theoretically banned the import of timber in 2005. However, an extensive black market operated by the Kachin Independence Organisation with the blessing of the Myanmar government continues to ship illegal logs across the border (KNG 2011).

Interestingly, while developed countries have called on developing countries to preserve their forests, in particular rainforests, some leaders of developing countries have pointed out that such calls are somewhat hypocritical, given that most developed countries almost completely depleted their own stands of forests in the process of industrialization. More positively, on World Environment Day in 2007 the then recently elected governor of the heavily forested Indonesian province of Aceh, Irwandi Yusuf, banned logging entirely. At the tip of Sumatra, Aceh contained considerable first growth triple canopy rainforests and was home to wild elephants and Sumatra's remaining tigers. Despite some shortcomings with the logging ban, including continued illegal logging, the move was shortlisted for a Future Policy Award by the Hamburg-based World Future Council. Under a change of provincial government, however, in 2014, protected forest areas were reduced from 60 per cent to 45 per cent, meaning an expected loss of some 1.2 million hectares of forest. The deforestation was primarily planned to accommodate new palm oil plantations.

Desertification

Drought and desertification, resulting from global climate change and direct human activity such as deforestation, threaten the livelihoods of more than 1.2 billion people across 110 countries. Around 2 billion people live in 'drylands', which occupy around 40 per cent of the earth's land surface, while 90 per cent of people who live in drylands are from developing countries. Of the earth's drylands, up to 20 per cent is already degraded and desertification shows no signs of abatement (Holtz 2007; Mueller et al. 2014). Drought is a generally natural variation towards lower rainfall in what are already low rainfall areas. However, rainfall patterns can also be affected by changed global weather patterns (such as the 'El Niño' effect), global warming due to the emission of 'greenhouse' gases and the removing of forests and other ground cover.

Desertification, or the degradation of drylands, involves the loss of biological or economic productivity and complexity in croplands, pastures and woodlands. Desertification occurs mainly as a consequence of climate variability and unsustainable human activities, with the most commonly cited forms of unsustainable land use being over-cultivation, over-grazing, deforestation and poor irrigation practices. Of the world's drylands (excluding hyper-arid deserts), 70 per cent, or some 3,600 million hectares, is degraded. Excessive use of lands generally and drylands in particular is allowed by unregulated access which is usually driven by economic necessity, or desperation. In many cases, even where people know their practices are not sustainable, they are looking to survive to next week, rather than next year. The future of the environment can, in such circumstances, start to look like a luxury many people cannot afford. There are also cases of ignorance of dryland farming, where new settlers farm drylands in rainy times only to have the drylands revert to normal soon after, exposing often inappropriate farming methods (UNCCD 2002a; Thomas 2008).

Once land is degraded, while it can recover, its capacity to do so is reduced. This has longer-term physical and socio-economic consequences. Physically, degraded topsoil can be blown away by wind or washed away by rain and it becomes prone to erosion, waterlogging and salinization. Excessive grazing of hooved animals can also damage soil and kill off existing vegetation, which in turn, reduces the capacity to maintain topsoil and further reduces vegetation, or allows the growth of inappropriate vegetation. Other consequences of land degradation include the loss of topsoil during rains that silt waterways, killing fish stocks and making such water unpotable. A concerted effort under the Millennium Development Goals had seen an increase of access to potable water for 2 billion people since 1990 (UN 2006b). But around 770 million people around the world still do not have adequate access to potable water (WHO/UNICEF 2008: 25; Water.Org 2015), almost entirely due to the degradation of waterways, most often due to silting. Examples of the degradation of marginal lands include during the 1930s in the US, in the 1950s in the USSR, in Australia, and notably in the Sahel region along the southern edges of the Sahara Desert, in places such as Mauritania, northern Burkina Faso, north-western Niger, central Chad, much of Sudan, parts of Eritrea, and across areas of northern China and Mongolia. Apart from environmental degradation, desertification reduces the capacity for food production, which in already marginal areas can result in famine. Whitehead notes that while acute famine crises usually coincide with catastrophic events, they tend to occur in areas that are already affected by scarcity and thus escalate a problematic situation into one of 'complete disaster' (in Friday and Laskey 1989: 82). Such complete disasters tend to displace people, which in some cases leads to conflict. There has been little formal study of the economic consequences of desertification but a UN report quotes an unpublished World Bank study as noting, in Africa, that the depletion of natural resources in one Sahelian country was equivalent to 20 per cent of its annual GDP. The United Nations Convention to Combat Desertification (UNCCD) estimates that the lost annual income due to desertification is approximately US\$42 billion each year (UNCCD 2011; Waters 2013: 172).

Desertification is widespread, occurring in Africa, across Asia, Latin America and parts of the Caribbean, the Mediterranean countries, Central and Eastern Europe and Australia. However, of all these places, desertification has its greatest impact in Africa, much of which has been affected by frequent and severe droughts, a situation further complicated by the debt crisis and frequent civil conflict. Two-thirds of Africa is desert or drylands, including extensive agricultural areas, almost three-quarters of which are already degraded to some extent. Many African countries are landlocked, have widespread poverty and depend on subsistence agriculture. Despite its natural problems, in 1970 Africa was self-sufficient in food production. But by 1984, due to frequent and severe drought, population increase, soil erosion, desertification, government policy failure and political turmoil, a quarter of Africa's population was being kept alive by imported grain (Manley and Brandt 1985: 157; Mason et al. 2012; see also UNCCD 2002c). This has been the prime contributing factor to sub-Saharan Africa having the most marginal dietary energy supply, lowest per capita GDP and highest infant mortality rate of any continent (UNDP 2008).

Because programmes designed to deal with desertification in Africa must be sustainable, they have increasingly focused on local communities:

> Local communities have valuable experience and a special understanding of their own environment. When the responsibility for natural resource management is taken away from them, their use of land and other natural resources can become highly inefficient. The result is often land degradation. Participatory development recognizes the rights of local communities over their resources. (UNCCD 2002d)

The UNCCD notes, however, that the participatory process is time consuming and labour intensive, that many affected member states continue to need stronger civil society and public security to participate, and that governments need to construct a conducive environment for community participation: 'The community has to go through a long learning and confidence-building process in order to take full advantage of the new resources it now receives and manages directly. Due attention is also paid to gender issues and the involvement of the more marginalized social groups' (UNCCD 2002d).

Water

Related to the issues of industrialization, deforestation, desertification and population growth, the use, pollution and depletion of the world's waterways for human and industrial purposes has reduced the amount of available potable water and has negatively impacted on human, plant and animal life, on animal life in particular in fisheries and streams as well as in oceans in areas near outlets. This has again impacted severely on marginal populations who rely on the supply of protein and potable water for everyday needs. As Harrington and Fisher noted: 'of all the threats to biological resources, habitat modification in its various forms is by far the most serious' (Harrington and Fisher, in Portney 1982: 122). Global fish stocks in particular have been hard hit, and unsustainably depleted. What was once considered to be an inexhaustible abundance of fish has begun to diminish in ways that have meant that some species of fish have become extinct and other are threatened with a reduction in numbers that might preclude their continued viability as a species (Vince 2012).

Habitat degradation and pollution are critical factors in sustaining fish stocks. The critical factors in the depletion of fish stocks include the drainage of coastal wetlands and swamps, along with the conversion of land for houses, farms and roads which is destroying breeding grounds for fish through increased run-off of silt, industrial chemicals and human waste into spawning areas. Industrial spills in the South East Asian archipelago have led to vast quantities of fish simply being killed, which does not include the impact of losing their breeding grounds and the effects of changing global water temperatures (Cheung et al. 2013).

However, probably the biggest impact on fish stocks is over-fishing which has taken place both through need and commercial opportunity and has become a common problem in many parts of the world. One area of international co-operation has been over the large, slow breeding Southern Bluefin Tuna (SBT), the numbers of which have been in decline since the 1960s when annual catches reached 80,000 tonnes. By the mid-1980s it became apparent that catches would have to be limited to preserve the remaining stocks and, while there has been considerable international debate and disagreement, and some illegal fishing, there is now agreement between the primary SBT fishing states to control fishing of the species. Stocks, however, have since been reduced to just 9 per cent of the initial spawning biomass (CCSBT 2014). A similar programme of conservation has also been enacted for the Atlantic Bluefin Tuna. Even stocks of that most feared fish, shark, have become depleted in a number of specific locations due to over-fishing. Improper or wasteful fishing methods have also depleted other, often localized, fish stocks at an unsustainable rate. The use of explosives and dragnets kill many species in addition to those that are actually sought after. Even Lake Victoria, which is bordered by Kenya, Uganda and Tanzania and feeds millions of people, is facing a depletion of its fish stocks due to over-fishing, illegal fishing and improper fishing methods (PNA 2001). Some Lake Victoria fish species are now on the verge of extinction while others are in serious decline (Kennedy 2015).

According to Proyect, advances in fishing technology mean that the world's fishing fleets have the capacity to exceed global fish stocks. The introduction of sonar and fishing boats that could carry much greater hauls meant that between 1970 and 1992, the average tonnage taken by each fishing boat almost doubled to 26,000 tonnes. Of this, about a third of the total catch, or some 27 million tonnes, was discarded as waste (Proyect 1998). By 2006, 7 per cent of the world's fish stocks were depleted, 17 per cent were over-exploited and more than half were fully exploited (FAO 2006). According to the FAO's 2010 fisheries report:

> the declining global catch in the last few years, together with the increased percentage of overexploited, depleted or recovering stocks and the decreased proportion of underexploited and moderately exploited species around the world, strengthens the likelihood that the production of wild capture fisheries will not be able to increase unless effective management plans are put in place to rebuild over-fished stocks.   (FAO 2010: 42)

One means of controlling fishing and of securing adequate supplies of fish stocks has been the age-old practice of aquaculture, which is the planned breeding of fish (FAO 2014b). At a local level, aquaculture has been able to use local ponds for breeding fish. Communities in protein-poor north-east Thailand have been experimenting with diversified, self-sufficient food programmes since the mid-1980s, and notably since the economic crisis of 1997, including breeding fish in local ponds and cages to supplement the traditional net fishing in the region's limited waterways. Similarly, in lowland Vietnam, local villagers have responded creatively to the permanent scarring of much of their countryside by using the thousands of remaining bomb craters as fish-breeding ponds. In addition, both Thailand and Vietnam have been turning rice paddies into fish-breeding ponds as a way of meeting both local and export demand.

However, while localized aquaculture is a practical response to securing protein, larger-scale or globalized aquaculture has had some negative consequences, especially through the introduction of 'exotic' species into unfamiliar environments that has resulted in the depletion of original indigenous fish stocks. For example, the introduction of a particular type of prawn (shrimp), *Penaeus japonicus*, from Japan to Europe has resulted in the species' colonization of vast marine areas (TWR 1998) and the loss of local species.

The loss of fish stocks and the depletion of coastal and ocean habitat is a major threat to both ecological balance and to the sustainability of a key source of protein for human consumption. But even more importantly, lack of access to potable water is perhaps the world's most immediate environmental issue. While just under a billion people still did not have access to safe drinking water, what is less appreciated is that the often poor quality of available water continues to be the single biggest contributing factor to general illness, notably through nutritional and fluid loss (primarily through diarrhoea), a situation which is reflected in infant mortality rates (Fordham 2002). That is, lack of access to potable water not only directly impacts upon the health of people who have no choice but to drink unsuitable water but this, in turn, limits their capacity to work and consequently has a direct economic impact on their capacity for development (see Whittington and Swarna 1994; also Latham 2000; and Strauss, especially p. 168, in Pinstrup-Andersen 1993 for discussion on nutrition and development).

The combination of industrial waste, increased use of herbicides, insecticides, growth promoters, deforestation and human population growth have all impacted negatively on the world's supply of potable water. As Baur and Rudolph (2001) have noted, the simple question of whether there is enough fresh water for each person is already a critical issue. Around 3,800 cubic km of fresh water is now withdrawn annually from the world's lakes, rivers and aquifers, about twice the amount extracted in the mid-twentieth century. Agriculture uses around 70 per cent of available water, industry uses almost one-fifth, and municipal and domestic use accounts for slightly less than 10 per cent (FAO 2014b). Rather than peak at around 9 billion around 2050, as was projected in Figure 10.2 – now a low estimate – then decline, a revision of estimates has shown that the world's population of more than 7 billion people (2014) was expected to reach 10 billion by around 2065, with constant fertility estimates now increasing global population from around 11 billion people in 2065 to more than 25 billion by 2100 (UN 2013c: xv).

Each person requires up to 50 litres of water a day for drinking, food preparation, sanitation and bathing (with around 20 litres considered a practical minimum). Access to water is not evenly distributed, with a number of countries occupying what are considered 'water-stressed' (semi-arid and arid) zones. One-third of these countries are expected to face severe water shortages this century. By 2025, there will be approximately 3.5 billion people living in water-stressed countries, a situation that appears to be exacerbated by global warming and population growth. In simple terms, there are more people than there are necessary minimums of available potable water, especially in less supportive environments. Where the environment has a greater capacity to support higher populations, those populations are placing such stresses on water supplies that its supportive capacity is diminishing.

The imbalance in water supply has been most notable in the increasing swings between drought and floods. And in many rural areas where there remains no access to running water, water drawn from wells or ground pumps is increasingly affected by chemical and human pollution seeping into the water table.

Loss of potable water, due to inadequate or failing waterways is a significant factor in the development profile of a number of cities in developing countries. In Pakistan, almost a half of the country's 185 million people (44 per cent) and up to 90 per cent in rural areas did not have access to drinkable water in the first few years of the twenty-first century, primarily due to industrial waste and agricultural run-off (Rosemann 2005: 3; Yes Pakistan 2002). Infrastructure projects, often funded by multilateral lending agencies such as the Asian Development Bank, have been undertaken in places like Karachi and Manila to reduce this unnecessary loss of drinking water. However, the extent of the problem, the rate at which it continues to grow worse and the cost involved in fixing it as well as of ensuring the reliable supply of potable water to urban systems means that the larger problem is expanding faster than it can be addressed.

While many developing countries do have restrictions on pollution, these restrictions are very commonly observed in the breach. And in any case, governments of developing countries are more inclined to go softly on such industry, as they cite economic inability to provide alternative means of waste disposal while pointing out the contribution of industrial development and enhanced food production to self-sufficiency, employment and economic development.

One suggested answer to declining water stocks is the privatization of water. That is, water should cease to be (in principle) a generally freely available resource and should become a commodity like any other. The case for privatizing water is that it will reduce wastage while encouraging private companies to secure greater potable water supplies for further sale (Segerfeldt 2005). While most countries do charge for water access, they do so through the provision of water as a government service as a broad social responsibility. The World Bank has estimated that the world water market was worth almost US$1 trillion at the beginning of the twenty-first century, although that only accounted for the approximately 5 per cent of the world's water consumers who obtained water through corporations. Two of the world's major private water suppliers, Suez Lyonnaise des Eaux (SLE) and Vivendi SA, own or control water companies in 120 countries, with each distributing water to more than 110 million people (Ondeo 2002; Vivendi 2002). However, the privatization of water assumes two points. The first point assumed is a capacity to pay, although it is likely that when there is no choice people will, if they can, pay for water as a primary necessity. However, many of the world's most poor would be unlikely to be able to pay for privatized water, while there are questions about the benefit to those who can do so. The second point is that everything can be commodified and that what has for most people traditionally been an assumed public right, somewhat like breathing air, can or should be regarded as the preserve of private interest. Regardless of private business's poor record on environmental issues, there are deep philosophical questions attached to the idea that what was once a common public good is available for private ownership. However, in principle, such questions go to the core of the nexus between humankind and the environment, and how human affairs are organized in ways that are equitable or otherwise, and which are sustainable or otherwise.

Political economy of the environment

Environmental degradation is not just a consequence of people mindlessly destroying the world they live in. For many people, notably the most poor in developing countries, drawing down on environmental resources is a matter of survival. Logging to clear land can occur because of population pressure or displacement, the need to earn cash income or the provision of fuel wood for cooking. Washing clothing and bathing in streams is a common practice in developing countries but adds chemicals to waterways that not only deplete fish stocks and other species but which also reduce their use for drinking water. Yet there appear to be few alternatives for people without access to other sources of water. Similarly, even where people construct toilet facilities away from waterways, seepage through ground water can and does lead to a high level of bacteria in streams and wells, with negative consequences for the health of people who use such sources. In some cases, environmental degradation is a consequence of a lower level of aware-ness or lack of education. But in most cases, poor people engage in such practices not through choice but through sheer necessity. For other communities, unsustainable resource exploitation is a consequence of living in marginal environments, or environments that are unable to comfortably sustain growing populations. Similarly, many people who had previously come from subsistence societies have increasingly been encouraged to participate in monoculture cash cropping. With world commodity prices falling between the 1970s and the early 2000s (non-energy commodity prices falling by about half between 1980 and 2000 (GCM 2000)), increased prices and food scarcity after 2006 and increasing tariff barriers to value-added food products, cash cropping has required more exploitation of a given area to produce the same income (or what is most often in reality less real income) or, more recently, to make up for higher-priced foodstuffs.

In most developing countries, the quickest and most lucrative wealth is to be made by selling resources, usually without value-adding (e.g. minerals, raw logs, wood-chips), or by cutting costs such as those expended on environmental safeguards (e.g. dumping pollutants into waterways or not rehabilitating degraded land). While local exploiters often operate for personal profit at the expense of their fellows and the environment, the wider relationship between the local and the global also determines which resources are in demand, how much is to be paid for them, what alternatives a local economy might have for income generation and, arguably, the direction in which local economies can operate. The price of commodities alone can determine environmental impact, not through steering providers away from lower-priced com-modities but through increasing production to make up for shortfalls in prices or to undercut competition. That is, if a product, say saw-logs, is reduced in price by half, at least twice as many logs (due to higher marginal costs) will need to be produced to return equivalent levels of income. The reduction in the price of saw-logs can be a consequence of simple reduced demand but at least as likely will be a consequence of major buyers pitting primary commodity producers against each other to bargain down prices. Where prices for particular commodities fall to levels that become socially or environmentally unsustainable, the option is often to increase production to produce more profit, rather than to seek alternatives.

Beyond the rapaciousness of international carpetbaggers and their proxy comprador elites, there is some awareness of the problems caused by the iniquity of global allocation of resources. In a world that con-tinues to be dominated by a version of *realpolitik,* strongly influenced by neoliberal economic policies, state leaders and lawmakers are only answerable to their constituents, amongst whom are international businesses. They are not answerable to the citizens of other countries, nor is there any agreed global regulatory system that apportions wealth on the basis of effort or need (see Morgenthau 1978). As a consequence, if the benefits to their own citizens are at the expense of another's citizens then, in simple terms, it is the citizens of the other state that are disadvantaged. The primary consequence of this is that states that have less advantage in international relations tend to be exploited, or at best not have their interests considered, in the arranging of international trade, with the consequence that if they are not further impoverished in absolute terms then they are at least allowed access to fewer opportunities for relative development. This, then, relates to the earlier mentioned desperation that many people in developing countries find themselves facing, meaning they are often forced into environmentally unsustainable practices to survive, or that pressures to retain 'comparative advantage' come to include a disregard for the environment or environmental regulations.

As a consequence of the high environmental costs of development, there has increasingly been discussion about 'appropriate development' and 'sustainable development', two ideas that often overlap. What is commonly referred to as 'appropriate development' is where the level of technology is suitable for the needs and conditions of the area undergoing the process of development and does not require environmentally destructive or economically unsustainable industry. Sustainable development similarly means the idea that development can be sustained, primarily in ecological terms but also economically, politically and socially.

'Appropriate development' and 'sustainable development' include a capacity to be locally operated and sustained without requiring either external expertise or capital. In this respect, sophisticated technology is regarded as much less important than technology that works, can be maintained at little or no expense and has few environmental side effects. An example of inappropriate development, for example, is the use of diesel-powered electric generators in poor, oil-importing countries. Appropriate development might rely on solar, wind, geothermal or water (stream-, dam-, wave- or tidal-generated) power (Dunkerley et al. 1981), while there has been development of alcohol and oilseed (such as rapeseed) as a replacement for petrol and diesel as transport fuels. Solar power is also advancing quickly and, while it might remain a relatively capital-expensive form of energy, its cost is quickly reducing while its practicability is increasing through the use of increasingly efficient and less expensive photo-voltaic cells that can provide power on a cloudy day or by moonlight. The issue of access to energy, in particular electricity, is the source of considerable tension in environmental debates. Up to 1.2 billion people in developing countries do not have access to electricity (UNF 2013). Even in countries that currently employ fossil fuels as their primary energy source, prices will continue to increase and, for many, become prohibitively expensive, a situation that has arguably already happened with the passing of peak oil and the declining access to oil stocks. As a consequence, there will be an increasing economic necessity to consider alternative forms of energy-producing technology. That is, while there has been some move towards exploring alternative forms of energy, the major research and development will only occur when fossil fuels become prohibitively expensive which they are expected to do by the end of the first quarter of the twenty-first century. However, while this applies to developed countries, and countries that produce, subsidize or have low taxes on oil products, there are many countries that already struggle to meet their fuel import bill. The environmental issues related to fossil fuel use, not least of which is air pollution in many of the world's major developing cities, are increasingly critical. In particular, with an increasingly urbanized population, Asia has some of the world's most polluted cities, including Beijing, Tianjin, Shanghai, Jakarta, Bangkok, Manila, Mumbai, Calcutta and Delhi (Haq et al. 2002: chs 1–7), although urban sprawls such as Mexico City have also recorded dangerously high air pollution levels.

One energy proposal that received renewed impetus in the early twenty-first century, after a couple of decades of being side-lined, was nuclear energy. Despite having high establishment costs and long lead times, once established, nuclear energy is a relatively efficient energy producer and the material reserves it relies on are substantially available. Despite earlier failures, such as the Chernobyl disaster in the Ukraine and Three Mile Island in the US, by the early twenty-first century nuclear energy was again being promoted as a 'clean' and efficient energy production method. Debate about the safety of nuclear energy resumed again, however, with the failure of 'fail-safe' mechanisms and subsequent large-scale radiation leaks at the Tokyo Electric Power Company (TEPCO) plant at Fukushima following a massive earthquake and tsunami in March 2011. The Fukushima disaster led to a 40 kilometre radius exclusion zone and the dumping of radioactive water into the ocean. As a result the nuclear industry was pushed back by two decades and established, again, that the real issue with this form of power production was that, despite some claims to the contrary, it could not be absolutely guaranteed as safe and that the risks of it not being safe were too high. As a result, a number of countries reconsidered their existing and proposed nuclear power plants, notably in Germany and some other developed countries, but also in the Philippines. India, on the other hand, continued to press ahead with its own nuclear power plants, as did Iran.

Even assuming that safeguards against failure, leakage and waste disposal were mostly overcome in developed countries (and this remains a hotly contested claim, not least in light of the Fukushima disaster), technical imprecision, tectonic instability and related problems do not augur well for nuclear power's use by developing countries. Given the half-life of nuclear radioactivity (between 65,000 and 24,000 years, depending on type), problems in one part of the world have great capacity to eventually negatively affect all parts of the world.

Renewable energy

Renewable energy has been noted as one means of retaining existing energy consumption levels while maintaining relatively high levels of environmental sustainability. There is, not surprisingly, some debate about the ecological credentials of all renewable fuels, especially hydro-electricity which was the most widespread form of renewable energy in use at the time of writing. About one-fifth of the world's agricultural land is irrigated, and irrigated agriculture accounts for about 40 per cent of the world's agricultural production. Half the world's large dams were built exclusively or primarily for irrigation and an estimated 30 to 40 per cent of the 271 million hectares of irrigated land worldwide (around 15 per cent of the total) rely on dams. Dams producing hydro-electricity also produce close to 20 per cent of the world's total electric supply, with 24 countries depending on hydroelectricity for 90 per cent of their power supply. Dams also inhibit flooding which between 1972 and 1996 affected around 65 million people, which is more than war, drought or famine combined (Baur and Rudolph 2001).

Less positively, however, large dams have proven to be only marginally cost effective. The main problems with large dams have been cost overrun, a tendency to fall short of projected power targets and a return of less revenue than anticipated. Dams also impact upon fish stocks and floodplain agriculture and reduce habitat through flooding. It is worth noting that less than half of the dams commissioned during the 1990s had environmental impact assessments (WCD 2000b; Baur and Rudolph 2001). Dams have also been shown to have a high social cost, especially in terms of displacing local peoples (Isaacman and Isaacman

2013). Based on the World Commission on Dams' (WCD's) own report (WCD 2000b), Baur and Rudolph (2001) suggested that between 40 and 80 million people have been displaced by dam construction, with more than half of those coming from India and China (see Fuggle and Smith 2000). Given the social and political sensitivity of displacements of large numbers of people, beyond the leaked details of the WCD report there has been effectively no total data on displacements, with individual displacement statistics being approximate and often wildly varying between official estimates and NGO estimates. The Narmada River dam project in India, which includes some 30 large dams and 3,000 small dams, has been highly controversial and the site of resistance by local people opposed to being removed from their homes. There has also been extensive criticism of the project over inaccurate costing, benefits and returns (see Rangachari et al. 2000). (On large dams in Indonesia, see Aditjondro in Hirsch and Warren 1998.) The Three Gorges Dam on China's Yangtze River (originally conceived in 1999) was, upon its completion in 2006, the world's largest dam, generating a projected 22,500 megawatts of electricity. Construction of the dam, however, displaced 1.3 million people, destroyed historic artefacts and substantially changed the region's ecology. More positively, the dam was expected to reduce coal-fired electricity production by 31 million tonnes a year, saving approximately 100 million tonnes of greenhouse gas emissions, and helping to establish China as one of the global environment leaders if also as its biggest energy consumer (passing the United States in 2008) (IEA 2010).

While some developed countries such as Norway have fully developed hydroelectric schemes, others, such as Australia, discovered that the headlong rush towards hydroelectricity had become self-perpetuating, regardless of energy needs, itself having a significant environmental impact yet not meeting energy or consumption needs. In land-locked Laos, which has least developed (LLDC) status, a major hydroelectric project on the Theun River (Nam Theun) was intended to produce sustainable energy for both consumption in Laos and for selling on to Thailand. The project was heavily criticized for saddling Laos with international debt and for flooding a significant forest area. However, the Lao government agreed that the area to be flooded be logged first and has restricted legal logging in much of the rest of its forests. With around half the country under forest cover and a formal ban on logging introduced in 1989, Laos arguably remains among the most densely forested countries in the world. However, its forest cover has diminished from a claimed 55 per cent in 2000 to around 40 per cent in 2011, and continuing to decline at an annual rate of about 0.6 per cent since then (Sophathilath 2012). While the Nam Theun II dam project has been subjected to international scrutiny, due to local deforestation, social displacement and questions about the demand for the power it will generate, such controversy has at least ensured that the project has been closely monitored, with an eye to ensuring it proceeds according to agreed criteria (Iverach, in Stensholt 1997: 69–70, 76). Large dams required to generate hydroelectricity have also been highly controversial in many other cases in Latin America, across Asia and throughout Africa. Up to 10 million people are said to have been displaced by large dam development since 1948, with most not returning to their former standard of living, while many older dams were silting up, reducing their capacity and future potential (IRN 2001). By the end of the twentieth century, there were over 45,000 large dams in over 150 countries, with an average age of 35 years which meant they were mostly coming to the end of their useful water storage life (Baur and Rudolph 2001).

Support for large dam projects, which has cost some 125 billion dollars in multilateral and bilateral aid since 1950 (although as little as 15 per cent of total costs), has been challenged on the grounds of cost efficiency. Especially with the advent of micro-turbines, there is greater consideration being given to smaller, cheaper and more environmentally friendly forms of hydroelectricity.

Wind power is also becoming an increasing common form of energy, with wind turbines making appearances on windswept landscapes in a number of countries. While wind turbines are non-polluting, energy production relative to initial cost is relatively low. However, long-term benefits of wind turbines include reducing relative costs and high levels of sustainability.

Beyond those forms noted above, there is also what its supporters are fond of calling 'the fifth fuel' – energy conservation. Consumption drives resource exploitation and is in turn driven by two criteria. The first is that the world's population continues to grow, in simple terms providing a multiplier effect for existing consumption. The second criterion is that technological development has led many and perhaps most of the world's population to, if not expect, then at least to want more of almost everything, as the developed world has and continues to do. For example, chlorofluorocarbons (CFC) are internationally recognized as depleting the earth's ozone layer and manufacturers of refrigerators that use CFCs have been banned by most countries. However, CFC refrigerators are cheaper to produce than non-CFC refrigerators so when China embarked on a programme to ensure that each family has a refrigerator, it initially turned to the cheaper CFC refrigerators. The international community expressed its dismay at the prospect of tens of millions of CFC-producing refrigerators that would be added to the world's total but the Chinese government replied that its people could not afford non-CFC refrigerators, and yet it was not prepared to deny them the right to preserve food. Similarly, when the international community condemned the Malaysian government for unsustainable logging of old-growth tropical forests in northern Borneo, it replied that it would not be denied the right to also achieve developed status, to which such logging would contribute. And it pointed out that the West in particular had developed in part through deforesting its own lands and that it was hypocritical for it to now tell other states they could not do the same.

What this implied was that industrialized states were beginning to be forced to reconsider their own patterns of consumption and to look at ways of modifying and ultimately reducing them. The Kyoto Protocol, for example, intended to reduce greenhouse gas emissions by 8 per cent of 1990 levels by 2012. However, the December 2009 Copenhagen talks on climate change failed to craft a successor to the Kyoto Protocol, with China, followed by India and other developing countries, insisting on greenhouse gas emission differentials in favour of developing countries over developed countries. At the end of the talks, greenhouse emission targets were lowered or dropped – initial plans to restrict global greenhouse emissions to limit warming to 2°C by 2020 were replaced by 'as soon as possible'. The talks were widely considered to have been a failure, despite the pressing importance of addressing climate change and attendant global warming.

One means of encouraging more environmentally friendly practices has been the policy of 'greenhouse trading'. Greenhouse trading is essentially a credit system by which industries that emit greenhouse gases are encouraged to reduce emissions by being able to claim reductions against taxation or other methods of payment, e.g. one tonne of greenhouse gas could be worth, for instance, US$2. The savings (or payments) would then be invested in seeking non-polluting means of industrial capacity. However, while greenhouse trading was emerging as one means to resolve greenhouse gas emissions problems, its emergence was fitful and unco-ordinated (Pew Center 2002). However, by 2010, a version of this carbon taxation and trading plan was adopted by the European Union and some other states.

The world's largest mining company and indirectly one of the greatest contributors to greenhouse gas emissions, BHP-Billiton, 'acknowledge[d] that the mainstream science is correct' on climate change and that '[w]e have historically expressed our preference for a unified global solution but recognize that local action is more likely in the short term' (Kloppers 2010). The company's head, Marius

Kloppers, also accepted that reducing CO_2 emissions is a complex task requiring a mix of strategies including the enhancement of renewable energy, standards and regulations, taxes and market-based measures (Kloppers 2010). A part of the BHP-Billiton proposal included an emissions trading scheme, in which emissions trading works on the basis that a limited number of permits are available to emit carbon, that there can be a trade in permits and that such a trade would put a price on the emission of carbon in ways that should encourage emitters to seek alternative or cleaner methods of production.

Appropriate development usually (although not always) posits that social and ecological outcomes have precedence over economic outcomes and that development should, and indeed must, occur at the local level, relying on renewable, local inputs with little or no negative impact on the environment, where it has a direct and tangible benefit, rather than at the macro level. In this respect, increased self-sufficiency may have little or no benefit to the GDP but does have the capacity markedly to improve quality of life (see, for example, Dunkerley et al. 1981: 203–11; Trainer 2001).

In terms of local sustainability, mixed agriculture can also be more economically and environmentally sustainable than monoculture cash cropping in what is broadly a declining market in real prices. Sustainability is also enhanced, both in terms of varying usages of land to allow it to regenerate and in supplying a wider variety of foodstuffs for local consumption as well as for sale. This is especially so if the mixed cropping is based on indigenous plants which do not require fertilizers, pesticides or herbicides, while ensuring an adequate supply of nutrition to ensure their growth. In this respect, notions of sustainable development include those that allow people to live in economic or material terms that are not captive to fluctuating market forces, that are affordable to develop and do not require expensive external inputs and that do not damage or otherwise unbalance the local ecology.

Like many important ideas, 'sustainability' has been quickly recognized but then co-opted by a range of parties to support their respective causes and to essentially dilute or detract from the meaning of the term. 'Sustainability' was intended in its original contemporary usage to primarily mean *environmental* sustainability. That is, there is no future without a natural environment within which to live; use of the natural environment must be in a way that can be sustained; to ensure the future of the species, people can use resources only in ways that are renewable or which do not permanently deplete the earth's resources. Sustainability may allow growth but does not imply it. Indeed, in most cases it would be difficult to talk about further growth in simple per capita GDP terms while also aiming for sustainability. However, sustain-ability does not preclude greater equity of distribution, nor does it preclude growth in non-consumption areas, such as the growth of knowledge (education) or culture. Indeed, sustainability encourages a return to a somewhat simpler and less technologically dependent society. This does not imply a wholesale retreat from technology but a recognition that not all technological development is necessary, or 'appropriate', and that some types of simpler, and therefore less commercially profitable, technology may in fact be equally or more suitable for many requirements. As Korten noted: 'Current development practice supports increases in economic output that depend on the unsustainable depletion of the earth's natural resources and the life-support capabilities of its ecosystem. Such temporary gains do not represent development so much as theft by one generation of the birthright of future generations' (1989: 4).

Triple bottom line

In the process of development, understood as industrialization, there has been a fixed competition between economic development and environmental considerations, 'with one side trying to force through new rules and standards, and the other trying to roll them back' (Elkington 1999: 108). However, taking a line from economists Porter and van der Linda, soon

> resource productivity will be directly linked both to environmental protection and competitiveness. Environmental constraints drive innovation and, as a result, eco-efficiency ... The conclusion ... is that top executives should spend less time resisting new environmental legislation, and more rethinking the nature and future of their businesses to ensure they are well adapted for the sustainability transition. (1999: 109)

Elkington argues for what he calls a 'triple bottom line' for business management, which focuses on economic prosperity, environmental quality and social justice. This idea has increasingly been applied to the development paradigm, embracing 'not just economic dimensions but also social and environmental dimensions' (1999: 385, see also Slaper and Hall 2011).

A similar, 'multidimensional' paradigm has been defined by the World Bank as 'sustainable development', which focuses on various types of capital. It should be noted here that this is a relatively 'soft' version of the various interpretations that have been applied to the idea of 'sustainability' but it does employ economic criteria in its definition. Indeed, the language of sustainability is defined in economic terms, with sustainability applying to various types of 'capital'. The first type of capital is financial, implying sound macroeconomic planning and prudent fiscal management. Physical capital refers to infrastructure, while human capital applies to health and education, and social capital applies to skills and abilities, and institutions, relationships and norms about the quantity and quality of social interactions. Finally, natural capital refers to both commercial and non-commercial natural resources and 'ecological services', including potable water, energy, fibres, waste assimilation, climate stabilization and other aspects of the natural environment that relate to maintaining life (World Bank 2001c).

One aspect that impinges on Elkington's model, though, is that of the role of government in establishing parameters for social and environmental as well as economic outcomes. To this end, notions of governance come into play, in which governments are not only accountable and responsible but also have the capacity to retain an institutional distance from sources of pressure (such as short-term focused businesses). In this sense, 'governance' becomes a critical issue in ensuring that broader communities act together for a common benefit, rather than individuals or individual organizations acting separately for their own, limited benefit.

There is little doubt that we are, as a global community, beginning to bump into the edges of the earth's capacity to indefinitely sustain what has been to date an ever-expanding human population. And while the consequences of these limits will affect some more than others, especially in the short to medium term, in the longer term they will affect all. As a consequence of these totalizing aspects of globalization, and the finite extent of the globe, Elkington's argument in favour of environmental and social responsibility as well as economic prosperity is functionally non-negotiable: 'to refuse the challenge implied by the triple bottom line,' he says, 'is to risk extinction' (1999: 2). More positively, there seems to be a growing awareness of this probable outcome, which reduces its chances of occurring.

Note

1. Compiled from 'List of weather records', Wikipedia, www.en.wikipedia.org/wiki/List_of_weather_records (accessed 21 April 2011).

Chapter 11

Security and Development

John McKay

It has long been recognized that violence, warfare and various kinds of instability represent one of the major obstacles to development and prosperity. But in the modern world it is also painfully apparent that there is now a wide range of threats to human life and welfare, and indeed to the broader ecosystem upon which human life depends, that includes but goes beyond warfare. With modern military technologies now capable of massive destruction, traditional conflicts – and most of all nuclear warfare – still represent perhaps the most potent threat but other kinds of danger are also attracting more and more attention. The threat of the spread of various kinds of diseases is one example. Even though the First World War caused massive losses of life on both sides, the outbreak of Spanish influenza that quickly followed resulted in a far greater number of deaths. Thus, current fears of the spread of any new strain of influenza or any other virus such as Ebola are now seen as a major threat to global welfare. Similarly, the environmental consequences of continued global warming are seen as having devastating consequences for the environment, for food security and for public health.

These are just two examples of concerns in the burgeoning field of human security which have been responsible for a radical rethinking and broadening of the older concepts. This process has been under way for a number of years but was given much impetus after the terrorist attacks on New York and Washington in September 2001, an event now known universally as 9/11. One measure of the current level of international interest in these issues has been the emergence of a number of new scholarly journals devoted entirely to this specific field, for example *Stability: International Journal of Security & Development,* and *Conflict, Security & Development.* This chapter explores the serious and multi-faceted implications of these security concerns for the entire development agenda and, in particular, evaluates the costs and opportunities for developing countries of the new security agenda.

It has often been argued that the modern field of development studies was born in the immediate aftermath of the Second World War, and in particular with the urgent concerns to rebuild nations that had suffered major devastation and to stimulate growth in the newly independent former colonies that began to emerge from the late 1940s. The desire was to ensure that the destruction resulting from major war should never return but to use the technologies and new planning techniques that were the direct result of the war effort to achieve this new and more prosperous world. Such optimism was of course cut short by the rapid onset of the Cold War and this had important implications for the developing world. A new emphasis on the creation of ever more deadly weapons absorbed vast amounts of finance that might have been used for development. This diversion of funds became even larger as more nations beyond just the principal protagonists sought to guarantee what they saw as their legitimate security interests. Each side in the Cold War sought to build alliances with a wide range of countries, however small, and this provided some opportunities as well as costs. Some nations were drawn into destructive conflicts that were essentially proxy wars, since a full conflict between the US and the Soviet Union was too destructive to contemplate. Wars in Korea and Vietnam were prime examples but there were also bloody and long-running regional conflicts in various parts of Asia, Africa and Latin America. However, some countries also benefited from large-scale development assistance that was given for essentially security reasons, and some in particular were able to demand particularly favourable treatment by threatening to move over to the other side. Also, the very concept of the Third World, aligned with neither the first world of the US and its allies nor the second world of the Soviet empire, dates from this period and has generated a sense of co-operation and mutual assistance that has been helpful in part.

Some of these essentially Cold War conflicts – notably those in Korea and across the Straits of Taiwan – have never been resolved and are still among the most serious threats facing the global community. However, with the fall of the Berlin Wall in 1989 and the subsequent collapse of Communist rule in Russia, there was some optimism that the age of conflict was over. Francis Fukuyama (1992) famously declared 'the end of history', in that the old basis for conflict had disappeared with the complete triumph of liberal democracy as the clearly superior system. The developing world was seen as the major beneficiary of the expected 'peace dividend' that was to follow.

The reality has turned out to be very different. Not only did some of the old conflicts persist but new threats began to be seen even in the more traditional security realm, most recently through the reassertion of Russian military power in the Ukraine and other parts of Eastern Europe. Rapid economic growth in China, followed by large investments in modernizing its military capability, has been seen by many US security analysts as representing a new threat to American strategic dominance, and attitudes in Washington to the problem of Taiwan partly reflect this thinking. But, importantly from a developing country perspective, the peace dividend was never distributed. Small countries that had never been important economically were now not even seen as being strategically significant and could safely be ignored.

But soon there was no peace dividend even for the United States. In the place of the old ideological contest between capitalism and communism, new fault lines appeared leading to new kinds of conflicts. Samuel Huntington (1996) portrayed this as a new 'clash of civilizations' with broad cultural and religious divides at the epicentre and the renewal of the centuries-old contest between Christianity and Islam as the most dangerous element. While this view generated much criticism as well as support, the events of 9/11 added a new urgency to what had until then been largely an academic debate. Terrorism is not a new phenomenon and there had been a series of attacks on US interests in the lead up to 9/11 but it was a strike at the centre of American power that finally produced a massive change in thinking about the whole question of security. From the very first day, issues of development were to the fore. In one enduring image, the television cameras recorded a speech by the then President of the World Bank, James Wolfensohn. Standing in front of the smouldering ruins of the World Trade Center, he urged the global community to now take issues of poverty more seriously and to avoid the conflicts and terrorism that deprivation inevitably engenders.

Since then, any hope of a peace dividend has been replaced by massive spending in the name of the 'war on terror'. The attack on Afghanistan to replace the Taliban regime that had provided shelter for the Al-Qaeda terrorists responsible for 9/11 was followed in 2003 by the invasion of Iraq, with the aim of removing Saddam Hussein and to provide the first stage of what was hoped would be a complete transformation of the Middle East and the rest of the Muslim world. The emerging reality has proved to be much more complex and challenging than was anticipated, culminating more recently in the tragedy that is Syria and the rise of the Islamic State movement. One result over these years has been a massive increase in US military spending and hence in its budget deficits.

To some extent, the development consequences of the 'war on terror' are similar to those of the Cold War: massive sums are being spent on security, money that could have been devoted to more productive purposes. Repression and torture are again being justified in the name of security and rather dubious regimes around the world are given support because of their role in the fight against terrorism. Anti-terrorism measures are also imposing some significant costs. For example, the rules designed to protect shipping containers and other cargoes from terrorists are resulting in significant extra costs for exporters and transport companies. But again, as in the Cold War period, some countries are able to leverage their positions: the US has brought out its old slogan that 'you are either with us or against us' and some leaders have pointed out that such support demands something in return.

However, the new security agenda includes much more than the fight against terrorism. In the post-Cold War period, much more attention has had to be given to new kinds of transnational crime, including illegal population movements and people smuggling. Agricultural methods, especially in various parts of Asia, have been widely blamed for outbreaks of new kinds of diseases, and especially those involving cross-infections from animals to humans. Increased population pressures and the frantic pursuit of industrial growth have resulted in serious environmental damage, with real fears of irreversible climate change. Once again such threats bear down particularly on the poorer nations. Countries like Bangladesh are predicted to face very serious threats from flooding, while a number of Pacific nations may disappear completely as sea levels rise.

These are the themes explored in this chapter, with a particular focus on the period since 9/11. In the first part, the redefinition and broadening of the whole concept of security is explored, and especially research on the numerous implications for development. It is argued that while this emphasis on a number of new kinds of threat is to be welcomed, we must not lose sight of the continued menace of old-fashioned security concerns either. Indeed, some of best new studies are explicitly concerned with the interrelationships between traditional and new concepts of security. Some of the policy responses, many of them involving innovative forms of international co-operation that have been suggested to deal with these complex dangers, are evaluated.

The second part of the chapter looks in more detail at terrorism and related forms of violence. This is of course only one aspect of the human security debate but it is a very topical issue and has dominated many of our discussions of international problems, particularly since 9/11. Here several key issues are explored. First, we ask whether the kind of violent act that was perpetrated on 9/11 can be considered as a completely new kind of phenomenon. Terrorism has been with us for centuries in one form or another but some analysts have suggested that we have now witnessed the birth of the 'new terrorism'. Secondly, and most importantly here, the immediate and wider development costs associated with the 'war on terror' and similar attempts to counter such violence in various regions are considered. Finally, the discussion focuses on particular outcomes for some of the most vulnerable members of society and considers the whole relationship between violence and development.

Revisiting the concept of security: linking security and development

The current debate about the redefinition of the whole concept of security is based around three separate but related threads. First, the scope of what constitutes the security domain is under question, with a number of writers arguing that we must look at definitions that are much broader than have been conventionally used. Secondly, the place of economic relations within the security domain forces us to think directly about the centrality of developmental issues within this agenda. It has often been contended that trade and other economic linkages play a positive role in the development of stable and productive links between nations but this has been challenged in a number of recent studies. Thirdly, even those writers who still concern themselves with the traditional concerns of security studies now argue that new kinds of threats to stability must be included in our analyses and there is much to be gained from exploring the complex interactions between the traditional and the newer security factors as well as their overall relationship with the development agenda.

Broadening the security agenda

A basic conceptual problem concerns the changing nature of international relations and the consequent focus of concern for states. During the Cold War, there was a simple and overriding imperative for survival and defence, and this is still true for relations between the two Koreas, for example. But in many other domains, the very concept of security has been extended to include many topics central to the development agenda: ideas of *economic security, environmental security* and *food security* as well as concerns with international crime, illegal migration and various pandemics. Some would argue that the most useful new overarching concept is that of *human security,* which reflects many of the concerns of traditional security but with a wider concern for the individual as the object of security and for the ways in which increasingly global systems impact on the family and other small local groups. It also looks at 'structural violence' emanating from non-territorial threats (Tow, Thakur and Hyun 2000; McRae and Hubert 2001). The emphasis on human security received much initial impetus from a UNDP report (United Nations 1994) which proposed that two forms of security are vital for the individual: *freedom from want* and *freedom from fear*, and this formulation is still very influential in most accounts of the concept.

Alan Dupont (2001) argues, for example, that a new class of non-military threats has the potential to destabilize East Asia and reverse decades of economic and social progress. Here he includes issues such as overpopulation, pollution, deforestation, unregulated population movements, transnational crime and HIV/AIDS. This broadening of the scope of security issues to include, at the very least, questions of national priorities in areas such as trade and economic priorities has a number of important consequences: the traditional separation of international relations from defence studies is no longer valid, indeed any meaningful study must also include a broad range of other viewpoints and disciplines. Similarly, at the level of government, ministries of foreign affairs, trade and health, all need to make policy inputs to security questions, something which simply does not happen in most countries.

The gathering pace of globalization is also adding a number of complications. Actors at a range of scales, from local communities through cities to regions of various kinds, are now part of global networks in their own right. In many countries, the nation-state is no longer the sole arbiter of policy, even of policies that have implications for security, especially if one accepts the new, broader concept of security discussed above. The entire post-war security system has been built around relations and treaties between sovereign states, but this concept looks rather shaky.

Economic growth, trade and security

In the literature on international relations and security, there has been a long-running debate about the relationships between economic change and the degree of resultant stability or instability in the security environment. On the one hand, some analysts have argued that economic growth will inevitably lead to greater interdependence between nations and a general desire to avoid any conflict that might interrupt economic progress. Hence, economic growth and change lead to regional stability. Also, as growth proceeds, there has been a tendency in many countries for more democratic forms of government to emerge and some commentators have gone on to argue that two democracies will never go to war – the so-called democratic peace theory (Richardson 1997). This view has been put very strongly by Kishore Mahbubani (1998), who has argued that one of the major reasons for Asia's economic dynamism is that a tidal wave of common sense has hit the region: it is accepted that Asia's success must not be jeopardized by any petty, nationalist squabbles.

In a controversial theoretical analysis by Etel Solingen (1998), the themes of democracy and peace have also been linked to the possible relationship between economic liberalization and regional stability. She argues that the architecture of regional order depends upon the construction of various kinds of coalitions. Basically, two forms of coalition are possible. *Internationalist coalitions*, made up of supporters of economic liberalization, usually create co-operative regional orders that encourage peace and stability. On the other hand, opponents of economic liberalization give rise to *statist/nationalist coalitions* that are prone to create and reproduce zones of wars and militarized disputes. Thus, the fostering of economic reform can be regarded as a major contribution to regional security.

In marked contrast, some analysts have argued that the process of growth itself can lead to instability, especially in the current phase of capitalist development in which there have been marked shifts in power distribution between nations as well as a seemingly inevitable widening of the gap between rich and poor both between and within nations. The intense competition that now characterizes the world economy can lead to serious rivalries and disputes that can escalate into armed conflicts. At the same time, the increased national wealth that has resulted from rapid growth can be used to purchase ever more sophisticated and destructive weapons, intensifying the damage resulting from any conflict. Few if any nations in a region such as Asia can be regarded as supporters of the status quo, especially in the economic realm, and intense competition has been an inevitable consequence of the greater integration into global markets. Zysman and Borrus (1996), for example, have argued that there are several important lines of fracture that result from economic competition. Efforts by middle-power and mid-technology countries such as Korea to break loose from the existing hierarchy of economic power by moving towards higher-value and higher-technology products could create serious rivalries of development strategies. China and India may in turn provide alternative and competing lines of development, making economic competition within Asia into a form of security competition. Also, there is always a danger that Asia may be transformed into a more self-contained economic bloc competing with the US and Europe (see also Betts 1993; Friedberg 1993).

These old debates have taken on new forms and increased relevance in the period following the Asian financial crisis of 1997–8 and the recent (and perhaps ongoing) GFC. The Asian crisis, and the role of the West and International Monetary Fund (IMF) in its management and seeming resolution, created in some Asian minds a new sense of vulnerability and, for some, a blaming of the US in particular, and US-dominated institutions such as the IMF, for these problems. The 'politics of resentment' (Higgott 2000) have created a new and more unstable environment in the region, compounding the already serious security issues facing Asia. The rapid recovery of Asia from its crisis and the rapid growth of China re-ignited debate over the Asian Century and the potential for conflict between a rising China and a declining US, and more generally a marked acceleration of the return of Asia as the centre of the global economy. This issue has already been discussed at length in Chapter 4, but we need to stress here the potential for conflict in key regions such as the Indian Ocean that are also central to global development concerns (Kaplan 2010).

These theoretical controversies are crucial to those organizations set up to foster regional co-operation, economic progress and more general dialogue. If economic prosperity leads automatically to a more peaceful region, regional trade organizations by themselves make a significant contribution to peace and security. If, on the other hand, economic growth is rather more problematic in its security implications, then a rather more complex set of policy and institutional solutions need to be designed (McKay 2003).

Linking traditional and newer security agendas

Some of the best literature on human security is not arguing that traditional security concerns have become obsolete; this is clearly not the case. Rather there is a search for conceptual linkages between the old issues and the new ones. Tow and Trood (2000) have suggested four potential linkages between the two schools of thought:

1. *Conflict prevention.* Traditional security studies have spent much time dealing with the ways in which conflict can be prevented and these are very much at the centre of the debate about human security. Co-operative security arrangements, and a broader sensitivity to

the interests and priorities of other nations or peoples, can be much more cost-effective than waging war and prevent large-scale human suffering.

2. *Reducing vulnerability.* Traditional studies have dealt with the nation-state as the subject of security, and have employed concepts of state sovereignty and social contract to deal with overriding issues of *order*. *Human security* stresses human welfare goals and sees the state only as a means to achieving these goals, and only one means among many. A meeting point between these concepts can be the use of various instruments such as collective security to overcome behaviour that could threaten states, communities or groups.

3. *Who is to be governed and secured?* A number of recent studies have argued that security is a civilizational problem. This acknowledges that fault lines do exist between peoples, an area of concern in traditional security as well as human security analysis.

4. *Collective security.* Both traditional and new concepts of security concede that there is a crisis of collective security at regional and international levels and the development of new institutions and mechanisms is regarded by both as a high priority.

Attempts to push the new agenda of human security have met some strident criticisms. Some critics have seen the human security agenda as yet another example of Western models of economic and political development being foisted on developing countries. The emphasis in much of this new agenda on the individual is seen as potentially undermining the jurisdiction and power of the nation-state. In some versions of the human security blueprint, for example, that put forward by the Canadian government, options for humanitarian intervention in crisis-ridden countries are left open, something which is vehemently opposed by many countries. Most governments, notably that of Japan, favour an emphasis on 'freedom from want' rather than 'freedom from fear', and this brings the debate very close to traditional concepts of development. Still others have questioned just how much the idea of human security adds to the much older formulations of *comprehensive security*. For example, Japan as long ago as 1980 put forward a policy of comprehensive security to safeguard the economic livelihood of the Japanese people, protect vital markets and sources of raw materials, and guarantee Japanese investments. The idea was taken up in a number of South East Asian countries, including Singapore, which proposed a concept of *total security*. Acharya (2002) has attempted to answer these criticisms, arguing that many of the basic ideas of human security were in fact first articulated by Asian scholars. He also stresses some important

differences between the formulations of human security and comprehensive security. However, he concedes that the basic unit of analysis in
human security has shifted to the individual and the community, away
from the emphasis on state security and regime stability which is central
to comprehensive security. This is its strength, he argues, and forges a
direct link to development concerns but this is bound to cause suspicion
in many regional governments.

Exploring the complex interaction between security and development

Defining the nexus between security and development is now one of
the important and complex tasks within the overall field of international development. As has been noted in an important study from the
International Peace Institute (Tschirgi, Lund and Mancini 2010) all
the statistics point to some obvious connections: since the 1980s some
80 per cent of the poorest nations have been wracked by violent conflict of some kind. Similar relationships are highlighted in the *World
Development Report 2011* (World Bank 2011). About 1.5 billion
people – some 25 per cent of the global population – live in situations
of conflict and violence, and the gap in poverty is increasing between
stable nations and those affected by violence. No fragile or conflict-
ridden nation has yet achieved a single Millennium Development Goal.
But the nature of violence has undergone a profound change – in this
respect the new millennium is radically different from the previous one.
Both inter-state conflict and civil war have declined in total, but a number of nations have suffered from repeated violence. In the last decade,
90 per cent of countries enduring civil wars have had one or more such
conflicts in the last 30 years, and in many cases this kind of instability
has been ongoing (Rangelov and Kaldor 2012). New forms of instability, such as organized crime and other kinds of criminal violence, have
also emerged, but the basic causal mechanisms seem to be constant.
Stresses resulting from internal and international conditions are unable to be contained by weak and often corrupt institutions resulting in
rapid loss of development momentum, which in turn fuels new rounds
of violence and breeds new kinds of criminal behaviour. Some nations
that in the past were devastated by civil war – such as Mozambique and
Rwanda – have made good progress recently, but in many conflict situations such as the Democratic Republic of Congo anything resembling
an effective government has ceased to exist.

But moving beyond these obvious relationships to explore some
key causal relationships is proving to be much more challenging.

Fukuda-Parr (2010) has stressed that the links between poverty and conflict are complex and two-way. Civil war hampers development, reducing GDP and government revenues. Administrative capacity is reduced along with expenditures for productive and social sectors. Social institutions, social networks and trust are all seriously eroded, incomes fall, nutrition declines and diseases increase along with child and infant mortality. Women and children are particularly vulnerable to all these effects. In such situations people may feel they have little to lose by continuing conflict, and young men – well represented in most developing countries' demographic structures – are easily persuaded to join rebel armies (Cincotta 2010). Conflict seems particularly common in situations of marked inequalities between community groups, particularly ethnic groups, and when countries are dependent on particular commodities with high returns available to those who control high value products such as diamonds (McKay 2012; Ikejiaku 2012).

In Africa the availability of lootable resources has played some role in virtually all recent internal conflicts. Michael Ross (2004) has explored some of these issues and after evaluating the available literature arrives at four major conclusions:

- Countries with large oil industries are prone to protracted internal conflicts, but the presence of oil does not seem to be related to the duration of such struggles.
- By contrast, the presence of gemstones and drugs of various kinds – such as opium, coca, and cannabis – does not seem to necessarily initiate conflict, but it does not lengthen pre-existing wars. The role of timber resources is not at all clear.
- Agricultural commodities do not seem to be related to either the initiation or duration of civil war.
- The frequent claim that primary commodities in general are associated with the onset of civil war appears shaky.

A number of other authors have also suggested that it is not just the presence of a particular commodity that is important but the precise nature of the deposits, their value, their ease of extraction, and their location. Le Billon (2001, 2005), for example, has suggested that different types of resources are conducive to the development of distinct types of civil wars. Resources clustered around a particular location can be more easily captured than more diffuse sources spread over a wide geographical area, while resources distant from the capital are more vulnerable to rebel attack. Hence, point source resources close to the capital will tend to be associated with conflicts over state control; point source resources distant from the capital will tend to generate separatist movements; diffuse resources closer to the capital may encourage rebellions and rioting; and diffuse resources distant from the capital will tend to be associated with warlordism.

However, it is also instructive to place these specific issues within the broader debate about the causes of civil war. In a number of influential contributions, Paul Collier and his co-workers have argued that participants in civil wars are motivated by either *greed* – a desire to become rich – or *grievance* – a strong dissatisfaction with an existing state of affairs (Collier *et al.* 2003; Collier and Hoeffler 2002a; 2002b; 2004). Others have brought these together in the concept of *motivation*, but have also argued that there must also be *opportunity* – a reasonable chance that the rebels will be able to be successful – and *identity* – a common cause essential for group formation (Gurr 1970; Berdal and Malone 2000; Elbadawi and Sambanis 2002). The funding available from looted resources is clearly relevant here. Income from the sale of resources props up existing governments – which in many cases are incompetent, repressive and corrupt and hence give rise to widespread resentment. These rents flowing from control of lucrative resources increase the attractiveness of taking power from existing regimes, while the expectation of such riches may well increase the attractiveness of joining and identifying with the rebel forces. It is hardly surprising then that a number of empirical studies have found a positive relationship between the availability of lootable resources and the prospects of civil war or secessionist movements, all of which have serious consequences for national progress (see, for example, Addison, Le Billon and Murshed 2002; Gilmore, Gleditsch and Lujala 2005).

The struggle over resources may also be magnified when environmental deterioration puts pressure on increasingly scarce resources. Many people may be forced to migrate, bringing them into conflict with other groups. Conflict may also spill over from neighbouring countries – for example it is estimated that in recent years Tanzania's GDP has been reduced by 0.7 per cent per year as the result of conflict in adjoining nations (World Bank 2011). One area that has received increased attention in recent years is the growing evidence that pressures on the environment and its resources are an important source of conflict. A much discussed case here is the ongoing conflict in the Darfur region of Sudan where rapid population growth and declining rainfall have placed impossible pressures on the predominantly farming and herding communities, and added to the existing ethnic rivalries and the problems created by a corrupt and ineffective government (Matthew 2010). There has also been much discussion of the potential for conflict that can result from global climate change: problems of competition for food and water could have serious consequences for security in many parts of the world (Chellaney 2011; McKay 2009). But there is a danger that many potential conservation measures can have particularly detrimental effects on some poorer communities and actually enhance the possibilities for even greater conflict. Thus, as Matthew has argued, planners need to search for conservation strategies that are pro-poor and thus pro-stability. 'Peace parks' along the borders of two formerly warring neighbouring countries or regions have been suggested as part of such an approach.

Similar policy imperatives are also apparent in many areas of conflict that are at least in part related to widespread poverty. Fukuda-Parr (2010) suggests that many aid programmes in fact exacerbate existing conflict situations or create the potential for new conflagrations that can have disastrous consequences for progress: the development planning process needs to be redefined to include assessments of security risks for all aid programmes. She supports the idea of creating some Millennium Security Goals (MSGs) to bring development and security agendas more into harmony. Such an approach is based on the work of Picciotto and others. See, for example, Picciotto, Olonisakin, and Clarke (2006) and Picciotto, Clarke and Olonisakin (2009) who have suggested eight MSGs as an agenda for a more balanced approach to development:

1. Reduce the number, length, and intensity of conflicts between and within states.
2. Reduce the number and severity of attacks.
3. Reduce the number of refugees and displaced persons.
4. Regulate the arms trade.
5. Reduce the extent and severity of core human rights violations.
6. Protect civilians and reduce women's and children's participation and victimization in war.
7. Reverse weapons proliferation and achieve progress toward nuclear, radiological, chemical, and biological disarmament.
8. Combat transnational crime and illegal trafficking.

These goals are easy to enumerate but extremely difficult to achieve, but we will return to this idea of human security as a new focus for the entire development agenda.

The nature and costs of terrorism

The 'New Terrorism'

Alvin Buckelew (1984: 18) has defined terrorism as 'violent, criminal behaviour designed primarily to generate fear in the community, or in a substantial segment of the community, for political purposes'. Such activity is certainly not new, with examples of terrorist groups identified for at least 2,000 years. However, a number of commentators have argued that the 9/11 attacks on the US have heralded the emergence of what is being called *the new terrorism* (see, for example, Hoffman 2002; Ramakrishna and Tan 2002). Hoffman has identified a series of features that set this new phenomenon apart from earlier terrorist attacks:

- The 9/11 attacks killed an unprecedented number of victims. No previous terrorist act had ever killed more than 500 persons.
- The event consisted of a co-ordinated series of spectacular and simultaneous attacks.
- The attacks showed a new level of patient and detailed planning.
- The hijackers showed a willingness to kill themselves as well as their victims.
- The hijackers had a relatively high level of education, and contrary to popular stereotypes they were not drawn from the ranks of the mentally unstable, the poor or the isolated loners.

To this list could be added the dominantly religious dimension of the terrorist organizations (Ramakrishna and Tan 2002) and the distinctively networked nature of their operational procedures (O'Brien 2002). Some of these individual features are not entirely new – for example suicide bombers had been used earlier by the Tamil Tigers in Sri Lanka and by a number of Palestinian groups – but it is the integration of all of these elements into a new and distinctive strategy that is important. All of these researchers argue that a clear understanding of this new phenomenon must be central to any strategy to deal with these terrorist threats.

Hoffman has also drawn our attention to the sheer audacity and imagination involved in the 9/11 attacks. Most earlier assumptions about the nature of likely targets and the methods that could be employed were shattered and this is turn has created a great deal of community unease – one of the key aims of terrorism for centuries – as possible new kinds of targets and new kinds of vulnerabilities are identified. He poses a list of potential targets that have not yet been attacked simply to highlight that the list of possible terrorist acts is almost limitless and certainly impossible to totally guard against. Perhaps here we come to the real core of the threat posed by the 'new terrorism'. Within governments and the population at large there is now an acceptance that there is nothing that the new breed of terrorist is not capable of. After the death of Osama bin Laden a number of commentaries predicted the demise of Al-Qaeda, especially in the light of the new wave of democratization then seen as sweeping the Middle East and North Africa (for example, Jenkins and Godges 2011; McCants 2011). However, with the increasing chaos in Libya and Syria, and the continued weakness of the government imposed on Iraq, nothing now seems safe, and there is no limit to the precautions that might and should be taken. The cost implications are of course enormous.

Calculating the costs of terrorism

The events of 9/11 and the responses to this tragedy have engendered a number of studies that have tried to quantify the costs of terrorism, and of armed conflict more generally. Gupta et al. (2002) and others have attempted to put the impacts of the 'new terrorism' within the broader historical literature on the consequences of conflicts of various kinds. This suggests that conflicts such as terrorism lower growth, both directly and indirectly in various ways:

- The process of financial deepening is adversely affected by the undermining of confidence in the domestic currency due to fears of inflation and depreciation.
- Funds tend to move away from productive assets to non-productive ones, notably gold.
- The supervision of the financial system is neglected.
- The transaction costs of doing business increase sharply.
- Additional security precautions can impede the flow of goods and services.
- Fiscal accounts can be disrupted through the erosion of the tax base, the lowering of efficiency in tax administration and the distortion of public spending.
- Military expenditure tends to increase dramatically, and historically has remained high even after the end of conflict.
- The destruction of infrastructure and human capital, plus the indirect effects such as reductions in trade, tourism or business confidence, all weaken the fiscal position of the nation involved in conflict. (See also Addison, Chowdhury and Murshed 2002.)

Other authors have concentrated on the more specific impacts of terrorism in the post-9/11 environment. The OECD in its *Economic Outlook* of 2002 attempted to evaluate the economic consequences of terrorism (OECD 2002). Usefully, the authors try to separate the short-term impacts from those of a medium- and longer-term nature. They argue that the short-term consequences of the attacks were limited by some swift policy responses. Short-term loans and guarantees were put in place, for example. The insurance industry raised its premiums, reduced its coverage and called on governments to step in and cover risks deemed too difficult for the private sector, but private sector initiatives soon emerged to provide coverage for these kinds of risks. However, they concede, in the longer term tighter border controls may well have a detrimental impact on trade. One result of globalization and the introduction of just-in-time supply chain management systems is that companies depend to an increasing extent on efficient border-crossing systems. Long delays that result from enhanced security precautions can have serious consequences for the efficiency of manufacturing systems. It is suggested that these new security measures have added 1-3 per cent to total trading costs. They also suggest that spending on homeland security and military operations, especially in the United States, as well as private spending on the security of premises, employees and information, may crowd out accumulation in directly productive capacity. This finding contradicts the opinions expressed by Hobijn (2002), who in response to the question of what homeland security in the US would cost, answered 'not much'.

More detailed modelling work on the trade impacts of terrorism has been undertaken by Nitsch and Schumacher (2002) and Walkenhurst and Dihel (2002). Nitsch and Schumacher analysed data on trade flows between some 200 countries from 1960 to 1993, concluding that a doubling in the number of terrorist incidents is associated with a decrease of bilateral trade by around 6 per cent. Walkenhurst and Dihel, by contrast, attempted to disaggregate the impacts of the various factors leading to increased costs:

- *Air transport.* Given the methods used in the 9/11 attacks, it was natural that air services should be given particular attention in the attempt to counter increased terrorist threats. Tighter screening of passengers and their luggage was introduced, cockpit access was restricted, and on a number of flights armed air marshals were introduced. Training of personnel was increased at all levels. Insurance premiums increased sharply. Similar measures were introduced to protect air cargo services. Many airlines passed on these costs to passengers in the form of 'security surcharges'.

- *Maritime transport.* Before September 2001, only 2 per cent of the 72 million containers moved annually were screened in any way but a whole range of safety checks was quickly introduced. For example, documents for all shipments going to the US must now be lodged with US authorities before the ship leaves the port of origin, all ships must now travel at very low speeds within US harbours, insurance premiums have increased sharply and a range of war-risk surcharges have been introduced in particular regions.
- *Road and rail transport.* Delays on land-crossing into the US, for example from Mexico, have increased markedly. Freight yards have been fenced in a more secure way and sensors have been introduced to alert operators to any interference with cargoes. Inspections of train lines, bridges and tunnel have increased.
- *Customs.* Increased inspections of various kinds have undone the efficiency gains from simplified and automated procedures introduced over the last few years, although much work is now going on to develop new systems that can again reduce costs.

The authors developed a model to evaluate the real global costs of these enhanced security measures. They conclude that total world welfare has declined by a staggering US$75 billion per year as a direct result of the attacks of 9/11. The largest losses were estimated to be in Western Europe, North America and North Asia, but in relative terms the economies of South Africa, North Africa and the Middle East were even more seriously affected. The authors note that, in an increasingly integrated global economy, even small changes in trade costs can have a significant impact on trade flows and economic welfare. Even countries not directly involved in conflict can suffer serious losses as the result of enhanced security concerns and higher frictional costs of trade.

Many costs associated with countering terrorism are predominantly faced by the rich countries – for example the naval operations to counter piracy off the Horn of Africa and in the Indian Ocean is estimated to cost around $2 billion per year, but many small companies in poorer countries – for example 30 per cent of firms in Africa – are seriously affected by crime and violence (World Bank 2011).

It should be noted that some commentators believe that the costs associated with precautions against terrorism need not be permanent. In fact, it has been argued that once new technologies are fully developed, the efficiencies achieved might mean that the actual costs of processing cargoes and passengers, for example, may be even less than they were before 9/11. Advance passenger information systems and other electronic innovations at airports should in time result in faster passenger movements. Similarly, new standardized manifest systems at all ports may in time cut costs and reduce handling times. The US Customs' Automated Commercial Environment (ACE) project, developed to identify high-risk cargo, may eventually reduce costs to business and facilitate the faster processing of trade. It has been estimated that over the next 20 years the ACE system will save US importers around US$22.2 billion and save the US government US$4.4 billion in administrative costs over the same period (Raby 2003).

Facing the basic causes of terrorism and other human security issues

The basic argument in this last major section of this chapter is that we need to move beyond considerations of the costs of human insecurity, and certainly beyond the simplistic sloganizing that has characterized much of the recent debate. In the case of terrorism, for example, while direct security efforts to safeguard aircraft, ships, trains and other possible targets are necessary and laudable, rather more has to be done. Essentially, this involves taking a much longer-term view of the phenomenon of terrorism, trying to understand what motivates the terrorists and attempting to deal with the underlying causes. This is the only real and constructive way to manage the problem. This also brings the discussion directly into the domain of development and what might be involved is nothing less than the creation of a new agenda for development studies.

But it is necessary at this point to make one important thing very clear. There has been a tendency in the press and in some political circles to equate any call for understanding terrorism with some kind of tacit support for terrorist causes, or at least with a 'soft' approach to the problem. Jessica Stern (2003), in her landmark study of religious terrorism, has done us all a favour in this regard by firmly demolishing all of these kinds of spurious and anti-intellectual arguments. As Stern notes, empathy and understanding do not necessarily imply sympathy or support. She argues that it is important to look behind the slogans and stereotypes and try to gain deeper insights into motivations.

In the current situation, such analysis and search for understanding are absolutely essential. It may be that at the end of such a programme of intense work many of the 'causes' of terrorism that we identify may be dismissed as unworthy, absurd or not to be tolerated. But clearly the methods we are currently adopting are not working and are unlikely to produce viable long-term answers to the problem; hence we must embark on quite a new agenda. There are at least four major arguments to support such a position.

Firstly, it now seems clear that by themselves conventional strategies are unlikely to be effective. However well thought out and executed these plans may be, there are just too many trains, bridges, airports or whatever to guard all day every day. Even if the precautions are effective for 99 per cent or more of the time, some terrorist event will take place somewhere – and people will die. Also, much of our thinking about what terrorists will target next has been based on what their targets were last time around. Certainly transport and trade are the most obvious areas to be threatened but, as Hoffman suggests, the range of possible targets is almost endless. If we cannot guard all the obvious targets, how can we deal with all those extra possibilities of which we are only dimly aware?

Secondly, many of the methods that have been used in the recent past to limit the activities of terrorist groups may in fact have made the problem worse by fuelling resentment. Many programmes have been poorly thought through and relied on simple stereotypes and prejudices. In turn, they have served to simply reinforce the stereotypes and prejudices held about the West. The thwarting of some terrorist activities may in fact have come at the cost of boosting the recruitment of the next generation of terrorists. Kumar Ramakrishna (2002: 208) has set out the dangers very clearly – the emphasis on military solutions and coercion can be very counterproductive and should be replaced by a series of indirect strategies that can deal with the problem of terrorism without making the problem worse, and in particular without generating the kind of 'civilizational conflict' that a number of authors, notably Huntington (1996), have warned us about.

Thirdly, in many parts of the world protests have been raised about the impact of what many people see as severe anti-terrorism regulations on the rights of the bulk of the population. Once sacrosanct civil and political rights, such as freedom of expression, freedom of association, protection from arbitrary detention and the right to independent legal advice, have been tossed aside in the name of the 'war on terror'. Importantly Hocking (2004) and others have asked whether we can ever protect ourselves by removing the very freedoms that define us as a democracy. Similarly, arguments have been put forward in a number of publications coming out of Asia. Notable here is a volume edited by Johannen, Smith and Gomez (2003) in which several contributors argue that in Asia a number of authoritarian regimes have seized the opportunity to emphasize that their continued concerns for national security have been vindicated, and that the crushing of political dissent is essential.

Fourthly, the ongoing costs of these measures in purely economic terms are enormous, as we have seen, and the developmental impacts may be quite severe. Various links between poverty and terrorism have been made yet terrorism and counter-terrorism measures seem to be having a relatively much larger impact on low-income countries, and the costs of terrorism and anti-terrorism now constitute a major new handicap to development (Gupta et al. 2002). Yet it is precisely the lack of development that is one of the major underlying factors in the growth of terrorism in many countries (World Bank 2011).

Thus, there are some important reasons to take a much longer-term view of the issue of terrorism rather than simply relying on the direct, military and quasi-military tactics now being employed. But these are complex and heavily contested issues and there is little consensus in the literature on the mix of factors that has led to the emergence of terrorism, hence the development of more sophisticated policy initiatives is made more difficult. As a next step here, we draw out some of the lessons or at least identify the major schools of thought on the causes of terrorism and insecurity.

Old versus new: the fear of modernity

A number of political leaders, notably former President George W. Bush, are fond of saying things like 'terrorists want all of us to return to a mediaeval way of life', or 'what terrorists hate about us is our freedom and our way of life'. Thus the 'war on terror' for them is a struggle for the defence of modernity against the primitive tenets of a tribal, desert society. This position is also based on a specific view of Islam which is portrayed as having progressed hardly at all since the death of the Prophet.

Such attitudes have flourished in the general spirit of self-confidence, or even triumphalism, that has pervaded much of the West since the end of the Cold War. Francis Fukuyama, in an article published soon after 9/11 (*Guardian,* 11 October 2001) defended his assertions against those who saw terrorism as a new 'clash of civilizations', arguing that Western liberal democracy remains the only system that will dominate world politics and terrorism represents only a rearguard action by those societies whose very existence is threatened by modernization.

Such ideas have been rejected by Stuart Sim (2004) who has argued that we now live in a new age of dogma and fundamentalism, and Western belief in the unchallenged superiority of its political and economic system is but one aspect of 'political fundamentalism'. The entire world, apart from a few who have not yet seen the light, is assumed to be only too anxious to join the 'born-again liberal democrats' (p. 152). This, he suggests, parallels a strong element of market fundamentalism, which is a modern and more intense version of the Protestant work ethic. Like all fundamentalisms, there are strong theological overtones and it is no accident that the religious right in the US is closely linked to a form of market fundamentalism that stresses the purity of its principles, even if the social impact of its policy outcomes can be very damaging to the social fabric. He also notes that, for every fundamentalism, there grows up an equally dogmatic opposing fundamentalism and in this case it is the growth of the anti-globalization movement that is particularly instructive.

Even more vehement comments along these general lines have been made by John Gray (2003) who argues that, far from being mediaeval in nature, Al-Qaeda and other radical Islamic organizations are essentially modern.

> Western societies are governed by the belief that modernity is a single condition, everywhere the same and always benign. As societies become more modern, so they become more alike. At the same time they become better. Being modern means realising *our* values – the values of the Enlightenment, as we like to think of them. (Gray 2003: 1)

The reality is rather different, he suggests. Al-Qaeda is very much a by-product of globalization, and like the Soviet Union and Nazi Germany, it sees history as a mere overture to a brave new world. All such movements, including the Enlightenment itself, are convinced that it is possible to transform the human condition, the myth that is at the centre of modernity. In this sense, radical Islam and neoliberal orthodoxy are very similar, even though their goals seem so different.

This kind of analysis, which defines modernity as a form of fundamentalism, is very challenging for many practitioners of development, who have often seen development itself as a process of modernization, and I will return to these emerging notions below.

Religion and holy war

One current belief shared by many in the West is that Islamic and other recent forms of terrorist movements reflect a fanaticism and fundamentalism that comes directly out of notions of jihad. After 9/11, there appeared a large number of books attempting to elucidate the meaning of such fundamentalism and the precise nature of 'holy war' (see for example, Kepel 2002; Ruthven 2002, 2004). Ruthven has chronicled the origins and development of the term 'fundamentalism', arguing that it is extremely slippery and paradoxical and has outgrown much of its original meaning. It was first coined with reference to a particularly zealous Protestant movement in the United States, which stressed that all important truths could only be found in the Bible; hence the path to wisdom depended on a willingness to undertake detailed analysis of this one true source. The Bible was revealed truth and hence should be interpreted literally. Since then, the use of the term has been widened to include many kinds of religious, economic and political belief systems, all of which make some claim to an exclusive pathway to true enlightenment or perfection. Ironically, Ruthven suggests, the replacement in at least some areas of Western thought of modernity with newer postmodern concepts has provided some important space for various kinds of thought systems. If, as the postmodernists argue, the validity of any overarching meta-narrative is no longer tenable, then all theories and world views become equally valid. But, and here is the irony, each of these new fundamentalist stories is not only asking for equal recognition but in fact claims to be the single source of truth and salvation. Hence, the postmodern world might be characterized as a 'clash of fundamentalisms'. Others have also suggested that, in the uncertain or even chaotic world that has resulted from the postmodern or globalized condition, unerring faith in the one true source provides some certainty and comfort.

Islamic fundamentalism is often portrayed in just these terms. While the adherence to the revealed truth of the Koran and the demands for the establishment of Islamic states based on sharia law provide an immediate identification with fundamentalism, many commentators have argued that the sense of extreme uncertainty or even shame prevalent in the Middle East in particular has provided a fertile breeding ground for broader and more politically based notions of Islamic fundamentalism.

Closely related to these ideas is the notion of *sharia*. The original meaning of this word is simply 'struggle' but it has come to be seen as a struggle or holy war on behalf of Islam to defend this one true religion against attacking infidels. As Kepel (2002) has suggested, the term is now used in some quarters as the ultimate justification for what might seem unacceptable violence and terrorism. Kepel goes on to argue that 9/11, however spectacular it may seem, should not be interpreted as a sign of growing Islamic strength and influence. In fact, the triumph of the revolution in Iran and the Taliban in Afghanistan should be seen as the highpoint of success, and since then there have been a series of important reverses. In order to reverse this downward trend, Osama bin Laden sought to bring off a spectacular attack aimed not at what had been his prime target – what he portrayed as the corrupt, anti-Islamic and pro-Western regime in Saudi Arabia – but at the more general evil of Western hegemony. The West, and the US in particular, would be seen by ordinary Muslims as weak and impotent and this would trigger a much wider *jihad*. But, Kepel stresses, such mobilization can only be achieved by long-term political action reaching down to the grass-roots, not through one act of terrorism, however daring. However, the importance of Osama bin Laden as a symbol of just struggle should not be underestimated, especially since he demonstrated a real genius in harnessing the media to get his message across.

The 'home-grown terrorists'

Closely related to these ideas of fundamentalism and *jihad* is the important work that has been done trying to explain why many terrorist acts that have been perpetrated in the West have been undertaken by Islamic immigrants, or more usually the children of immigrants actually born in the country of the attack – the so-called 'home-grown terrorists'. As a growing number of recruits to the cause of Islamic State have joined the conflict in Syria and Iraq – recruited in part through a very sophisticated and effective use of new technologies and of social media in particular – a number of commentators have suggested that this now represents one of the most important fronts in the 'war on terror' (for example, Crone and Harrow 2011; Jenkins 2012).

Two very important studies – by Kepel (2004) and Roy (2002) – have done much to shape how we think about such issues. Roy notes that one of the key results of globalization has been the international migration of large numbers of people. No fewer than one-third of the world's Muslims now live as minorities in other countries. Many members of these communities, and in particular younger Muslims, feel alienated and rootless. This should not be seen as a backlash against Westernization, he suggests, but one of its outcomes. What he terms 'neo-fundamentalism' is fuelling a new kind of radicalism that embraces the leadership of Al-Qaeda and often includes rejection of integration into Western societies. This Islamic revival, or what he calls 're-Islamization', is an attempt by westernized Muslims to reassert their identities. Importantly, this is not manifested as a yearning for a lost homeland or nation but a declaration of a more general affinity with a universal religious identity or community, often represented by an imaginary *ummah* or Muslim community. Thus, echoing the arguments of John Gray already presented, Islamic fundamentalism in this context is not simply a reaction against Westernization but a product of the multiple forces we call globalization (see also King and Taylor 2011).

Kepel (2004), though, presents a further complication to this already sophisticated analysis. He argues that a fierce contest is being waged between two elements of the Islamic youth communities in Western nations. One group consists of the disillusioned and angry group identified by Olivier Roy. But there is another, more positive segment that is optimistic about the future and sees itself as the bearer of a new Westernized and more democratic ideology that can be passed back to the countries from which their families emigrated. The clash between these two views is really about the right of self-definition, Kepel contends, and constitutes a vital 'battle for Europe'. The issue of identity has also been taken up by Amartya Sen (2007), who suggests that in the current phase of globalization identity can be a source of strength, linking people into support networks of various kinds, but it can also be a source of violence, since by identifying membership of any community one is also defining an outgroup. The answer, he contends, is to give people the freedom to develop multiple, overlapping identities, including a global identity. These debates have of course been given much greater prominence with the recent flow of young men – and indeed a smaller number of young women – to fight with Islamic State movement in Syria and Iraq. In a number of countries – such as the United Kingdom, the US, Australia, Canada and France – programmes to 'de-radicalize' elements of Islamic youth have been introduced along with measures to cancel the passports of potential recruits and to prosecute returning 'foreign fighters'.

Reactions to US imperialism and the wars in Iraq and Afghanistan

In considering various contending theories on the causes of terrorism, one must acknowledge a number of writings that suggest that the lack of progress in solving the Palestine question, the close identification in the Muslim world of the US with the Israeli cause and the wars in Iraq and Afghanistan are all major contributors to the spread of terrorism (Freedman 2008). At first sight, these sorts of arguments have very limited relevance to the kinds of themes being addressed in this chapter but some recent commentary would suggest otherwise.

John Gray (2007) saw the war in Iraq as a struggle over several of the issues that are central to the future direction of global development. There is of course the question of resources, and oil in particular, and he evaluates the extent to which a desire to secure supplies of this key commodity led to the decision to invade Iraq. But there is also the broader question of how power and states are to be defined in this new age. Echoing the views of Bobbitt (2002), he suggests that for neoliberals at least the old state system is being replaced by a concept of the 'market state', in which the aim of policy is no longer to reflect the views of citizens but to satisfy the demands of the global economy. The crusade to spread democracy in the Middle East and beyond undertaken by the 'armed missionaries of liberalism' is part of a broader view that everything must be done to speed up the transition to a brave new world in which there is no place for evil – a utopian and apocalyptic project of the kind that has, he suggests, failed so many times in the past.

Closely linked to the crusade to spread democracy throughout the world is the notion that the powerful countries of the developed world have a moral responsibility to protect the lives and human rights of the citizens of authoritarian and war-torn countries (Stewart and Knaus 2012; Rotmann, Kurtz and Brockmeier 2014). We have witnessed many examples of such lofty and idealistic missions in recent times, for example the intervention of French forces to halt the advance of Islamic militants in Mali, and also heard complaints from many quarters when the international community has not seen it as feasible or desirable to intervene in particularly disastrous situations, most recently in Syria. However, what seems to be emerging is that in many cases such military interventions can also have disastrous results, most strikingly in Libya, resulting in intensified instability and suffering.

Poverty, globalization and insecurity

Finally, the importance of poverty as a driver of terrorist activity and a major contributor to all kinds of conflict and human insecurity must be reiterated, along with some of claims that the particular kind of global economy that is emerging is a major contributor to a range of disputes. In attempting this synthesis, it is also important to review some of the arguments that have been put forward in various chapters of this volume.

Brainard, Chollet and LaFleur (2007: 1) have set out in a very concise manner the complex linkages that exist between poverty and insecurity.

> Extreme poverty exhausts governing institutions, depletes resources, weakens leaders, and crushes hope – fueling a volatile mix of desperation and instability. Poor, fragile states can explode into violence or implode into collapse, imperilling their citizens, regional neighbors, and the wider world as livelihoods are crushed, investors flee, and ungoverned territories become a spawning ground for

global threats like terrorism, trafficking, environmental devastation, and disease. Yet if poverty leads to insecurity, it is also true that the destabilizing effects of conflict and demographic and environmental challenges make it harder for leaders, institutions, and outsiders to promote human development.

Some political leaders have questioned the role of poverty as a motivator for terrorists, pointing out that almost all of the perpetrators of the 9/11 attacks were well educated and from relatively affluent middle-class families. However, as part of a massive research study seeking to understand the mind of the terrorist (Stout 2004), a number of contributing authors presented a very different picture. Staub (2004), for example, argues that poverty – and in particular the constant confrontation with people who are better off – magnifies a sense of hopelessness and lack of power and may result in a turning to extreme forms of ideology. In addition, many people find it difficult to pursue education and newer forms of employment in a situation that increasingly requires a fruitful integration of the old and the new. In societies undergoing change, this will often result in confusion over identity, an issue I have already introduced. But more generally within the research community there has been an acceptance that poverty and failed states are important contributors to the problem of terrorism.

Poor or failing states face a wide array of serious problems that contribute to instability and violence. Poverty is itself a factor, but so is environmental degradation and the particular demographic structure of many developing countries in which there are large numbers of young people who often feel that their life chances are very limited and are able to compare their lot with the Western affluence portrayed in the media (Rice 2007). In a similar vein, Miguel (2007) considers two competing theories as to the central causes of violent conflict in developing countries. One theory focuses on the impact of political repression, while the second views economic conditions as being of prime importance, and the author comes down firmly in favour of the explanatory power of poverty. For unemployed young people with little hope of advancement through formal channels, joining an armed group can be very attractive. Apart from meeting a range of psychological needs, such involvement can provide a number of opportunities for significant income from activities such as looting, drug running, extortion and various forms of smuggling. He does point out that the political repression and poverty theories need not be mutually exclusive, and one factor may feed off the other, which raises the issue of how important the fostering of democracy can be to reducing violence and the chances of terrorism. The Bush administration in the US was often been criticized for giving too much attention to its 'freedom agenda' rather than devoting more resources to poverty alleviation programmes. This issue is taken up directly by Windsor (2007) who argues that democratic systems can produce much greater advances in development than can authoritarian regimes; hence the fostering of democracy deals simultaneously with the issue of repression and that of poverty. However, this is a very contentious finding.

Conclusions: human security as a focus for development studies

This chapter began with a general review of the concept of human security and then, to illustrate some major points and approaches, looked at the very topical issue of terrorism and its multifaceted connections with a range of development concepts and policy dilemmas. By way of conclusion, we broaden the discussion again and suggest ways in which the study of problems of human security can provide a very innovative and productive focus for the whole field of development studies.

There can certainly be no doubting the seriousness of the challenges posed to developing nations by violent conflict, terrorism and other issues of human security, and as we have noted, almost all of the countries that score lowest on the UN's Human Development Index have suffered from some kind of conflict since 1990 and their populations suffer from extremely high levels of child mortality and low life expectancies (United Nations 2005; World Bank 2011). Conflict has resulted in the destruction of food systems, basic services and health facilities, and there is clear evidence that the harshest burdens fall on the poor and the marginal, the women and children most of all. Populations have been displaced on a massive scale, and in conflict situations there is an added risk of the spread of HIV/AIDS. In such situations, leadership and the basic institutions of governance are often destroyed, making it much more difficult to end conflicts and initiate programmes of reconstruction. Thus, the scale and importance of these tragic events is quite clear.

But, as we have also seen, the causes of violence and terrorism are complex and far-reaching and to truly understand what is going on we need to go back to the basic dynamics of global development. This point has been made very strongly by Caroline Thomas (2007) who contends that a human security approach offers some important advantages for our analysis. The inbuilt focus on the individual rather than the nation-state is essential in dealing with issues of vulnerability and threat. It also forces us to think through the interconnected forces operating at various geographical scales to produce particular outcomes and this is also helpful in the design of appropriate policy responses. Human security also provides normative power and a strong moral justification for transformative action. If development is about power and the politics of its appropriation, then this approach leads us immediately to ask the appropriate but often uncomfortable questions about just what is going on in the world, and also leads us to the design of the reforms in global and local governance that are essential. But here we are faced with some stark policy choices. As Menkhaus (2010) has argued in relation to the disastrous situation in Somalia, the usual assumption that state structures and governance need to be strengthened is problematic, at least in the short term. State-building and peace-building are seen as antagonistic enterprises by groups that feel they may be excluded from the rewards associated with a new state.

If this book has any single theme, it is to support the idea of development as freedom. The challenges we face are enormous and, as we have seen, some severe doubts have been expressed about the ability of studies of development to rise to this immense task. If we need a new mandate for the subject, human security might just fit the bill: the ideas of *freedom from want* and *freedom from fear* are both noble and essential for our collective survival.

References

4HLF (2011) 'Busan Partnership for Effective Development Co-operation, Fourth High Level Forum on Aid Effectiveness', Busan, Republic of Korea, 29 November–1 December 2011.

Acemoglu, D. and Robinson, J. (2006) *Economic Origins of Dictatorship and Democracy* (Cambridge: Cambridge University Press).

Acharya, A. (2002) 'Human Security: What Kind for the Asia-Pacific?', in D. Dickens (ed.), *The Human Face of Security: Asia-Pacific Perspectives*, Papers on Strategy and Defence, no. 144 (Canberra: Strategic and Defence Studies Centre, Australian National University).

Acharya, A., de Lima, A. F. and Moore, M. (2004) *Aid Proliferation: How Responsible are Donors?*, IDS Working Paper no. 214 (Sussex: Institute of Development Studies).

ADB (Asian Development Bank) (2011) 'Governance', in *Sectors and Themes*, Asian Development Bank, 12 August 2011.

Addison, T., Chowdhury, A. and Murshed, M. (2002) 'By How Much Does Conflict Reduce Financial Development?', WIDER Discussion Paper no. 2002148 (Helsinki: World Institute for Development Economic Research, United Nations University).

Addison, T., Le Billon, P. and Murshed, M. (2002) 'Conflict in Africa: The Cost of Peaceful Behaviour', *Journal of African Economies* 11(3), 365–86.

Agarwal, B. (1997) '"Bargaining" and Gender Relations: Within and Beyond the Household', *Feminist Economics*, 3(1): 1–51.

Agenor, P.-R., Miller, M., Vines, D. and Weber, A. (eds) (1999) *The Asian Financial Crisis: Causes, Contagion and Consequences* (Cambridge: Cambridge University Press).

Ahamed, L. (2009) *Lords of Finance: The Bankers Who Broke the World* (London: Penguin).

Ahmed, F. E. (2008) 'Hidden Opportunities: Islam, Masculinity and Poverty Alleviation', *International Feminist Journal of Politics*, 10(4): 542–62.

Akyeampong, E., Bates, R., Nunn, N. and Robinson, J. (eds) (2014) *Africa's Development in Historical Perspective* (Cambridge: Cambridge University Press).

Alkire, S. (2002) 'Dimensions of Human Development', *World Development*, 30(2): 181–205.

Alkire, S. (2011) 'Multidimensional Poverty and its Discontents', OPHI Working Paper No. 46 (Queen Elizabeth House, University of Oxford).

Alvi E. and Senbeta, A. (2012) 'Does Foreign Aid Reduce Poverty?' *Journal of International Development*, 24: 955–76.

Amin, S. (1976) *Unequal Development* (London: Monthly Review Press).

—— (1977) *Imperialism and Unequal Development* (Hassocks: Harvester).

Ampiah, K. and Naidu, S. (2008) *Crouching Tiger, Hidden Dragon? Africa and China* (Cape Town: University of KwaZulu-Natal Press).

Amsden, A. (1989) *Asia's Next Giant: South Korea and Late Industrialization* (New York: Oxford University Press).

—— (2001) *The Rise of 'The Rest': Challenges to the West from Late-Industrializing Economies* (Oxford: Oxford University Press).

319

Anand, S. and Sen, A. (2000) 'Human Development and Economic Sustainability', *World Development,* 28(12): 2029–49.

Anderson, B. (1991) *Imagined Communities,* 2nd edn (London: Versa).

Anderson, M. (1999) *Do No Harm: How Aid Can Support Peace – or War* (Boulder, CO: Lynne Rienner Publishers).

Antrobus, P. (n.d.) 'MDGs – the Most Distracting Gimmick. Contextualising the MDGs. Seeking Accountability on Women's Human Rights: Women Debate the Millennium Development Goals', Women's International Coalition for Economic Justice. Available at www.wicej.addr.com/mdg/toc.html (accessed 1 March 2011).

Appel, G. (1990) 'Costing Social Change', in M. Dove (ed.), *The Real and Imagined Role of Culture in Development: Case Studies from Indonesia* (Honolulu: University of Hawaii Press).

Arifin, E. (2010) 'Contraceptive Discontinuation in Bali, Indonesia'. Available at: www. blisstiger.com/topic/view/id-17266 (accessed 16 April 2011).

Arrighi, G. (2002) 'The African Crisis: World Systemic and Regional Aspects', *New Left Review* 15: 5–38.

Arrighi, G. (2005) 'Hegemony Unravelling', *New Left Review,* 32, 33.

ASC, TI, CSS, PRC (2003, December) *Failed and Collapsed State in the International System.* The African Studies Center (Leiden: The Transnational Institute; Amsterdam: The Center for Social Studies; Coimbra University, the Peace Research Center-CIP-FUHEM).

Atkinson, A. (2006) 'Funding the Millennium Development Goals: A Challenge for Global Public Finance', *European Review,* 14(4): 555–64.

AusAID (Australian Agency for International Development) (2006), *Pacific 2020: Challenges and Opportunities for Growth* (Canberra: AusAID).

——— (2010a) 'Cairns Compact on Strengthening Development Coordination: What is the Cairns Compact?' Available at: www.ausaid.gov.au/country/pacific/cairnscompact.cfm (accessed 1 March 2011).

——— (2010b) *Women, Peace and Security: AusAID's Implementation of United Nations Security Council Resolution 1325* (Canberra: AusAID).

AWID (2010) *Brief 11. The Impact of the Crisis on Women: Main Trends Across Regions* (Toronto, Mexico and Capetown: Association for Women's Rights in Development: AWID).

Ayers, J. and Huq, S. (2009) 'Supporting Adaptation to Climate Change: What Role for Official Development Assistance?' *Development Policy Review,* 27(6): 675–92.

Baek, S.-W. (2005) 'Does China Follow "The East Asian Development Model"?', *Journal of Contemporary Asia,* 35: 485–98.

Balchin, C. (2010). *Towards a Future without Fundamentalisms: Analyzing Religious Fundamentalist Strategies and Feminist Responses* (Toronto: AWID).

Bannon, I. and Correia, M. C. (eds) (2006) The *Other Half of Development: Men's Issues in Development* (Washington, DC: World Bank).

Battaile, W. (2002) *ARDE 2001: Making Choices* (World Bank Annual Review of Development Effectiveness).

Bauer, J. and Bell, D. (1999) *The East Asian Challenge for Human Rights* (Cambridge: Cambridge University Press).

Bauer, P. (1993) *Development Aid: End it or Mend It,* Occasional Papers No. 43 (San Francisco: International Center for Economic Growth/ICS Press).

Baur, J. and Rudolph, J. (2001) 'Water Facts and Findings on Large Dams as Pulled from the Report of the World Commission on Dams', *Development and Cooperation,* 2.

Bayliss, K. and McKinley, T. (2007) 'Privatising Basic Utilities in Sub-Saharan Africa: The MDG Impact', *Policy Research Brief* (Brasilia, International Poverty Centre, UNDP).

Beeson, M. and Islam, I. (2005) 'Neo-Liberalism and East Asia: Resisting the Washington Consensus', *Journal of Development Studies,* 41: 197–219.

Bell, D. (2000) *East Meets West: Human Rights and Democracy in East Asia* (Princeton, NJ: Princeton University Press).

———— (2008) *China's New Confucianism: Politics and Everyday Life in a Changing Society* (Princeton, NJ: Princeton University Press).

Benería, L. Deere, C. D., and Kabeer, N. (2012) 'Gender and International Migration: Globalization, Development, and Governance', *Feminist Economics,* 18:2, 1–33, doi: 10.1080/13545701.2012.688998.

Benería, L. (1995) 'Toward a Greater Integration of Gender in Economics', *World Development,* 23(11): 1839–50.

———— (1999) 'The Enduring Debate over Unpaid Labour', *International Labour Review,* 138(3): 287–309.

Benería, L. and Permanyer, I. (2010) 'The Measurement of Socio-economic Gender Inequality Revisited', *Development and Change,* 41(3): 375–99.

Berdal, M. and Malone, D. (eds) (2000) *Greed and Grievance: Economic Agendas in Civil Wars.* (Boulder, CO: Lynne Rienner).

Berger, M. and Borer, D. (eds) (1997) *The Rise of East Asia: Critical Visions of the Pacific Century* (London: Routledge).

Bessell, S. (2010) 'Methodologies for Gender-sensitive and Pro-poor Poverty Measures', in S. Chant (ed.) *The International Handbook of Gender and Poverty: Concepts, Research, Policy* (Cheltenham, UK, and Northampton, MA, USA: Edward Elgar) pp. 59–64.

Bessette, J. (1994) *The Mild Voice of Reason: Deliberative Democracy and the American National Government* (Chicago, IL: University of Chicago Press).

Betts, Richard K. (1993) 'Wealth, Power and Instability: East Asia and the United States After the Cold War', *International Security,* 18(3): 34–77.

Bevins, V. (2014, 10 September) 'Brazil says Rate of Amazon Deforestation up for First Time in Years', *LA Times.*

Bhagwati, J. (2004) *In Defense of Globalization* (New York: Oxford University Press).

Birdsall, N. (2011) 'The Global Financial Crisis: The Beginning of the End of the "Development" Agenda', in N. Birdsall and F. Fukuyama (eds), *New Ideas on Development After the Financial Crisis* (Baltimore, MD: Johns Hopkins University Press), pp. 1–26.

Blair, H. (1997) *Success and Failure in Rural Development: A Comparison of Maharashtra, Bihar and Bangladesh,* paper presented to Peasant Symposium, Bucknell University, 10 May 1997.

Blattberg, C. (2003) 'Patriotic, Not Deliberative Democracy', *Critical Review of International Social and Political Philosophy,* 6(1): 155–74.

Bloch, M. (ed.) (1975) *Marxist Analyses and Social Anthropology* (New York: Wiley).

Block, F. and Somers, M. (2014) *The Power of Market Fundamentalism: Polanyi's Critique* (Cambridge Mass: Harvard University Press).

Blyth, M. (2013) *Austerity: The History of a Dangerous Idea* (Oxford: Oxford University Press).

Bobbitt, P. (2002) *The Shield of Achilles: War, Peace and the Course of History* (London: Allen Lane).

Booth, C. (1887) 'The Inhabitants of Tower Hamlets (School Division Board), Their Condition and Occupations', *Journal of the Royal Statistical Society* 50: 326–40.

Booth, D. (2011) 'Aid, Institutions and Governance: What Have We Learned?' *Development Policy Review* 29: s5–s26.

Borer, T. A. (2009) 'Gendered War and Gendered Peace: Truth Commissions and Postconflict Gender Violence: Lessons From South Africa', *Violence Against Women,* 15(10): 1169–93.

Boserup, E. (1970) *Women's Role in Economic Development* (New York: St Martin's Press).

Bouta, T. and Frerks, G. (2003) *Women's Roles in Conflict Prevention, Conflict Resolution and Post-Conflict Reconstruction: Literature Review and Institutional Analysis* (The Hague: Netherlands Institute of International Relations).

Boyce, J. (2002) 'Unpacking Aid', *Development and Change* 33(2): 329–46.

Boyce, P. and Coyle, D. (2013) 'Development, Discourse and Law: Transgender and Same-Sex Sexualities in Nepal: Sexuality, Poverty and Law'. Brief Supporting Evidence Report (Brighton: Institute of Development Studies).

Braidotti, R., Charkeiwicz, E., Hausler, S. and Wieringa, S. (1997) 'Women, the Environment and Sustainable Development', in N. Visvanathan, L. Duggan, L. Nisonoff and N. Wiegersma (eds), *The Women, Gender and Development Reader* (London: Zed Books), pp. 54–61.

Brainard, L., Chollet, D. and LaFleur, V. (2007) 'The Tangled Web: The Poverty-Insecurity Nexus', in L. Brainard and D. Chollet (eds), *Too Poor for Peace? Global Poverty, Conflict, and Security in the 21st Century* (Washington, DC: Brookings Institution Press), pp. 1–30.

Bremmer, I. (2010) *The End of the Free Market* (New York: Portfolio).

Brenner, R. (2006) *The Economics of Global Turbulence* (London: Verso).

Broadman, H. (2007) *Africa's Silk Road: China and India's New Economic Frontier* (Washington, DC: World Bank).

Brown, R. (2010). 'Unequal Burden: Water Privatisation and Women's Human Rights in Tanzania', *Gender and Development*, 18(1): 59–67.

Brundtland, G. (1987) *Our Common Future* (Oxford: Oxford University Press).

Buckelew, A. (1984) *Terrorism and the American Response* (San Rafael, CA: Mira Academic Press).

Budlender, D. (2001) 'The South African Women's Budget Initiative: What Does it Tell Us about Poverty Alleviation?', in F. Wilson, K. Nazneen and E. Braathen (eds), *Poverty Reduction: What Role for the State in Today's Globalised Economy?* (Cape Town: CROP International Studies on Poverty, NAEP), ch. 15.

———— (2008) 'Why Care Matters for Social Development', *UNRISD Research and Policy Brief* no. 9 (Geneva: UNRISD).

Budlender, D. (2009). *Ten-Country Overview Report: Integrating Gender Responsive Budgeting into the Aid Effectiveness Agenda* (New York: UNIFEM).

Bulír, A., Gelb, A. and Mosley, P. (2008) 'Introduction: The Volatility of Overseas Aid', *World Development*, 36(10): 2045–7.

Bulman, D., Eden, M. and Nguyen, H. (2014) *Transitioning from Low-income Growth to High-income Growth: Is there a Middle Income Trap?* Policy Research Working Paper 7104 (Washington DC: World Bank).

Burkey, S. (1988) *People First: A Guide* (London and New Jersey: Zed Books).

Burnside, C. and Dollar, D. (1997) *Aid, Policies and Growth*, Policy Research Working Paper 1777 (Washington, DC: World Bank).

Burton, M., Gunther, R. and Higley, J. (eds) (1992) *Elites and Democratic Consolidation in Latin America and Southern Europe* (Cambridge: Cambridge University Press).

Bussolo, M. and De Hoyos R. (2009). 'Introduction and Overview', *Gender Aspects Of The Trade And Poverty Nexus: A Macro-Micro Approach* (Washington, DC: World Bank).

Buvinic, M. (1986) 'Projects for Women in the Third World: Explaining their Misbehavior', *World Development*, 14(5): 653–64.

Bytown Consulting and CAC International (2008) *Evaluation of CIDA's Implementation of its Policy on Gender Equity. Executive Report*, presented to Evaluation Division, Canadian International Development Agency.

Cardero, M. (2000) 'The Impact of NAFTA on Female Employment in Mexico', in L. de Pauli (ed.), *Women's Empowerment and Economic Justice: Reflecting on Experience in Latin America and the Caribbean* (New York: UNIFEM).

Cardoso, F. (1982) 'Dependency and Development in Latin America', in H. Alavi and T. Shanin (eds), *Introduction to the Sociology of Developing Countries* (New York: Monthly Review Press), pp. 112–27.

Cardoso, F. and Faletto, R. (1979) *Dependency and Development* (Berkeley: University of California Press).

Cassidy, J. (2010) *How Markets Fail: The Logic of Economic Calamities* (New York: Picador).

Cassity, E. (2010) 'New Partnerships and Education Policy in Asia and the Pacific', *International Journal of Educational Development*, 30: 508–17.

CCSBT (Commission for the Conservation of Southern Bluefin Tuna) (2014) *Latest Stock Assessment* (Canberra: Commission for the Conservation of Southern Bluefin Tuna).

Chan, S. (2002) *Liberalism, Democracy and Development* (Cambridge: Cambridge University Press).

Chandler, D. (2010) *International Statebuilding: The Rise of Post-Liberal Governance* (London: Routledge).

Chandy, L. and Gertz, G. (2011) 'Poverty in Numbers: The Changing State of Global Poverty from 2005 to 2015', *Brookings Global Views Policy Brief 2011–01* (Washington, DC: The Brookings Institute).

Chang, H.-J. (1999) 'The Economic Theory of the Developmental State', in M. Woo-Cumings (ed.), *The Developmental State* (Ithaca, NY: Cornell University Press) pp. 182–99.

——— (2002) *Kicking Away the Ladder: Development Strategy in Historical Perspective* (London: Anthem Press).

——— (2006) *East Asian Development Experience: The Miracle, the Crisis and the Future* (London: Zed Press).

——— (2007a) *The East Asian Development Experience: The Miracle, the Crisis and the Future* (London: Zed Books).

——— (2007b) *Bad Samaritans: The Guilty Secrets of Rich Nations and the Threat to Global Prosperity* (London: Random House).

——— (2010) *23 Things They Don't Tell You About Capitalism* (London: Allen Lane).

Chant, S. (2004) 'Dangerous Equations? How Female-headed Households became the Poorest of the Poor: Causes, Consequences and Cautions', *IDS Bulletin,* 35(4): 19–26.

——— (2007) 'Gender, Cities, and the Millennium Development Goals in the Global South', *New Working Paper Series*, LSE Gender Institute.

——— (2008) 'The "Feminisation of Poverty" and the "Feminisation" of Anti-Poverty Programmes: Room for Revision?' *Journal of Development Studies,* 44(2): 165–97.

——— (2010a) 'Gendered Poverty Across Space and Time: Introduction and Overview', in S. Chant (ed.) *The International Handbook of Gender and Poverty: Concepts, Research, Policy* (Cheltenham, UK, and Northampton, MA, USA: Edward Elgar), pp. 1–26.

——— (2010b) 'Towards a (Re) Conceptualisation of the "Feminisation of Poverty": Reflections on Gender-differentiated Poverty from The Gambia, Philippines and Costa Rica', in S. Chant (ed.) *The International Handbook of Gender and Poverty: Concepts, Research, Policy* (Cheltenham, UK, and Northampton, MA, USA: Edward Elgar), pp. 111–16.

Chau, N., Goto, H., and Kanbur, R. (2009) 'Middlemen, Non-Profits, and Poverty', Department of Applied Economics, Cornell University, Ithaca, NY.

Chellaney, B. (2011) *Water: Asia's New Battleground* (Washington, DC: Georgetown University Press).

Chen, Z., Ge, Y., Lai, H., and Wan, C. (2013) 'Globalization and Gender Wage Inequality in China', *World Development*, 44: 256–266.

Cheung, W, Watson, R. and Pauly, D. (2013) 'Signature of Ocean Warming in Global Fisheries Catch', *Nature*, 497: 365–8.

Chibba, M. (2011) 'The Millennium Development Goals: Key Current Issues and Challenges', *Development Policy Review*, 29(1): 75–90.

Cho, K. (1999) *Pollution Statistics in Korea in Relation to 1993 SNA* (Seoul: Bank of Korea Research Department).

Chun, H, Munyi, E., and Lee, H. (2010) 'South Korea as an Emerging Donor: Challenges and Changes on its Entering OECD/DAC', *Journal of International Development*, 22(6): 788–802.

Cincotta, R. (2010) 'Demographic Challenges to the State', in N. Tschiri, M. Lund and F. Mancini (eds) *Security and Development: Searching for Critical Connections* (Boulder, CO: Lynne Rienner), pp. 77–98.

Clague, C. (ed.) (1997) *Institutions and Economic Development: Growth and Governance in Less-Developed and Post-Socialist Countries* (Baltimore, MD: Johns Hopkins University Press).

Clapham, C., Herbst, G. and Mills, G. (eds) (2006) *Big African States* (Johannesburg: Wits University Press).

Clay, E., Geddes, M., and Natali, L. (2009) *Untying Aid: Is it Working? An Evaluation of the Implementation of the Paris Declaration and of the 2001 DAC Recommendation of Untying ODA to the LDCs* (Copenhagen: Danish Institute for International Studies).

Cockburn, J., Fofana, I., Decaluwe, B., Mabugu, R. and Chitiga, M. (2007) 'Gender-Focused Macro-Micro Analysis of the Poverty Impacts of Trade Liberalization in South Africa', in Peter J. Lambert (ed.) *Equity (Research on Economic Inequality)*, Emerald Group Publishing Limited, 15: 269–305.

Cockburn, J., Decaluwé, B., Fofana, I. and Robichaud, V. (2008) *Trade, Growth and Gender in Developing Countries: A Comparison of Ghana, Honduras, Senegal and Uganda*, Poverty and Economic Policy (PEP) Research Network and CIRPÉE (Université Laval).

Colclough, C. and Manor, J. (eds) (1991) *States or Markets? Neo-Liberalism and the Development Policy Debate* (Oxford: Oxford University Press).

Collier, D. and Levitsky, S. 1996. 'Democracy "With Adjectives": Conceptual Innovation in Comparative Research', Working Paper #230, Helen Kellogg Institute for International Studies, August 1996.

Collier, D. and Levitsky, S. (2009) 'Conceptual hierarchies in comparative research', in Collier, D. and Gerring, J. eds. *Concepts and Method in the Social Sciences: The Tradition of Giovanni Satori* (Routledge: London).

Collier, P. (1998) 'The Political Economy of Ethnicity', paper to the Annual World Bank Conference on Development Economics, Washington, DC, 20–21 April.

—— (1999). 'On the Economic Consequences of Civil War', *Oxford Economic Papers*, 51(1), 168–83.

—— (2009) *Wars, Guns and Votes: Democracy in Dangerous Places* (New York: Harper-Collins).

Collier, P., Elliot, L., Hegre, H., Hoeffler, A., Reynal-Querol, M. and Sambanis, N. (2003) *Breaking the Conflict Trap. Civil War and Development Policy* (Washington DC: World Bank and Oxford University Press).

Collier, P. and Hoeffler, A. (2002a) 'On the Incidence of Civil War in Africa', *Journal of Conflict Resolution*, 46(1), 13–28.

Collier, P. and Hoeffler, A. (2002b) *The Political Economy of Secession*. (Washington, DC: Development Research Group, World Bank).

Collier, P. and Hoeffler, A. (2004) 'Greed and Grievance in Civil War', *Oxford Economic Papers*, 56(4), 563–95.

Collinson, S. Elhawary, S. and Muggah, R. (2010) 'States of Fragility: Stabilisation and its Implications for Humanitarian Action', *Disasters*, 34: S275–S296.

Commission on Global Governance (1995) *Our Global Neighborhood* (Oxford: Oxford University Press).

Commonwealth Expert Group (1989) *Engendering Adjustment for the 1990s: Report of a Commonwealth Expert Group on Women and Structural Adjustment* (London: Commonwealth Secretariat).

Considine, M.-L. (2010) '*REDD alert*' *ECOS: Towards a Sustainable Future,* CSIRO Publishing, available at: www.ecosmagazine.com/paper/EC10047.htm (accessed 1 March 2011).

Cook, S. and Pincus, J. (2014) 'Poverty, inequality and social protection in Southeast Asia: An Introduction', *Journal of Southeast Asian Economies*, 3(1): 1–17.

Cornwall, A. (2001) 'Making a Difference? Gender and Participatory Development', *IDS Discussion Paper*, no. 378 (Brighton: Institute of Development Studies).

Cornwell, R. (1999) 'The End of the Post-Colonial State System in Africa?', *African Security Review* 8(2).

Costa, M., Sharp, R. and Elson, D. (2009) 'Gender Responsive Budgeting in the Asia Pacific Region: Democratic Republic of Timor-Leste', available at: www.unisanet. unisa.au/ genderbudgets (accessed 27 January 2011).

Cowen, M. and Shenton, R. (1996) *Doctrines of Development* (London: Routledge).

Crone, M. and Harrow, M. (2011) 'Homegrown terrorism in the West', *Terrorism & Political Violence*, 23(4), 521–36.

Crouch, C. (2011) *The Strange Non-Death of Neoliberalism* (Cambridge: Polity).

CVCB (Co-operative Venture for Capacity Building) (2007) *About Capacity Building,* available at www.rirdc.gov.au/capacitybuilding/about.html (accessed 28 April 2007).

Dahl, R. (1970) *After the Revolution: Authority in Good Society* (New Haven, CT: Yale University Press).

——— (1971) *Polyarchy and Opposition: Participation and Opposition* (New Haven, CT: Yale University Press).

——— (1986) *Democracy, Liberty and Equality* (Toyen: Norwegian University Press).

——— (1989) *Democracy and Its Critics* (New Haven, CT: Yale University Press).

——— (2000) *On Democracy* (New Haven, CT: Yale University Press).

Dains, R. (2004) 'Lasswell's Garrison State Reconsidered: Exploring a Paradigm Shift in US Civil-Military Relations', PhD thesis, University of Alabama, Tuscaloosa.

Dale, G. (2010) *Karl Polanyi: The Limits of the Market* (Cambridge: Polity).

Dangwal, D. (2005) 'Commercialisation of Forests, Timber Extraction and Deforestation in Uttaranchal, 1815–1947', *Conservation and Society*, 3(1): 110–33.

DARA (2010) 'The Humanitarian Response Index 2010: The Problems of Politicisation. Executive Summary' (Madrid: DARA).

Das, S. (2006) *Traders, Guns and Money: Knowns and Unknowns in the Dazzling World of Derivatives* (London: Prentice Hall).

——— (2011) *Extreme Money: The Masters of the Universe and the Cult of Risk* (London: Penguin).

Das Pradhan (2000) 'Engendering Good Governance in Practice', *Development Bulletin*, 51: 6–9.

Davies, R. and La O', M. (2013) 'Global Aid in 2013: A Pause Before Descending' Policy Brief 7, Development Policy Centre, Australian National University, Canberra.

Davis, K. and Dadush, S. (2010) 'The Privatization of Development Assistance: Symposium Overview', *NYU Journal of International Law and Politics,* 42.

de Bary, W. (1998) *Asian Values and Human Rights: A Confucian Communitarian Perspective* (Cambridge, MA: Harvard University Press).

de Pauli, L. (ed.) (2000) *Women's Empowerment and Economic Justice: Reflecting on Experience in Latin America and the Caribbean* (New York: UNIFEM).

de Rivero, O. (2001) *The Myth of Development: The Non-Viable Economies of the 21st Century* (London: Zed Books).

de Soto, H. (2000) *The Mystery of Capital: Why Capitalism Triumphs in the West But Fails Everywhere Else* (London: Bantam Press).

Deininger, K. and Squire, L. (1998) 'New Ways of Looking at Old Issues: Inequality and Growth', *Journal of Development Economics* 57: 259–87.

Demetriades, J. and E. Esplen (2008) 'The Gender Dimensions of Poverty and Climate Change Adaptation' *IDS Bulletin*, 39(4): 24–31.

Denison, E. (1971) 'Welfare Measurement and the GNP', *Survey of Current Business* 51: 13–16, 39.

Desai, R. and Kharas, H. (2010) 'Democratizing Foreign Aid: Online Philanthropy and International Development Assistance', *International Law and Politics*, 42(4): 1111–42.

Desch, M. (1999) *Civilian Control of the Military: The Changing Security Environment* (Baltimore, MD: Johns Hopkins University Press).

Dey, J. (1982) 'Development Planning in the Gambia: The Gap between Planners and Farmers' Perceptions, Expectations and Objectives', *World Development*, 10(5).

DFID (Department for International Development) (1997) *Eliminating World Poverty: A Challenge for the Twenty-First Century*, White Paper (London: DFID).

⸻ (2000) *Making Globalization Work for the World's Poor: An Introduction to the UK Government's White Paper on International Development* (London: DFID).

⸻ (2010) *Eliminating World Poverty: Building our Common Future* (London: DFID).

DiMarco, L. (ed.) (1972) *International Economics and Development: Essays in Honour of Raul Prebisch* (London: Academic Press).

Di Palma, G. (1991) *To Craft Democracies: An Essay on Democratic Transition* (Berkeley: University of California Press).

Dollar, D. and Kraay, A. (2002) 'Spreading the Wealth', *Foreign Affairs* 81(1): 120–33.

Dollar, D and Levine, V. (2006) 'The Increasing Selectivity of Foreign Aid' 1984–2003', *World Development*, 34(12): 2034–46.

Doyal, L. and Gough, I. (1991) *A Theory of Human Need* (London: Macmillan).

DRC 2014. 'An Exploratory Analysis of China's Strategy for Future Energy Development', Development Research Centre, State Council, People's Republic of China. http://www.chinadaily.com.cn/m/drc/2014-03/17/content_17352981.htm accessed 13 June 2014.

Drechsler, D. and Jütting, J. (2010) 'Why is Progress in Gender Equality so Slow? An Introduction to the "Social Institutions and Gender" Index', in S. Chant (ed.) *The International Handbook of Gender and Poverty: Concepts, Research, Policy* (Cheltenham, UK and Northampton, MA, USA: Edward Elgar), pp. 77–83.

Duffield, M. (2002) 'Social Reconstruction and the Radicalization of Development: Aid as a Relation of Global Liberal Governance', *Development and Change* 33(5): 1049–71.

⸻ (2005) 'Social Reconstruction: The Reuniting of Aid and Politics', *Development*, 48(3): 16–24.

Duménil, G. and Lévy, D. (2011) *The Crisis of Neoliberalism* (Cambridge, MA: Harvard University Press).

Dunkerley, J., Ramsay, W., Gordon, L. and Cecelski, E. (1981) *Energy Strategies for Developing Nations* (Baltimore, MD, and London: Johns Hopkins University Press).

Dupont, A. (2001) *East Asia Imperilled: Transnational Challenges to Security* (Cambridge: Cambridge University Press).

Dureau, C. (2003) Address to 'Working Together for East Timor' Conference, Darebin City Council, Melbourne, 4–5 April.

Dutt, A. (2005) 'International Trade in Early Development Economics', in K. S. Jomo and Erik Reinert (eds), *Development Economics: How Schools of Economic Thought Have Addressed Development* (London: Zed Books), pp. 99–127.

Dymski, G. (2010) 'Why the Subprime Crisis is Different: A Minskyian Approach', *Cambridge Journal of Economics*, 34: 239–55.

Easterly, W. (2001) *The Elusive Quest for Growth* (Cambridge, MA: MIT Press).

—— (2006) *The White Man's Burden: Why the West's Efforts to Aid the Rest have Done So Much Ill and So Little Good* (New York: Penguin Press).

—— (2010) 'Foreign Aid for Scoundrels', *The New York Review of Books*, November 25. Available at: www.nybooks.com/articles/archives/2010/nov/25/foreign-aid-scoundrels (accessed 1 March 2011).

The Economist (2013) 'Doha Delivers', www.economist.com/blogs/freeexchange/2013/12/world-trade-organisation (accessed 16 December 2013).

Edström, J., Das A., and Dolan, C. (2014) 'Introduction: Undressing Patriarchy and Masculinities to Re-politicise Gender' *IDS Bulletin* 45(1) January 2014: 1–10.

Eerdewijk, A. V. and Davids, T. (2013). 'Escaping the Mythical Beast: Gender Mainstreaming Reconceptualised,' J. Int. Dev., doi: 10.1002/jid

Ehrlich, P. (1969) *The Population Bomb* (New York: Ballantyne Books).

Eichengreen, B. (1999) *Toward a New International Financial Architecture: A Practical Post-Asia Agenda* (Washington, DC: Institute for International Economics).

—— (2007) *Global Imbalances and Lessons of Bretton Woods* (Cambridge, MA: MIT Press).

Eichengreen, B. and Fishlow, A. (1998) 'Contending with Capital Flows: What is Different about the 1990s?' in M. Kahler (ed.), *Capital Flows and Financial Crises* (Manchester: Manchester University Press), pp. 23–68.

Elbadawi, I and Sambanis, N. (2002) 'How Much War Will We See? Explaining the Prevalence of Civil War', *Journal of Conflict Resolution* 46(3), 307–34.

Elkington, J. (1999) *Cannibals with Forks: The Triple Bottom Line of 21st-Century Business* (Oxford: Capstone).

Elson, D. (1991) 'Structural Adjustment: Its Effect on Women', in T. Wallace and C. March (eds), *Changing Perceptions: Writings on Gender and Development* (Oxford: Oxfam), pp. 39–59.

—— (2010) 'Gender and the Global Economic Crisis in Developing Countries: A Framework for Analysis', *Gender and Development*, 18(2): 201–12.

Elson, D. and Sharp, R. (2010) 'Gender-responsive Budgeting and Women's Poverty', in S. Chant (ed.) *The International Handbook of Gender and Poverty: Concepts, Research, Policy* (Cheltenham, UK, and Northampton, MA, USA: Edward Elgar), pp. 522–7.

Elson, D, Fukuda-Parr, S, Vizard, P. (eds) (2011). *Human Rights and the Capabilities Approach: An Interdisciplinary Dialogue* (Abingdon: Routledge).

Emmanuel, A. (1972) *Unequal Exchange* (London: Monthly Review Press).

Englebert, P. (2000) 'Pre-Colonial Institutions, Post-Colonial States, and Economic Development in Topical Africa', *Political Research Quarterly*, 53(1) March: 7–36.

Eriksen, T. (2002) *Ethnicity and Nationalism,* 2nd edn (London: Pluto Press).

Escobar, A. (1995) *Encountering Development: The Making and Unmaking of the Third World* (Princeton, NJ: Princeton University Press).

Esplen, E. (2006) *Engaging Men in Gender Equality: Positive Strategies and Approaches – Overview and Annotated Bibliography* (Brighton: BRIDGE, Institute of Development Studies).

Estefa (2001) *Evaluating the World Bank's Community Empowerment Project,* 7(2).

European Report on Development (2013), *Post-2015: Global Action for an Inclusive and Sustainable Future* (Brussels: Overseas Development Institute (ODI), German Development Institute/Deutsches Institut für Entwicklungspolitik (DIE), European Centre for Development Policy Management (ECDPM)).

Evans, G, and Grant, B. (1989) *Australia's Foreign Relations*, 2nd edn (Melbourne: Melbourne University Press).

Evans, P. (1995) *Embedded Autonomy: States and Industrial Transformation* (Princeton, NJ: Princeton University Press).

Eyben, R. (2008) 'Power, Mutual Accountability and Responsibility in the Practice of International Aid: A Relational Approach', *IDS Working Paper* (Brighton: Institute of Development Studies at the University of Sussex).

Eyben, R. (2013). 'Getting Unpaid Care onto Development Agendas', *IDS In Focus Policy Briefing*, 31 (Brighton: IDS).

FAO (Food and Agriculture Organization) (2001) *State of the World's Forests 2001* (Rome: Food and Agriculture Organization of the United Nations).

—— (2006) *State of the World's Fisheries and Aquaculture* (New York: FAO, United Nations).

—— (2010) *State of the World's Fisheries and Aquaculture* (New York: FAO, United Nations).

—— (2014a) 'Sixth Meeting of the Working Group on Aquaculture', Regional Commission for Fisheries, Muscat, Oman, 21–23 October 2014.

—— (2014b) 'Aquastat', www.fao.org/nr/water/aquastat/main/index.stm (accessed 5 February 2015).

Fengler, W. and Kharas, H. (eds) (2010) *Delivering Aid Differently: Lessons from the Field* (Washington, DC: Brookings Institution Press).

Ferguson, N. (2005) 'Sinking Globalization', *Foreign Affairs,* 2005(2): 64–77.

—— (2011) *Civilization: The West and the Rest* (London: Allen Lane).

Ferry, L. (2009) 'Sustainable Development in the Context of Globalization', speech to French Senate, 1 October.

FfP (Fund for Peace) (2006) *Failed State Index 2006,* available at: www.fundforpeace. org/programs/fsi/fsindex2006.php (accessed [date])

Fishlow, A. (1985) 'Lessons from the Past: Capital Markets in the 19th Century and the Interwar Period', in M. Kahler (ed.), *The Politics of International Debt* (Ithaca, NY: Cornell University Press), pp. 37–94.

Floro, M. and Schaeffer, K. (2001) 'Restructuring of Labour Markets in the Philippines and Zambia: The Gender Dimension', in L. Beneria and S. Bisnath (eds), *Gender and Development: Theoretical, Empirical and Practical Approaches,* vol. 2I (London: Elgar Publishing), pp. 393–418.

Fontana, M., Joekes, S. and Masika, R. (1998) *Global Trade Expansion and Liberalisation: Gender Issues and Impacts* (Brighton: BRIDGE, Institute of Development Studies).

Fordham (2002) 'Scatter Plot: Infant Mortality versus Access to Safe Water', *Stabilization Policy in Developing Countries, Political Economy and Development* (New York City: Fordham University).

Foster, J., Greer, J. and Thorbecke, E. (1984), 'A Class of Decomposable Poverty Measures', *Econometrica,* 52(3): 761–6.

Fox, J. (2009) *The Myth of the Rational Market: A History of Risk, Reward, and Delusion on Wall Street* (New York: Harper).

Fox, J. and Brown, D. L. (1998) *The Struggle for Accountability: The World Bank, NGOs and Grassroots Movements* (Cambridge, MA: MIT Press).

Frank, A. G. (1967) *Capitalism and Underdevelopment in Latin America* (London: Monthly Review Press).

Frank, A. G. (1980) *Crisis in the World Economy* (New York: Holmes & Meier).

Freedman, L. (2008) *The Choice of Enemies: America Confronts the Middle East* (London: Weidenfeld & Nicolson).

Freire, P. (1976) *Education: The Practice of Freedom* (London: Writers and Readers Publishing Cooperative).

—— (1985) [1970] *Pedagogy of the Oppressed* (Harmondsworth: Pelican Books).

Friday, L. and Laskey, R. (1989) *The Fragile Environment: The Darwin College Lectures* (Cambridge: Cambridge University Press).

Friedberg, A. (1993) 'Ripe for Rivalry: Prospects for Peace in a Multipolar Asia', *International Security*, 18(3): 5–33.

Friedman, E. (2009) 'How Economic Superpower China Could Transform Africa'. *Journal of Chinese Political Science*, 14: 1–20.

Friedman, J. (1992) *Empowerment: The Politics of Alternative Development* (Oxford: Blackwell Publishing).

Fritz, V. and Cammack, D. (2006) 'State-building and Fragile States. Development Horizons: Future Directions for Research and Policy Seminar', 15 December (London: Overseas Development Institute).

Fritz, V. and Menocal, A. R. (2006) '(Re)building Developmental States: From Theory to Practice', Working Paper no. 274 (London: Overseas Development Institute).

Fromm, E. and Maccoby, M. (1970) *Social Character in a Mexican Village: A Sociopsychoanalytic Study* (Englewood Cliffs, NJ: Prentice-Hall).

Frost, Ellen (2008) *Asia's New Regionalism* (Boulder, CO: Lynne Rienner).

Frot, E. and Santiso, J. (2010) 'Crushed Aid: Fragmentation in Sectoral Aid', *OECD Development Centre Working Paper* (Working Paper no. 284).

Fuggle, R. and Smith, W. (2000) *Experience with Dams in Water and Energy Resource Development in the People's Republic of China* (Cape Town: World Commission on Dams).

Fukuda-Parr, S. (2010) 'Reducing Inequality – The Missing MDG: A Content Review of PRSPs and Bilateral Donor Policy Statements' *IDS Bulletin*, 41(1): 26–35.

Fukuda-Parr, S., Greenstein, J. and Stewart, D. (2013) 'How Should MDG Success and Failure be Judged: Faster Progress or Achieving the Targets?' *World Development*, 41: 19–30.

Fukuyama, F. (1992) *The End of History and the Last* Man (London: Verso).

––––––– (2004) *State Building* (London: Profile Books).

Furtado, C. (1964) *Development and Underdevelopment* (Berkeley: University of California Press).

––––––– (1965) *Diagnosis of the Brazilian Crisis* (Berkeley: University of California Press).

––––––– (1969) *Economic Development in Latin America* (Cambridge: Cambridge University Press).

Galbraith, J. and Berner, M. (2001) *Inequality and Industrial Change* (Cambridge: Cambridge University Press).

Gallasch, D. (2001) *Taking Shelter Under Trees* (Chiang Mai: Friends without Borders).

Galtung, J. (1997) 'Grand Designs on a Collision Course', *Development* 40(1): 71–5 (reprinted from *International Development Review* (1978): 3–4).

Gardner, K. and Lewis, D. (1996) *Anthropology, Development and the Post-Modern Challenge* (London: Pluto Press).

Garrett, G. (2004) 'Globalization's Missing Middle', *Foreign Affairs* 83(6): 84–96.

Gates, S. Hegre, H. and Nygard, H. (2012) 'Development Consequences of Armed Conflict', *World Development*, 40(9), 1713–22.

Gaye, A., Klugman, J., Kovacevic, M., Twigg, S. and Zambrano, E. (2010) 'Measuring Key Disparities in Human Development: The Gender Inequality Index', *Human Development Research Paper*, UNDP.

GCM (Global Commodity Markets) (2000) 'Summary', *Global Commodity Markets* (Washington, DC: World Bank).

Gellner, E. (1964) *Thought and Change* (London: Weidenfeld & Nicolson).

––––––– (1983) *Nations and Nationalism* (Ithaca: Cornell University Press).

Gender and Development Network (2014) Women's Rights and Gender Equality in the Post-2015 Framework, Gender and Development Network position paper, UK. www. gadnetwork.uk.org (accessed 5 June 2014).

George, S. (1998) *A Fate Worse than Debt* (London: Penguin).

Gereffi, G. and Wyman, D. (eds) (1990) *Manufacturing Miracles: Paths to Industrialization in Latin America and East Asia* (Princeton, NJ: Princeton University Press).

German, T. and Randel, J. (2002) 'Never Richer, Never Poorer', part 4, World Aid Trends, in *The Reality of Aid: An Independent Review of Poverty Reduction and Development Assistance* (Manila: IBON Books), pp. 145–57.

Gerschenkron, A. (1962) *Economic Backwardness in Historical Perspective* (Cambridge, MA: Harvard University Press).

Ghosh, B. N. (ed.) (2001) *Global Financial Crises and Reforms* (London: Routledge).

Gibb, R., Hughes, T., Mills, G. and Vaahtoranta, T. (eds) (2002) *Charting a New Course: Globalization, African Recovery and the New Africa Initiative* (Johannesburg: South African Institute of International Affairs).

Gill, I. and Kharas, H. (2007) *An East Asian Renaissance: Ideas for Economic Growth* (Washington, DC: World Bank).

Gill, I., Huang, Y. and Kharas, H. (2007) *East Asian Visions: Perspectives on Economic Development* (Washington, DC: World Bank; and Singapore, Institute of Policy Studies).

Gilmore, E., Gleditsch, N. P. and Lujala, P. (2005) 'A Diamond Curse? Civil War and a Lootable Resource', *Journal of Conflict Resolution*, 49(4), 538–62.

Global Development Research Center (n.d.), 'Defining Capacity Building', www.gdrc.org/uem/capacity-define.html (accessed 26 February 2016).

Global Humanitarian Assistance (2013) *Global Humanitarian Assistance Report 2013* (Bristol: Development Initiatives)

Global Humanitarian Initiative (GH1) (2010) *GHA Report 2010* (Somerset: Global Humanitarian Assistance, Development Initiatives).

Global Witness (2007) 'Hot Chocolate: How Cocoa Fuelled the Conflict in Côte d'Ivoire' (Washington, DC: Global Witness).

Goetz, A.-M. and Sandler, J. (2007) 'Swapping Gender: From Cross-cutting Obscurity to Sectoral Security?', in A. Cornwall, E. Harrison and A. Whitehead (eds) (2007), *Feminisms in Development: Contradictions, Contestations, and Challenges* (London, Zed Books), pp. 161–73.

Gonzalez, J., Lauder, K. and Melles, B. (2000) *Opting for Partnership: Governance Innovations in Southeast Asia* (Ottawa and Kuala Lumpur: Institute on Governance).

Gonzalez-Vicente, R. (2011) 'China's Engagement in South America and Africa's Extractive Sectors: New Perspectives for Resource Curse Theories', *The Pacific Review*, 24: 65–87.

Gore, C. (2013) 'The New Development Cooperation Landscape: Actors, Approaches, Architecture,' *Journal of International Development*, 25: 769–86.

Goulet, D. (1971) *The Cruel Choice: A New Concept in the Theory of Development* (New York: Atheneum).

Government Commission on Capital Flight from Poor Countries (2009) Tax Havens and Development, Report from the Government Commission on Capital Flight from Poor Countries. Appointed by Royal Decree of 27 June 2008. Submitted to the Ministry of Foreign Affairs, on 18 June 2009. *Official Norwegian Reports 2009*: 19.

Gowan, P. (1999) *The Global Gamble: Washington's Faustian Bid for World Dominance* (London: Verso).

Grant, J. A. and Taylor, I. (2004) 'Global Governance and Conflict Diamonds: The Kimberley Process and the Quest for Clean Gems', *The Round Table*, 93(375): 385–401.

Grawert, E. (2009) *Departures From Postcolonial Authoritarianism* (Frankfurt am Main: Peter Lang).

Gray, J. (1998) *False Dawn: The Delusions of Global Capitalism* (London: Granta).

—— (2003) *Al Qaeda and What it Means to be Modern* (London: Faber & Faber).

——— (2007) *Black Mass: Apocalyptic Religion and the Death of Utopia* (London: Allen Lane).

Green, R. H. (1978) 'Basic Human Needs: Concept or Slogan, Synthesis or Smokescreen?', *IDS Bulletin* 9(4): 7–11.

Greig, A., Kimmel, M. and Lang, J. (2000) 'Men, Masculinities and Development: Broadening our Work Towards Gender Equality', *Gender in Development Monograph Series* 10 (New York: UNDP).

Greig, A. and Edström, J. (2012) *Mobilising Men in Practice: Challenging Sexual and Gender-based Violence in Institutional Settings* (Brighton: Institute of Development Studies).

Griffiths, M. (2003) 'Self-determination, International Society and World Order', *Macquarie Law Journal*, 3.

Griffith-Jones, S., Ocampo, J. A. (2009) 'The Financial Crisis and its Impact on Developing Countries, *Working Paper, International Policy Centre for Inclusive Growth*, 53.

Griffith-Jones, S. (2013, 31 October) 'Germany wants the Robin Hood Tax – and Europe's Voters Do Too' *The Guardian*, www.theguardian.com/commentisfree/2013/oct/30/germany-robin-hood-tax-europe-financial-transaction-tax (accessed 10 January 2014).

Groves, L. and Hinton, R. (eds) (2004) *Inclusive Aid: Changing Power and Relationships in International Development* (London: Earthscan).

Grown, C., Elson, D. and Cagatay, N. (2000) 'Introduction', *World Development*, 28(7): 1145–56.

Grugel, J. (2002) *Democratization: A Critical Introduction* (Basingstoke: Palgrave Macmillan).

Gujit, I. and Shah, M. K. (1998) *The Myth of Community: Gender Issues in Participatory Development* (London: Intermediate Technology Publications).

Gupta, S., Clements, B., Bhattacharya, R. and Chakravarti, S. (2002) 'Fiscal Consequences of Armed Conflict and Terrorism in Low- and Middle-Income Countries', *IMF Working Paper*, 142 (Washington: International Monetary Fund).

Gupta, S., Pattillo, C. and Wagh, S. (2009) 'Effect of Remittances on Poverty and Financial Development in Sub-Saharan Africa', *World Development*, 37(1):104–15.

Gurr, T. R. (1970) *Why Men Rebel* (Princeton, NJ: Princeton University Press).

Gusfield, J. (1976) 'Tradition and Modernity: Misplaced Polarities in the Study of Social Change', *American Journal of Sociology*, 72.

Habermas, J. (2001a) 'A Constitution for Europe?', *New Left Review*, 11: 5–26.

——— (2001b) *A Postnational Constellation* (Cambridge, MA: MIT Press).

Hadjimichael, M. (1996) *Adjustment for Growth: The African Experience*, Occasional Paper (Washington, DC: International Monetary Fund).

Haggard, S. (2000) *The Political Economy of the Asian Financial Crisis* (Washington, DC: Institute for International Economics).

Hall, P. and Taylor, R. (1996) 'Political Science and the Three New Institutionalisms', *Political Studies*, 44(5): December, 936–57.

Halper, S. (2010) *The Beijing Consensus: How China's Authoritarian Model Will Dominate the Twenty-First Century* (New York: Basic Books).

Hameiri, S. (2008) 'Risk Management, Neo-liberalism and the Securitisation of the Australian Aid Program', *Australian Journal of International Affairs*, 62(3): 357–71.

Han, F, Fernandez, W and Tan, S. (1998) *Lee Kuan Kuan Yew: The Man and His Ideas* (Singapore: Times Editions).

Hancock, G. (1989) *Lords of Poverty* (London: Macmillan).

Hansen, H. and Tarp, F. (2000) 'Aid Effectiveness Disputed', in F. Tarp (ed.), *Foreign Aid and Development: Lessons Learned and Directions for the Future* (London: Routledge), pp. 103–28.

Hansen, J., Ruedy, R., Sato, M. and Lo, K. (2006) *GISS Surface Temperature Analysis, Global Temperature Trends: 2005 Summation* (New York: Goddard Institute for Space Studies, National Aeronautics and Space Administration).

HAP International (2008) *The Guide to the HAP Standard: Humanitarian Accountability and Quality Management* (Oxfam GB for HAP International).

Haq, G., Han, W. and Kim, C. (eds) (2002) *Urban Air Pollution Management and Practice in Major and Mega Cities of Asia* (Seoul: Korea Environment Institute).

Harper, C. Nowacka, K., Alder, H. and Ferrant, G. (2014) Measuring Women's Empowerment and Social Transformation in the Post-2015 Agenda (London: Overseas Development Institute).

Harvey, D. (2003) *The New Imperialism* (Oxford: Oxford University Press).

—— (2010) *The Enigma of Capitalism and the Crises of Capitalism* (Oxford: Oxford University Press).

Harvey, D. (2005) *A Brief History of Neoliberalism* (Oxford: Oxford University Press).

Harvey, M., Ramlogan, R. and Randles, S. (eds) (2014) *Karl Polanyi: New Perspectives on the Place of the Economy in Society* (Manchester: Manchester University Press).

Hasani, E. (2003) 'Uti Possidetus Juris: From Rome To Kosovo', Fletcher Forum of World Affairs, Summer/Fall 2003.

Hayek, Friedrich (1960) *The Constitution of Liberty* (Chicago: University of Chicago Press).

He, B. (2010) 'Participatory and Deliberative Institutions in China', in E. Leib and B. He (eds), *The Search for Deliberative Democracy in China* (London: Palgrave Macmillan).

Heinonen, P. (2006) 'Changing Perceptions: Globalization, Women and Development', International Women's Congress, Women's Role in the Alliance of Civilizations, Istanbul, 28–9 January.

Hellinger, S., Hellinger, D. and O'Regan, F. (1988) *Aid for Just Development* (London: Lynne Rienner).

Herbst, G. (2000) *States and Power in Africa: Comparative Lessons in Authority and Control* (Princeton, NJ: Princeton University Press).

Hettne, B. (1995) *Development Theory and the Three Worlds*, 2nd edn (London: Longman).

Hickey, S. and Mohan, G. (2005) 'Relocating Participation within a Radical Politics of Development', *Development and Change*, 36(2): 237–62.

Higgins, B. (1958) *Economic Development: Principles, Problems, and Policies* (London: Constable).

Higgott, R. (2000) 'The International Relations of the Asian Economic Crisis: A Study in the Politics of Resentment', in R. Robison, M. Beeson, K. Jayasuriya and H.-R. Kim (eds), *Politics and Markets in the Wake of the Asian Crisis* (London: Routledge), pp. 261–82.

Hirsch, P. and Warren, C. (eds) (1998) *The Politics of Environment in Southeast Asia: Resources and Resistance* (London: Routledge).

Hirschman, A. (1958) *The Strategy of Economic Development* (Yale, CT: Yale University Press).

Hirschmann, D. (1987) 'Early Post-Colonial Bureaucracy as History: The Case of the Lesotho Central Planning and Development Office, 1965–1975', *International Journal of African Historical Studies*, 20(3): 455–70.

HM Treasury (2004) 'International Issues: International Finance Facility'. PDF file of International Finance Facility Proposal, available at: www.hm-treasury.gov.uk/medi/D64/78/IFF_propsal_doc_080404.pdf.

—— (2006) 'International Issues. International Finance Facility', available at: www.hm-treasury.gov.uk/documents/international_issues/int_gnd_intfinance.cfm (accessed [date]).

Hobijn, B. (2002) 'What Will Homeland Security Cost?', Paper presented to the German Institute of Global Research (DIW) workshop on 'The Economic Consequences of Global Terrorism', Berlin, available at www.diw.de/deutsch/service/veranstaltungen/ws_consequences.

Hobsbawm, E. (1998) 'Introduction' to a modern edition of Karl Marx and Frederick Engels, *The Communist Manifesto* (London: Verso), pp. 1–29.

―――― (2004) *Nations and Nationalism Since 1870: Programme, Myth, Reality* (Cambridge: Cambridge University Press).

Hocking, J. (2004) *Terror Laws: ASIO, Counter-Terrorism and the Threat to Democracy* (Sydney: University of New South Wales Press).

Hodge, P. (1970) 'The Future of Community Development', in A. Robson and B. Crick (eds), *The Future of Social Services* (Harmondsworth: Penguin Books).

Hoffman, B. (2002) 'The Emergence of the New Terrorism' in A. Tan and K. Ramakrishna (eds), *The New Terrorism: Anatomy, Trends, and Counter-Strategies* (Singapore: Eastern Universities Press), pp. 30–49.

Hoffman, P. (1997) 'The Challenge of Economic Development', *Development* 40: 19–24.

Holtz, E. (2007) 'Implementing the United Nations Convention to Combat Desertification from a Parliamentary Point of View: Critical Assessment and Challenges Ahead', Seventh Parliamentarians Forum of the United Nations Convention to Combat Desertification (New York: United Nations).

Homer-Dixon, T. (1999) *Environment, Security, and Violence* (Princeton, NJ: Princeton University Press).

Hopkins, A. and K. Patel (2006) 'Reflecting on Gender Equality in Muslim Contexts in Oxfam GB', *Gender and Development*, 14(3): 423–35.

Hopkins, R. F. (2000) 'Political Economy of Foreign Aid', in F. Tarp (ed.), *Foreign Aid and Development: Lessons Learned and Directions for the Future* (London: Routledge).

Hopkins, T. and Wallerstein, I. (1982) *World-Systems Analysis: Theory and Methodology* (Beverly Hills, CA: Sage).

Hoppe, H. (2001) *Democracy: The God That Failed* (Rutgers, NJ: Transaction Publishers).

Horowitz, D (1985) *Ethnic Groups in Conflict* (Berkeley, CA: University of California Press).

Howard, R. (1983) 'The Full-Belly Thesis: Should Economic Rights Take Priority over Civil and Political Rights? Evidence from Sub-Saharan Africa', *Human Rights Quarterly* 5(4): November, 467–90.

Howell, J. (2006) 'The Global War on Terror, Development and Civil Society', *Journal of International Development*, 18: 121–35.

Htaw, L. (2008, 6 June) 'Burma Tops List in Deforestation', *Independent Mon News Agency* (USA).

Huang, Y. (2008) *Capitalism with Chinese Characteristics: Entrepreneurship and the State* (New York: Cambridge University Press).

Hudson Institute (2010) *The Index of Global Philanthropy and Remittances* 2010, available at: www.hudson.org/files/pdf_upload/Index_of_Global_Philanthropy_and_Remittances_2010.pdf. (Washington DC: Hudson Institute Center for Global Prosperity) (accessed 22 December 2010).

Hudson Institute (2013) *Index of Global Philanthropy and Remittances 2013* (Washington: Center for Global Prosperity).

Human Rights Watch (2002) 'Bush Should Urge Democratic Reforms in Pakistan', Press Release, 12 September.

Hummelbrunner, R. and Jones, H. (2013) 'A guide to managing in the face of complexity,' Working Paper, Overseas Development Institute, London.

Hundt, D. (2005) 'A Legitimate Paradox: Neo-liberal Reform and the Return of the State in Korea', *Journal of Development Studies*, 41: 242–60.

Hunt, D. (1989) *Economic Theories of Development: An Analysis of Competing Paradigms* (New York: Harvester Wheatsheaf).

Huntington, S. (1957) *The Soldier and the State: The Theory and Politics of Civil–Military Relations* (Cambridge, MA: Belknap Press).

―――― (1968) *Political Order in Changing Societies* (Cambridge, MA: Yale University Press).

―――― (1971) 'The Change to Change: Modernization, Development, and Politics', *Comparative Politics*, 3: 283–328.

―――― (1996) *The Clash of Civilizations and the Remaking of the New World Order* (New York: Simon & Schuster).

ICJ (1986). 'Frontier Dispute; Judgment', Reports, International Court of Justice, The Hague.

IEA (International Energy Agency) (2010) 'World Energy Outlook 2010 Factsheet' (Paris: International Energy Agency).

Ikejiaku, B. (2012) 'Poverty–Conflict Nexus: The Contentious Issue Revisited', *European Journal of Sustainable Development*, 1(2), 127–50.

ILO (International Labour Organization) (1976) *Employment, Growth and Basic Needs* (Geneva: International Labour Organization).

―――― (2013) 'Men and Masculinities: Promoting Gender Equality in the World of Work', *ILO Working Paper 3* (Geneva: International Labour Organization).

IMF (International Monetary Fund) (2005) 'Solomon Islands: 23005 Article IV Consultation', Staff Report and Public Information Notice on the Executive Board Discussion, *IMF Country Report*, 365 (Washington, DC: IMF).

―――― (2007) *Global Financial Stability Report, April 2007*, International Monetary Fund (Washington, DC: International Monetary Fund).

International Dialogue on Peacebuilding and Statebuilding (n.d.) 'About the International Dialogue', www.pbsbdialogue.org/en/id/about-international-dialogue/ (accessed 17 February 2016).

International Dialogue on Peacebuilding and Statebuilding (2010) 'Peacebuilding and Statebuilding Priorities and Challenges: a Synthesis of Findings from Seven Multi-stakeholder Consultations. International Dialogue on Peacebuilding and Statebuilding', www.pbsbdialogue.org/media/filer_public/54/bb/54bb413c-f64d-481e-8ad1-d75bed08be34/a_synthesis_of_findings_from_seven_multi-stakeholder_consultations_en.pdf (accessed 17 February 2016).

INGO (International Non-government Organizations) (2006) Accountability Charter, www.ingoaccountabilitycharter.org/wpcms/wp-content/uploads/ingo-accountability-charter-eng.pdf (accessed 1 March 2011).

Institute of Development Studies (2013) 'Building Relationships in Development Cooperation: Traditional Donors and the Rising Powers', Policy Briefing (Sussex: IDS).

IRN (International Rivers Network) (2001) *Manibeli Declaration* (International Rivers Network).

Isaacman, A, and Isaacman, B. (2013) *Dams, Displacement and the Delusion of Development: Cahora Bassa and Its Legacies in Mozambique* (Athens, OH, Ohio University Press).

Ivanic, M. and Martin, W. (2008) 'Implications of Higher Global Food Prices in Low-Income Countries', *World Bank Policy Research Working Paper 4594* (Washington, DC: World Bank).

Jackson, K. (ed.) (1999) *Asian Contagion: The Causes and Consequences of a Financial Crisis* (Boulder, CO: Westview).

Jacoby, T. and James, E. (2010) 'Emerging Patterns in the Reconstruction of Conflict-affected Countries', *Disasters*, 34: S1–S14.

Jahan, R. (1995) *The Elusive Agenda: Mainstreaming Women in Development* (London: Zed Books).

Jain, L., Krishnamurthy, B. and Tripathi, P. (1985) *Grass Without Roots: Rural Development Under Government Auspices* (New Delhi: Sage Publications).

Jefferess, D. (2008) *Post-Colonial Resistance: Culture, Liberation and Transformation* (Toronto: University of Toronto Press).

Jefferys, A. (2002) 'Giving Voice to Silent Emergencies', *Humanitarian Exchange* 20: 2–4.

Jenkins, B. and Godges, J. (2011) *The Long Shadow of 9/11: America's Response to Terrorism* (Santa Monica, CA: Rand).

Jenkins, M. (2012) *Al Qaeda in its Third Decade: Irreversible Decline or Imminent Victory?* (Santa Monica, CA: Rand Corporation).

Jhamb, B. and N. Sinha (2010) *Millennium Development Goals and Gender Budgeting: Where does India Stand?* (New Delhi: Centre for Budget and Governance Accountability).

Jhamb, B., Mishra, Y. Sinha, N. (2013). 'The Paradox of Gender-responsive Budgeting', *Economic & Political Weekly*, May 18, xlviii(20): 35–8.

Johannen, U., Smith, A. and Gomez, J. (2003) *September 11 and Political Freedom: Asian Perspectives* (Singapore: Select Publishing).

Johnson, C. (1987) 'Political Institutions and Economic Performance: The Government Business Relationship in Japan, South Korea and Taiwan', in F. Deyo (ed.), *The Political Economy of the New Asian Industrialism* (Ithaca, NY: Cornell University Press), pp. 136–65.

Johnsson-Latham, G. (2010), 'Power, Privilege and Gender as Reflected in Poverty Analysis and Development Goals', in S. Chant, S. (ed), T*he International Handbook of Gender and Poverty* (Cheltenham: Edward Elgar Publishing Inc.), pp. 41–6.

Jolly, R. (1999) 'New Composite Indices for Development Cooperation', *Development*, 42(3): 36–42.

Jomo, K. S. (ed.) (1998) *Tigers in Trouble: Financial Governance, Liberalisation and Crises in East Asia* (London: Zed Books).

Jomo, K. and Nagaraj, S. (2001) *Globalisation Versus Development* (Basingstoke: Palgrave).

Jones, N., Harper, C., Pantuliano, S. and Pavanello, S. (2009) 'The Global Economic Crisis and Impacts on Children and Caregivers: Emerging Evidence and Possible Policy Responses in the Middle East and North Africa', Background note (London: ODI).

Jones, N., Harper, C., and Watson, C. with Espey, J., Wadugodapitiya, D., Page, E., Stavropoulou, M., Presler-Marshall, E. and Clench, B. (2010) *Stemming Girls' Chronic Poverty: Catalysing Development Change by Building Just Social Institutions* (Manchester: Chronic Poverty Research Centre).

Kabeer, N. (1999) *The Conditions and Consequences of Choice: Reflections on the Measurement of Women's Empowerment*, UNRISD Discussion Paper no. 108 (Geneva: UNRISD).

——— (2005) 'Gender Equality and Women's Empowerment: A Critical Analysis of the Third Millennium Development Goals', *Gender and Development,* 13(1): 13–24.

——— (2006) 'Poverty, Social Exclusion and the MDGs: The Challenge of "Durable Inequalities" in the Asian Context', *IDS Bulletin*, 37(3): 64–78.

——— (2008) *Mainstreaming Gender in Social Protection for the Informal Economy* (London: Commonwealth Secretariat).

Kabeer, N. and Anh, T. T. V. (2000) 'Leaving the Ricefields, but not the Countryside: Gender, Livelihood Diversification and Pro-poor Growth in Rural Viet Nam', *UNRISD* Occasional Paper, 13 (Geneva: UNRISD).

Kabeer, N. and Natali, L. (2013) 'Gender Equality and Economic Growth: Is there a Win-Win?' *IDS Working Paper*, 2013, 417 (Sussex: Institute of Development Studies).

Kandiyoti, D. (2005) *The Politics of Gender and Reconstruction in Afghanistan,* Occasional Paper no. 4 (Geneva: UNRISD).

—— (2007) 'Between the Hammer and the Anvil: Post-conflict Reconstruction, Islam and Women's Rights', *Third World Quarterly,* 28(3): 503–17.

—— (2011) 'Disentangling Religion and Politics: Whither Gender Equality?' *IDS Bulletin,* 42(1): 10–14.

Kaplan, B. (2005) 'From Friedman to Whitman: The Transition of Chicago Political Economy', *Econ Journal Watch,* 2(1), April: 1–21.

Kaplan, R. (2010) *Monsoon: The Indian Ocean and the Future of American Power* (New York: Random House).

Kaplinsky, R. (2005) *Globalization, Poverty and Inequality* (Cambridge: Polity).

Karam, A. (2001) 'Women in War and Peace-building: The Roads Traversed, the Challenges Ahead', *International Feminist Journal of Politics,* 3(1): 2–25.

Karkara, R., Karlsson, L. and Malik, B. (2005) 'Working with Men and Boys to Gender Equality and to End Violence against Boys and Girls: Methods, Strategies, Tools and Practices', Save the Children, Sweden-Denmark, Regional Programme for South and Central Asia, Kathmandu, available at: www.siyanda.org/docs/SCS_Regional Workshop Report March_2004_Long2.pdf (accessed [date]).

Kaul, I. (1999) 'In Search of a New Paradigm of International Development Cooperation', *Development,* 42(3): 22–4.

Kennedy, N. (2015) 'Tanzania: Meet On Fish Sustainability in Lake Victoria in Pipeline', *Tanzania Daily News,* 22 January 2015.

Kepel, G. (2002) *Jihad: The Trail of Political Islam* (London: I. B. Tauris).

—— (2004) *The War for Muslim Minds: Islam and the West* (Cambridge, MA: Belknap Press of Harvard University Press).

Keynes, J. (1936) *The General Theory of Employment, Interest and Money* (London: Macmillan).

Kharas, H. (2009) 'Development Assistance in the 21st Century', Contribution to the VIII Salamanca Forum: The Fight Against Hunger and Poverty.

Kharas, H. (2012) 'Volume and Impacts of Philanthropic Assistance', The Brookings Institution, Washington, November 14.

Kilcullen, D. (2015) 'Blood Year: Terror and the Islamic State', *Quarterly Essay,* 58

Kim, E. M. and Lee, J. E. (2013) 'Busan and Beyond: South Korea and the Transition from Aid Effectiveness to Development', *J. Int. Dev.* 25: 787–801.

Kincheloe, J. and Horn, R (eds) (2007) *The Praeger Handbook of Education and Psychology* (Westport, CT: Praeger).

Kindleberger, C. P. and Aliber, R. Z. (2005) *Manias, Panics, and Crashes: A History of Financial Crises,* 5th edn (New York: John Wiley).

King, M. and Taylor, D. (2011) 'The Radicalization of Homegrown *Jihadists*: a Review of Theoretical Models and Social Psychological Evidence', *Terrorism & Political Violence,* 23(4), 602–22.

King, R. and Sweetman, C. (2010) 'Gender Perspectives on the Global Economic Crisis', *Oxfam International Discussion Paper* (Oxford, Oxfam International).

Klare, M. and Anderson, D. (1996) 'US and Soviet Military Aid', *A Scourge of Guns* (Washington, DC: Federation of American Scientists).

Klein, Naomi (2007) *The Shock Doctrine: The Rise of Disaster Capitalism* (London: Allen Lane).

Kloppers, M. (2010) 'Address to Australian British Chamber of Commerce', 15 September.

KNG (Kachin News Group) (2011, 23 April) 'Extensive Logging in Northern Burma by China', *Kachin News Group.*

Knight, D. and Aslam, A. (2000, 18 March) 'Brazil's Bail-out is a Time Bomb', *South-North Development Monitor.*

Korten, D. (1989) *Getting to the 21st Century: Voluntary Action and the Global Agenda* (West Hartford, CT: Kumarian Press).

Kovach, H. and Lansman, Y. (2006) *World Bank and IMF Conditionality: A Development injustice. European Network on Debt and Development* (Eurodad), Brussels.

Kovsted, J. (2000) 'Financial Sector Aid' in F. Tarp (ed.) *Foreign Aid and Development: Lessons Learned and Directions for the Future* (London: Routledge), pp. 332–50.

Krader, L. (1976) *Dialectic of Civil Society* (New York: Prometheus Books).

Kragelund, P. (2008) 'The Return of Non-DAC Donors to Africa: New Prospects for African Development?', *Development Policy Review*, 26(5): 555–84.

Kragh, M. V., Mortenson, J. B., Schaumberg-Muller, H. and Slente, H. P. (2000) 'Foreign Aid and Private Sector Development', in F. Tarp (ed.), *Foreign Aid and Development* (London: Routledge), pp. 312–31.

Krugman, P. (2008) *The Return of Depression Economics and the Crisis of 2008* (London: Penguin).

Kuczynski, P.-P. and Williamson, J. (2003) *After the Washington Consensus: Restarting Growth and Reform in Latin America* (Washington, DC: Institute for International Economics).

Kurlantzick, J. (2007) *Charm Offensive: How China's Soft Power is Transforming the World* (New Haven CT: Yale University Press).

Kuznets, S. (1955) 'Economic Growth and Income Inequality', *American Economic Review*, 45: 1–28.

La'o Hamutuk (2000) 'Evaluating the World Bank's Community Empowerment Project', *La'o Hamutuk Bulletin*, 1(4).

Lasswell, H. (1941) *The Garrison State* (Chicago, IL: University of Chicago Press).

Lapavitsas, C. (2013) *Profiting Without Producing: How Finance Exploits Us All* (London: Verso).

Latham, M. E. (2000) *Modernization as Ideology: American Social Science and Nation Building in the Kennedy Era* (Chapel Hill: University of North Carolina Press).

Laurie, N. (2011) 'Gender Water Networks: Femininity and Masculinity in Water Politics in Bolivia', *International Journal of Urban and Regional Research*, 35(1): 172–88.

Leach. M., Scoones, I. and Stirling, A. (2007) 'Pathways to Sustainability: An Overview of the STEPS Centre Approach', STEPS Approach Paper (Brighton: STEPS Centre).

LEAN (Labor Environment Action Network) (2011) 'What is Climate Change?' available at: www.lean.net.au/lean/about/climate-change.html (accessed 20 April 2011).

Le Billon, P. (2001) 'The Political Ecology of War: Natural Resources and Armed Conflicts', *Political Geography*, 20, 561–84.

Le Billon, P. (2005) 'Fuelling War: Natural Resources and Armed Conflicts', *Adelphi Papers* 45(375) (London: International Institute for Strategic Studies & Routledge).

Leckie, J. (ed.) (2009) *Development in an Insecure and Gendered World: The Relevance of the Millennium Development Goals* (Farnham: Ashgate).

Lee, C. K. (2014) 'The Spectre of Global China', *New Left Review*, 89, 29–65.

Leftwich, A. (2000) *States of Development: On the Primacy of Politics in Development* (Cambridge: Polity).

Leipziger, D. (ed.) (2000) *Lessons from East Asia* (Ann Arbor: University of Michigan Press).

Levitt, K. P. (2013) *From the Great Transformation to the Great Financialization* (London: Zed Books).

Lewenhak, S. (1992) *The Revaluation of Women's Work* (London: Earthscan).

Lewis, W. A. (1954) 'Economic Development with Unlimited Supplies of Labour', *Manchester School of Economic and Social Studies*, 22(2): 131–91.

Lewit, D. (2002) 'Porto Alegre's Budget of, by and for the People', *Yes*, 31 December, available at: www.yesmagazine.org/issues/what-would-democracy-look-like/562 (accessed 12 August 2011).

Leys, S. (1997) *The Analects of Confucius* (New York: W.W. Norton).

Liew, L. H. (2005) 'China's Engagement with Neo-Liberalism: Path Dependency, Geography and Party Self-Reinvention', *Journal of Development Studies*, 41: 331–52.

Lin, J. Y. (2009) *Economic Development and Transition: Thought, Strategy, and Viability* (Cambridge: Cambridge University Press).

Lin, J. Y. (2012a) *The Quest for Prosperity: How Developing Economies Can Take Off* (Princeton: Princeton University Press).

Lin, J. Y. (2012b) *Demystifying the Chinese Economy* (Cambridge: Cambridge University Press).

Lin, J. Y. (2013) *Against the Consensus: Reflections on the Great Recession* (Cambridge: Cambridge University Press).

Lovell, K., Richardson, S., Travers, P. and Wood, L. (1993) 'Resources and Functionings: A New View of Inequality in Australia', in W. Eichhorn (ed.), *Models and Measurement of Welfare and Inequality* (Berlin: Springer Verlag).

Luis, J. (2000) 'The Politics of State, Society and Economy', *International Journal of Social Economics*, 27(3): 277–43.

MacIntyre, A., Pempel, T. J. and Ravenhill, J. (eds) (2008) *Crisis as Catalyst: Asia's Dynamic Political Economy* (Ithaca, NY: Cornell University Press).

Mabsout, R. and van Staveren, I. (2010) 'Disentangling Bargaining Power from Individual and Household Level to Institutions: Evidence on Women's Position in Ethiopia', *World Development*, 38(5): 783–96.

Macintosh, A. (2010) *Can Money Grow on Trees? Reducing Emissions from Deforestation and Degradation (REDD) in Developing Countries* (Canberra: ACFID).

Mahbubani, K. (1998) *Can Asians Think?* (Singapore: Times Books International).

—————— (2008) *The New Asian Hemisphere: The Irresistible Shift of Global Power to the East* (New York: Public Affairs).

Mahmud, T. (2011) 'Colonial Cartographies, Post-Colonial Border and Enduring Failures of International Law: The Unending Wars Along the Afghanistan-Pakistan Border', *Brooklyn Journal of International Law*, 36(1).

Mandelbrot, B. and Hudson, R. (2004) *The Misbehavior of Markets: A Fractal View of Financial Markets* (New York: Basic Books).

Manghezi, A. (1976) *Class, Elite, and Community in African Development* (Uppsala: Scandinavian Institute of African Studies).

Manley, M. and Brandt, W. (1985) *Global Challenge* (London and Sydney: Pan Books).

Manning, R. (2006) 'Will "Emerging Donors" Change the Face of International Cooperation?', *Development Policy Review*, 24(4): 371–85.

Manning, R., Harland Scott, C. and Haddad, L. (2013) 'Whose Goals Count? Lessons for Setting the Next Development Goals,' *IDS Bulletin*, 44(5–6).

Marchand, M. H. (2009) 'The Future of Gender and Development after 9/11: Insights from Postcolonial Feminism and Transnationalism', *Third World Quarterly*, 30(5): 921–35.

Martinussen, J. (1997) *Society, State and Market: A Guide to Competing Theories of Development* (London: Zed Books).

Marx, K. (1970a) *A Contribution to the Critique of Political Economy* (London: Lawrence & Wishart).

—————— (1970b) *Capital*, vol. I (London: Lawrence & Wishart).

—————— (1970c) *Capital*, vol. II (London: Lawrence & Wishart).

—————— (1972) *Capital*, vol. III (London: Lawrence & Wishart).

—————— (1973) *Grundrisse* (Harmondsworth: Penguin Books).

Marx, K. and Engels, F. (1967) *Manifesto of the Communist Party* (Moscow: Progress Publishers).

Mason, P. (2009) *Meltdown: The End of the Age of Greed* (London: Verso).

Mason, P. (2015) *Postcapitalism: A Guide to Our Future* (London: Allen Lane).

Mason, N., Jayne, T., and Shiferaw, B. (2012) 'Wheat Consumption in Sub-Saharan Africa: Trends, Drivers, and Policy Implications' (East Lansing: Department of Agricultural, Food, and Resource Economics, Department of Economics, Michigan State University).

Matthew, R. (2010) 'Environment, Conflict, and Sustainable Development', in N. Tschiri, M. Lund and F. Mancini (eds) *Security and Development: Searching for Critical Connections* (Boulder, CO: Lynne Rienner), pp. 47–75.

Matthews, J, and Tan, H. (2014) 'Economics: Manufacture Renewables to Build Energy Security', *Nature*, 513(7517), 10 September 2014.

Mattick, P. (2011) *Business as Usual: The Economic Crisis and the Failure of Capitalism* (London: Reaktion Books).

Mazower, M. (2012) *Governing the World: The History of an Idea* (Harmondsworth: Penguin).

McCants, W. (2011) 'Al Qaeda's Challenge: The Jihadists' War with Islamist Democrats', *Foreign Affairs,* 90(5): 20–32.

McGillivray, M., Feeny, S., Hermes, N. and Lensink, R. (2006) 'Controversies Over the Impact of Development Aid: It Works; It Doesn't; It Can, but That Depends…', *Journal of International Development,* 18: 1031–50.

McGregor, R. (2010) *The Party: The Secret World of China's Communist Rulers* (London: Allen Lane).

McKay, J. (2003) 'APEC's Role in Political and Security Issues', in R. Feinberg (ed.), *APEC as an Institution: Multilateral Governance in the Asia-Pacific* (Singapore: Institute of Southeast Asian Studies), pp. 229–66.

———— (2009) 'Food and Health Considerations in Asia-Pacific Regional Security' *Asia Pacific Journal of Clinical Nutrition*, 18(4): 654–63.

McKay, J. (2012) 'Natural Resources: Curse or Cure for Africa?' Discussion Paper 5/2012 (Johannesburg: The Brenthurst Foundation).

McKay, J. (2013) 'After the Washington Consensus: Rethinking Dominant Paradigms and Questioning "One Size Fits All" Orthodoxies', in D. Kingsbury (ed.), *Critical Reflections on Development* (Basingstoke: Palgrave Macmillan), pp. 50–68.

McKay, J. (2014) 'Development: "Good Governance" or Development for the Greater Good', in M. Steger, P. Battersby and J. Siracusa (eds), *The Sage Handbook of Globalization* (Los Angeles & London: Sage), pp. 505–23.

McRae, R. and Hubert, D. (eds) (2001) *Human Security and the New Diplomacy: Protecting People, Promoting Peace* (Montreal: McGill-Queen's University Press).

Mazzucato, Mariana (2013) *The Entrepreneurial State: Debunking Public vs. Private Sector Myths* (London: Anthem Press).

Melamed, C. (2015) 'Leaving no one Behind: How the SDGs can Bring Real Change', *ODI Briefing*, March 2015 (London: Overseas Development Institute).

Menkhaus, K. (2010) 'Beyond the Conflict Trap in Somalia', in N. Tschiri, M. Lund and F. Mancini (eds) *Security and Development: Searching for Critical Connections* (Boulder, CO: Lynne Rienner), pp. 135–70.

Michel, S. and Beuret, M. (2009) *China Safari: On the Trail of Beijing's Expansion in Africa* (London: Nation Books).

Mies, M. (1986) *Patriarchy and Accumulation on a World Scale: Women in the International Division of Labour* (London: Zed Books).

Midgley, J. (1986) *Community Participation, Social Development and the State* (New York: Methue and Co Ltd).

Miguel, E. (2007) 'Poverty and Violence: An Overview of Recent Research and Implications for Foreign Aid', in L. Brainard and D. Chollet (eds), *Too Poor for Peace? Global Poverty, Conflict, and Security in the 21st Century* (Washington, DC: Brookings Institution Press), pp. 50–59.

Milbrath, L. (1996) *Learning to Think Environmentally While There is Still Time* (Albany, NY: State University of New York Press).

Miller, D. (1993) 'In Defence of Nationality', *Journal of Applied Philosophy*, 10(1): 3–16.

—— (1995) *On Nationality* (Oxford: Oxford University Press).

Milliken, J. and Krause, K. (2002) 'State Failure, State Collapse, and State Reconstruction: Concepts, Lessons and Strategies', *Development and Change*, 33(5): 753–74.

Mills, G. (2002) *Poverty to Prosperity: Globalization, Good Governance and African Recovery* (Johannesburg: Tafelberg Publications and the South African Institute of International Affairs).

—— (2010) *Why Africa is Poor: And What Africa Can Do About It* (Johannesburg: Penguin).

Ministerial Review Team (2001) *Report of the Ministerial Review Team: Towards Excellence in Aid Delivery: A Review of New Zealand's Official Development Assistance Programme* (Wellington).

Minsky, H. P. (1986) *Stabilizing an Unstable Economy* (New Haven: Yale University Press).

Mirowski, P. (2013) *Never Let a Serious Crisis Go to Waste: How Neoliberalism Survived the Financial Meltdown* (London: Verso).

Mohanty, C. (1997) 'Under Western Eyes: Feminist Scholarship and Colonial Discourses', in N. Visvanathan, L. Duggan, L. Nisonoff and N. Wiegersma (eds), *The Women, Gender and Development Reader* (London: Zed Books), pp. 79–85.

Molyneux, M. and Razavi, S. (2005) 'Beijing Plus Ten: An Ambivalent Record on Gender Justice', *Development and Change*, 36(6): 983–1010.

Moon, S. and Mills, Z. (2010) *Practical Approaches to the Aid Effectiveness Agenda: Evidence in Aligning Aid Information with Recipient Country Budgets* (London: Overseas Development Institute).

Moore, M. and Unsworth, J. (2006) 'Britain's New White Paper: Making Governance Work for the Poor', *Development Policy Review*, 24(6): 707–15.

Morgenthau, H. (1978) *Politics Among Nations: The Struggle for Power and Peace*, 5th edn (New York: Alfred A. Knopf).

Morris, I. (2010) *Why the West Rules – For Now* (London: Profile Books).

Morris-Suzuki, T. (1989) *A History of Japanese Economic Thought* (London: Routledge).

Morrissey, O. (2000) 'Foreign Aid in the Emerging Global Trade Environment', in F. Tarp (ed.), *Foreign Aid and Development* (London: Routledge), pp. 375–90.

Mortimer, R. (1984) 'Stubborn Survivors: Dissenting Essays on Peasants and Third World Development', in H. Feith and R. Tiffen (eds), *Monash Papers on Southeast Asia, no. 10* (Melbourne: Centre for Southeast Asian Studies, Monash University).

Moser, C. (1991) 'Gender Planning in the Third World: Meeting Practical and Strategic Gender Needs', in T. Wallace and C. March (eds), *Changing Perceptions: Writings on Gender and Development* (Oxford: Oxfam), pp. 158–71.

—— (1993) *Gender Planning and Development: Theory, Practice and Training* (London: Routledge).

Mosley, P. and Eeckhout, M. (2000) 'From Project Aid to Programme Assistance', in F. Tarp (ed.), *Foreign Aid and Development* (London: Routledge), pp. 131–53.

Moss, T. (2007) *African Development: Making Sense of the Issues and Actors* (Boulder, CO: Lynne Rienner).

Moyo, D. (2009) *Dead Aid: Why Aid is not Working and How There is Another Way for Africa* (New York: Farrar, Strauss & Giroux).

Muchhala, B. and Sengupta, M. (2015). 'A Critique of the Emerging Post-2015 Agenda', Centre for Development and Human Rights, www.cdhr.org.in/post-2015-agenda/a-critique-of-the-emerging-post-2015-agenda/ (accessed 17 February 2016).

Mueller, E, Wairnwright, J, Parsons, A, Turnbull, L. (eds) (2014) *Patterns of Land Degradation in Drylands* (Heidelberg, Springer).

Mughal, M. (2013). 'Remittances as Development Strategy: Stepping Stones or Slippery Slope?', *J. Int. Dev* 25: 583–95

Mukhopadhyay, M. (2007) 'Mainstreaming Gender or "streaming" Gender Away: Feminists Marooned in the Development Business', in A. Cornwall, E. Harrison and A. Whitehead (eds), *Feminisms in Development: Contradictions, Contestations, and Challenges* (London, Zed Books), pp. 135–49.

Myrdal, G. (1957) *Economic Theory and Underdeveloped Regions* (London: Duckworth).

Narayan, D. (2005). 'Conceptual Framework and Methodological Challenges, in *Measuring Empowerment. Cross-Disciplinary Perspectives*. (Washington, DC: World Bank), pp. 3–38.

Narayan, D., Chambers, R., Shah, M. K. and Petesch, P. (2000) *Voices of the Poor: Crying Out for Change* (New York: Oxford University Press).

Narayan-Parker, D. and Patel, R. (2000) *Voices of the Poor: Can Anyone Hear Us?* (Oxford: Oxford University Press).

NASA (2015) 'How Much Will The Earth Warm?' Earth Observatory (Greenbelt, MD: National Aeronautical and Space Administration).

Natsios, A. (2006) 'Five Debates on International Development: The US Perspective', *Development Policy Review* 24(2): 131–9.

Nayyar, N. (ed.) (1977) *Economic Relations Between Socialist Countries and the Third World* (London: Macmillan).

Nelson, H. (2006) 'Governments, States and Labels', *State, Society and Governance in Melanesia*, Discussion Paper no. 1, Research School of Pacific and Asian Studies (Canberra: Australian National University).

Nelson, N and Wright, S. 1995. Power and Participatory Development: Theory and Practice (Bourton-on-Dunmore: ITDG Publishing).

Ness, G. and Ando, H. (1984) *The Land is Shrinking: Population Planning in Asia* (Baltimore, MD: Johns Hopkins University Press).

New York Multi-stakeholder Roundtable (2013) 'Gender and the Post 2015 Framework. Key Messages from New York Multi-stakeholder Roundtable'.

Nicolai, S., Hoy, C., Berliner, T. and Aedy, T. (2015) *Projecting Progress: Reaching the SDGs by 2030* (London: Overseas Development Institute), www.odi.org/publications/9895-sdgs-progress-scorecard-projecting-2030-development-goals (accessed 17 February 2016).

Nitsch, V. and Schumacher, D. (2002) 'Terrorism and Trade', paper presented to the German Institute of Global Research (DIW) workshop on 'The Economic Consequences of Global Terrorism', Berlin, available at www.diw.de/deutsch/service/veranstaltungen/ws_consequences.

Noland, M. and Pack, H. (2003) *Industrial Policy in an Era of Globalization: Lessons from Asia* (Washington, DC: Institute for International Economics).

Nunnenkamp, P., and Thiele, R. (2013) 'Financing for development: the gap between words and deeds since Monterrey', *Development Policy Review*, 31(1): 75-98.

Nurkse, R. (1952) *Problems of Capital Formation in Developing Countries* (New York: Oxford University Press).

Nussbaum, M. (2000) *Women and Human Development: The Capabilities Approach* (Cambridge: Cambridge University Press).

O'Brien, K. (2002) 'Networks, Netwar and Information-Age Terrorism', in A. Tan and K. Ramakrishna (eds), *The New Terrorism: Anatomy, Trends, and Counter-Strategies* (Singapore: Eastern Universities Press), pp. 73–106.

O'Donnell, G. (1996) 'Illusions and Conceptual Flaws', *Journal of Democracy*, 7(4), October: 160–8.

O'Donnell, G. and Schmitter, P. (1986) *Transitions from Authoritarian Rule: Tentative Conclusions about Uncertain Democracies* (Baltimore, MD: Johns Hopkins University Press).

OAU (Organization of African Unity) (1981) *The Lagos Plan of Action for the Economic Development of Africa 1980–2000* (Geneva: OAU).

Ocampo, J. (2010) 'Latin American Development after the Global Financial Crisis', in N. Birdsall and F. Fukuyama (eds), *New Ideas on Development after the Financial Crisis* (Baltimore, MD: Johns Hopkins University Press), pp. 133–57.

ODI (Overseas Development Institute) (2008) 'Untangling Links Between Trade, Poverty and Gender: Latin American Experience shows Women need Support to Benefit from Trade Liberalisation', Briefing Paper (London: ODI).

——— (2010) 'Brazil: An Emerging Aid Player. Lessons on Emerging Donors, and South-South and Trilateral Cooperation', Briefing Paper (London: ODI).

OECD (Organisation for Economic Co-operation and Development) (1989) *Development Cooperation in the 1990s: Efforts and Policies of the Members of the Development Assistance Committee* (Paris).

——— (2002) 'Economic Consequences of Terrorism', *OECD Economic Outlook, 71* (Paris: OECD), 117–40.

OECD (2013a) Development Co-operation Report 2013: Ending Poverty, OECD Publishing, http://dx.doi.org/10.1787/dcr-2013-en (accessed 10 January 2014).

OECD (2013b) 'Aid for CSOs: Aid at a Glance: Flows of Official Development Assistance to and Through Civil Society Organisations in 2011' (Paris: OECD Development Co-operation Directorate).

OECD (2014) 'Compare Your Country', www.compareyourcountry.org/oda?cr=oecd&lg=en (accessed 2 March 2016).

OECD (2015) *In it Together: Why Less Inequality Benefits All* (Paris: OECD)

OECD DAC (Organisation for Economic Co-operation and Development, Development Assistance Committee) (2006) 'Statistical Annex of the 2006 Development Co-operation Report, Table 18 Major Aid Uses by Individual DAC Donors'; Table 19 Aid by Major Purposes in 2005, available at: www.oecd.org/document/9/0,2340, en_2649_ 34485_1893129_1_1_1_1,00.html (accessed 28 February 2011).

——— (2007) Development Co-operation Report 2006 Summary, available at: www.sourceoecd.org/developmentreport (accessed 28 February 2011).

——— (2009) *DAC Guiding Principles for Aid Effectiveness, Gender Equality and Women's Empowerment* (OECD DAC).

——— (2010a) *Atlas of Gender and Development: How Social Norms Affect Gender Equality in non-OECD Countries* (OECD Development Centre).

——— (2010b) *Aid in Support of Gender Equality in Fragile and Conflict Affected States* (OECD DAC).

——— (2014a) 'Aid to developing countries rebounds in 2013 to reach an all-time high' http://www.oecd.org/newsroom/aid-to-developing-countries-rebounds-in-2013-to-reach-an-all-time-high.htm

——— (2014b) Total DAC flows at a glance: by sector. www.oecd.org/dac/stats/totaldacflowsataglance.htm (accessed 29 June 2014).

——— (2014c) Statistics Climate-related aid. www.oecd.org/dac/environment-development/Climate-related%20aid%20Flyer%20-%20May%202014%20final.pdf (accessed 1 March 2011).

OECD Development Aid at Glance (2013) Statistics by Region 1. Developing Countries. http://www.oecd.org/dac/stats/World%20-%20Development%20Aid%20at%20 a%20Glance%202013.pdf (accessed 10 January 2014).

OECD Development Cooperation Directorate (DCD-DAC) (n.d.) *The Paris Declaration and the Accra Agenda for Action,* available at http://www.oecd.org/document/ 18/0,3 343,en_2649_3236398_35401554_1_1_1_1,00.html (accessed 1 March 2011).

Oliver, D. (1983) *Trickling Up* (Suva: Lotu Pasifika Production).

Ondeo (2002) *Ondeo in the World: Facts and Figures* (Paris: Suez Lyonnaise des Eaux).

Onis, Z. and Senses, F. (2005) 'Rethinking the Emerging Post-Washington Consensus', *Development and Change,* 36(2): 263–90.

Oosterlaken, I. and van den Hoven, J. (eds) (2012) *The Capability Approach, Technology and Design* (New York: Springer).

Ostergaard, H. (ed.) (1992) *Gender and Development: A Practical Guide* (New York: Routledge).

Otieno, P. E. (2014) 'Male Engagement In Deconstructing Institutional Violence In Kenya', *IDS Bulletin,* 45(1): 61–8.

Oxaal, Z. and Baden, S. (1997) 'Gender and Empowerment: Definitions, Approaches and Implications for Policy', *BRIDGE Report,* 40 (Brighton: Institute for Development Studies).

Oxfam (2002) *Rigged Rules and Double Standards: Trade, Globalisation, and the Fight against Poverty* (Oxford: Oxfam International).

Oxfam and United Nations Vietnam (2009) 'Responding to Climate Change: Opportunities for Improving Gender Equality' (Hanoi: Oxfam). Available at: www.oxfam.org. uk/resources/policy/climate_change/climate-change-gender-equality-vietnam. html (accessed 13 January 2011).

Padilla, A. and Tomlinson, B. (2006) 'Aid Trends: Shifting Trends, Global Security and the MDGs', in *The Reality of Aid 2006,* available at: www.realityofaid.org/trends.ph (accessed 28 February 2011).

Panitch, L. and Gindin, S. (2005) 'Superintending Global Capital', *New Left Review,* 35.
——— (2010) 'Capitalist Crises and the Crisis This Time' in L. Panitch, G. Albo and V. Chibber (eds), *The Crisis This Time: Socialist Register 2011* (London: Merlin Press), pp. 1–20.

Panitch, L., Konings, M., Gindin, S. and Aquanno, S. (2008) 'The Political Economy of the Subprime Crisis', in L. Panitch and M. Konings (eds), *American Empire and the Political Economy of Global Finance* (Basingstoke: Palgrave Macmillan), pp. 253–92.

Panitch, L. and Gindin, S. (2012) *The Making of Modern Capitalism: The Political Economy of American Empire* (London: Verso).

Parfitt, T. (2002) *The End of Development: Modernity, Post-Modernity and Development* (London: Zed Books).

Park, Y. C. (2003) 'Does East Asia Need a New Development Paradigm?', in S. Collins, and D. Rodrik (eds), *Brookings Trade Forum 2002* (Washington, DC: Brookings Institution).

Paris Declaration on Aid Effectiveness (2005), available at: www.oecd.org/dataoecd/ 11/41/ 34428351 (accessed 28 February 2011).

Parpart, J. (1995) 'Post-modernism, Gender and Development', in J. Crush (ed.), *Power of Development* (London: Routledge).

Parpart, J. (2013) 'Exploring the Transformative Potential of Gender Mainstreaming in International Development Institutions', *Journal of International Development*, doi: 10.1002/jid.2948.

Parsons, T. (1937) *The Structure of Social Action* (New York: Free Press).
——— (1951) *The Social System* (New York: Free Press).

Partnership Agreements: Synthesis Report (London: One World Action and the Commonwealth Secretariat).

Patnaik, P. (2005) 'Karl Marx as a Development Economist', in K. S. Jomo (ed.), *The Pioneers of Development Economics: Great Economists on Development* (London: Zed Books), pp. 62–73.

Patnaik, U. (2005) 'Ricardo's Fallacy: Mutual Benefit from Trade Based on Comparative Costs and Specialisation', in K. S. Jomo (ed.), *The Pioneers of Development Economics: Great Economists on Development* (London: Zed Books), pp. 31–41.

Paulo, S. and Reisen, H. (2010) 'Eastern Donors and Western Soft Law: Towards a DAC Donor Peer Review of China and India?', *Development Policy Review,* 28 (5): 535–52.

Pearson, R. (1995) 'Bringing it All Back Home: Integrating Training for Gender Specialists and Economic Planners', *World Development* 23(11): 1995–9.

—— (2001) 'Male Bias and Women's Work in Mexico's Border Industries', in L. Beneria and S. Bisnath (eds), *Gender and Development: Theoretical, Empirical and Practical Approaches,* vol. 2 (London: Elgar), pp. 246–76.

—— (2007) 'Reassessing Paid Work and Women's Empowerment: Lessons from the Global Economy', in A. Cornwall, E. Harrison and A. Whitehead (eds), *Feminisms in Development: Contradictions, Contestations, and Challenges* (London: Zed Books).

Peck, J. (2010) *Constructions of Neoliberal Reason* (Oxford: Oxford University Press).

Peck, J. (2013) 'Disembedding Polanyi: Explaining Polanyian Economic Geographies', *Environment & Planning A*: 1536–44.

Pei, M. (2011) 'China's Response to the Global Economic Crisis', in N. Birdsall and F. Fukuyama (eds), *New Ideas on Development after the Financial Crisis* (Baltimore, MD: Johns Hopkins University Press), pp. 111–32.

Pempel, T. J. (ed.) (1999) *The Politics of the Asian Crisis* (Ithaca, NY: Cornell University Press).

Pettis, M. (2013) *The Great Rebalancing: Trade, Conflict and the Perilous Road Ahead for the World Economy* (Princeton NJ: Princeton University Press).

Petras, J. and Veltmeyer, H. (2001) *Globalisation Unmasked: Imperialism in the 21st Century* (London: Zed Books).

Pew Center (2002) 'Report Shows Emerging Greenhouse Gas Market' (press release) (Arlington, VA: Pew Centre for Global Climate Change), 19 March.

Philanthropy News Digest (2013, 5 December). 'Private Giving From Emerging Economies Growing, Report Finds', www.philanthropynewsdigest.org/news/private-giving-from-emerging-economies-growing-report-finds (accessed 10 January 2014).

Picciotto, R., Clarke, M. and Olonisakin, F. (2009) *Global Development and Human Security* (Piscataway NJ: Transaction Publishers).

Picciotto, R., Olonisakin, F. and Clarke, M. (2006) 'Global Development and Security: Towards a Policy Agenda', *Global Development Studies*, 3 (Sweden: Ministry of Foreign Affairs).

Pieterse, J. N. (1998) 'My Paradigm or Yours? Alternative Development, Post-Development, Reflexive Development', *Development and Change*, 29: 343–73.

Piketty, T. (2014) *Capital in the Twenty-First Century* (Cambridge Mass: The Belknap Press of Harvard University Press).

Pinstrup-Andersen, P. (ed.) (1993) *The Political Economy of Food and Nutrition Policies* (Baltimore, MD: Johns Hopkins University Press).

Polanyi, Karl (1944/2001) *The Great Transformation: The Political and Economic Origins of Our Time* (Boston: Beacon Press, republished 2001).

Price, A, and Pittman, R (2014) 'Leadership and Community Development', in Pittman, R, and Phillips, R. (eds), *An Introduction to Community Development* 3rd edn (New York: Routledge).

PNA (Panafrican News Agency) (2001, 13 February) 'Concern as Kenyan Fish Stocks Fall', *Panafrican News Agency*.

Pogge, T. (2010) 'Advancing the Scope of Gender and Poverty Indices: An Agenda and Work in Progress', in S. Chant (ed.), *The International Handbook of Gender and Poverty: Concepts, Research, Policy* (Cheltenham, UK, and Northampton, MA, USA: Edward Elgar), pp. 53–8.

Pomeranz, K. (2000) *The Great Divergence: China, Europe and the Making of the Modern World Economy* (Princeton: Princeton University Press).

Porter, G., Bird, N., Kaur, N., and Peskett, L. (2008) *New Finance for Climate Change and the Environment* (Washington, DC: Heinrich Böll Foundation and WWF).

Portney, R. (ed.) (1982) *Current Issues in Natural Resource Policy* (Washington, DC: Resources for the Future).

Prashad, V. (2012) *The Poorer Nations: A Possible History of the Global South* (London: Verso).

Prebisch, R. (1950) *The Economic Development of Latin America and its Principal Problems* (Lake Success, NY: United Nations).

Proyect, L. (1998) 'Fish Stocks and Malthus', unpublished paper, 23 May.

Publish What You Fund (2013). Aid Transparency Index 2013, http://ati.publishwhat youfund.org/ (accessed 10 January 2014).

Pyle, J. L and Dawson, L. (1990) 'The Impact of Multinational Technological Transfer on Female Workforces in Asia', in L. Beneria and S. Bisnath (eds), *Gender and Development: Theoretical, Practical and Empirical Approaches,* vol. 2 (London: Edward Elgar).

Raaber, N. (2010) *The Impact of the Crisis on Women: Main Trends across Regions* (Toronto: Colonia Condesa; Capetown: AWID).

Raby, G. (2003) 'The Costs of Terrorism and the Benefits of Cooperating to Combat Terrorism', paper presented to the APEC Senior Officials' Meeting, Chiang Mai: Thailand, 21 February 2003.

Rahnema, M. and Bawtree, V. (eds) (1997) *The Post-Development Reader* (London: Zed Books).

Rajan, R. (2010) *Fault Lines: How Hidden Fractures Still Threaten the World Economy* (Princeton: Princeton University Press).

Ramakrishna, K. (2002) 'Countering the New Terrorism of Al Qaeda Without Generating Civilisational Conflict: The Need for an Indirect Strategy', in A. Tan, and K. Ramakrishna (eds) *The New Terrorism: Anatomy, Trends, and Counter-Strategies* (Singapore: Eastern Universities Press), pp. 207–32.

Ramakrishna, K. and Tan, A. (2002) 'The New Terrorism: Diagnosis and Prescriptions', in A. Tan and K. Ramakrishna (eds), *The New Terrorism: Anatomy, Trends, and Counter-Strategies* (Singapore: Eastern Universities Press), pp. 3–29.

Ramalingham, B. (2013) *Aid on the Edge of Chaos* (Oxford: Oxford University Press).

Ramo, J. C. (2004) *The Beijing Consensus* (London: The Foreign Policy Centre).

Randel, J. and German, T. (1997) *The Reality of Aid 1997/1998: An Independent Review of Poverty Reduction and Development Assistance* (London: Earthscan).

Randel, J., German, T. and Ewing, D. (1998) *The Reality of Aid 1998/1999: An Independent Review of Poverty Reduction and Development Assistance* (London: Earthscan).

―――― (2002) *The Reality of Aid 2002: An Independent Review of Poverty Reduction and Development Assistance* (Manila: EUROSTEP and ICVA, IBON Books).

―――― (2004) *The Reality of Aid 2004: An Independent Review of Poverty Reduction and Development Assistance* (Zed Books: London).

Randriamaro, Z. (2010) 'DAWN Development Debates in the Fierce New World', *Development,* 53(3): 386–89.

―――― (n.d.) 'Hidden Agendas: Gender and Economic Reforms in Africa'.

Rangachari, R., Sengupta, N., Iyer, R., Banerji, P. and Singh, S. (2000) *Large Dams: India's Experience* (Cape Town: World Commission on Dams).

Rangelov, I. and Kaldor, M. (2012) 'Persistent Conflict', *Conflict, Security & Development*, 12(3), 193–9.

Rao, A. and Kelleher, D. (2005) 'Is there Life after Mainstreaming?', *Gender and Development*, 13(2): 57–69.

Rathgeber, E. (1990) 'WID, WAD, GAD: Trends in Research and Practice', *Journal of Developing Areas*, 24(4): 489–502.

Razavi, S. (2009) 'From Global Economic Crisis to the "Other Crisis"', *Development and Change,* 52(3): 323–28.

Razavi, S., Arza, C., Braunstein, E., Cook, S., and Goulding, K. (2012) 'Gendered Impacts of Globalization: Employment and Social Protection', *UNRISD Research Paper*, 2012–4 (Geneva, UNRISD).

Rendall, M. (2013) 'Structural Change in Developing Countries: Has it Decreased Gender Inequality?' *World Dev*, 45: 1–16, http://dx.doi.org/10.1016/j.world-dev.2012.10.005.

Reinhart, C. and Rogoff, K. (2009) *This Time is Different: Eight Centuries of Financial Folly* (Princeton, NJ: Princeton University Press).

Rensberg, P. (1980) 'Another Look at the Serowe Brigades', *Prospects: Quarterly Review of Education* 10(4): 379–91.

Resosudarno, I. (2002) 'Shifting Power to the Periphery: Preliminary Impacts of Indonesia's Decentralisation on Forests and Forest People', paper presented to Indonesia Update Conference, Australian National University, 18 September.

Rice, S. (2007) 'Poverty Breeds Insecurity', in L. Brainard and D. Chollet (eds), *Too Poor for Peace? Global Poverty, Conflict, and Security in the 21st Century* (Washington, DC: Brookings Institution Press), pp. 31–49.

Richardson, J. (1997) 'The Declining Probability of War Thesis: How Relevant for the Asia-Pacific?' in S. Harris and A. Mack (eds), *Asia-Pacific Security: The Economics-Politics Nexus* (Sydney: Allen & Unwin), pp. 81–100.

Rist, G. (1997) *The History of Development: From Western Origins to Global Faith* (London: Zed Books).

Roberts, L. and Cave, D. (2010) 'Advancing Innovative Development and Aid Strategies in the Asia-Pacific: Accelerating the Millennium Development Goals', Final Conference Report, 16–18 June (Sydney: Lowy Institute for International Policy).

Robertson, R. and Turner, B. (1991) *Talcott Parsons: Theorist of Modernity* (Thousand Oaks, CA: Sage).

Robinson, D. (2010) 'Social Protection, Livelihoods and the Hidden Economy of Care', *Development,* 53(3): 325–32.

Robison, R. and Hewison, K. (2005) 'Introduction: East Asia and the Trials of Neo-Liberalism', *Journal of Development Studies*, 41: 183–96.

Rocha, G. (2002) 'Neo-Dependency in Brazil', *New Left Review,* 16: 5–30.

Rodda, A. (1991) *Women and the Environment* (London: Zed Books).

Rodrik, D. (2006) 'Goodbye Washington Consensus Hello Washington Confusion? A Review of the World Bank's Economic Growth in the 1990s: Learning from a Decade of Reform', *Journal of Economic Literature*, 44: 973–87.

Rodrik, D. (2011) *The Globalization Paradox: Democracy and the Future of the World Economy* (New York: W.W. Norton).

Rogers, B. (1980) *The Domestication of Women: Discrimination in Developing Societies* (London: Tavistock).

Rojas-Suarez, L. (2010) 'The International Financial Crisis: Eight Lessons for and from Latin America', in N. Birdsall and F. Fukuyama (eds), *New Ideas on Development after the Financial Crisis* (Baltimore, MD: Johns Hopkins University Press), pp. 158–88.

Ros, J. (2005) 'The Pioneers of Development Economics and Modern Growth Theory', in K. S. Jomo and Erik Reinert (eds), *Development Economics: How Schools of Economic Thought Have Addressed Development* (London: Zed Books), pp. 81–98.

Rosemann, N. (2005) *Drinking Water Crisis in Pakistan and the Issue of Bottled Water: The Case of Nestlé's 'Pure Life'* (Islamabad: ActionAid Pakistan).

Rosenstein-Rodan, P. N. (1943) 'The Problems of Industrialization of Eastern and SouthEastern Europe', *Economic Journal,* June-Sept, reprinted in A. N. Agarwala and S. P. Singh (eds) (1963), *The Economics of Underdevelopment* (Oxford: Oxford University Press), pp. 245–55.

Ross, Michael (2004) 'What Do We Know About Natural Resources and Civil War?' *Journal of Peace Research*, 41(3), 337–56.

Rosser, A. (ed.) (2006) 'Achieving Turnaround in Fragile States', *IDS Bulletin*, 37(2).

Rostow, W. (1960) *The Stages of Economic Growth* (Cambridge: Cambridge University Press).

—— (1971) *Politics and the Stage of Growth* (Cambridge: Cambridge University Press).

—— (1984) 'Development: The Political Economy of the Marshallian Long Period', in G. Meier and D. Seers (eds), *Pioneers in Development* (New York: Oxford University Press), pp. 229–61.

—— (1990) *Theorists of Development from David Hume to the Present* (New York: Oxford University Press).

Rotmann, P., Kurtz, G. and Brockmeier, S. (2014) 'Major Powers and the Contested Evolution of a Responsibility to Protect', *Conflict, Security & Development*, 14(4), 355–77.

Roubini, N. and Mihm, S. (2010) *Crisis Economics: A Crash Course in the Future of Finance* (New York: Penguin).

Rowen, H. (1998) *Behind East Asian Growth: The Political and Social Foundations of Prosperity* (London: Routledge).

Rowlands, J. (1998) 'A Word of the Times, but What Does it Mean? Empowerment in the Discourse and Practice of Development', in H. Afshav (ed.), *Women and Empowerment: Illustrations from the Third World* (London: Macmillan), pp. 11–34.

Rowntree, B. (1902) *Poverty: A Study of Town Life* (London: Macmillan).

Roy, O. (2002) *Globalised Islam: The Search for the New Ummah* (London: Hurst).

Ruggeri Laderchi, C., Saith, R. and Stewart, F. (2006) 'Does it Matter that We Do Not Agree on the Definition of Poverty? A Comparison of Four Approaches', in M. McGillivray and M. Clarke (eds), *Understanding Human Well-being* (Tokyo: UNU Press).

Rumansara, A. (1998) 'The Struggle of the People in Kedung Ombo', in J. Fox and D. L. Brown (eds), *The Struggle for Accountability: The World Bank, NGOs and Grassroots Movements* (Boston, MA: MIT Press), pp. 123–49.

Ruskin, J. (1902) [1862] *Unto This Last: Four Essays of the First Principles of Political Economy* (Sunnyside: Allen).

Ruthven, M. (2002) *A Fury for God: The Islamist Attacks on America* (London: Granta).

—— (2004) *Fundamentalism: The Search for Meaning* (Oxford: Oxford University Press).

Ruxton, S. (2004) *Gender Equality and Men* (Oxford: Oxfam).

Ryrie, W. (1995) *First World, Third World* (London: Macmillan).

Saad-Filho, A. (2005) 'The Rise and Decline of Latin American Structuralism and Dependency Theory' in K. S. Jomo and Erik Reinert (eds), *Development Economics: How Schools of Economic Thought Have Addressed Development* (London: Zed Books), pp. 128–45.

Sachs, J. (2005) *The End of Poverty: How We Can Make it Happen in our Lifetime* (London: Penguin).

Sachs, W. (1992) *The Development Dictionary: A Guide to Knowledge as Power* (London: Zed Books).

Samman, E. (2015) 'Why and How a Country Lens Matters for the SDGs', Research Note, July 2015, ODI Development Progress (London: Overseas Development Institute).

Sandel, Michael (2012) *What Money Can't Buy: The Moral Limits of Markets* (London: Allen Lane).

Sandor, E., Scott, S. and Benn, J. (2009) 'Innovative Financing to Fund Development: Progress and Prospects', DCD Issues Brief, OECD, available at: www.oecd.org/ dataoecd/56/47/44087344.pdf (accessed 16 December 2010).

Saul, J. (2004) 'Globalization, Imperialism, Development: False Binaries and Radical Resolutions', *Socialist Register 2004*, 40: 220–44.

Sauvy, A. (1952, 14 August) 'Trois Mondes, Une Planete', *L'Observateur*, 118, p. 14.

Save the Children (2010) *At a Crossroads: Humanitarianism for the Next Decade,* (London: Save the Children).

Scheffran, J. and Remling, E. (2013) 'The Social Dimensions of Human Security under a Changing Climate', in Redclift, M. and Grasso, M. eds, *Handbook on Climate Change and Human Security* (Cheltenham: Edward Elgar).

Schober and Winter-Ebmer (2011) 'Gender Wage Inequality and Economic Growth: Is There Really a Puzzle?—A Comment', *World Dev*, 39(8-4): 1476–84. doi: 10.1016/j.worlddev.2011.05.001

Schumacher, E. (1973) *Small is Beautiful: A Study of Economics as if People Mattered* (London: Blond & Briggs).

Schumpeter, J. (1934) *The Theory of Economic Development* (Cambridge, MA: Harvard University Press).

——— (1976) *Capitalism, Socialism and Democracy.* (New York: Harper & Row).

Schure, T. (2010) 'Conflict Minerals: The New Blood Diamonds', available at: www.worldpress.org/print_article.cfm?article_id=3834&dont=yes (accessed 17 December 2010).

Schuurman, F. (2001) *Globalisation and Development Studies: Challenges for the 21st Century* (London: Sage).

Security Council Report (2010) *Cross-Cutting Report on Women, Peace and Security* (New York: Security Council Report).

Seers, D. (1972) 'The Meaning of Development', in N. Baster (ed.), *Measuring Development: The Role and Adequacy of Development Indicators* (London: Frank Cass).

Segerfeldt, F. (2005, 25 August) 'Private Water Saves Lives', *Financial Times*.

Seguino, S. (2010) 'The Global Economic Crisis, its Gender and Ethnic Implications, and Policy Responses', *Gender and Development*, 18(2): 179–99.

Seguino, S. (2011) 'Gender Inequality and Economic Growth: A Reply to Schober and Winter-Ebmer', World Development, 39(8), August 2011: 1485–7, doi: 10.1016/j.worlddev.2011.05.002.

Seguino, S. (2013) 'Financing for Gender Equality: Reframing and Prioritizing Public Expenditures to Promote Gender Equality', www.gender-budgets.org/index.php?option=com_joomdoc&view=documents&path=suggested-readings/seguino-s-paper&Itemid=587 (accessed 8 August 2014).

Sen, A. (1980) 'Equality of What?', in S. McMurrin (ed.), *Tanner Lectures on Human Values* (Cambridge: Cambridge University Press).

——— (1984) *Resources, Values and Development* (Oxford: Basil Blackwell).

——— (1985a) *Commodities and Capabilities* (Amsterdam: North Holland).

——— (1985b) 'Well-being Agency and Freedom', *Journal of Philosophy*, 82: 169–221.

—— (1987a), 'The Standard of Living: Lecture 1, Concepts and Critiques', in G. Hawthorn (ed.), *The Standard of Living* (Cambridge: Cambridge University Press).

—— (1987b) 'The Standard of Living: Lecture 2, Lives and Capabilities', in G. Hawthorn (ed.), *The Standard of Living* (Cambridge: Cambridge University Press).

—— (1990) 'Development as Capability Expansion', in K. Griffin and J. Knight (eds), *Human Development and the International Development Strategy for the 1990s* (London: Macmillan).

—— (1993) 'Capability and Well-Being', in M. Nussbaum and A. Sen (eds), *The Quality of Life*, (Oxford: Clarendon Press).

—— (1999a) *Development as Freedom* (New York: Alfred A. Knopf).

—— (1999b) 'The Possibility of Social Choice', *American Economic Review*, June: 349–78.

—— (2007) *Identity and Violence: The Illusion of Destiny* (London: Allen Lane).

Sen, G. (2013) Gender Equality in the Post-2015 Development Agenda: Lessons from the MDGs, *IDS Bulletin*, 44 (5–6): 42–8.

Sen, G. and Grown, C. (1987) *Development Crisis, and Alternative Visions: Third World Women's Perspectives* (New Delhi: DAWN).

Seymour, M. (2000) 'On Redefining the Nation', in N. Miscevic, (ed.), *'Nationalism and Ethnic Conflict. Philosophical Perspectives* (La Salle and Chicago: Open Court).

Sharp, J. and Briggs, J. (2006) 'Postcolonialism and Development: New Dialogues?' *Geographical Journal*, 172: 6–9.

Sharp, J, Briggs, J. Yacoub, H. and Hamed, N. (2003) 'Doing Gender and Development: Understanding Empowerment and local Gender Relations', in *Transactions of the British Institute of Geographers*, n.s. 28: 281–95.

Shepherd, L. J. (2006) 'Veiled References: Constructions of Gender in the Bush Administration Discourse on the Attacks on Afghanistan post-9/11', *International Feminist Journal of Politics*, 8(1): 19–41.

Shiller, R. J. (2009) *Irrational Exuberance* (New York: Broadway Books).

Shirk, S. (2007) *China: Fragile Superpower* (New York: Oxford University Press).

Shiva, V. (1989) *Staying Alive: Women, Ecology and Development* (London: Zed Books).

—— (2000) BBC Reith Lecture, Radio 4.

Silberschmidt, M. (2001) 'Disempowerment of Men in Rural and Urban East Africa: Implications for Male Identity and Sexual Behaviour', *World Development*, 29(4): 657–71.

Sim, S. (2004) *Fundamentalist World: The New Dark Age of Dogma* (London: Icon).

Simon, D. (2006) 'Separated by Common Ground? Bringing (Post) Development and (Post) Colonialism Together', *Geographical Journal*, 172: 10–22.

Simon, Julian L. (1994) 'More People, Greater Wealth, More Resources, Healthier Environment', *Economic Affairs: Journal of the Institute of Economic Affairs*, April.

Simons, P. et al. (1997) Committee to Review the Australian Overseas Aid Program, *One Clear Objective: Poverty Reduction Through Sustainable Development*, Report of the Committee of Review (Canberra: AusAID).

Singh, A. and Zammit, A. (2000) 'International Capital Flows: Identifying the Gender Dimension', *World Development*, 28(7): 1249–68.

Siwakoti, G. (2002) 'Who's Aiding Whom? Poverty, Conflict and ODA in Nepal', in J. Randel, T. German and D. Ewing (eds), *The Reality of Aid 2002* (Manila: EUROSTEP and ICVA, IBON Books), pp. 81–97.

Skidelsky, R. (2009) *Keynes: The Return of the Master* (London: Allen Lane).

Slaper, T, and Hall, T. (2011) 'The Triple Bottom Line: What Is It and How Does It Work?', *Indiana Business Review*, Spring 2011.

Smillie, I. (1995) *The Alms Bazaar: Altruism under Fire – Non-profit Organisations and International Development* (London: Intermediate Technology Publications).

—— (1999) 'Public Support and the Politics of Aid', *Development*, 42(3): September, 71–6.

Smith, A. (1986) *Nationalism and Modernism* (London: Routledge).

—— (1998) *Nationalism and Modernism* (London: Routledge).

Smith, M. (2010) *Global Capitalism in Crisis: Karl Marx and the Decay of the Profit System* (Halifax, Nova Scotia: Fernwood).

Smyth, I. (2009) 'Gender in Climate Change and Disaster Risk Reduction, Manila, October 2008', *Development in Practice*, 19(6): 799–802.

Sneyd, A. (2006) 'Jeffrey Sachs: Rolling Back Neo-liberalism through Neo-modernisation?', *IPEG Papers in Global Political Economy*, no. 23, Working Draft, June.

Snyder, M. and Tadesse, M. (1997) 'The African Context: Women in the Political Economy', in N. Visvanathan, L. Duggan, L. Nisonoff and N. Wiegersma (eds), *The Women, Gender and Development Reader* (London: Zed Books), pp. 75–8.

Solingen, E. (1998) *Regional Orders at Century's Dawn: Global and Domestic Influences on Grand Strategy* (Princeton, NJ: Princeton University Press).

Solow, R. (1956) 'A Contribution to the Theory of Economic Growth', *Quarterly Journal of Economics* 70: 65–94.

Sophathilath, P. (2012) 'Assessment of the Contribution of Forestry to Poverty Alleviation in Lao People's Democratic Republic', *Making Forestry Work for The Poor. Assessment of the Contribution of Forestry to Poverty Alleviation in Asia and the Pacific* (Bangkok: FAO).

Sparr, P. (1994) *Mortgaging Women's Lives: Feminist Critiques of Structural Adjustment* (London: Zed Books).

Sphere Project, The (2004) *Humanitarian Charter and Minimum Standards in Disaster Response* (Geneva: The Sphere Project).

Standing, H. (2007) 'Gender, Myth and Fable: The Perils of Mainstreaming in Sector Bureaucracies', in A. Cornwall, E. Harrison and A. Whitehead (eds), *Feminisms in Development: Contradictions, Contestations, and Challenges* (London: Zed Books), pp. 101–11.

Staub, E. (2004) 'Preventing Terrorism: Raising "Inclusively" Caring Children in the Complex World of the Twenty-First Century', in C. Stout (ed.), *Psychology of Terrorism: Coping with the Continued Threat* (Westport, CT: Praeger), pp. 199–244.

Stedman Jones, G. (2002) 'Introduction' to new edition of Karl Marx and Frederick Engels, *The Communist Manifesto* (London: Penguin), pp. 3–187.

Stensholt, R. (1997) *Developing the Mekong Subregion* (Melbourne: Monash Asia Institute).

Stepan, A. (1985) 'State Power and the Strength of Civil Society in the Southern Cone of Lain America', in P. Evans, D. Rueschemeyer and T. Skocpol (eds), *Bringing the State Back In* (Cambridge University Press: Cambridge).

Stern, J. (2003) *Terror in the Name of God: Why Religious Militants Kill* (New York: HarperCollins).

Stern, N. (2007) *The Economics of Climate Change* (Cambridge: Cambridge University Press).

Stewart, F. (1985) *Basic Needs in Developing Countries* (Baltimore, MD: Baltimore University Press).

Stewart, F. (2001) 'Horizontal Inequality: a Neglected Dimension of Development', 2001 WIDER Annual Lecture (Helsinki: World Institute for Development Economics Research of the United Nations University).

Stewart, R. and Knaus, G. (2012) *Can Intervention Work?* (London: W.W. Norton).

Stiglitz, J. (2002) *Globalization and its Discontents* (New York: W.W. Norton).

Stiglitz, J. (2006) *Making Globalization Work: The Next Steps to Global Justice* (London: Allen Lane).

Stiglitz, J. (2010) *Freefall: Free Markets and the Sinking of the Global Economy* (London: Allen Lane).

Stiglitz, J. (2013) *The Price of Inequality* (Penguin: London).

Stiglitz, J. and Yusuf, S. (2001) *Rethinking the East Asian Miracle* (Oxford: World Bank and Oxford University Press).

Stotsky, J. G. (2006) 'Gender and Its Relevance to Macroeconomic Policy: A Survey', *IMF Working Paper* (Washington, DC: International Monetary Fund).

Stout, C. (ed.) (2004) *Psychology of Terrorism: Coping with the Continued Threat* (Westport, CT: Praeger).

Strange, S. (1986) *Casino Capitalism* (Oxford: Basil Blackwell).

———— (1998) *Mad Money* (Manchester: Manchester University Press).

Streeck, Wolfgang (2014a) 'How Will Capitalism End?' *New Left Review*, 87: 35–64.

Streeck, Wolfgang (2014b) *Buying Time: The Delayed Crisis of Democratic Capitalism* (London: Verso).

Streeten, P. (1979) 'Basic Needs: Premises and Promises', *Journal of Policy Modeling*, 1(1): 136–46.

Streeten, P., Burki, S. J., ul Haq, M., Hicks, N. and Stewart, F. (1981) *First Things First: Meeting Basic Human Needs in Developing Countries* (Oxford: Oxford University Press).

Stubbings, L. (1992) 'Look *What You Started, Henry*': A History of the Australian Red Cross, 1914–1991 (Australian Red Cross).

Subrahmanian, R. (2007) 'Making Sense of Gender in Shifting Institutional Contexts: Some Reflections on Gender Mainstreaming', in A. Cornwall et al. (eds), *Feminisms in Development: Contradictions, Contestations, and Challenges* (London: Zed Books), pp. 112–21.

Subrahmanian, A. (2011) 'The Crisis and the Two Globalization Fetishes', in N. Birdsall and F. Fukuyama (eds), *New Ideas on Development After the Financial Crisis* (Baltimore, MD: Johns Hopkins University Press), pp. 62–82.

Suhrke, A. (2006) 'The Limits of Statebuilding: The Role of International Assistance in Afghanistan', paper presented to the International Studies Association annual meeting San Diego, 21–4 March.

Sumner, A. (2010). 'Global Poverty and The "New Bottom Billion": What If Three-Quarters Of The World's Poor Live In Middle-Income Countries?' *IDS Working Paper 349* (Brighton: Institute of Development Studies).

———— (2012) 'Where do the poor live?' *World Development*, 40(5): 865–77.

Sylvester, C. (2006) 'Bare Life as a Development/Postcolonial Problematic', *Geographical Journal*, 172: 66–78.

Tadros, M. (2011) 'Introduction: Gender, Rights and Religion at the Crossroad', *IDS Bulletin*, 42(1): 1–9.

Taleb, N. (2010) *The Black Swan: The Impact of the Highly Improbable*, 2nd revised edn (London: Penguin).

Tan-Mullins, M., Mohan, G. and Power, M. (2010) 'Redefining 'Aid' in the China-Africa Context', *Development and Change*, 41(5): 857–81.

Tanzi, V. (2011) *Government Versus Markets: The Changing Economic Role of the State* (Cambridge: Cambridge University Press).

Tarp, F. (2000) *Foreign Aid and Development: Lessons Learned and Directions for the Future* (London: Routledge).

Taylor, L. (2010) *Maynard's Revenge: The Collapse of Free Market Macroeconomics* (Cambridge, MA: Harvard University Press).

Taylor, V. (1999) *A Quick Guide to Mainstreaming in Development Planning* (London: Commonwealth Secretariat).

Tesoriero, F. (2010) *Community Development: Community Based Alternatives in an Age of Globalization* (Sydney: Pearson).

TFET (Trust Fund for East Timor) (2000) *Update No. 3* Trust Fund for East Timor World Bank (Asian Development Bank, AUSAID, USAID) 6 October.

Third World Network (2013) 'Female Garment Workers Bear Brunt of Tragedy,' *Third World Resurgence*, 273, May 2013: 39–40, http://www.twnside.org.sg/title2/resurgence/2013/273/women1.htm (accessed 8 August 2014).

Thomas, C. (2007) 'Globalization and Human Security' in A. McGrew and N. Poku (eds), *Globalization, Development and Human Security* (Cambridge: Polity) pp. 107–31.

Thomas, R.J. 2008. 'Opportunities to reduce the vulnerability of dryland farmers in Central and West Asia and North Africa to climate change', *Agriculture Ecosystems and Environment* Vol 126, Issues 1-2, pp 36-45.

Thompson, D. (2014, 21 January). 'The World's 85 Richest People Are as Wealthy as the Poorest 3 Billion', *Forbes*.

Tiessen, R. (2007) *Everywhere/nowhere: Gender Mainstreaming in Development Agencies* (Bloomfield, CT: Kumarian Press).

Tomlinson, B. (2010) 'Crisis Management: An Analysis of Global Aid Trends', in *The Reality of Aid* (2010), *Aid and Development Effectiveness: Towards Human Rights, Social Justice and Democracy. Reality of Aid 2010 Report* (Quezon City, Philippines: IBON Books), ch. 4.

Tomlinson, B. (2012) 'Global Aid Trends: A Growing Donor Private Sector Orientation in a Multi-Stakeholder Aid Architecture', in *Reality of Aid Report 2012*, pp. 115–152.

Tow, W., Thakur, R. and Hyun, I.-T. (2000) *Asia's Emerging Regional Order: Reconciling Traditional and Human Security* (Tokyo: United Nations University Press).

Tow, W. and Trood, R. (2000) 'Linkages between Traditional Security and Human Security', in W. Tow, R. Thakur and I.-T. Hyun (eds), *Asia's Emerging Regional Order: Reconciling Traditional and Human Security* (Tokyo: United Nations University Press), pp. 13–22.

Toye, J. (1987) *Dilemmas of Development: Reflections on the Counter-Revolution in Development Theory and Policy* (Oxford: Basil Blackwell).

—— (1991) 'Is there a New Political Economy of Development', in C. Colclough and J. Manor (eds), *States or Markets? Neo-Liberalism and the Development Policy Debate* (Oxford: Oxford University Press).

——(1993) *The Dilemmas of Development*, 2nd edn (Oxford: Blackwell).

Trainer, F. (2001) 'Development: Conventional versus Critical Perspectives', *Humanomics*, 17(1): 29–39.

Trani, J.-F., Bakhshi, P., Bellanca, N., Biggeri, M. and Marchetta, F. (2011) 'Disabilities Through the Capability Approach Lens: Implications for Public Policies?', *European Journal of Disability Research*, 5, 143–157.

Travers, P. and Richardson, S. (1993) *Living Decently* (Melbourne: Oxford University Press).

Trewin, R. 2004. 'Cooperatives: Issues and Trends in Developing Countries' (Fern Hill Park, ACT: Australian Centre for International Agricultural Research).

Tripathy, J. (2010) 'How Gendered is Gender and Development? Culture, Masculinity, and Gender Difference' *Development in Practice*, 20(1): 113–21.

Tscharnthe, T., Leischner, C., Veldkamp, E. and Guhuhardja, E. (2010) *Tropical Rainforests and Agroforests Under Global Change* (Heidelberg: Springer).

Tschirgi, N., Lund, M. and Mancini, F. (eds) (2010) *Security and Development: Searching for Critical Connections* (Boulder, CO: Lynne Rienner).

Tsunami Evaluation Coalition (2006) *Synthesis Report: Executive Summary* (London: Tsunami Evaluation Coalition).

TWR (Third World Network) (1998) 'The Negative Impacts of Aquaculture', *Third World Resurgence*, 93, May 1998, in *Third World Network*.

UN (United Nations) (1945) *Charter of the United Nations,* with subsequent amendments.

———— (1958) Series on Community Development no. 26, *Report on the Mission to Survey Community Development in Africa,* January-April 1956 (New York: United Nations).

———— (1985) *United Nations Programme of Action for African Economic Recovery and Development, 1986–1990* (New York: United Nations).

———— (1994) *Human Development Report 1994* (New York: United Nations Development Programme).

———— (1995) *United Nations Fourth World Conference International Platform for Action* (New York: United Nations).

———— (1999) *World Survey on the Role of Women in Development* (New York: United Nations).

———— (2005) *Human Development Report 2005* (New York: United Nations).

———— (2006a) 'United Nations Member States', press release Org/1469 (New York: United Nations).

———— (2006b) *The Millennium Development Goals Report 2006* (New York: United Nations).

———— (2006c) *Review of the First United Nations Decade for Eradication of Poverty,* E/CN.5/2006/3 (New York: United Nations).

———— (2008) *The Millennium Development Goals Report* (New York: United Nations).

———— (2009) *2009 World Survey on the Role of Women in Development: Women's Control over Economic Resources and Access to Financial Resources, including Microfinance* (ST/ESA/326) (New York: UN Department of Economic and Social Affairs Division for the Advancement of Women).

———— (2010a) *Millennium Development Goal 8: The Global Partnership for Development at a Critical Juncture,* MDG Gap Task Force Report 2010 (New York: United Nations).

———— (2010b) *The Millennium Development Goals Report 2010* (New York: United Nations).

———— (2010c) The *World's Women 2010: Trends and Statistics* (ST/ESA/STAT/SER.K/19) (New York: Department of Economic and Social Affairs).

————(2013a) A New Global Partnership: Eradicate Poverty and Transform Economies through Sustainable Development Report of the High-Level Panel of Eminent Persons on the Post-2015 Development Agenda, (New York, United Nations).

———— (2013b) The Millennium Development Goals Report 2013 (United Nations New York).

———— (2013c) World Population Prospects: The 2012 Revision (New York: United Nations Department of Economic and Social Affairs).

———— (2014) The Millennium Development Goals Report 2014, United Nations New York.

————(2015a) *Millennium Development Goals Report 2015* (New York: United Nations).

———— (2015b) *Transforming our World: The 2030 Agenda for Sustainable Development* (New York: United Nations).

UNCCD (United Nations Convention to Combat Desertification) (2002a) *The Causes of Desertification* (New York: United Nations).

———— (2002b) *The Consequences of Desertification* (New York: United Nations).

———— (2002c) UN Convention to Combat Desertification *Combating Desertification in Africa* (New York: United Nations).

———— (2002d) *Participatory Development: A Bottom-up Approach to Combating Desertification* (New York: United Nations).

———— (2011) *The Consequences of Desertification,* United Nations Convention to Combat Desertification (New York: United Nations).

UNCSD (United Nations Commission on Sustainable Development) (2002a) *CSD Theme Indicator Framework* (New York: United Nations).

—— (2002b) *Indicators of Sustainable Development: Guidelines and Methodologies* (New York: United Nations).

UNCTAD (United Nations Conference on Trade and Development) (2002) *World Investment Report 2002* (New York: United Nations).

—— (2010) *Least Developed Countries Report: Towards a New International Development Architecture for LDCs* (New York UN Conference on Trade and Development).

—— (2013). World Investment Report: Global Value Chains; Investment & Trade for Development: Overview. United Nations, New York & Geneva.

UNCTSD (United Nations Commodity Trade Statistics Database) (2007) New York, available at: www.comtrade.un.org/db/default.aspx (accessed 10 August 2011).

UNDESA (2006) Expert Group Meeting on the Millennium Development Goals, Indigenous Participation and Good Governance, background note, PF II/2006/WS. 3/7. New York, 11–13 January 2006.

UNDP (United Nations Development Programme) (1990) *Human Development Report 1990* (Oxford: Oxford University Press).

—— (1995) *Human Development Report 1995* (New York: United Nations Development Programme).

—— (2006) *Human Development Report 2006: Beyond Scarcity: Power, Poverty and the Global Water Crisis* (New York: United Nations Development Programme).

—— (2008) 'Fighting Climate Change: Human Solidarity in a Divided World', *Human Development Report* (New York: United Nations).

—— (2010a) *Human Development Report 2010* (Basingstoke: Palgrave Macmillan).

—— (2010b) 'International Human Development Indicators', *Worldwide Trends in the Human Development Index 1970–2010* (New York: United Nations).

—— (2010c) 'A Multidimensional Measure of Poverty', *Human Development Report 2010* (New York: United Nations).

—— (2011) *Compact For Inclusive Growth and Prosperity* (New York: United Nations).

—— (2013) *Human Development Report 2013: The Rise of the South – Human Progress in a Diverse World* (New York: UNDP).

—— (2014) *Human Development Report 2014* (New York: UNDP).

United Nations Economic Commission for Africa (2014) Dynamic Industrial Policy for Africa (Addis Ababa: UN Economic Commission for Africa).

UNESCAP (United Nations Economic and Social Commission for Asia and the Pacific) (2011) 'What Is Good Governance' (New York: United Nations Economic and Social Commission for Asia and the Pacific).

United Nations Economic and Social Council (2012) Trends and progress in international development cooperation, Report of the Secretary General, Development Cooperation Forum, 25 May 2012.

UNEP (United Nations Environment Program) (1999) *Global Environmental Outlook 2000* (London: Earthscan Publications).

—— (2015) *Geo 5: Global Environment* Outlook – *Environment for the Future We Want* (New York: United Nations Environment Program).

UNESCO (2013) 'Literacy Data Show persistent gender gap', UNESCO Institute of Statistics, www.uis.unesco.org/literacy/Pages/literacy-day-2014.aspx (accessed 2 February 2015).

UNF (United Nations Foundation) (2013) 'What We Do: Achieving Universal Energy Access', United Nations Foundation, www.unfoundation.org/what-we-do/issues/energy-and-climate/clean-energy-development.html (accessed 6 February 2015).

UNFCCC (United Nations Framework Convention on Climate Change) (1992) *Report* (New York: United Nations).

UNHDR (United Nations Human Development Reports) (1999) *United Nations Human Development Report: Globalization with a Human Face* (New York: United Nations Development Programme).

UNICEF (United Nations International Children's Emergency Fund) (1996) *The State of the World's Children 1996* (New York: United Nations International Children's Emergency Fund).

UNIFEM (2000) *Progress of the World's Women* (New York: UNDP).

——— (2006) 'Promoting Gender Equality in New Aid Modalities and Partnerships', UNIFEM Discussion Paper, March (New York: UNDP).

UNITAID (2012) *Results Beyond Investment, Annual Report 2012* (Geneva: World Health Organization).

UN Millennium Project (2005) *Taking Action: Achieving Gender Equality and Empowering Women*, Task Force on Education and Gender Equality (London: Earthscan).

——— (2006) 'Expanding the Financial Envelope to Achieve the Goals', available at: www.unmillenniumproject.org/reports/costs_benefits2.htm (accessed 1 March 2011).

UN Women (2012) 'Gender, Conflict and the Post-2015 Development Framework', Peace and Security Section (New York: UN Women).

——— (2013) 'A Transformative Stand-Alone Goal on Achieving Gender Equality, Women's Rights and Women's Empowerment: Imperatives and Key Components' (New York: UN Women).

——— (2014) 'Millennium Development Goals Gender Chart UN Statistics Division' (New York: UN Women).

USCB (United States Census Bureau) (2011) *International Data Base* (Washington, DC: United States Census Bureau)

USDS (United States Department of State) (2002) *Patterns of Global Terrorism* (Washington, DC: United States Department of State).

——— (2006) *The National Strategy for Combating Terrorism* (Washington, DC: United States Department of State).

Vandemoortele, M. (2009) *Within-Country Inequality, Global Imbalances and Financial Instability* (London: ODI)

Van Staveren, I. (2013) 'An Exploratory Cross-Country Analysis of Gendered Institutions' *J. Int. Dev.* 25: 108–21.

Varfolomeyev, S. and Gurevich, K. (2001) 'The Hypergeometric Growth of the Human Population on a Macrohistorical Scale', *Journal of Theoretical Biology,* 212: 367–72.

Varoufakis, Y. (2011) *The Global Minotaur: America, the True Origins of the Financial Crisis and the Future of the World Economy* (London: Zed Books).

Varoufakis, Y., Halevi, J. and Theocarakis, N. (2011) *Modern Political Economics: Making Sense of the Post-2008 World* (London: Routledge).

te Velde, D. W. et al. (2010) The Global Financial Crisis and Developing Countries, *ODI Working Paper 316* (London).

Verhaeghe, P. (2014) *What About Me? The Struggle for Identity in a Market-Based Society* (Melbourne: Scribe).

Vince, G. (2012, 21 September) 'How the World's Oceans Could be Running out of Fish', *BBC*.

Vivendi (2002) *Environment*, Vivendi Universal Public Statement.

Wade, R. (1990) *Governing the Market: Economic Theory and the Role of Government in East Asian Industrialisation* (Princeton, NJ: Princeton University Press).

——— (2003) 'What Strategies are Viable for Developing Countries Today? The World Trade Organization and the Shrinking of Development Space', *Review of International Political Economy*, 10(4): 621–44, doi:10.1080/09692290310001601902

——— (2004) 'The Reprinting of *Governing the Market:* A Dinner Table Conversation', *Issues and Studies,* 40(1): 103–34.

———(2008) 'Financial Regime Change?' *New Left Review*, 53: 5–22.

————(2009) 'From Global Imbalances to Global Reorganisations', *Cambridge Journal of Economics,* 33: 539–62.

Walkenhurst, P. and Dihel, N. (2002) 'Trade Impacts of the Terrorist Attacks of 11 September 2001: A Quantitative Assessment', paper presented to the German Institute of Global Research (DIW) workshop on The Economic Consequences of Global Terrorism', Berlin, available at www.diw.de/deutsch/service/veranstaltungen/ws_ consequences

Walker, R. (2007) 'Capacity Building and Cookie Enabling', *Christian Science Monitor,* 19, April.

Wallerstein, E. (2006) 'The Curve of American Power', *New Left Review,* 40.

Wallerstein, I. (1974) *The Modern World System* (New York: Monthly Review Press).

————(1979) *The Capitalist World Economy* (Cambridge: Cambridge University Press).

———— (1984) *The Politics of the World Economy* (Cambridge: Cambridge University Press).

———— (2011) *Centrist Liberalism Triumphant, 1789–1914* (Berkeley, CA: University of California Press).

Wang Hui (2009) *The End of the Revolution: China and the Limits of Modernity* (London: Verso).

Waring, M. (1988) *Counting for Nothing: What Men Value and What Women are Worth* (Wellington: Allen & Unwin).

Warren, B. (1980) *Imperialism: Pioneer of Capitalism* (London: Verso).

Warren, C. (1993) *Adat and Dinas: Balinese Communities in the Indonesian State* (Oxford: Oxford University Press).

Water.Org (2015) 'Millions lack safe water', http://water.org/water-crisis/water-facts/ water/ accessed 4 February 2015.

Waters, R. (2013) 'Desertification', in M. Griffiths (ed.) *Encyclopedia of International Relations and Global Politics*

Watkins, K. (2013) 'Leaving no-one Behind: an Equity Agenda for the Post-2015 Goals', Think Piece (London: Overseas Development Institute).

WB-GNI (2002) *GNI Per Capita 2000, Atlas Method and PPP,* World Development Indicators Database (Washington, DC: World Bank).

WBPNL (World Bank Poverty Net Library) (2001) 'Cultural Capital and Educational Attainment', *Social Capital,* World Bank Poverty Net Library (Washington, DC: World Bank).

WCD (World Commission on Dams) (2000a) 'Executive Summary', *Large Dams Cross Check Survey* (New York: World Commission on Dams).

————(2000b) *Dams and Development: A New Framework for Decision-Making* (New York: World Commission on Dams).

Webber, R. (1985) 'Health and Development', in B. Kinika and S. Oxenham (eds), *The Road Out: Rural Development in Solomon Islands* (Suva: University of South Pacific).

Wee, V. and Heyzer, N. (1995) *Gender, Poverty and Sustainable Development: Towards a Holistic Framework of Understanding and Action* (Singapore: ENGENDER).

Weidou, N. 2005. Energy and Advanced Coal Utilization Strategy in China Science and Technology Commission, Ministry of Education, People's Republic of China.

Weiss, L. (2003) 'Guiding Globalization in East Asia: New Roles for Old Developmental States', in L. Weiss (ed.), *States in the Global Economy: Bringing Domestic Institutions Back In* (Cambridge: Cambridge University Press), pp. 245–70.

Weissman, S. et al. (1975) *The Trojan Horse: A Radical Look at Foreign Aid* (Palo Alto, CA: Ramparts Press).

Weitz, R. (1986) *New Roads to Development* (New York: Greenwood Press).

Wheeler, T. (2015, 28 July). 'Inclusive Peace: How to Leave no one Behind', www. saferworld.org.uk/news-and-views/blog-post/10-inclusive-peace-how-to-leave-no-one-behind (accessed 17 February 2016).

Wheen, F. (2006) *Marx's Das Kapital: A Biography* (London: Atlantic Books).

Whittington, D. and Swarna, V. (1994) *The Economic Benefits of Potable Water Supply Projects to Households in Developing Countries*, paper no. 53 (Manila: Asian Development Bank, Economic and Development Resource Centre).

WHO/UNICEF (2006) 'Joint Monitoring Program for Water Supply and Sanitation', available at: www.wssinfo.org/en/40_mdg2006.html (accessed 26 April 2007).

—— (2008) 'Progress in Drinking Water and Sanitation', WHO/UNICEF Joint Monitoring Programme for Water Supply and Sanitation, New York, 17 July.

Widoyoko (2014) 'Deforestation, rent seeking and local elections in West Kalimantan', *Inside Indonesia* www.insideindonesia.org/feature-editions/deforestation-rent-seeking-and-local-elections-in-west-kalimantan (accessed 4 February 2015).

Wiig, H. (2013) Joint Titling in Rural Peru: Impact on Women's Participation in Household Decision-Making, *World Dev*, 52: 104–119.

Williamson, J. (1994) *The Political Economy of Policy Reform* (Washington, DC: Institute for International Economics).

—— (2004) 'The Years of Emerging Market Crises', *Journal of Economic Literature*, 42: 822–37.

Williamson, J. and Mahar, M. (1998) *A Survey of Financial Liberalization*, Princeton Essays in International Finance no. 211.

Windsor, J. (2007) 'Breaking the Poverty-Insecurity Nexus: Is Democracy the Answer?', in L. Brainard and D. Chollet (eds), *Too Poor for Peace? Global Poverty, Conflict, and Security in the 21st Century* (Washington, DC: Brookings Institution Press), pp. 153–62.

Winters, A. and Yusuf, S. (2007) *Dancing with Giants: China, India and the Global Economy* (Washington, DC: World Bank).

Wisor, S., Bessell, S., Castillo, F., Crawford, J., Donaghue, K., Hunt, J., Jaggar, A., Liu, A., and Pogge, T. (2014). *The Individual Deprivation Measure: A Gender-Sensitive Approach to Poverty Measurement* (Melbourne: International Women's Development Agency). http://www.iwda.org.au/wp-content/uploads/2014/11/20141110_IndividualDeprivationMeasure.pdf

WN (2002) *Globalization, Growth and Poverty: Building an Inclusive World Economy* (Washington, DC: World Bank).

Women in National Parliaments. Situation as of 1 June 2014. http://www.ipu.org/wmn-e/world.htm (accessed 8 August 2014).

Woo, Jung-en (1991) *Race to the Swift: State and Finance in Korean Industrialization* (New York: Columbia University Press).

Woo Wing Thye, Sachs, J. D. and Schwab, K. (eds) (2000) *The Asian Financial Crisis: Lessons for a Resilient Asia* (Cambridge, MA: MIT Press).

Woodford-Berger, P. (2007) 'Gender Mainstreaming: What is it (about) and Should We Continue Doing It?', in A. Cornwall, E. Harrison, and A. Whitehead (eds), *Feminisms in Development: Contradictions, Contestations, and Challenges* (London: Zed Books).

Woods, N. (2008) 'Whose Aid? Whose Influence? China, Emerging Donors and the Silent Revolution in Development Assistance,' *International Affairs*, 84 (6): 1205–21.

World Bank (various years) *World Development Indicators* (Washington, DC: World Bank).

—— (various years) *World Development Report* (New York: Oxford University Press).

—— (1981a) *Accelerated Development in Sub-Saharan Africa: An Agenda for Action* (Washington, DC: World Bank).

—— (1981b) *A Collection of Farewell Speeches on the Occasion of the Retirement of Robert S. McNamara as President of the World Bank, 1968–81*, World Bank Report 13380 (Washington, DC: World Bank).

—— (1984a) *Toward Sustained Development in Sub-Saharan Africa: A Joint Programme of Action* (Washington, DC: World Bank).

—— (1984b) *World Development Report: Population Change and Development* (New York: Oxford University Press).

—— (1986) *Financing Adjustment with Growth in Sub-Saharan Africa* (Washington, DC: World Bank).

—— (1990) *Proceedings of the World Bank Annual Conference on Development Economics* (Washington, DC: World Bank).

—— (1991a) *World Development Report 1991* (Oxford: Oxford University Press).

—— (1991b) *World Development Report: From Plan to Market* (New York: Oxford University Press).

—— (1994) *Population and Development: Implications for the World Bank* (Washington, DC: World Bank).

—— (1995) *Strengthening the Effectiveness of Aid: Lessons for Donors*, available at: www.worldbank.org (accessed on 27 September 2002).

—— (1996) *Madagascar Poverty Report* (Washington, DC: World Bank).

—— (1998) *Assessing Aid: What Works, What Doesn't and Why*, a World Bank Policy Research Report (Oxford: Oxford University Press).

—— (2000) *First Trust Fund For East Timor Project to be Handed over to East Timorese*, press release (Washington, DC: World Bank Group).

—— (2001a) 'Community Empowerment and Social Inclusion', in *Social Policy Design* (Washington, DC: World Bank).

—— (2001b) *Engendering Development: Through Gender Equality in Rights, Resources and Voice* (Washington, DC: World Bank).

—— (2001c) *Sustainable Development in the 21st Century* (Washington, DC: World Bank).

—— (2002a) *World Development Report 2000/2001: Attacking Poverty* (Washington, DC: World Bank).

——(2002b) *Engendering Development* (Washington, DC: World Bank), available at: www.worldbank.org/gender/Prr/.

—— (2002c) *The Role and Effectiveness of Development Assistance: Lessons from World Bank Experience* (Washington, DC: DEC).

—— (2006a) '06 World Development Indicators', available at: www.devdata. worldbank.org/wdi2006/contents/section1_1_1.htm.

—— (2006b) 'The Costs of Attaining the Millennium Development Goals', available at: www.web.worldbank.org/html/extdr/mdgassessment.pdf.

—— (2006c) *Timor-Leste: Country Brief* (Washington, DC: World Bank).

—— (2006d) *Status of Projects in Execution FY-06 – Timor-Leste* (Washington, DC: World Bank).

—— (2007) *World Development Indicators 2007* (Washington, DC: World Bank).

—— (2010a) *The MDGs after the Crisis: Global Monitoring Report 2010* (Washington: International Bank for Reconstruction and Development/The World Bank).

—— (2010b) *Empowering Indonesian Communities through Developing Infrastructure and Services* (Washington, DC: World Bank) April.

—— (2011) *World Development Report 2011: Conflict Security and Development* (Washington, DC: World Bank).

World Bank (2012) *Jobs: World Development Report 2013* (Washington DC: World Bank).

World Bank (2013) 'Developing Countries to Receive Over $410 Billion in Remittances in 2013, Says World Bank,' Press Release, October 2, 2013. Available at: www. worldbank.org/en/news/press-release/2013/10/02/developing-countries-remittances-2013-world-bank (accessed 11 December 2013).

World Bank (2014a) *Community Driven Development*, available at: www.worldbank. org/en/topic/communitydrivendevelopment/overview (accessed 11 April 2014).

World Bank (2014b) 'Rural population (% of total population)' http://data.worldbank.org/indicator/SP.RUR.TOTL.ZS/countries?display=graph (accessed 3 February 2015).

World Bank (2014c) *Resource Financed Infrastructure* (Washington DC: World Bank).

World Bank (2014d) *Risk and Opportunity* (Washington DC: World Bank).

World Bank PovertyNet (2006) 'Pro-poor Growth', available at: www.web.worldbank.org/ WBSITE/EXTERNAL/TOPICS/EXTPOVERTY/0,menuPK:336998~pagePK:149018~piPK:149093~theSitePK:336992,00.html.

World Commission on Environment and Development (1987) *Our Common Future* (Brundtland Report) (Oxford: Oxford University Press).

World Economic Forum (2014) *Outlook on the Global Agenda 2015* (Geneva: World Economic Forum).

Wu, D. (2013) 'WED: Measuring Change in Women Entrepreneur's Economic Empowerment: A Literature Review', Working Paper, Donor Committee for Enterprise Development, September 2013.

WWF (World Wildlife Fund) (2014) *Deforestation* www.worldwildlife.org/threats/deforestation (accessed 27 November 2014).

Yes Pakistan (2002) available at: www.yespakistan.com/people/potable_water.asp (accessed 2 December 2002).

Zakaria, F. (1994) 'A Conversation with Lee Kwan Yew', *Foreign Affairs*, March/April 1994.

Zimmerman, R. (1993) *Dollars, Diplomacy and Dependency: Dilemmas of US Economic Aid* (London: Lynne Rienner).

Zysman, J. and Borrus, M. (1996) 'Lines of Fracture, Webs of Cohesion: Economic Interconnections and Security Politics in Asia', in S. L. Shirk and C. Twomey (eds), *Power and Prosperity: Economics and Security Linkages in Asia-Pacific* (New Brunswick: Transaction Publishers), pp. 77–99.

Index